Status in Management
and Organizations

People go to extraordinary lengths to gain and defend their status. Those with higher status are listened to more, receive more deference from others, and are perceived as having more power. People with higher status also tend to have better health and longevity. In short, status matters. Despite the importance of status, particularly in the workplace, it has received comparatively little attention from management scholars. It is only relatively recently that they have turned their attention to the powerful role that social status plays in organizations. This book brings together this important work, showing why we should distinguish status from power, hierarchy, and work quality. It also shows how a better understanding of status can be used to address problems in a number of different areas, including strategic acquisitions, the development of innovations, new venture funding, executive compensation, discrimination, and team diversity effects.

JONE L. PEARCE is Dean's Professor of Leadership and Director of the Center for Global Leadership at the Paul Merage School of Business, University of California, Irvine. She has published nearly ninety scholarly articles and is the author of four books, including *Organization and Management in the Embrace of Government* (2001) and *Organizational Behavior: Real Research for Real Managers* (2009). She is a fellow of the Academy of Management, the International Association of Applied Psychology, the American Psychological Association, and the Association for Psychological Science.

Cambridge Companions to Management

Cambridge Companions to Management is an essential new resource for academics, graduate students, and reflective business practitioners seeking cutting-edge perspectives on managing people in organizations. Each Companion integrates the latest academic thinking with contemporary business practice, dealing with real-world issues facing organizations and individuals in the workplace, and demonstrating how and why practice has changed over time. World-class editors and contributors write with unrivaled depth on managing people and organizations in today's global business environment, making the series a truly international resource.

Status in Management and Organizations

Edited by

JONE L. PEARCE
University of California, Irvine

CAMBRIDGE
UNIVERSITY PRESS

CAMBRIDGE UNIVERSITY PRESS
Cambridge, New York, Melbourne, Madrid, Cape Town, Singapore,
São Paulo, Delhi, Dubai, Tokyo, Mexico City

Cambridge University Press
The Edinburgh Building, Cambridge CB2 8RU, UK

Published in the United States of America by Cambridge University Press, New York

www.cambridge.org
Information on this title: www.cambridge.org/9780521132961

© Cambridge University Press 2011

First published 2011

Printed in the United Kingdom at the University Press, Cambridge

A catalog record for this publication is available from the British Library

Library of Congress Cataloging in Publication data
Status in management and organizations / [edited by] Jone L. Pearce.
    p.   cm. – (Cambridge companions to management)
    Includes bibliographical references and index.
    ISBN 978-0-521-11545-2 – ISBN 978-0-521-13296-1 (pbk.)
    1. Organizational sociology.   2. Organizational behavior.   3. Industrial
    sociology.   4. Social status.   5. Prestige.   I. Pearce, Jone L.
    HM791.S73   2011
    306.3′6–dc22
    2010034945

ISBN 978-0-521-11545-2 Hardback
ISBN 978-0-521-13296-1 Paperback

To Harry, my love

Contents

Figures

Tables

Contributors

MICHELLE A. BARTON is a doctoral candidate at the Ross School of Business, University of Michigan. Her research explores the processes by which individuals and groups organize to manage uncertainty in real time. In particular, she focuses on how teams recognize and use diverse expertise to create more mindful organizational practices and to facilitate flexible and adaptive performance.

J. STUART BUNDERSON is a professor of organizational behavior at the John M. Olin Business School at Washington University in St. Louis and a research professor with the Faculty of Management and Organization at the University of Groningen, the Netherlands. He holds a Ph.D. degree in strategic management and organization from the University of Minnesota, and B.S. and M.S. degrees from Brigham Young University. His research focuses on learning, power and status, and meaningful work, and has been published in leading management journals including *Administrative Science Quarterly*, *Academy of Management Review*, *Academy of Management Journal*, *Journal of Applied Psychology*, and *Harvard Business Review*. He serves as a senior editor at *Organization Science* and is on the editorial board of the *Academy of Management Review*.

JOERG DIETZ is a professor and Head of the Department of Organizational Behavior at the University of Lausanne in Switzerland. He teaches organizational behavior at the micro and macro levels as well as cross-cultural management. His research interests include workforce diversity (in particular, prejudice and discrimination in the workplace), contextual antecedents of organizational behavior, and employee–customer linkages. His research has been published in numerous journals, including *Academy of Management Journal*, *Journal of Applied Psychology*, and *Organizational Behavior and Human Decision Processes*. He has won several teaching and research awards, including best paper awards from two divisions of the Academy of Management.

KIMBERLY D. ELSBACH is Professor of Management and Chancellor's Fellow at the Graduate School of Management at the University of California, Davis. She is also the NCAA Faculty Athletics Representative for UC Davis. She received her Ph.D. in industrial engineering from Stanford University in 1993. She studies how people form impressions and images of each other and their organizations. Her book, _Organizational Perception Management_, was recently published by Lawrence Erlbaum Associates Press.

DESHANI B. GANEGODA is a Ph.D. student in organizational behavior at the University of Central Florida. She earned her Bachelor of Business degree and honors degree (first class) in management at Monash University, Australia. Her research interests include organizational justice, morality, ethics, and organizational change. She has co-authored several book chapters and presented papers on this and other topics at premier management conferences.

JERALD GREENBERG is Senior Psychologist at the RAND Corporation's Institute for Civil Justice and was formerly Abramowitz Professor of Business Ethics at Ohio State University's Fisher College of Business. He has served as Associate Editor of _Organizational Behavior and Human Decision Processes_ and of the _Journal of Organizational Behavior_. In addition to over twenty-five books, he has published over 160 articles and chapters, mostly in the field he helped develop, organizational justice. Recognizing a lifetime of research accomplishments, he won the Distinguished Scientific Contributions to Management Award granted in 2007 by the Academy of Management, the Distinguished Scientific Achievement Award granted in 2006 by the Society for Industrial and Organizational Psychology (SIOP), and the Herbert Heneman Career Achievement Award granted in 2005 by the Human Resources Division of the Academy of Management. Based on citation counts, Dr. Greenberg has been identified as the thirty-seventh most influential management scholar.

ROYSTON GREENWOOD is the TELUS Professor of Strategic Management in the Department of Strategic Management and Organization, School of Business, University of Alberta, and Visiting Professor at the Saïd Business School, University of Oxford. He received his Ph.D. from the University of Birmingham, UK. His research focuses on the dynamics of institutional change, especially at the field level of analysis. He is a founding co-editor of *Strategic Organization* and is a co-editor of the *SAGE Handbook of Organizational Institutionalism*.

MICHAEL JENSEN is an associate professor at the University of Michigan, Ann Arbor. His main research focuses on the role of social structures and dynamics in markets, and his current projects include work on identity and status.

BO KYUNG KIM is a doctoral candidate at the University of Michigan, Ann Arbor. Her current research focuses on market identity and social structure, with emphasis on the interaction between them over time.

HEEYON KIM is a doctoral candidate at the University of Michigan, Ann Arbor. Her research interests are in the areas of organizational identity and status, with current projects focusing on the mobility of status and identity.

MICHAEL LOUNSBURY is the Alex Hamilton Professor of Strategic Management and Organization at the University of Alberta School of Business and the National Institute of Nanotechnology. His research focuses on the relationship between organizational and institutional change, entrepreneurial dynamics, and the emergence of new industries and practices. He serves on a number of editorial boards and is currently the series editor of *Research in the Sociology of Organizations* and co-editor of *Organization Studies*.

BILIAN NI SULLIVAN received her Ph.D. from Stanford University and currently is an assistant professor at the Hong Kong University of Science and Technology. Her research interests are in the areas of learning, social networks, and stratification.

MICHAEL NIPPA is Professor of Management, Leadership, and Human Resources at Freiberg University. His research integrates corporate management and leadership, development and management of organizations, human resource management in an international context, and formulation and implementation of strategy.

JAMES O'BRIEN is Assistant Professor of Human Resource Management in the Aubrey Dan Program in Management and Organization Studies, Faculty of Social Science, at the University of Western Ontario. He received his Ph.D. from the Richard Ivey School of

Business, University of Western Ontario, in 2009. His research interests include decision making in human resource management, team decision making and problem solving, and individual differences. He is a founding member of the Evidence-Based Management Collaborative. He has published in the *Journal of Management Education* and *Industrial and Organizational Psychology: Perspectives on Science and Practice*.

JONE L. PEARCE is Dean's Professor of Leadership and Director of the Center for Global Leadership at the Paul Merage School of Business, University of California, Irvine. She conducts research on workplace interpersonal processes, such as trust and status, and how these processes may be affected by political structures, economic conditions, and organizational policies and practices. Her work has appeared in nearly ninety scholarly articles in such publications as the *Academy of Management Journal, Academy of Management Review, Journal of Applied Psychology*, and *Organization Science*; she has edited several volumes and written four books, including *Volunteers: The Organizational Behavior of Unpaid Workers* (1993), *Organization and Management in the Embrace of Government* (2001), and *Organizational Behavior Real Research for Real Managers* (2006, revised and expanded in 2009). She is a Fellow of the Academy of Management, the International Association of Applied Psychology, the American Psychological Association (Div. 14, SIOP), and the Association for Psychological Science.

KATHERINE W. PHILLIPS is an associate professor of management and organizations at the Kellogg School of Management at Northwestern University in Evanston, IL. She earned her Ph.D. at the Stanford Graduate School of Business. Her research focuses on diversity, information sharing, and status processes in teams and organizations. She has published her work in multiple edited volumes and peer-reviewed journals, including *Organizational Behavior and Human Decision Processes, Journal of Applied Psychology, Journal of Experimental Social Psychology, Organization Science*, and *Personality and Social Psychology Bulletin*.

M. KIM SAXTON is a clinical assistant professor of marketing at the Indiana University (IU) Kelley School of Business. She holds a Ph.D. and MBA in marketing from IU, as well as a B.S. in management science from the Massachusetts Institute of Technology (MIT).

She has twenty years' experience in competitive intelligence, market research, and marketing. She began her career in consulting. Other roles have included VP at Walker Information, Global Market Research Manager at Eli Lilly and Company, Executive Director of Marketing at Xanodyne Pharmaceutical, and partner of her own competitive intelligence and strategic planning consulting firm. She has provided insights to the decision making of a variety of Fortune 500 firms: Nike, LensCrafters, American Express, General Foods, Hallmark Cards, the Coca-Cola Company, Eli Lilly and Company, as well as a number of other companies. She has developed custom marketing training programs for Pfizer Pharmaceuticals and Deborah Woods Associates. She has won multiple teaching awards both at IU and the Lilly Marketing Institute. She has published in *Marketing Science, Journal of Business Research, International Journal of Research in Marketing, Corporate Reputation Review, Reputation Management,* and *Journal of Research in Science Teaching.*

TODD SAXTON is an associate professor of strategy and entrepreneurship at the Indiana University Kelley School of Business and is the Indiana Venture Center Faculty Fellow. He sits on the board of the Venture Club of Indiana. He received his undergraduate degree in economics from the University of Virginia, with distinction, in 1985. He worked in business consulting for two different firms from 1985 to 1991, primarily helping Fortune 500 companies with acquisition and alliance programs and competitive strategy. He received his Ph.D. from Indiana University in 1995 in strategy and entrepreneurship. Today, he teaches and researches at the Indiana University Kelley School of Business, primarily in Indianapolis. He has won multiple teaching awards including the Lilly Teaching Award as top graduate instructor. He specializes in corporate and competitive strategy, innovation, and new venture formation and development. He has also published in the *Academy of Management Journal, Strategic Management Journal* and *Journal of Management.*

DANIEL STEWART is an associate professor of management at Gonzaga University. He received his Ph.D. from Stanford University. In addition to his interest in the evolution of social status, his research has also been focused on Native American entrepreneurship. Alongside his academic activities, he is a small business owner and serves as a board member for various commercial ventures and Native American organizations.

MELISSA C. THOMAS-HUNT is an associate professor of business administration at the Darden School of Business at the University of Virginia. She received her Ph.D. from the Kellogg Graduate School of Management at Northwestern University. Her research focuses on conflict management, negotiation, and inclusive leadership within global teams and organizations. Her publications have appeared in *Organizational Behavior and Human Decision Processes, Journal of Applied Psychology, Journal of Experimental Social Psychology, Management Science, Personality and Social Psychology Bulletin,* and numerous edited volumes.

TYLER WRY is a doctoral student at the University of Alberta School of Business and the National Institute of Nanotechnology. His research is motivated by a passion to understand the interplay of cultural and strategic factors in shaping innovation. In particular, he focuses on the endogenous shaping of cultural forces within fields and how this interacts with strategic and actor-level factors to influence the types of innovation pursued by various field members and the outcomes that result.

Foreword

Although a great deal of an executive's behavior and success is driven by status needs, nevertheless, there has been a paucity of research on this topic. The purpose of this volume, as suggested by the editor Jone Pearce, is to create the research and conceptual foundation stones for a new field of enquiry, "a quest to learn more about how status influences organizational behavior." She has brought together some of the leading thinkers around this broad arena, from a number of countries (e.g., the USA, Canada, Germany, and the UK), as well as a senior psychologist for a think tank, the RAND Corporation. They explore how status differences are legitimated, the influence of status on markets, the role of status in new industries and ventures, when ascriptive status trumps achieved status in teams, status in the workplace, and developing status and knowledge management.

By highlighting a subject which has not received the attention it deserves, either conceptually or empirically, this volume is the standard bearer for future theory, research, and development in this field. The editor also highlights the importance of status scholarship for exploring strategic issues in organizations and, in some ways, as an integrative mechanism to engage with a number of the management disciplines as a focal point of research interest.

We feel that this book will make a substantial contribution to the literature in the field, and I would like to congratulate Jone Pearce and her contributor colleagues for a job extremely well done, which should influence an important neglected area of interest in organizational behavior.

Cary L. Cooper,
CBE, Lancaster University Management School, UK

Preface

This book arose from a question debated under an ancient tree over a long lunch in the Buda Hills nearly twenty years ago: why did some managing directors work so hard to try to adapt their organizations to the new non-communist market realities while others just sat and waited? Imre Branyiczki and I concluded that it was all about status – its pursuit, its defense, and which particular people's respect and admiration were sought. That conclusion led to a quest to learn more about how status influenced organizational behavior. I discovered that many others across the range of management and organization fields were also coming to the conclusion that status mattered for the problems they were investigating, but that their work was scattered across such a wide range of subfields that they could not easily find one another. With this volume I had two purposes. First, I hoped to gather together those doing the leading work in the diverse fields that address management and organizations to make it easier for all of us to learn of each other's work on status. Second, I wanted to make it easier for those unfamiliar with status scholarship who are addressing problems in strategy, organizations, and organizational behavior to learn more about how status can help address their own puzzles.

I owe a debt of gratitude to many who helped make this book possible. First and foremost, the chapter authors graciously shared their best work, and worked to help to make their scholarship more accessible to those outside their own specialization. They are a credit to our profession. Most of us could attend a workshop in Chicago last summer where chapters were presented and discussed. I would like to thank the University of California, Irvine's Center for Leadership and Team Development for its financial support of the workshop and for the wizardry of Melissa La Puma who made the workshop a success. My Dean, Andy Policano of the Merage School of Business, gave me that most valuable of gifts: time to think and write. Ann Clark provided invaluable assistance putting the manuscript together, and Harry Briggs helped keep me together throughout the process. Finally, our editors, Paula Parish and Cary Cooper, helped make this volume much better than it would have been. Thank you all.

1 Introduction: The power of status

JONE L. PEARCE

My classmates who got jobs at investment banks now don't like to admit where they work. They'll mumble, "I work in finance but am getting out ..." When they got jobs at Goldman Sachs at graduation, they expected everyone to be jealous, but now they are too embarrassed to tell anyone they work there. (Personal communication, Ivy League university graduate, January 21, 2010)

Status matters to people. The rapid reversal in the social standing of the new financiers in the above quotation in response to the 2008 financial collapse is something they clearly feel. Whether or not it will be enough to overwhelm the riches they were still receiving is an important practical question for their employer, and an interesting intellectual one for scholars of management and organizations.

Status was once a central concern of social scientists. This is reflected in its early prominence in sociology and social psychology (Simmel [1908], 1950; Harvey and Consalvi, 1960; Weber [1914], 1978). Mirroring this early interest, status was also featured in early management and organization theory. For example, Barnard ([1938], 1968) suggested that status (which he called prestige) was an important inducement in organizations, and Vroom (1964) proposed that seeking status is one of the major reasons why people work. Maslow (1943) proposed that the esteem of others was one of the fundamental human needs.

However, since that time a relative respected social standing, or status, has occupied a rather minor place in the management and organization literature. The desire to occupy a respected social standing as a driving force in managerial and organizational work has not been completely neglected, but only in the past few years have scholars turned their attention to the powerful role of social status in explaining organizational behavior, team dynamics, the development of new industries and entrepreneurial firms, management strategies, and market behavior. While many of those working in different organizational science traditions, such as Belliveau, O'Reilly, and Wade (1996), Brint and Karabel (1991), Chung, Singh, and Lee (2000), D'Aveni (1996), Dollinger, Golden, and Saxton (1997), Eisenhardt and Schoonhoven (1996), Elsbach and Kramer (1996), Gioia and Thomas (1996), Kilduff and Krackhardt (1994), Kirkbride, Tang, and Westwood (1991), Kraatz (1998), Long *et al.* (1998), Podolny (1993), Sundstrom and Sundstrom (1986), Tyler (1988), Waldron (1998), and Weisband, Schneider, and Connolly (1995), have noted status's importance to the markets, organizational, or team settings they have studied, these works are not indepth theoretical or empirical studies focusing on status itself.

The scattered attention to status in management and organization research is costly. First, the diversity of subfields in which status is introduced means that scholars working in these fields focused on their specific problems, and while they find that status and status striving are useful ways to think about their problems, they remain unaware of each other's work and so cannot build on it and develop our understanding of status in organizations. Second, the lack of sustained theoretical conversation about the role of status in management and organizational research means that many empirical phenomena that might be better explained as status effects are explained in other, less powerful ways. For example, Van der Vegt, Bunderson, and Oosterhof (2006) deplore their finding that those group members who have the most expertise received the most help from their fellow group members, when those with less expertise needed it more. Those familiar with the status literature and, in particular, the fact that expertise bestows status and those with more status receive more attention and assistance would not be surprised by this finding. Similarly, Tsui, Egan, and O'Reilly (1992) found that American white men found racially homogeneous workplaces more attractive than did blacks. Again, research on status indicates that most people prefer to interact with those of high status, making high-status individuals appear more homophilous than those of lower status (Sidanius *et al.*, 2004). Thus, status-seeking may better explain Tsui, Egan, and O'Reilly's (1992) findings than the similarity-attraction they propose. Given the demonstrated power of status and status striving in social settings, the unavailability of theoretical explanations based on well-established status-seeking explanations can produce misleading organizational theory and action.

From across the wide range of organization and management topics, scholars are increasingly turning to status to account for empirical puzzles. As is reflected in the following chapters, recent programs
of research on the role of status on strategic diversification and alliance formation, intra-team conflict, discrimination and harassment,
organizational change, employee identification, and organizational
commitment are timely and important. These scholars, all focusing
on differing problems, have come to the conclusion that status is an
important theoretical explanation of their empirical observations.

This resurgence of interest may have arisen because scholars across
the management and organization disciplines have turned their
attention to understanding the problems of markets, strategies, and
organizations they have observed, and observation inevitably directs
attention to the role of status in driving action in social settings. How
do members of boundary-less open-source communities organize
themselves, evaluating and elevating the influence of those with useful expertise without the evaluation and control that formal hierarchies provide? When firms decide to expand or shift into new markets,
which choices are more successful and why? What leads some nascent firms to receive more support from funders and supporters than
others before there has been any market test of their new product or
services? How do team members size up the various clues they receive
about the expertise of their new colleagues in multifunctional teams?
Why have racial and gender discrimination not given way to meritocracy in organizations so dependent on employee performance for
their own success? These are the kinds of practical strategic, organizational, and workplace problems we increasingly face as organizations
depend on innovation and ad hoc teams to do their work. It is ironic
that those who seek to understand these challenges have discovered
that status, traditionally associated with the most static of traditional
societies, has become such an important explanatory concept.

However, this renewed scholarly attention to the role of status is
scattered across the disparate disciplines of the management and
organization fields. Many scholars have increasingly found that status provides valuable insights, but because the problems they address
are so different, they rarely discover one another's work. This volume seeks to bring together those international scholars conducting
current research on the role of status in their diverse management
and organization disciplines. Bringing these scholars together can

help to clarify the role of status, expand and build theories of status, and further develop theories in their disciplines by including status effects. This volume is intended to introduce the promise of status to those conducting research across all of the subfields of management and organization scholarship, as well as to engage those who have an interest in status with new research and provocative theorizing addressing management and organization problems. It is intended to encourage and further a diverse conversation on the role of status in understanding organization and management.

This chapter has two purposes. First, it serves as a brief introduction to what is known about status as it is used in the fields of strategy, organizational theory, and organizational behavior, and provides readers with a foundation for the issues and debates regarding status in and between organizations developed by the authors of the chapters. Second, it explains how each of the subsequent chapters fits into and advances this foundation. The chapter authors have been collected together to represent the wide range of problems and issues that scholars are increasingly using status to better understand, but they have all worked hard to make their often highly specialized scholarship accessible to scholars in other disciplines. Nevertheless, the works included in this volume are quite diverse and so this chapter and the last chapter serve to identify commonalities and opportunities for cross-fertilization. This chapter begins with a discussion of the fairly extensive definitional debates about status, then it addresses the well-established benefits of holding higher status for individuals, teams, and organizations. What research can tell us about how relatively higher status is secured follows, before the chapter concludes with a brief introduction to the following chapters included in this volume.

Competing understandings of status?

The study of status is as old as the social sciences themselves (see Scott, 1996 for a historical review), so it is no surprise that there have long been debates about what status is or is not. Medieval writers used the term "estate" to describe their existing social hierarchies, which they characterized as comprised of three estates: "a religious estate of priests, a military and political estate of knights or lords and the 'common' estate of the ordinary people" (Scott, 1996, p. 6).

Historically, an individual's status derived from the particular category that person occupied in a social setting. With modernization, as social divisions became more complex and fluid, the term estates gave way as the terms "orders," "degrees," and "ranks" were added to refer to the multitude of social hierarchies in more mobile societies. Later, political economists introduced the term "class," a social ordering based on economic condition (Marx, 1894/1967). Yet, Weber's ([1914], 1978) work is still widely cited in sociology, largely for his descriptions of the complex ways in which people are differentiated through party, class, and status.

Weber's original works were written in German, presenting an English translation issue. Weber uses the German word *Stände* which was translated directly into the word "status" and interpreted as status groups varying in their relative hierarchical social standing in the community by Roth and Wittich in their widely accepted English translation of Weber's ([1914], 1978) *Economy and Society*. Weber (p. 932) proposed that status "is a quality of social honor or a lack of it, and is in the main conditioned as well as expressed through a specific style of life." Most individuals accept this translation, but Scott (1996) and Murvar (1985) proposed an English translation of *Stände* into the word "estate" and use the phrase "social estate" to make the direct English translation less specific to the feudal context.

Sociologists have struggled with the distinction between status as a subjective evaluation and status as an objective and structural reality. That is, is status simply a perception of individuals, however much those perceptions may disagree with one another, or is status something about which some degree of social consensus should be expected and that acts on individuals whether or not they personally approve or accept it? Wegener (1992) argues for the former perceptual conceptualization, proposing that while the two may have been conflated in earlier times when there was more social stability, modern mobility has had the effect of destroying any consensus on the relative standing of different social groupings. The way he handles the problem is to call the subjective evaluation prestige, and the structural condition (office, occupation, neighborhood, etc.) status. However, for Weber ([1914], 1978), like most others sociologists, prestige is an aspect of relative status, it is not synonymous with it. To add more confusion, many organizational scholars follow neither Wegener (1992) nor Weber ([1914], 1978) but equate status with prestige (e.g., Conway,

Pizzamiglio, and Mount, 1996; Gioia and Thomas, 1996; Kraatz, 1998; Still and Strang, 2009). Another slightly different variation that is popular in management and organizational literature is the definition of Berger (Berger, Conner, and Fisek, 1983), which classifies status as having characteristics that are differentially evaluated in terms of honor, esteem, or desirability; that is, status is deconstructed into its component characteristics. Finally, Parsons's (1937) work is widely cited, and to him status is the result of a person's structural position along several dimensions – kinship unit, personal qualities, achievements, possessions, authority, and power, not a subjective individual evaluation. This is echoed in D'Aveni's (1996) use of hierarchical organizational rank as his measure of relative status. This inconsistent terminology makes cross-fertilization in our scholarship difficult.

This concern with the distinction between individual subjective and objective structural status is of less interest to the more person-focused social psychologists. For example, Secord and Backman (1974) suggest "which attributes contribute to status will depend on the persons making the evaluations" (p. 274), making status a wholly subjective assessment by individuals. However, this hyper-individualism is as unsatisfactory as a wholly structural definition. Status is a judgment within a social context and so most would expect evaluations of it to have at least some social consensus. While status must be perceived by individuals to affect their actions, those perceptions are expected to be grounded in a modicum of social consensus to avoid being considered autistic. Further, the concept's usefulness as a predictor of individuals' attitudes and behavior becomes limited if it is reduced to an idiosyncratic intra-psychic state, since theories of causality among purely intra-psychic perceptions cannot be tested.

This potential dissensus on the meaning of status across the social sciences and within the management and organization fields is addressed here by proposing that status is grounded in a social consensus, must be perceived by individuals, and can be assessed via structural characteristics (but is not reduced solely to these measurement indicators). To state a formal definition: status refers to position or standing with reference to a particular group or society. To have high social status is to have a respected or honored standing in that group or society. Thus, a person's status is always linked to a particular social grouping and involves evaluations that one occupies a respected position there.

We note that the frequent reference to honor among status theorists merits our attention. Status connotes respect and integrity. This helps differentiate status from power (see also Magee and Galinsky, 2008). Although some in the management and organization fields use status and power interchangeably (e.g., Ibarra, 1993), we suggest the distinction is an important one, particularly in management and organizational scholarship. When people defer to those with high status, they do so because they think deference is the proper thing to do, not because the person wields power over them. Status may be correlated with power in many circumstances, and research indicates that each one can lead to another (Magee and Galinsky, 2008); nevertheless, it is necessary to distinguish deference to those with the power to help or hurt you from deference to those you honor and respect.

Just as status is not synonymous with power, it is not equivalent to position in an organizational hierarchy of authority. Clearly, those occupying higher hierarchical positions may not be the most honored and respected members in organizations (any university professor could tell you that). In the organizational sciences, too many have equated hierarchical position with status. For example, Driskell and Salas (1991) used status interchangeably with organizational rank in their study of stress and decision making. Nor is status the same as self-esteem (Schlenker and Gutek, 1987) or social capital (Belliveau, O'Reilly, and Wade, 1996), although having a high status may contribute to both.

Finally, because status has been extensively studied in the fields of sociology and psychology, a wide range of theoretical perspectives on status form the foundation for the chapters in this volume. For example, one major area of inquiry centers on how people of differing status behave in interaction with one another (e.g., Blau, 1994; Brewer and Kramer, 1985; D'Aveni, 1996; Greenberg, 1988; Levine and Moreland, 1990; Tyler, 1998; Webster and Hysom, 1998), with several chapters building on and developing this stream of status research. An important variant of this work is the study of how status differences affect participants' expectations of one another, most prominently Berger, Conner, and Fisek (1983) and Berger and Zelditch's (1998) expectation states theory. This theory is particularly useful in understanding how people use cues to determine another's status, which in turn colors a host of other perceptions and evaluations important to individuals' commitment and performance that are further developed here. Similarly, normative expectations regarding interaction patterns that support others' claimed status, called "facework" by Goffman (1959), is receiving increased attention with studies of East Asians' cultural preference for interactional support of a respected social standing (e.g., Doucet and Jehn, 1997; Earley, 1997). The ways in which interaction patterns condition status assessments is further developed in several chapters. Social Dominance Theory has proven useful in understanding racial discrimination in societies in general and here is applied to understanding the persistence and change in status differences in organizations. In addition, Podolny's (1993) seminal idea that status is an indicator of product or service quality in marketplaces is critiqued, expanded, and developed. Finally, social identity theory has become central to much research on team performance and workplace discrimination. In several chapters, theory about how identity is driven by conflicting status implications of various selves is described. Yet, despite the variety of different theories of status and uses of status to enrich and develop other theories included in this volume, all authors conceive status as a judgment of the relative worth and value of another in a particular social setting; performance quality, expertise, power, formal hierarchical rank, and a host of other features may influence judgments of a person's relative status, but they are not themselves status.

High status is advantageous

If a desire for higher status drives action, it is important to understand why this should be so. First, many have argued that the drive for status is fundamental. For example, Troyer and Younts (1997) suggest that one of the primary motivations for individuals' participation in groups is the avoidance of status loss. Waldron (1998) further proposes a biological need to strive for status:

Founded in the principles of natural selection, the central thesis from evolutionary psychology is that particular psychological and physiological mechanisms – in this case for status – would have been selected for in the history of our species because of the adaptive advantages that ... status afforded individuals would have been greater access to scarce and sought-after resources. (Waldron, 1998, p. 511)

Certainly, it would appear obvious that having high status leads to desirable advantages and that people will make efforts to obtain those advantages. After all, a major component of the world economy is the production of costly display goods whose primary purpose is to signal high relative status. Economists call these *positional goods*, goods valued not for their intrinsic value but because they compare favorably with what others have (Hirsch, 1976). Nevertheless, the empirical documentation of the value of status for those in organizations and for organizations themselves makes the point vividly.

In organization-focused research, there is extensive documentation that an actor's relatively higher social status leads to assumptions by others that the actor is competent and a high performer. For example, status in one domain tends to generalize to other domains. Webster and Hysom (1998) found that higher levels of educational attainment led laboratory subjects to assume that those with more education had greater task competence, even when such competence was unrelated to education. Those with more status do not have to work as hard as those with lower relative status to be seen as good performers: Szmatka, Skvoretz, and Berger (1997) found that those with higher status were held accountable to easier performance standards than those with lower status, as did Washington and Zajac (2005). Further, Kilduff and Krackhardt (1994) found that being perceived to have a high-status friend boosted a person's reputation as a good performer. Status also generalizes from organizations to the members who participate in them (e.g., Elsbach and Kramer, 1996), such that employees of higher status organizations are assumed to be better performers than those in relatively lower status organizations.

Furthermore, those with high status receive disproportionately higher rewards, particularly financial ones. For example, Stuart, Hoang, and Hybels (1999) showed that having high-status affiliates shortens a firm's time to initial public stock offering and produced greater valuations compared to firms that lacked high-status affiliates. D'Aveni (1996) found that high-status university degrees increased upward mobility opportunities. This effect seems to be particularly pronounced under ambiguous circumstances, as others seek some evidence of the person's competence when concrete evidence is unavailable. For example, Chung, Singh, and Lee (2000) found that high-status investment banks were more likely to form alliances with others of high status under the more ambiguous circumstances of an initial public offering than in less uncertain underwriting deals. Similarly, Pfeffer (1977) found that occupying a higher social class was a better predictor of organizational advancement in the (pre-deregulated) US banking industry than in manufacturing where there were clearer measures of individual job performance. This effect seems to be quite generalizable; for example, those with higher status are less likely to be harassed (Aquino *et al.*, 1999). Those with higher status also achieve better outcomes in negotiations (Ball and Eckel, 1996).

What is more, those with high status appear to be able to obtain more deference from others, and thus are able to get more of what they want. Berger and Zelditch (1998), Lovaglia *et al.* (1998), Okamoto and Smith-Lovin (2001), Szmatka, Skvoretz, and Berger (1997), and Webster and Foschi (1988) all found that those with higher status received more deference from others and were more influential in group discussions. Levine and Moreland (1990) concluded from their review of social psychological laboratory research on the subject that people with higher status have more opportunities to exert social influence, try to influence other group members more frequently, and become more influential than people with lower status. Others have documented differences in behavior patterns consistent with this expected pattern of deference. For example, high-status individuals were characterized as more dominating and smiled less in interaction (Carli, LaFleur, and Loeber, 1995), and they are more prone to in-group bias than lower status individuals (Ng, 1985; Sidanius *et al.*, 2004).

The advantages of status are reflected in research on those who find themselves with conflicting statuses – they tend to emphasize their high-status characteristics and downplay their low ones (Elsbach and Kramer, 1996). What is more, those who lose status at work tend to be less satisfied, have lower self-esteem, and report more work-related depression (Schlenker and Gutek, 1987). Elsbach and Kramer (1996) found that when an organization's status was denigrated, its members experienced dissonance and acted to emphasize those dimensions on which their organization had higher rank. Pearce, Ramirez, and Branyiczki (2001) suggested that relative status incongruence was the primary motivator of executives' organizational change strategies in transition economies. Further, there is substantial evidence that those who have inconsistent status roles in organizations experience greater stress and strain (Bacharach, Bamberger, and Mundell, 1993).

Thus, occupying comparatively higher status positions provides many advantages, such as the assumption of competence in unrelated domains, greater financial rewards and other benefits, and more deference from others. And this is only a partial list of the advantages of relatively higher status. Given these status advantages and the likelihood of many other benefits, we should not be surprised that people in organizations and markets, as in other social settings, would seek high status and would struggle to prevent a loss of status. High status is actively pursued and vigorously defended because it provides so many advantages – power, wealth, dispensations, and longevity – within organizations or in any other social setting. The importance and centrality of status to social life is reflected in literature and mass entertainment, and is the foundation of the popular leadership and management self-help industries.

How status differences arise

If status is so advantageous, how do some people and organizations get more of it than others do? Unfortunately, the research on how relatively high status is obtained is not as extensive as that on the advantages of status. Weber ([1914], 1978) proposed that social worth was based on occupational prestige, lineage prestige, style of life, formal education, and, with some time-lag, material wealth. Having more money seems to be a universal route to higher status. For example, Nee (1996) recorded that as market reforms were introduced in China, the status value of being a cadre (Communist Party activist) declined in favor of working in private businesses, because the economic changes meant cadres controlled an increasingly smaller proportion of financial resources. Similarly, higher levels of education (Bidwell and Friedkin, 1988), working in high-status occupations (Kanekar, Kolsawalla, and Nazareth, 1989; Riley, Foner, and Waring, 1988), and memberships in elite organizations (D'Aveni and Kesner, 1993; Kadushin, 1995) are avenues to higher social status in unrelated social domains.

Job performance in the workplace also appears to be a reliable route to higher status. Shackelford, Wood, and Worchel (1996) found that individuals enhanced their status by demonstrating superior ability at the task assigned to the group. This suggests that behaviors that are useful to the group or organization may be the basis for a gratitude that generalizes to respect and high social standing.

Yet there appear to be easier routes to relatively higher status. For example, Sundstrom and Sundstrom (1986) documented the value of status-object displays. Those who spoke more and were more articulate and assertive without being hostile and dominating received attributions of higher status (Driskell, Olmstead, and Salas, 1993; Skvoretz and Fararo, 1996). He and Huang (2009) and Tansuwan and Overbeck (2009) found that expressing contempt (implicitly) or pride (implicitly or explicitly) led others to grant the actor higher status. Finally, non-verbal behavior such as maintaining eye contact and voluntarily sitting at the head of the table also resulted in attributions of higher status from others (Berger and Zelditch, 1998). Given the numerous advantages of having high status, it is not surprising that striving for higher status has been found in many settings.

Finally, Podolny (1993) proposed that organizations acquire relatively higher marketplace status by delivering or being perceived to be able to deliver high-quality products. Client organizations expect the higher status of vendors such as advertising agencies (Baker, Faulkner, and Fisher, 1998) and law firms (Uzzi and Lancaster, 2004), and endorsements by prominent institutions (Stuart, Hoang, and Hybels, 1999) all to contribute to an organization's relative status.

Because status pertains to particular social settings, it may well be that the routes to higher status will vary in different groups, organizations, industries, and cultures, making generalizations more difficult. Like power, status is advantageous and frequently sought, but exactly how it is achieved may be highly situation-specific. Several of the chapters in this volume directly address how relatively high status is obtained, finding that in their research settings, status attainment is a more complicated matter.

In conclusion, status is a respected social position that may be associated with hierarchical authority, power, and money, but is distinct from them in terms of how it influences. Having relatively higher status provides many advantages and so individuals, groups, and organizations actively pursue and defend it. This is well known and provides the foundation for the scholarship provided in this volume. However, taken as a whole, what is clear from this new work is that much historical research has focused on status in comparatively stable social settings. Much of the new research focuses on emergent, innovative, virtual, and changing workplaces and markets, finding that the ambiguity of such settings makes social status an important anchor of perceptions and evaluations. The attainment and defense of status is both more important and more complex in these ambiguous and shifting environments.

The contributions to this volume

In this volume we bring together the leading scholars in status from across the range of management and organization studies – those with basic disciplinary roots in economics, political science, sociology, social, and other branches of psychology. The chapters are grouped into five sections along with a concluding integrative chapter.

Part I, *How status differences are legitimated*, includes two chapters that extend our knowledge of how status operates in markets and organizations. In the first chapter in this section, Chapter 2, Bilian Ni Sullivan and Daniel Stewart directly confront the bias toward stable social systems in status research by addressing the persistent status variability or uncertainty of some participants in an online open-source software developers' community. In these settings expertise is critical to the community's effectiveness, but expertise needs to be evaluated and judged in the absence of face-to-face interaction or formal hierarchy of authority. Their research questions several established theories of how individuals interact to form collective judgments. For example, much theory and scholarship predicts convergence and consensus of important social features like status, yet they find that high-status long-tenure participants grow increasingly divergent in their assessments of the performance of others in the open-source developer community. Performance-based status positions in these communities were not produced by consensus, as is so often the case in face-to-face social settings. The members of this community interact and interact frequently over long periods of time, but do not converge in their assessments of the status of others. Ni Sullivan and Stewart's work in these new organizational communities helps to identify the limitations of our bureaucracy-based theorizing.

Next, in Chapter 3, James O'Brien and Joerg Dietz develop insight into why there has been so little progress in understanding the persistence of racial, ethnic, and gender bias which undermines the professed concern to recognize and reward organizational participants based on their performance. Their chapter introduces scholars in management and organization to the role that Social Dominance Theory can play in explaining the maintenance of ascriptive (class or demographic) status through self-reinforcing dynamics. They describe how social status hierarchies are legitimated and sustained even when they conflict with professed organizational merit-based status hierarchies. The authors draw on research showing that individuals vary in the extent to which they support ascriptive status hierarchies to suggest how such biases can better be attenuated in organizations.

Part II, *The influence of status on markets*, contains two chapters addressing how markets are affected by status. In Chapter 4 Michael Jensen, Bo Kyung Kim, and Heeyon Kim develop a new theory to help explain which firm-strategic moves into different product or service markets will be attractive and successful. They address the widespread assumption of those who study the role of status in strategy and firm performance: that status is equivalent to firm quality. They make a persuasive case that bringing the original understanding of status as social prestige back into strategy research allows theorizing that provides fertile theory about the effectiveness of different kinds of diversification strategies. Their exciting work distinguishes between horizontal status (the status of the product or service) and vertical status (the status of a firm within a particular product or service niche or industry). By placing firms within this theoretical grid, they produce provocative and original predictions about questions such as whether it is better to pursue higher status within your own industry or move horizontally or diagonally to another product or market.

In Chapter 5 Michael Nippa addresses the market for labor and how a popular economic theory of executive compensation insufficiently considers the confounding effects of status seeking. He demonstrates how the inclusion of status can extend and improve the increasingly popular tournament theory applications to managerial compensation. Tournament theory has been used to account for the extremely high levels of motivations in structures, such as competitive sports, that resemble tournaments. More recently the theory has been used to rationalize the recently rapidly increasing gap between the compensation of firms' chief executives and other highly paid employees. Nippa systematically demonstrates that very high executive compensation cannot result from tournament compensation structures and argues for the exploitation of high status and power as a more powerful driver of high executive compensation. His chapter concludes with practical suggestions for the design of tournaments within organizations.

The next two chapters address the powerful role of status in shaping emerging innovation-based industries and firms (Part III, *The role of status in new industries and ventures*). In Chapter 6 Tyler Wry, Michael Lounsbury, and Royston Greenwood directly address the lack of context in so much research on status. They note that scholars from the range of social science disciplines treat status – that most social of phenomena – as surprisingly decontextualized. In a study of innovation in the emerging nanotechnology industry they found support for the varying circumstances under which high-status star researchers influence, and do not influence, the development of innovation paths. Their work contradicts the widespread assumption that relative status always drives attention in innovation-driven industries. Their chapter draws on their research to directly address one of the central problems in institutional analyses of organizations: when does social system change come from low-status marginal participants, and when does it come from high-status central participants?

In Chapter 7 M. Kim Saxton and Todd Saxton propose a conceptualization of the role of status in the external funding of emerging firms, and argue that the study of venture capital funding has been under-socialized. For emerging firms in the high-startup-cost technology and pharmaceutical industries (entrepreneurial ventures that do not yet have products or customers), important decisions to fund and provide support are made before any objective performance can be evaluated; such judgments would be expected to be influenced by the social standing of the entrepreneurial team. When the technologies and markets are unproven, and failure rates and the potential gains are high, funders cannot rely solely on conventional financial and market benchmarks in evaluating potential investments. Scholars of venture capital have noted that social information seems to play a role in these highly ambiguous circumstances. However, with a limited understanding of social processes they are reduced to labeling these ill-understood processes as reputation, or sometimes legitimacy. The authors distinguish legitimacy, reputation, and status, and theorize that their relative importance in venture funding decisions varies, based on the emerging venture's stage of development. They draw on the popular status-producing rankings and "Best" listings in business periodicals as reflections of status-seeking to describe how and when status drives new venture funding.

In Part IV, *When ascriptive status trumps achieved status in teams*, the authors theorize about how team members use cues to assess status and expertise in face-to-face teams. In Chapter 8 J. Stuart Bunderson and Michelle Barton focus on the challenge of those forced to work together on interdependent tasks who face the challenge of correctly identifying who has relevant task expertise. Expertise is often difficult to assess, and so individuals rely on more visible cues, cues that may reflect the person's expertise, but may just as well reflect non-task relevant ascriptive or other social status. They note the powerful effects of status on influence and attention, and so seek to better understand how individuals assess and combine conflicting visible cues. In their chapter they develop an integrative typology of different status cues, based on their insight that some cues are more reliable (that is, accurately assessed) but may not validly represent expertise. Drawing on well-established research regarding our bias toward what is reliably measured, they make provocative predictions about which status cues will dominate in the absence of cues that are clearly both reliable and valid.

In Chapter 9 Melissa Thomas-Hunt and Katherine Phillips address how and when racial stereotypes are activated in teams of functionally diverse high-achieving individuals. Such teams are increasingly used with more complex technologies, rapidly changing markets, and increasingly globalized work. Here they seek to explain the conflicting research on the impact of race on the effective use of members' expertise by teams by proposing that low-ascribed status is cued when individuals display stereotype-consistent actions, when they report activities that cue that lower ascriptive status, or when they act in ways that violate normative expectations for team behavior. By drawing on our knowledge of status-cueing, the authors help to identify actions individuals and organizations can take to reduce one of societies' and organizations' most persistent problems.

The two chapters in Part V, *Status in the workplace*, both draw on how status affects individuals' self-esteem to address two of the most prominent lines of scholarship in organizational behavior: identity and justice. In Chapter 10 Jerald Greenberg and Deshani Ganegoda draw on recent research to explain how the status of individuals affects their reactions to just or unjust treatment by their organizations, offering numerous powerful new ideas. For example, they propose that both distributive injustice (getting less than you feel you deserve) and procedural injustice (the rules for reward distributions are unfair) serve as signals that the person occupies a disrespected, low status. Similarly, low-status organizational members look to just procedures as a source of security, but in contrast, high-status employees expect just treatment as a right, given their high status. Because justice theorizing forms the basis for our understanding of the effectiveness of organizational reward and incentives systems, Greenberg and Ganegoda's propositions hold promise to move status to the center of the field of organizational behavior.

In Chapter 11 Kimberly Elsbach draws on both her own work and research undertaken by others on status signaling to make innovative contributions to identity theory. She provides evidence that directly questions Turner's (1987) assertion of functional antagonism, or that if the salience of one self-categorization increases, the salience of another decreases. She provides a persuasive argument that those doing work develop quite savvy systems to signal both high distinctiveness and high status, even when these may conflict. Individuals can deploy a varying mix of physical markers and behavioral actions to send complex and sophisticated identity signals. By building on scholarship on status, her chapter provides a powerful critique and extension of self-categorization theory.

In the final chapter, Chapter 12, the editor, Jone Pearce, highlights and explores the chapter authors' theorizing about both the role of status in better understanding management and organizations, and of possible cross-fertilizations provided by bringing these diverse scholars and their problems together here. The contributions status can make to theorizing in organizational behavior, organization theory, and strategy are noted, as well as how they have helped advance our understanding of this powerful and complex phenomenon, status.

References

Aquino, K., Grover, S. L., Bradfield, M., and Allen, D. G. 1999. "The effects of negative affectivity, hierarchical status, and self-determination on workplace victimization." *Academy of Management Journal* 42(3): 260–272.

Bacharach, S. B., Bamberger, P., and Mundell, B. 1993. "Status inconsistency in organizations: From hierarchy to stress." *Journal of Organizational Behavior* 14: 21–36.

Baker, W. E., Faulkner, R. R., and Fisher G. A. 1998. "Hazards of the market: The continuity and dissolution of interorganizational market relationships." *American Sociological Review* 63: 147–177.

Ball, S. and Eckel, C. C. 1996. "Buying status: Experimental evidence on status in negotiation." *Psychology and Marketing* 13(4): 381–405.

Barnard, C. I. [1938], 1968. *The Functions of the Executive*. Cambridge, MA: Harvard University Press.

Belliveau, M. A., O'Reilly, C. A., and Wade, J. B. 1996. "Social capital at the top: Effects of social similarity and status on CEO compensation." *Academy of Management Journal* 39: 1568–1593.

Berger, J., Conner, T. L., and Fisek, M. H. (eds.). 1983. *Expectation States Theory: A Theoretical Research Program*. Washington, D.C.: University Press of America.

Berger, J. and Zelditch, M., Jr. (eds.). 1998. *Status, Power, and Legitimacy: Strategies and Theories*. New Brunswick, NJ: Transaction.

Bidwell, C. E. and Friedkin, N. E. 1988. "The sociology of education," in N. J. Smelser (ed.), *Handbook of Sociology*. Newbury Park, CA: Sage Publications, pp. 449–472.

Blau, P. M. 1994. *Structural Contexts of Opportunities*. University of Chicago Press.

Brewer, M. B. and Kramer, R. M. 1985. "The psychology of intergroup attitudes and behavior." *Annual Review of Psychology* 36: 219–243.

Brint, S. and Karabel, J. 1991. "Institutional origins and transformations: The case of American community colleges," in W. W. Powell and P. J. DiMaggio (eds.), *The New Institutionalism in Organizational Analysis*. University of Chicago Press, pp. 337–360.

Carli, L. L., LaFleur, S. J., and Loeber, C. C. 1995. "Nonverbal behavior, gender, and influence." *Journal of Personality & Social Psychology* 68: 1030–1041.

Chung, S., Singh, H., and Lee, K. 2000. "Complementarity, status similarity and social capital as drivers of alliance formation." *Strategic Management Journal* 21: 1–22.

Conway, M., Pizzamiglio, M. T., and Mount, L. 1996. "Status, communality, and agency: Implications for stereotypes of gender and other groups." *Journal of Personality & Social Psychology* 71: 25–38.

D'Aveni, R. A. 1996. "A multiple-constituency, status-based approach to interorganizational mobility of faculty and input-output competition among top business schools." *Organization Science* 7: 166–189.

D'Aveni, R. A. and Kesner, I. F. 1993. "Top managerial prestige, power and tender offer response: A study of elite social networks and target firm cooperation during takeovers." *Organization Science* 4: 123–151.

Dollinger, M. J., Golden, P. A., and Saxton, T. 1997. "The effect of reputation on the decision to joint venture." *Strategic Management Journal* 18: 127–140.

Doucet, L. and Jehn, K. A. 1997. "Analyzing harsh words in a sensitive setting: American expatriates in communist China." *Journal of Organizational Behavior* 18: 559–582.

Driskell, J. E., Olmstead, B., and Salas, E. 1993. "Task cues, dominance cues, and influences in task groups." *Journal of Applied Psychology* 78: 51–60.

Driskell, J. E. and Salas, E. 1991. "Group decision making under stress." *Journal of Applied Psychology* 76: 473–478.

Earley, P. C. 1997. *Face, Harmony and Social Structure.* New York: Oxford University Press.

Eisenhardt, K. M. and Schoonhoven, C. B. 1996. "Resource-based view of strategic alliance formation: Strategic and social effects in entrepreneurial firms." *Organization Science* 7: 136–150.

Elsbach, K. D. and Kramer, R. M. 1996. "Members' responses to organizational identity threats: Encountering and countering the Business Week rankings." *Administrative Science Quarterly* 41: 442–476.

Gioia, D. A and Thomas, J. B. 1996. "Identity, image, and issue interpretation: Sensemaking during strategic change in academia." *Administrative Science Quarterly* 41: 370–403.

Goffman, E. 1959. *The Presentation of Self in Everyday Life.* Garden City, NY: Doubleday.

Greenberg, J. 1988. "Equity and workplace status: A field experiment." *Journal of Applied Psychology* 73: 606–613.

Harvey, O. J. and Consalvi, C. 1960. "Status conformity to pressure in informal groups." *Journal of Abnormal and Social Psychology* 60: 182–187.

He, J. and Huang, Z. 2009. *CEO Social Status and Managerial Risk Taking.* Chicago, IL: Academy of Management Annual Meeting.

Hirsch, F. 1976. *The Social Limits to Growth.* Cambridge, MA: Harvard University Press.

Ibarra, H. 1993. "Network centrality, power, and innovation involvement: Determinants of technical and administrative roles." *Academy of Management Journal* 36: 471–501.

Kadushin, C. 1995. "Friendship among the French financial elite." *American Sociological Review* 60: 202–221.

Kanekar, S., Kolsawalla, M. B., and Nazareth, T. 1989. "Occupational prestige as a function of occupant's gender." *Journal of Applied Social Psychology* 19: 681–688.

Kilduff, M. and Krackhardt, D. 1994. "Bringing the individual back in: A structural analysis of the internal market for reputation in organizations." *Academy of Management Journal* 37: 87–108.

Kirkbride, P. S., Tang, S. Y., and Westwood, R. I. 1991. "Chinese conflict preferences and negotiating behaviour: Cultural and psychological influences." *Organization Studies* 12: 365–386.

Kraatz, M. S. 1998. "Learning by association? Interorganizational networks and adaptation to environmental change." *Academy of Management Journal* 41: 621–643.

Levine, J. M. and Moreland, R. L. 1990. "Progress in small group research." *Annual Review of Psychology* 41: 585–634.

Long, R. G., Bowers, W. P., Barnett, T., and White, M. C. 1998. "Research productivity of graduates in management: Effects of academic origin and academic affiliation." *Academy of Management Journal* 41: 704–714.

Lovaglia, M. J., Lucas, J. W., Houser, J. A., Thye, S. R., and Markovsky, B. 1998. "Status processes and mental ability test scores." *American Journal of Sociology* 104: 195–228.

Magee, J. C. and Galinsky, A. D. 2008 "Social hierarchy: The self-reinforcing nature of power and status." *The Academy of Management Annals* 2: 351–398.

Marx, K. 1894/1967. *Capital: A Critique of Political Economy*, Vol. III, edited by F. Engels. New York: International Publishers.

Maslow, A. H. 1943. "A theory of human motivation." *Psychological Review* 50: 370–396.

Murvar, V. (ed.). 1985. *Theory of Liberty, Legitimacy, and Power: New Directions in the Intellectual and Scientific Legacy of Max Weber.* London, Boston: Routledge & Kegan Paul.

Nee, V. 1996. "The emergence of a market society: Changing mechanisms of stratification in China." *American Journal of Sociology* 101: 908–949.

Ng, S. H. 1985. "Biases in reward allocation resulting from personal status, group status, and allocation procedure." *Australian Journal of Psychology* 37: 297–307.

Okamoto, D. G. and Smith-Lovin, L. 2001. "Changing the subject: Gender, status, and the dynamics of topic change." *American Sociological Review* 66(6): 852–873.

Parsons, T. 1937. *The Structure of Social Action.* New York: McGraw-Hill.

Pearce, J. L., Ramirez, R. R., and Branyiczki, I. 2001. "Leadership and the pursuit of status: Effects of globalization and economic transformation," in W. S. Mobley and M. McCall (eds.), *Advances in Global Leadership*, Vol. II. Greenwich, CT: JAI Press, pp. 153–178.

Pfeffer, J. 1977. "Toward an examination of stratification in organizations." *Administrative Science Quarterly* 22: 553–567.

Podolny, J. M. 1993. "A status-based model of market competition." *American Journal of Sociology* 98(4): 829–872.

2005. *Status Signals*. Princeton University Press.

Riley, M. W., Foner, A., and Waring, J. 1988. "Sociology of age," in N. J. Smelser (ed.), *Handbook of Sociology*. Newbury Park, CA: Sage Publications, pp. 243–290.

Schlenker, J. A. and Gutek, B. A. 1987. "Effects of role loss on work-related attitudes." *Journal of Applied Psychology* 72: 287–293.

Scott, J. 1996. *Stratification and Power: Structures of Class, Status and Command*. Cambridge: Polity Press.

Secord, P. F. and Backman, C. W. 1974. *Social Psychology* (2nd edn.). New York: McGraw-Hill.

Shackelford, S., Wood, W., and Worchel, S. 1996. "Behavioral styles and the influence of women in mixed-sex groups." *Social Psychology Quarterly* 59: 284–293.

Sidanius, J., Pratto, F., van Laar, C., and Levin, S. 2004. "Social Dominance Theory: Its agenda and method." *Political Psychology* 25: 845–879.

Simmel, G. [1908], 1950. "The secret and the secret society," in K. H. Wolff (trans.), *The Sociology of Georg Simmel*. Glencoe, IL: The Free Press, pp. 305–376.

Skvoretz, J. and Fararo, T. J. 1996. "Status and participation in task groups: A dynamic network model." *American Journal of Sociology* 101: 1366–1414.

Still, M. C. and Strang, D. 2009. "Who does an elite organization emulate?" *Administrative Science Quarterly* 54: 58–89.

Stuart, T. E., Hoang, H., and Hybels, R. C. 1999. "Interorganizational endorsements and the performance of entrepreneurial ventures." *Administrative Science Quarterly* 44: 315–349.

Sundstrom, E. and Sundstrom, M. G. 1986. *Work Places: The Psychology of the Physical Environment in Offices and Factories*. New York: Cambridge University Press.

Szmatka, J., Skvoretz, J., and Berger, J. (eds.). 1997. *Status, Network, and Structure: Theory Development in Group Processes*. Stanford University Press.

Tansuwan, E. and Overbeck, J. R. 2009. *You're Not That Special, but I'll Still Do What You Say: Effects of Contempt on Status Conferral*. Chicago, IL: Academy of Management Annual Meeting.

Troyer, L. and Younts, C. W. 1997. "Whose expectations matter? The relative power of first- and second-order expectations in determining social influence." *American Journal of Sociology* 103: 692–732.

Tsui, A. S., Egan, T. D., and O'Reilly, C. A., III. 1992. "Being different: Relational demography and organizational attachment." *Administrative Science Quarterly* 37: 549–579.

Turner, J. 1987. *Rediscovering the Social Group: A Self-categorization Theory*. Oxford: Blackwell.

Tyler, T. R. 1998. "The psychology of authority relations: A relational perspective on influence and power in groups," in R. M. Kramer and M. A. Neale (eds.), *Power and Influence in Organizations*. Thousand Oaks, CA: Sage Publications, pp. 251–260.

Uzzi, B. and Lancaster, R. 2004. "Embeddedness and price formation in the corporate law market." *American Sociological Review* 69: 319–344.

Van der Vegt, G. S., Bunderson, J. S., and Oosterhof, A. 2006. "Expertness diversity and interpersonal helping in teams: Why those who need the most help end up getting the least." *Academy of Management Journal* 49: 877–893.

Vroom, V. H. 1964. *Work and Motivation*. New York: Wiley.

Waldron, D. A. 1998. "Status in organizations: Where evolutionary theory ranks." *Managerial & Decision Economics* 19: 505–520.

Washington, M. and Zajac, E. J. 2005. "Status evolution and competition." *Academy of Management Journal* 48: 282–296.

Weber, M. [1914], 1978. *Economy and Society: An Outline of Interpretive Sociology*, Vol. II. Berkeley, CA: University of California Press.

Webster, M., Jr. and Foschi, M. (eds.). 1988. *Status Generalization: New Theory and Research*. Stanford University Press.

Webster, M., Jr. and Hysom, S. J. 1998. "Creating status characteristics." *American Sociological Review* 63: 351–378.

Wegener, B. 1992. "Concepts and measurement of prestige." *Annual Review of Sociology* 18: 253–280.

Weisband, S. P., Schneider, S. K., and Connolly, T. 1995. "Computer-mediated communication and social information: Status salience and status differences." *Academy of Management Journal* 38: 1124–1151.

PART I

How status differences are legitimated

2 Divergence in status evaluation: Theoretical implications for a social construction view of status building

BILIAN NI SULLIVAN AND DANIEL STEWART

One theme that consistently arises in the literature on status is the persistence and stability of status ordering among individuals and organizations (see Zhou, 2005). Yet, existing studies purporting to address this phenomenon do not directly model the effect of relevant variables on the degree of *instability* in status that results from the process of inter-subjective evaluation. As a result, while previous studies shed much light on the understanding of the emergence of status, they fall short of revealing a detailed picture of the mechanisms by which actors in an organization (or a community or a market) "socially construct" the status order and, in particular, what factors may affect the generation of status instability. Thus, previous field studies largely shun consideration of possible destabilizing forces that may interfere with the process of generating a status order. Since status mobility is most likely to occur when an actor faces a fluid flow of evaluations from others, the lack of examination of instability within status evaluations hinders our understanding of how actors move (or often do not move) along the status order.

Building on the social constructive perspective of status building, in this chapter we argue that the root cause of instability in the process of status evaluation is uncertainty surrounding an actor's true quality and that the establishment of a stable status ordering comes as a result of how actors deal with perceived uncertainty about the quality of a focal actor. We refer to status in the same spirit as Weber (1968), who used the term "status" in reference to an individual's or group's prestige or honor, and Blau (1964), who used the term in reference to an actor's claim to respect and compliance in relations with others. We focus on the processes affecting the amount of *instability* in an actor's status by using the amount of variance in external

25

evaluations as an indicator of status instability. That is, if an actor receives highly divergent evaluations from others, the divergence in received evaluations indicates either uncertainty or lack of agreement about the actor's perceived status. Conversely, we contend that status reaches a stable state when an actor receives evaluations with a high degree of consensus.

We address the issue of divergence in status evaluations by taking the study of status ratings out of the laboratory and into the field. Several important lines of work have examined the role of status within groups (see Webster and Hysom, 1998 for an excellent overview). These small group studies have shed enormous light on the processes by which micro-level processes and expectations affect the creation of status (Berger, Rosenholtz, and Zelditch, 1980). However, by focusing on status processes at the group level, it remains difficult to make inferences for the role of social forces within larger social structures, in which ambiguity and complexity play a significant role in the creation of social order. By analyzing a real-world organization of significant size, in this study we can address social factors that affect status evaluations in a way that might be constrained in experimental studies. For such an organization, the number of possible dyadic relationships can increase to a level at which each member of the observed set is unlikely to know much about the majority of other members. Thus, uncertainty and ambiguity in status might be the rule rather than the exception. In such a context, social processes may come to the fore as mechanisms which enhance or decrease status uncertainty. In this chapter, we show how social constructive processes affect the amount of observed variance in an actor's received status evaluations.

This chapter is structured as follows. We first review the organizational and sociological literature on status formation. We then develop hypotheses about the effects of different factors on the consistency of status evaluations, based on different theoretical perspectives. Finally, we present an empirical study of status formation in a large open-source software organization in which (much like a virtual organization) organizational boundaries are not clearly defined and members are primarily connected through the use of the Internet. We conclude by considering the implications of those results on existing theories of status.

The importance of status

Status can be independent of or only loosely linked to an actor's true quality or observed performance (Benjamin and Podolny, 1999; Gould, 2002; Podolny, 2005; Washington and Zajac, 2004). One important feature of status in sociological studies is that status can be transferred "through association and through relations that involve either exchange or deference" (Podolny, 2005, p. 14). A good standing within a status ordering can become an important intangible asset that can generate future rents or form a firm's strategy (Sullivan, 1998). High status in a marketplace can also be beneficial to a firm's performance in terms of profitability and revenue (Benjamin and Podolny, 1999; Podolny, 1993).

Given the importance of status in individual and organizational behavior, scholars have also been pursuing explanations of how these constructs are formed in the first place. Sociologists and organizational theorists have argued that the status evaluations received by an actor may not closely reflect the actor's actual quality, due to multiple cognitive, social, and institutional factors affecting others' perceptions about the actor and that actor's reaction to received status evaluations. Scholars in this theoretical camp have used different approaches to address how status is socially constructed. Some have suggested that the emergence of status is shaped by social and institutional factors that guide inter-subjective evaluations, resulting in differentiated status orderings (Gould, 2002; Rao, 1994; Stewart, 2005; Zhou, 2005). Others argue that status can be derived from an actor's position within his or her social network (Benjamin and Podolny, 1999; Podolny, 1993; Stuart, Hoang, and Hybels, 1999). Hence, status can be used as a signal for quality, and yet the signal itself can be independent of product or actor quality.

We agree that status may not be tightly linked to quality and that the emergence of an actor's status is shaped by a social process of inter-subjective evaluation. Departing from previous literature, however, we examine the process of status building by looking at what factors lead to more divergent evaluations about an actor, which we propose indicates the degree of instability in the actor's status. In the process of status evaluation, the distribution of an actor's received evaluations is varied: an actor may receive similar evaluations (convergent evaluations) or dissimilar evaluations (divergent evaluations) from others. Theories of social order in general suggest that status evaluations should converge and reach stability over certain factors. For instance, since social orders are established through commonly agreed legitimatization processes (Zhou, 2005) that take place over extended periods of time, an actor's received evaluations should converge and stabilize over time. Yet, none of the studies in the literature have specifically examined what factors might affect the process of reaching a stabilized state. This examination of the determinants of status evaluation instability, as reflected by divergence in evaluation, reveals a more detailed description of the mechanisms at hand in the process of status building, particularly showing how actors deal with perceived uncertainty about the quality of other actors. It also furthers our understanding of status building and status mobility by providing a fresh angle to examine different theoretical perspectives on the formation of status.

In the following discussion, we argue that much of the instability (indicated by divergence) in status evaluations comes from the way in which actors respond to perceived uncertainty about a focal actor's merits or quality. Divergence in status evaluation will be increased or reduced depending on the actions taken by the focal actor and others in the face of this uncertainty. Drawing from existing studies in the sociological and organizational literature on status, we focus on the influences of social cues, legitimacy, and network connections, and their effects on changes in the level of divergence in received status evaluations.

Theory and hypotheses

Although there are some differences in their theoretical approaches, the general agreement among organizational scholars on status is that status is socially constructed. While some have emphasized the importance of perceptual properties of inter-subjective evaluations (Gould, 2002; Rao, 1994; Stewart, 2005; Zhou, 2005), others have stressed the important role of structural positions in the process of establishing status (Benjamin and Podolny, 1999; Podolny, 1993; Stuart *et al.*, 1999). In the following, we develop predictions on divergence of status evaluations by examining how actors rely on social cues, legitimacy, and social structure to deal with the uncertainty surrounding an actor's status.

Social cues, perceived uncertainty, and evaluation divergence

One frequently expressed conjecture in sociological and organizational studies is that status ordering is a result of a system of inter-subjective evaluations, which is strongly influenced by social factors (Gould, 2002; Zhou, 2005; Stewart, 2005). If we use the term "ego" to represent an actor who receives an evaluation and "alter" to represent an actor who gives an evaluation, using this approach, we would say that alter's perception of ego's standing in relation to others and the perception of how others regard ego become essential components in alter's judgment of ego. This social construction perspective holds that the formation of status is fundamentally based on how actors perceive social cues in the process of evaluation. The notion that people's judgment is socially influenced has been long demonstrated in social psychology studies (e.g., Asch, 1951; Milgram, 1974). Building on earlier studies, sociologists have argued that judgment about an actor's relative quality and status can be socially determined because people often depend on the judgments of others when making their own judgments (Gould, 2002). For instance, Stewart (2005) found that, *ceteris paribus*, a community member is more likely to give an actor high status ratings if the majority of other community members have previously given high rankings to that actor.

The idea that an individual's judgment will be influenced by others has direct implications for divergence in an actor's received ratings. Divergence in status evaluation largely comes from uncertainty surrounding the quality of the focal actor. Variability in evaluation persists if the quality of the actor remains uncertain. Therefore, the level of variability in status evaluation could depend on how alters react to perceived uncertainty surrounding ego and ego's actions to reduce perceived uncertainty for alter(s). From the social influence perspective, if ego has experienced a high degree of consistency in previous received ratings, actors who subsequently rate ego will be likely to follow that consistency and give similar consistent ratings. However, if the focal actor (ego) has received ratings with a high degree of variation or inconsistency among the raters, that actor is likely to receive diverse ratings in the next round. Information-seeking processes invoked by uncertainty increase the likelihood of future diverse ratings for the following reasons. First, given that alters have limited information about ego's real quality, evaluations of high variation enhance alters' perceptions that ego's quality is highly uncertain. This perceived uncertainty surrounding ego would likely persist if ego and alter(s) do not have additional information to clarify the standing of ego's true quality, resulting in diverse ratings in the next round. Second, anchoring effects invoked upon observing diverse ratings received by ego suggest that alters who subsequently rate ego will have a wider range of reference points to consider when giving evaluations. Since an individual's rating scale is directly correlated with the rating information presented in the stimuli (Janiszewski, Silk, and Cooke, 2003; Mellers and Cooke, 1994; Parducci, 1965; Wong and Kwong, 2006), diverse reference points give raters more room to adjust the ratings than does a homogeneous reference group, leading to more diverse subsequent ratings received by ego. Thus, we predict the following:

Hypothesis 1 (H1): An ego's current received status ratings are more likely to diverge if the ego's previous ratings are diverse.

Legitimacy, perceived uncertainty, and evaluation divergence

Divergence in perceived levels of uncertainty surrounding ego can be enlarged if actors share different norms about evaluation procedures and standards. Therefore, if an organization or community has prevailing evaluation norms which are regarded as legitimate, actors are likely to express similar views toward a given actor, leading to more convergent evaluations about a focal actor. The perceived legitimacy of the procedures and normative rules that generate the foundations for mutual evaluations in an organization or a community is an important concept in the social construction perspective of social order building (Rao, 1994; Zhou, 2005). The concept of legitimacy refers to "a generalized perception or assumption that the actions of an entity are desirable, proper, or appropriate within a socially constructed system of norms, values, beliefs and definitions" (Suchman, 1995, p. 574), which has been extensively discussed in the neoinstitutional literature. Scholars have argued that an actor's legitimacy can be enhanced through proper affiliations (Meyer and Rowan, 1977; Suchman, 1995; Galaskiewicz, 1985). Legitimacy can improve and stabilize resource flows, making highly legitimate actors more likely to succeed and survive (DiMaggio and Powell, 1983; Wiewel and Hunter, 1985; Scott, 2001; Baum and Oliver, 1992). Consistent with the legitimacy argument in neoinstitutional theories, scholars studying status have further developed the concept of institutional logic, explicitly emphasizing the role of legitimacy as an important mechanism for the emergence of a social ordering (Rao, 1994; Zhou, 2005). For instance, in his study of occupational prestige, Zhou (2005) pointed out that "to acquire prestige or status, all social positions, roles, and behavior must justify their claims on the basis of legitimacy and appropriateness in reference to the institutional realm of shared values and beliefs" (p. 95).

While a logical extension of the legitimacy argument is that a highly legitimate actor should be more likely to garner high status ratings in the future, the legitimacy argument also has direct implications for the development of status evaluation standards in any emerging community or organization, in which the norms and beliefs will be developed to guide acceptable behavior. In particular, informal norms will be emphasized in a community where no formal authority relations are in place (O'Mahony and Ferraro, 2004). The establishment of legitimized evaluation procedures and standards is likely to lead to more trust in the linkage between observed evaluations and the true quality of ego; consequently, alter may perceive less uncertainty about ego's true quality. However, the establishment and acceptance of any norms regarding what constitutes high legitimacy takes time and effort, accompanied by the process of socialization (Zucker, 1988). The development of norms and beliefs suggests that part of the socialization process for any newcomer is the acceptance of what are deemed as legitimate beliefs and, by extension, what variables would constitute a legitimate basis for a proper status evaluation. This suggests that the longer an actor belongs to a community, the more likely it is that he or she will come to share evaluative standards with the prevailing norms and beliefs regarding status evaluation in that community. Therefore, if a rated actor receives ratings only from others with long tenure in a community, that actor should have evaluations that are less likely to diverge. On the other hand, if the actor receives ratings from others who have high variance in community tenure, the reputation ratings received by the focal actor are more likely to diverge. We thus have the following prediction:

Hypothesis 2 (H2): An ego's received status evaluations are more likely to diverge if the alters who rate ego have a high degree of diversity in their tenure in the community.

Another factor that can affect the development of status norms is the opinion of high-status actors. Theories of social influence have often emphasized the role of high-status actors, since the opinions of high-status actors are more likely to be valued (Festinger, 1957; Heider, 1958; Homans, 1950; Torrance, 1955) and, consequently, actors in other status groups may be reluctant to express their true views if those views do not conform to the values held by high-status others (Phillips and Zuckerman, 2001). The strong influence of the high-status group has been empirically demonstrated in previous studies on status, indicating that high (or low) ratings from high-status players led to high (or low) ratings for a focal actor (Stewart, 2005). An extension of this finding is that if more high-status actors give ego high ratings, others are more likely to give ego high ratings too. Thus, we predict the following:

Hypothesis 3 (H3): An ego's received status evaluations are less likely to diverge as the average status of those giving ego high ratings increases.

Network connections, perceived uncertainty, and evaluation divergence

The previous hypotheses emphasize alter's actions under uncertainty regarding ego's quality. It is also possible for ego to manage perceived uncertainty by virtue of possessing appropriate network connections. This structural approach of status formation is rooted in an academic tradition that emphasizes social structure as a unique and primary factor in determining human behavior (Cook *et al.*, 1983). Like approaches which emphasize social cues and legitimacy, the structural approach also stresses that an actor's true quality is often difficult to observe and that there is a perceptual component in the status evaluation process. Unlike other approaches, however, the structural approach argues that information inferred from the patterns and outcomes that emerge from the positional and social relations among actors becomes an essential element in determining the status ordering among actors (Leifer and White, 1987; White, 1981). An actor with the right connections – connections that help the actor to receive high recognition within the network – will be perceived as being able to produce higher quality products. Subsequently, that actor should be rewarded in correspondence (Lin, 1982; Podolny, 1993, 2001).

A common argument in the network literature regarding the establishment of status is that there are "third-party" perceptual benefits (Podolny, 2001; Stuart *et al.*, 1999), meaning that ego will be perceived as a high-status player if ego is connected to high-status actors. In the context of social networks, an actor has high status if that actor is associated with other central players (Bonacich, 1972; Wasserman and Faust, 1994). This argument suggests that if ego has a high degree of network status, alters will use that information to infer that ego's quality is high and subsequently will give ego a high status rating. Consequently, we predict that the amount of divergence in reputation ratings received by ego will decrease when ego has high network status.

Among the numerous benefits generated by networks, the benefits of information flow have been among the most highly studied. Social networks have been found to be effective information channels for the personal pursuit of jobs (Granovetter, 1974), creativity (Burt, 2004), organizational learning (Powell, 1990; Uzzi, 1996), and the diffusion of organizational practices (Davis, 1991; Davis and Greve, 1997; Haunschild, 1993). We propose that the information derived from networks can also directly impact the amount of divergence in ego's received status ratings. This may occur through a combination of improved performance resulting from information benefits and the subsequent control of status uncertainty via egocentric information that is pushed through the network by ego. Since an actor (ego) can utilize information transmission through network ties to broadcast his or her potential qualities, if ego has the ability to reach actors in different groups or clusters, he or she is in a much better position to acquire and disseminate information. A network that can reach more actors in different groups or clusters is a network with more structural holes, formally defined as "a relationship of nonredundancy between two contacts" (Burt, 1992, p. 18). Therefore, an ego in a network with

more structural holes is better equipped to both acquire unique information that is beneficial to his or her performance and also to manage
the diffusion of information about him or herself. With connections
to groups that are not connected otherwise, ego can more effectively
control the flow of information into different groups and therefore
manage uncertainty regarding his or her status. Consequently, a larger number of others will have access to knowledge about ego, plus
their opinion about the level of ego's quality is likely to be similar.
Therefore, for our final prediction, we propose the following:

Hypothesis 4 (H4): An ego's received status evaluations are less likely to
diverge as ego's network status increases.

Hypothesis 5 (H5): An ego's received status evaluations are less likely to
diverge as ego bridges more structural holes.

Method

Advogato.org

We test our hypotheses in the context of a community of computer
software programmers. Founded in 1999, Advogato.org is an online
community of individuals who are involved in developing open-
source software. The goal of the open-source software community is
to preserve the freedom to run, copy, distribute, study, change, and
improve software (Stallman, 1999; Axelrod and Cohen, 1999). As a
self-organizing community, Advogato.org maintains a stable organizational structure, even in the absence of visible formal control.

Developers join the community voluntarily and create online user
accounts that they can use to post publicly viewable weblogs, share
source code, and participate in public forums related to open-source
software development. In the true spirit of open-source software, even
the source code for the website is made publicly available. There is no
special requirement to create an Advogato account. Anyone interested
in participating or observing the activity within the community is
welcome to join simply by filling out an online form to create a unique
user identity.

For this study, the essential aspect of Advogato is its use of a system of peer certifications whereby any member of the community

can provide a publicly displayed evaluation of the status of any other community member. Peer certificates are used as the basis of a tiered status ordering consisting of masters (high-status software developer), journeyers (high-middle-status software developer), apprentices (low-middle-status software developer), and observers (low-status member or one who has not been verified by others as being a contributor to free software development). The published criteria for defining a user's status revolve around that user's skill and dedication to the free software community, with an emphasis on how influential a user's contributions have been to the development of open-source software projects. For a sample Advogato webpage, see Appendix A.

Certificates were designed as a way to confirm whether or not an Advogato member is a legitimate member of the free software community (Levien, 2004). Therefore, each new user is given by default the status of "observer." The only way in which a member can gain a status beyond "observer" is to be recognized as such by another Advogato member who already holds a status higher than "observer." In other words, a new "observer" must be given a rating of "apprentice" or higher by at least one person who is already ranked as being an "apprentice" or higher. This system of trust certification protects the integrity of the system by deterring attempts at status mobility by the use of invalid accounts.[1]

In order to give a status certification, a logged-in Advogato member must visit another member's individual Advogato page and then provide the certification by choosing from among the four status levels in a pull-down window that appears at the bottom of the receiver's page. Once a user gives a certificate, it appears on the pages of both the rater and the certificate receiver. Once peer certificates are received, each certificate is weighted by the status of the sender and then combined with all other certificates received in order to calculate a publicly displayed status rank that corresponds with the overall level of certificates that the member has acquired.

A second major part of the Advogato community is the use of "project" pages, which users can create to describe their participation in open-source software projects. Project pages typically contain information on the name of the project, its web address, notes describing the project, a list of which Advogato users participate in the project, and their roles in the project. Once a user lists him or herself as being a project participant, a line is added to his or her personal page stating which project the user is involved with and what his or her self-assigned role is within the project. Roles are defined according to titles. Users participate in projects with the title of (in descending importance): lead developer, developer, contributor, documenter, or helper.

During the time of this study, the Advogato community had over 5,000 members who were working on approximately 1,100 unique projects. Thus, it seems unlikely that any individual member would be familiar with all of the other community members. As such, members may not know each other's work very well and therefore the levels of status recognition between community members are ambiguous and may be affected by social diffusion processes.

Data

The data was organized in a series of panels provided by the founder and administrator of the Advogato website. The site administrator provided thirteen discrete panels, which were taken at approximately one-month intervals since the founding of the site in late 1999. The data is inclusive of each member of the community and each project that existed at that time. Due to capacity limitations in computing technology available, we drew a random sample of 33 percent of the original data (sampled by the ego's ID number) so that the data would be small enough to analyze without exceeding the limitations of the available computer hardware and statistical software.

Dependent variables

The dependent variable for this study is the *divergence in status ratings* received by an actor at a given time period. We view the peer certificates in the Advogato community as evidence that a status evaluation between members has occurred. We treat the certificates of "master," "journeyer," "apprentice," and "observer" as a continuous measure of status rating in order to capture the continuous effect of various mechanisms on all status levels. In this study, we coded "master" as "4," the highest status level, followed by "journeyer" as "3," "apprentice" as "2," and "observer" as "1," with the lowest status level. The divergence of status rating was then obtained by calculating the standard deviation of the average level of received ratings in a given period. For all the diversity or divergence measures in this study, we also tried the coefficient of variation, which is the standard deviation divided by the mean in a given period, as a measure of diversity or divergence in all the models. The results for the effects of the variables of interest to us are similar with two different measures (results available from the authors). Given the concern by some scholars over the use of the coefficient of variation (Sorenson, 2002), we report the results with standard deviation as a diversity or divergence measure.

Independent variables

The *diversity of the focal actor's status rating in a prior time panel* was also obtained by calculating the standard deviation of the actor's ratings. The *diversity of alters' tenure* was calculated as the standard deviation of the tenure for all alters who gave ego a rating in the prior period. Tenure is operationalized as the cumulative number of days since an actor joined the Advogato community.

Our third independent variable is the *average status of those who gave ego high ratings in a prior time period*, where the high ratings are defined as those at either a "master" or "journeyer" rank (level 4 or 3, respectively). If the mean status of those giving the ego high ratings is high, others may follow what the high-status actors do and give the ego high ratings as well. For actors who did not receive a high rating in the prior panel, we assigned a "0" for this variable.

We used the project data mentioned above to construct our network measures. To compute members' network measures, we constructed an adjacency matrix representing all Advogato members who were participating in one or more projects during a particular time period. While some projects may exist only for one time panel, others may exist for consecutive panels. We then coded the matrix with a "1" indicating two members were both on the same project, thus forming a tie, and a "0" indicating they were not tied in a particular panel.

We included a measure for the number of *structural holes* in an actor's network in a prior time panel, using the procedure outlined in Burt (1992). Following Podolny (2001), the formula used to calculate the brokerage opportunities is as follows:

$$H_i = 1 - \sum_j \left(p_{ij} + \sum_q p_{iq}p_{qj} \right)^2, \ i \neq j \neq q$$

where p_{ij} is the proportion of i's network that works on a project with j and p_{qj} is the proportion of q's network that works on a project with j.

Network status is measured by the Bonacich eigenvector centrality (Bonacich, 1972; Wasserman and Faust, 1994), which weights a focal member's status by the centrality status of non-focal others who worked on a project with ego in the prior time period. This measure gives a member a higher status score if ego's connected ties are more central in the network. Bonacich centrality has been used as a measure of status in prior research (e.g., Podolny and Phillips, 1996; Podolny, 2001; Jensen, 2003). This measure is formally given as follows:

$$s(a,B) = \sum_{k=1}^{\infty} aB^K R^{k+1} \mathbf{1}$$

where a is an arbitrary scaling coefficient, R is the network matrix, and B is a weighting parameter that can range between zero and the absolute value of the inverse of the value of the maximum eigenvalue of the matrix R. $\mathbf{1}$ is a column vector where each element has the value "1." Then, s is also a column vector where each element denotes the network status of the actors in our sample in a particular year.

Control variables

In addition, we also controlled for the *average status rating of an actor in a prior time period*, since an actor's current ratings are likely to be affected by the level of his or her previous ratings. The *focal actor's tenure* (in days since the actor created his or her user account) is controlled for in the models since it is possible that an actor with longer tenure may develop more extensive ties in the community, thus affecting the diffusion of information. It is also possible that beliefs about an actor's status could become institutionalized over time. We also control for *the average tenure of all alters* who gave ego ratings in the prior time period since it is possible that alter's tenure is associated with status and therefore could affect the ratings alter gives. We also controlled for the *time panel* in order to control for any other systematic environmental factors that might vary with time and be related to the focal actor's status. *Network degree centrality* is measured by the total number of project ties held by ego in the prior panel (Freeman, 1979). The *total number of certificates received* by ego was included since there should be variance in the number of certificates received by individuals of different status. Finally, in order to address the possibility that our status measures might be a function of the number of projects, we created dummy variables for the number of projects that ego participated in during each period. Since only a limited number of community members participated in fourteen or more projects in a given panel, we grouped them into one category. In our models, therefore, we entered thirteen dummy variables, with one omitted category.

Models

We used fixed-effects models in order to control for other actor-specific factors, such as race, gender, or other fixed qualities that may affect an actor's status level and therefore presents a strong test of the sociological arguments. The model to be fitted is the following:

$$y_{it} = \alpha + x_{it}\beta + v_i + \varepsilon_{it}$$

where $i = 1, ..., n$ and for each i, $t = 1, ..., T$ of which Ti periods are observed.

Since not all members of the Advogato community participated in the projects which we used to construct our network matrix, we incorporated Heckman's procedure for addressing sample selection bias to estimate the panel models. Furthermore, given the high correlation between alters' average tenure and the diversity of alters' tenure, we orthogonalized these two variables using a modified Gram-Schmidt procedure (cf. Saville and Wood, 1991). This technique partials out common variance and constructs an orthonormal basis for any set of linearly independent vectors.

Results

Our results table (Table 2.1, on pages 41–2) presents the outcomes of models where the dependent variable is the divergence of status ratings received by an actor in time t. Model 1 includes all the control variables except for the network variables. Model 2 presents the results for our first prediction, which states that an actor with diverse prior status ratings is more likely to have high divergence in current received ratings. The results show that, as predicted in Hypothesis 1, diversity in an actor's prior status ratings has a positive and significant effect ($p < 0.01$) on the actor's current rating diversity.

We added the amount of diversity in tenure for all alters who rated ego in a given prior time period in Model 3. As shown, alters' tenure diversity has a positive and significant ($p < 0.05$) effect on ego's current status divergence, supporting our prediction in Hypothesis 2 that, since status norms develop over time, increased amounts of diversity in alters' tenure lead to decreased agreement regarding ego's status. With an increase in the diversity of alters' tenure, a focal actor is more likely to have a high level of divergence in his or her current ratings.

Model 3 also provides evidence to support a possible stabilizing effect of high-status others, our third prediction (Hypothesis 3), which proposes that raters tend to follow the opinion of high-status actors. Thus, if more high-status actors give ego high ratings, then others will also be more prone to give ego high ratings. Consequently, the diversity in an actor's received ratings should be lower. As shown in Model 3, the effect of the average status of alters who gave ego high status ratings has a negative and significant effect ($p < 0.01$) on ego's current rating diversity, as predicted

In Model 4, we entered three network variables: degree centrality, network (Bonacich) status, and structural holes. As shown, an actor's degree centrality does not have a significant effect on the actor's current status rating divergence. While both network status and structural holes have a negative effect on an actor's current status divergence, only the effect of structural holes is significant ($p < 0.01$). Our final prediction (Hypothesis 5), in which we proposed that a network with more structural holes would reduce divergence in status evaluations, was strongly supported. The results reflect the importance of being able to control the wide spread of information among actors in different groups, thereby reducing divergence in status evaluations. At first glance, the lack of significance for the network status variable seems to go against previous findings that status emerging from network connections can be used as a signal for an actor's quality (i.e., Podolny, 1993). Our finding suggests that, while network status can be used as a signal to infer an actor's true quality, the perception of that signal might be characterized by a high degree of variation among others. We will discuss what factors might contribute to this high degree of variation in the following section.

Table 2.1 *Fixed effect estimates of status divergence level of an actor*

	1		2		3		4	
Average status ranking of *i* (*t*–1)	-0.029	**	-0.011	**	-0.008	**	-0.007	*
	(0.004)		(0.003)		(0.003)		(0.003)	
i's tenure (days)	-0.0001		-0.0003	**	-0.0003	**	-0.0002	**
	(0.000)		(0.000)		(0.000)		(0.000)	
Panel time	0.006	**	-0.002	#	-0.003	*	-0.003	*
	(0.002)		(0.001)		(0.001)		(0.001)	
Inverse Mills ratio	0.041	**	0.023	**	0.022	**	0.029	**
	(0.005)		(0.004)		(0.004)		(0.004)	
Alters' (*j*) average tenure (days)	0.0004	**	0.001	**	0.021	**	0.020	**
	(0.000)		(0.000)		(0.002)		(0.002)	
Total number of cites for *i*	0.002	**	0.0004	*	0.000	*	0.000	*
	(0.000)		(0.000)		(0.000)		(0.000)	
Diversity of *i*'s status rating (*t*–1)			0.568	**	0.573	**	0.575	**
			(0.005)		(0.005)		(0.005)	
Diversity of alters' tenure (*t*–1)					0.055	**	0.049	**
					(0.007)		(0.007)	

Table 2.1 (*cont.*)

	1	2	3	4
Average status of *j* who give *i* high ratings			−0.005 **	−0.006 **
			(0.002)	(0.002)
Network degree centrality (*t*–1)				0.001
				(0.001)
Network status (*t*–1)				−0.0005
				(0.001)
Network structural holes (*t*–1)		0.069 **		−0.044 **
		(0.008)		(0.008)
Constant	0.233 **		0.290 **	0.280 **
	(0.011)		(0.020)	(0.020)
N (total actor-panel)	20446	20446	20446	20446
R squared (within)	0.13	0.45	0.48	0.48
F-value	143.82 **	813.89 **	740.90 **	654.48 **

** $p < 0.01$, * $p < 0.05$, # $p < 0.1$, two-tailed tests

Dummy variables of *i*'s project number in each panel were included but not reported.

Discussion

While previous theories in the study of social order have suggested that status positions can eventually become stabilized either as a result of institutionalization (Zhou, 2005) or as an outcome of social perception processes (Stewart, 2005), few have used field studies to empirically and systemically examine the factors which affect the process of status evaluation instability. This study draws upon multiple theoretical perspectives to shed light on how multiple factors can contribute to our understanding of stabilization processes in status formation. The findings suggest that multiple mechanisms affect the process of status formation through the simultaneous impact of "social cues," legitimacy, and network structure on status evaluation divergence.

Contrary to the long-standing belief that opinions about the status of a focal actor converge over time, our study reveals that, over time, a focal actor's received status evaluations may diverge, depending on the characteristics of non-focal raters. Our finding that opinions from others with diverse backgrounds lead to diverse status evaluations for the focal actor suggests that the convergence of beliefs about status are dependent on the institutional-specific context and norms that shape and guide socialization processes among actors.

We found that divergence in status evaluations can be influenced by a social constructive process. Shared norms and beliefs among evaluators create a set of legitimized standards for evaluating status, as indicated by the finding that a high degree of diversity in alters' tenures led to a high degree of divergence in ego's status ratings. Furthermore, the social perception process inherent in status evaluation determines that a high degree of diversity or uncertainty in a focal actor's prior ratings leads to a high degree of divergence or uncertainty in that actor's future status ratings.

We also found strong evidence that social structure has an important role in determining the level of divergence in an actor's status rating. Our findings suggest that network brokerage can decrease the amount of divergence in an actor's status rating, as indicated by the negative and significant effect of structural holes on an actor's status rating divergence. We did not find supporting evidence for an effect of network (Bonacich) status on divergence in status evaluations. As suggested above, this could be caused by variance in alters' perceptions of network status signals. Perhaps this variance offsets any signaling benefits from network status. The variation might also come from actors within a given status level exhibiting a higher degree of cohesion with other actors at the same level (Podolny, 1993, 2001). As a result of this class cohesion, an actor can become isolated from others who hold a status different from his or her own. This isolation might impede ego's ability to gain recognition from new community members or from out-group members.

Implications

This study has important implications for the study of status formation. The examination of divergence in an actor's received ratings provides a platform for us to investigate the impact of different mechanisms previously put forward from different theoretical perspectives in the study of status. Our study shows that in the process of status formation, multiple mechanisms can take effect simultaneously. For instance, while the social constructive theory of status formation emphasizes that actors in communities or markets evaluate each other based on mutually understood and shared assumptions about the core evaluation standards (Rao, 1994; Zhou, 2005), the social structure perspective of status formation stresses that status is rooted in the relational structure in which the actor is embedded (Podolny, 1993). Our study suggests that multiple mechanisms not only work independently but also work together: the process of status building resides in legitimation processes that are *determined by* the relational connections surrounding an actor.

Our study also suggests that the process of legitimation might affect not just the receipt of status ratings, but also the manner in which actors give status ratings. We find that while ego's received status ratings tend to become more consistent with increased tenure, increased tenure in alters seems to increase divergence in ego's received status ratings. From a legitimation perspective, if alters share longer tenure in the community, they could become more likely to share norms and beliefs, and therefore should be more likely to give consistent ratings. However, given both the positive effect of alters' average tenure and the negative effect of diversity in alters' tenure, we propose that organizational legitimacy combines with an increased level of individual-level confidence for actors with more stable status positions. If, over time, actors' status positions become increasingly institutionalized, it is possible that actors in more institutionalized positions are more willing to make judgments that reflect more of their own internal evaluative schema rather than the normative influence from what others are saying. This suggests that, in terms of giving ratings, actors in more stabilized positions are perhaps less subject to the forces of social influence.

The practical implications for divergence in status evaluations depend on what it really means to an actor who experiences divergence and the possible impact of divergence on the actor's overall status level. The distribution of an actor's status evaluations and changes to that distribution can mean a few things. First, changes in dispersion of the distribution can suggest changes in the perceived quality of an actor if the actor receives new evaluations which deviate from his or her previous status, suggesting that an actor is either being downgraded (for previously high-status players) or upgraded (for previously low-status players). Second, changes in the amount of dispersion suggest changes in the amount of uncertainty surrounding an actor, especially if the actor is new to the community or is not well established. New community members might receive divergent evaluations from other community members during a familiarization period that reflects inherently higher levels of unfamiliarity by others.

Intuitively, a heterogeneous rating portfolio might be more beneficial for an actor than a homogeneous low rating profile since, while the former has room for upward mobility, the latter is more likely to become stuck at the bottom of the social strata. However, a continually diverse rating profile could be detrimental to an actor's overall status due to the signaling effects of inconsistent evaluations. Therefore, actors who strive for upward mobility have an incentive to reduce the level of divergence in their ratings. One effective way to achieve this is to get positive endorsements from raters with high status. Because of the strong social influence of the opinions of high-status players, a receiving actor might experience a lower level of divergence in status ratings while increasing the possibility of upward status mobility.

In this online community (as with others), it is possible for actors to have pre-existing friendships through projects *before* they join the Advogato community. In this case, actors with more project ties could generate favorable rankings through their friendships, resulting in a lower level of divergence in their ratings. However, results from this study show that actors with more network connections do not have a lower degree of divergence in their ratings, suggesting that friendships alone may not be capable of stabilizing status. Simple connections to high-status others through projects also do not help in reducing rating diversity. The results seem to suggest that a network with diverse connections and an efficient information diffusion capability is more likely to reduce dispersion in status evaluations.

Future studies

Future studies of this online community may allow for the following. First, it may be possible to further examine why it is that the tenure of ego has a different impact from the tenure of alter. One possibility is that although longer tenure in a community creates institutionalized positions for focal actors, it is really the establishment of status for the non-focal actors that allows the development of values and beliefs to emerge in the community. That is, since the emergence of a status order reflects a process of legitimization, individuals of differing status are likely to be more homogeneous within a group than across groups in terms of commonly held values and beliefs, which could affect their rating behaviors.

It would also be interesting to examine other mechanisms which affect the giving of ratings to others. For instance, our results suggest that, in terms of giving evaluations, high-status actors might be less subject to the power of social influence. Thus, there is some irony to our observation that an actor of high status, who may have benefited from social influence in his or her own received ratings, may be prone to actually give ratings that are affected less by social influence and more by personal volition.

Finally, it might be beneficial to examine the interactions between the multiple factors discussed in this chapter. For instance, with the help of network ties, especially in the presence of structural holes, an actor with high variance in his or her received status ratings in one time period might use the network to reduce high variance in the next time period. As a result, the observed positive effect of prior diverse ratings on current diversity in ratings might be reduced for an actor with more structural holes in the network.

Structural holes might also moderate the "legitimacy" effect, but in a different way. If, over time, actors come to possess shared evaluation standards due to a socialization process in which actors gradually develop norms that are commonly agreed upon, then groups of actors with different tenures will likely differ in their evaluation standards. As a result, any rating differences resulting from different evaluation standards could become heightened by the more accurate information that diffuses from an ego in a brokerage position. In other words, structural holes may enhance differences in opinion and therefore the observed positive effect of alters' tenure diversity on ego's status divergence might be even stronger if ego has a network with more structural holes. Thus, it may be that network structure can moderate the impact of social constructive processes on status evaluations by affecting the social cues received by others. On the one hand, structural holes can increase the ability of ego to control information, thereby decreasing variance in opinion regarding his social status. On the other hand, if differences in status norms exist across the community, then cleaner information flowing through structural holes may actually serve to increase the level of differentiation in opinion across subgroups.

Conclusion

This study provides a detailed examination of how different factors may affect variability in status evaluations (thereby influencing the process of status formation) in an online organization of significant size. We have shown that multiple mechanisms can co-present in the process of status building. In particular, we examine actors within a very large online social network, which allows us to control for both social diffusion effects and social structure. We find that legitimacy, the perception of social cues, and network structure simultaneously affect the level of divergence in an actor's received status ratings. By using constructs from multiple theoretical perspectives, we reveal a nuanced description of the mechanisms at hand in the process of status formation, with a special emphasis on analyzing how actors within an organization or a community deal with perceived uncertainty regarding a focal actor's quality.

This study calls for more attention on community and market-level forces which affect status dynamics. Our findings suggest that the emergence of a stable status system within a community or a market is contingent on the influence of multiple factors, especially those forces influencing normative pressure and information flow. In a context where normative pressures are relatively weak, status positions may be transient and actors may experience more mobility in social status. For example, in markets or communities where entry and exit are fluid, or where there are differences in ideology among high-status actors, the degree to which members are uniformly "socialized" will differ and, as a result of uneven normative pressure, there may be instability in social status. However, extensive information flow in a community or market may offset normative uncertainty and reduce perceptual gaps regarding actor quality, which could lead to the system reaching a more stable status state.

APPENDIX A. SAMPLE PERSONAL PAGE FROM ADVOGATO.ORG

(Source: www.advogato.org/person/zhaoway)

Personal info for zhaoway

This person is currently certified at Journeyer level.
   Name: zhaoway
   Homepage: www.zhaoway.com

   This person is:

- a Developer on project Debian.
- a Documenter on project Evangelism.

   Recent diary entries for zhaoway:

14 April 2002

Gradually I'm having a different attitude towards correctness proving. But I need to read more. And I need to code more. I heard Erlang is a good real time language and is functional. But I will be far away from mastering it that I would be able to put it into work. Generally, though I feel functional programming is difficult, Clean makes me feel that it is interesting, and could be easier later on, at least I hope so. So I'd like to do more in that. And in the pure way.

Uh, the Object I/O library of Clean, which is difficult. I think the difficulty is mainly because of the type system and the pure nature of Clean. Whatever, it is difficult, albeit the *uniqueness* discipline is pretty simple and straight. I spent the early morning solving a small problem of local state passing, and finally did it. Hee hee.

From Scheme I learnt *continuation* which is by far the most *cool* thing I learnt from programming languages, but I have to say that impure functional languages gives little in helping learning the functional style.

I'm more or less lost in knowing what the hell the benefits of macros are. That means programming is a difficult topic, I mean, only after I do a project which materialize the power of macros, can I really understand the power of macros. My beliefs in macros would be just lies 'till that day comes.

Lone Wolf

I read that Hermann Weyl being called the *lone wolf* among Hilbert's students. It's amazing that an *egg head* mathematician being called *lone wolf*. Previously I thought only characters in Hemmingway or Jack London's books or from Schwazeneiger's movies will ever be called *lone wolf*. Funny. You'd love mathematicians.

Elephant

Okay, I think I could name my warm-up project in the Clean language now. The name is *elephant*. It's a program playing Chinese Chess a la Xiangqi through TCP. Only 10k characters have been written so far. But I did draw all of the 14 pretty pictures of the chessmen using only the mouse and successfully loaded them through the API jungle of Clean's Object I/O library. I am proud of it. Hehehe.

65 older entries...

This person has certified others as follows:

- zhaoway certified foka as Journeyer
- zhaoway certified spacehunt as Journeyer
- zhaoway certified perlamer as Journeyer
- zhaoway certified wichert as Master
- zhaoway certified tausq as Journeyer
- zhaoway certified evo as Journeyer
- zhaoway certified andersee as Master
- zhaoway certified claviola as Journeyer
- zhaoway certified sye as Apprentice
- zhaoway certified bratsche as Journeyer

- zhaoway certified atai as Journeyer
- zhaoway certified ianmacd as Journeyer
- zhaoway certified fxn as Journeyer
- zhaoway certified thom as Journeyer
- zhaoway certified forrest as Journeyer
- zhaoway certified crhodes as Journeyer

Others have certified this person as follows:

- foka certified zhaoway as Apprentice
- spacehunt certified zhaoway as Journeyer
- perlamer certified zhaoway as Journeyer
- jrf certified zhaoway as Journeyer
- fxn certified zhaoway as Journeyer
- sye certified zhaoway as Journeyer
- evo certified zhaoway as Journeyer
- Joy certified zhaoway as Apprentice
- chalst certified zhaoway as Journeyer
- forrest certified zhaoway as Journeyer

Certify zhaoway as:

See the Certification overview for more information.
[Home | Articles | Account | People | Projects]

Note

1 For instance, it would be difficult for a hacker to generate status by creating a set of bogus accounts in order to manufacture peer certificates. This scheme would only work if the hacker was able to convince a legitimate community member to certify the hacker at a rank of apprentice or above. According to the administrator of the site, this type of deception happens very infrequently and with limited results.

References

Asch, S. E. 1951. "Effects of group pressure upon the modification and distortion of judgments," in H. Guetzkow (ed.), *Groups, Leadership, and Men*. Pittsburgh, PA: Carnegie Press.

Axelrod, R. M. and Cohen, M. D. 1999. *Harnessing Complexity: Organizational Implications of a Scientific Frontier*. New York: Free Press.

Baum, J. and Oliver, C. 1992. "Institutional embeddedness and the dynamics of organizational populations." *American Sociological Review* 57: 540–559.

Benjamin, B. A. and Podolny, J. M. 1999. "Status, quality, and social order in California wine industry." *Administrative Science Quarterly* 44: 563–589.

Berger, J., Conner, T. L., and Fisek, M. H. 1974. *Expectation States Theory: A Theoretical Research Program.* Cambridge, MA: Winthrop Publishers.

Berger, J., Rosenholtz, S. J., and Zelditch, M., Jr. 1980. "Status organizing processes." *Annual Review of Sociology* 6: 479–508.

Berger, P. L. and Luckmann, T. 1966. *The Social Construction of Reality: A Treatise in the Sociology of Knowledge.* New York: Doubleday & Company.

Blau, P. M. 1964. *Exchange and Power in Social Life.* New York: Wiley.

Bonacich, P. 1972. "Factoring and weighing approaches to clique identification." *Journal of Mathematical Sociology* 2: 113–120.

Borgatti, S. P., Everett, M. G., and Freeman, L. C. 2002. *Ucinet 6 for Windows.* Harvard: Analytic Technologies.

Burt, R. S. 1992. *Structural Holes: The Social Structure of Competition.* Cambridge, MA: Harvard University Press.

2004. "Structural holes and good ideas." *American Journal of Sociology* 110: 349–399.

Cook, K. S., Emerson, R. M., Gillmore, M. R., and Yamagishi, T. 1983. "The distribution of power in exchange networks: Theory and experimental evidence." *American Journal of Sociology* 89: 275–305.

Davis, G. F. 1991. "Agents without principles? The spread of the poison pill through the intercorporate network." *Administrative Science Quarterly* 36: 583–613.

Davis, G. F. and Greve, H. R. 1997. "Corporate elite, networks and governance changes in the 1980s." *American Journal of Sociology* 103: 1–37.

DiMaggio, P. J. and Powell, W. W. 1983. "The iron cage revisited: Institutional isomorphism and collective rationality in organizational fields." *American Sociological Review* 48: 147–160.

Festinger, L. 1957. *A Theory of Cognitive Dissonance.* Evanston, IL: Row Peterson.

Freeman, L. C. 1979. "Centrality in social networks: Conceptual clarification." *Social Networks* 1: 215–239.

Galaskiewicz, J. 1985. "Interorganizational relations." *Annual Review of Sociology* 11: 281–304.

Gould, R. V. 2002. "The origins of status hierarchies: A formal theory and empirical test." *American Journal of Sociology* 107: 1143–1178.

Gould, R. V. and Fernandez, R. M. 1989. "Structures of mediation: A formal approach to brokerage in transaction networks." *Sociological Methodology* 19: 89–126.

Granovetter, M. 1974. *Getting a Job: A Study of Contacts and Careers.* Cambridge, MA: Harvard University Press.

Hall, R. 1992. "The strategic analysis of intangible resources." *Strategic Management Journal* 13: 135–144.

Haunschild, P. R. 1993. "Interorganizational imitation: The impact of interlocks on corporate acquisition activity." *Administrative Science Quarterly* 38: 564–592.

1994. "How much is that company worth? Interorganizational relationships; uncertainty; and acquisition premiums." *Administrative Science Quarterly* 39: 391–411.

Heider, F. 1958. *The Psychology of Interpersonal Relations.* New York: Wiley.

Homans, G. C. 1950. *The Human Group.* New York: Harcourt, Brace.

1961. *Social Behavior: Its Elementary Forms.* New York: Harcourt, Brace & World.

Janiszewski, C., Silk, T., and Cooke, A. D. J. 2003. "Different scales for different frames: The role of subjective scales and experience in explaining attribute framing effects." *Journal of Consumer Research* 30: 311–325.

Jensen, M. 2003. "The role of network resources in market entry: Commercial banks' entry into investment banking, 1991–1997." *Administrative Science Quarterly* 48(3): 466–495.

Klein, B. and Leffler, K. B. 1981. "The role of market forces in assuring contractual performance." *Journal of Political Economy* 89: 615–641.

Leifer, E. M. and White, H. C. 1987. "A structural approach to markets," in M. S. Mizruchi and M. Schwartz (eds.), *Intercorporate Relations: The Structural Analysis of Business.* Cambridge University Press, pp. 85–108.

Levien, R. 2004. *Attack Resistant Trust Metrics.* Unpublished manuscript. University of California at Berkeley.

Lin, N. 1982. "Social resources and instrumental action," in P. V. Marsden and N. Lin (eds), *Social Structure and Network Analysis.* Beverly Hills, CA: Sage Publications.

Marsden, P. V. 1982. "Brokerage behavior in restricted exchange networks," in P. V. Marsden and N. Lin (eds), *Social Structure and Network Analysis.* Beverly Hills, CA: Sage Publications.

Mellers, B. A. and Cooke, A. D. J. 1994. "Trade-offs depend on attribute range." *Journal of Experimental Psychology: Human Perception and Performance* 20(5): 1055–1067.

Meyer, J. W. and Rowan, B. 1977. "Institutionalized organizations: Formal structure as myth and ceremony." *American Journal of Sociology* 83(2): 340–363.

Milgram, S. 1967. "The small-world problem." *Psychology Today* 1: 60–67.

1974. *Obedience to Authority: An Experimental View*. London: HarperCollins.

O'Mahony, S. and Ferraro, F. 2004. "Managing the boundary of an 'open' project." Harvard Business School Working Paper.

Parducci, A. 1965. "Category judgment: A range-frequency model." *Psychological Review* 72(6): 407–418.

Phillips, D. J. and Zuckerman, E. W. 2001. "Middle-status conformity: Theoretical restatement and empirical demonstration in two markets." *American Journal of Sociology* 107(2): 379–429.

Podolny, J. M. 1993. "A status-based model of market competition." *American Journal of Sociology* 98: 829–872.

2001. "Networks as the pipes and prisms of the market." *American Journal of Sociology* 107: 33–60.

2005. *Status Signals: A Sociological Study of Market Competition*. Princeton University Press.

Podolny, J. and Phillips, D. J. 1996. "The dynamics of organizational status." *Industrial and Corporate Change* 5: 453–471.

Powell, W. W. 1990. "Neither market nor hierarchy: Network forms of organization," in B. Staw and L. Cummings (eds.), *Research in Organizational Behavior*. Greenwich, CT: JAI Press.

Rao, H. 1994. "The social construction of reputation: Certification contests, legitimation, and the survival of organizations in the American automobile industry: 1895–1912." *Strategic Management Journal* 15: 29–44.

Ross, L. and Nisbett, R. E. 1991. *The Person and the Situation: Perspectives of Social Psychology*. Philadelphia, PA: Temple University Press.

Saville, D. and Wood, G. R. 1991. *Statistical Methods: The Geometric Approach*. New York: Springer-Verlag.

Scott, W. R. 2001. *Institutions and Organizations* (2nd edn.). Thousand Oaks, CA: Sage.

Sorensen, J. B. 2002. "The use and misuse of the coefficient of variation in organizational demography research." *Sociological Methods and Research* 30: 475–491.

Stallman, R. 1999. "The GNU operating system and the free software movement," in C. Dibona, S. Ockman, and M. Stone (eds.), *Open Sources*. Sebastopol, CA: O'Reilly.

Stewart, D. 2005. "Social status in an open source community." *American Sociological Review* 70(5): 823–842.

Stuart, T. E., Hoang, H., and Hybels, R. 1999. "Interorganizational endorsements and the performance of entrepreneurial ventures." *Administrative Science Quarterly* 44(2): 315–349.

Suchman, M. C. 1995. "Managing legitimacy: Strategic and institutional approaches." *Academy of Management Review* 20: 571–610.

Sullivan, M. W. 1998. "How brand names affect the demand for twin automobiles." *Journal of Marketing Research* 35: 154–165.

Torrance, E. P. 1955. "Some consequences of power differences on decision making in permanent and temporary three-man groups," in A. P. Hare, E. F. Borgatta, and R. F. Bales (eds.), *Small Groups*. New York: Knopf, pp. 482–492.

Uzzi, B. 1996. "The sources and consequences of embeddedness for the economic performance of organizations: The network effect." *American Sociological Review* 61: 674–698.

Washington, M. and Zajac, E. 2004. "Status evolution and competition: Theory and evidence." *Academy of Management Journal* 48: 282–296.

Wasserman, S. and Faust, K. 1994. *Social Network Analysis: Methods and Applications*. Cambridge University Press.

Weber, M. 1968. *Economy and Society: An Outline of Interpretive Sociology*. New York: Bedminster Press.

Webster, M., Jr. and Hysom, S. J. 1998. "Creating status characteristics." *American Sociological Review* 63: 351–378.

White, H. C. 1981. "Where do markets come from?" *American Journal of Sociology* 87: 517–547.

Wiewel, W. and Hunter, A. 1985. "The interorganizational network as a resource: A comparative case study on organizational genesis." *Administrative Science Quarterly* 30: 482–496.

Wong, K. F. E. and Kwong, J. Y. Y. 2006. "Effects of rater goals on rating patterns in performance evaluation: Evidence from an experimental field study." *Journal of Applied Psychology* 91: 282–297.

Zhou, X. 2005. "The institutional logic of occupational prestige ranking: Reconceptualization and reanalyses." *American Journal of Sociology* 111: 90–140.

Zucker, L. G. (ed.). 1988. *Institutional Patterns and Organizations: Culture and Environment*. Cambridge, MA: Ballinger.

3 | Maintaining but also changing hierarchies: What Social Dominance Theory has to say

JAMES O'BRIEN AND JOERG DIETZ

Sands (2009) reports some interesting observations about gender bias in theater. If you went to see a Broadway play recently, the odds are about seven to one that the play you saw was written by a man. These odds are roughly consistent with real differences in submission rates for these scripts, organized by gender. In a subsequent study, however, Sands reported that female evaluators in the theatrical industry rated identical plays by pseudonymous female playwrights more stringently than male raters did, who did not discriminate along gender lines (Cohen, 2009).

As a manifestation of systemic discrimination, the overall picture here is not surprising. It is well known that in the theater and movie industry a gender hierarchy exists that favors not only male writers, but also male actors, producers, and directors. But why do female raters act so harshly with respect to female playwrights and thereby contribute to inequality at the expense of their gender? Social Dominance Theory (SDT) (see, e.g., Sidanius and Pratto, 1999), which is a theory of group-based social hierarchies, contends that "group oppression is very much a cooperative game" (p. 43). Low-status groups are enmeshed in the very system that produces negative outcomes for them, and they paradoxically and often inadvertently support their own oppression. This example indicates how SDT explains, at least partially, the maintenance of social hierarchies.

Consider an organizational example. The record of diversity interventions and training in achieving desired workplace outcomes (performance, equal representation across levels, improved work climate, etc.) is mixed. Kalev, Kelly, and Dobbin (2006) examined diversity management practices and found that programs that assign authority,

Note: Both authors contributed equally to this chapter.

responsibility, and expertise (affirmative action plans, diversity staff, and diversity committees) were best at improving the representation of women and minorities in managerial positions. Diversity initiatives that provide feedback and training were not useful and at times counter-productive, while networking initiatives had small positive effects. SDT argues that in hierarchy systems, institutions (in contrast to individuals) are particularly powerful because they pool resources, have broad influence, and are stable (Pratto, Sidanius, and Levin, 2006). Thus, institutions are well armed to effect change and improve the status and hierarchical position of underrepresented groups. This example indicates how SDT can explain change in status hierarchies.

In this chapter, we position SDT as a theory of both maintenance and change of social hierarchies. We acknowledge that according to SDT, the forces that favor hierarchy maintenance are stronger, and we will attend to these forces. But SDT also suggests ways in which status hierarchies change and may be changed. This perspective may have been somewhat neglected in light of the omnipresent notion that hierarchies are self-reinforcing systems. Reacting to this perspective, Magee and Galinsky (2008) recently challenged organization scientists to conceptualize models of hierarchy that also allowed for hierarchy-attenuating forces. In the remainder of this chapter, we will first review the origins and tenets of SDT and then review a sample of the organizational studies of the theory, before turning to other organizational themes and issues that SDT inspires and informs.

Social Dominance Theory and Social Dominance Orientation

All animals are equal, but some animals are more equal than others.

George Orwell, *Animal Farm*

Broadly speaking, SDT is a theory of the operation of group-based social hierarchies in societies. Three kinds of status hierarchies exist on the basis of age, gender, and criteria that are set in arbitrary ways (e.g., ethnicity). Under SDT, therefore, the emphasis is on status hierarchies on the basis of ascribed, rather than earned, criteria. The existence, maintenance, and change of these hierarchies are predicated on multiple processes that operate within and across levels of analysis, from the individual to the societal level. These processes include individual dispositions and acts, differential behaviors by groups as a function of group status, institutional acts, and myths that legitimate or challenge existing social arrangements. SDT explains how members of particular social groups accumulate a disproportionate share of status and power. Below, we break down SDT into its origins, the kinds of status hierarchies it considers, the mechanisms comprising the theory, and manifestations of group-based hierarchies.

The origins of SDT

Sidanius and Pratto (1999, p. 38) assert that SDT draws on a wide range of disciplines and theories in social science. Disciplines that have informed SDT and define its assumptions include psychology, sociology, economics, and anthropology. Important social psychological roots include social identity theory (e.g., Tajfel and Turner, 1986) and authoritarian personality theory (Adorno *et al.*, 1950), and micro-sociological roots include Blumer's (1960) group positions theory and Rokeach's (1979) two-value model of political orientation. Economic and sociological theories including Marxist theories and neoclassical elite theories (e.g., Pareto, 1901/1979) underlie the assumption of SDT that societies must produce a surplus of resources for arbitrary-set social hierarchies to emerge: there has to be something material for groups to fight over. Anthropology suggests that age- and gender-based hierarchies as well as friction between groups in the hierarchy are innate features of human social systems.

Kinds of social hierarchies

In societies, groups are typically vertically ordered into status hierarchies, which ascribe relative status and power. Dominant groups enjoy more than their fair share of positive social value, which refers to "all those material and symbolic things for which people strive ... [including] political authority and power, good and plentiful food, splendid homes, the best available health care, wealth, and high social status" (Sidanius and Pratto, 1999, pp. 31–32).

Under SDT, social hierarchies are organized along age, gender, and "arbitrary-set" characteristics (p. 33). In age-based hierarchies, adults exercise authority over children, but there is also some flexibility to this category. Individuals move across age-based groups over their life course, and the cut-offs for middle age vary within and across societies. Gender-based hierarchies manifest patriarchy, under which "males have disproportionate social and political power over females" (Sidanius and Pratto, 1999, p. 33).

Finally, criteria for arbitrary-set hierarchies include race, ethnicity, sexuality, and religion. Among the three kinds of group-based social hierarchies, the arbitrary-set system "is associated with the greatest degree of violence, brutality, and oppression" (Sidanius and Pratto, 1999, p. 34). In comparison to age- and gender-based hierarchies, interactions across levels of arbitrary-set hierarchy more frequently take place among coalitions (e.g., race riots) rather than individuals, which partially explains the severity of the behaviors seen here.

Mechanisms

SDT asserts that, beyond "force, intimidation and discrimination" (Pratto *et al.*, 2006, p. 275), powerful interlocking mechanisms such as mythologies, behaviors by both institutions and groups, and contributions by individuals themselves uphold status hierarchies. The mechanisms of SDT or, as Sidanius and Pratto (1999, p. 40) characterized it, the *schematic* show how group-based social hierarchies are produced and sustained under the theory. Figure 3.1, which we explain in more detail below, provides a simplification of the mechanics using the example of gender hierarchy, roughly organized by level of theory.

Myths

Legitimating myths either reflect and support or attenuate a particular hierarchical arrangement of social groups. These shared stories "consist of attitudes, values, beliefs, stereotypes, and ideologies that provide moral and intellectual justification for the social practices that distribute social value within the social system" (Sidanius and Pratto, 1999, p. 45). The reference to "myths" is an interesting and probably deliberate word choice, as myths have both durable and transcendent qualities: they endure, even in the face of concerted efforts to correct them, and as a property of higher-order social systems (i.e., societies) they span group boundaries and interests. Pratto *et al.* (2006) noted that myths often take the form of self-fulfilling prophecies. Thus, myths are the foundation for status hierarchies, but they are also reinforced by status hierarchies. Examples of myths that legitimize male dominance in hierarchies include sexism and stereotypes that depict leaders as men or the myth that women ought to be sexually attractive.

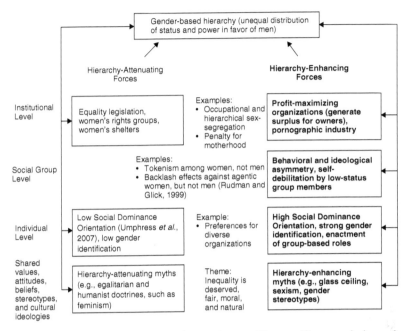

Figure 3.1 Mechanisms of Social Dominance Theory, illustrated through gender-hierarchy examples

Institutions

At the organizational level, Sidanius and Pratto (1999, p. 41) consider what they call institutional discrimination: "Group-based social hierarchy is produced not only by individual and private acts of discrimination, but also by the rules, procedures, and actions of social institutions." Social institutions include organizations like corporations, but also regulatory bodies, such as governments and parliaments. An example of institutional gender discrimination is the career penalties that women incur for motherhood (e.g., Correll, Benard, and Paik, 2007). It is plausible to argue that these penalties result, at least in part, from the incongruence of professional and gender roles that is an inherent property of social institutions.

Social groups

At the level of groups, several mechanisms (asymmetrical in-group bias, self-debilitating behaviors among subordinates, and ideological asymmetry) foster the maintenance of status hierarchies. Sidanius and Pratto (1999) subsumed these mechanisms under the label of "behavioral asymmetry." The asymmetry reflects the paradox that both those who enjoy strong hierarchical positions as well as those who are at the bottom of status hierarchies engage in behaviors that maintain these hierarchies. Members of dominant and subordinate groups contribute to the maintenance of status hierarchies in different ways, based on the different "behavioral repertoires" (p. 43) they possess. For example, the "deferential and obsequious behavior of subordinates" (p. 44) may support a particular configuration of groups, and have the effect of stabilizing the relative positions of the groups within the hierarchy over time. Another example of behavioral asymmetry can be found in the stereotype threat that members of low-status groups experience versus the stereotype lift experienced by members of high-status groups (Walton and Cohen, 2003).

Asymmetrical in-group bias refers to the fact that members of dominant groups typically show a bias for their group, whereas members of subordinate groups do so to a lower degree and, at times, even display out-group favoritism. Hence, in-group bias varies as a function of the position of the group in the social hierarchy and is strongest within dominant groups. In addition, members of subordinate groups are much more likely to engage in group-debilitating behaviors that cement their position in the hierarchy. Research on salary negotiations (e.g., Stevens, Bavetta, and Gist, 1993), for example, indicates that women report lower self-efficacy for negotiating salaries than men do. Pratto *et al.* (2006) point to the participation of women in the beauty myth as a debilitating behavior. Finally, ideological asymmetry is sensitive to the discrepancy between in-group ideologies and system-enhancing ideologies. These discrepancies are asymmetrical in that they exist only for members of low-status groups. It is, for example, harder for women than for men to endorse currently male-dominated corporate ideologies simply because these ideologies (e.g., the beliefs in "old boy networks") serve only men.

Individuals

At the individual level, SDT includes both personal acts of discrimination, accumulating over time and persons, and the individual difference variable Social Dominance Orientation (SDO, the endorsement of social hierarchies), which we will consider shortly in a separate section. For now, it suffices to mention that there is variance in SDO not only between dominant and subordinate groups (i.e., levels of

SDO tend to be higher among members of dominant groups) but also within groups. Furthermore, SDO predicts the extent to which individuals engage in hierarchy-maintaining and hierarchy-attenuating behaviors.

Although we have explained the mechanisms of SDT by level of analysis, it is critical to point out that SDT is a multi- and cross-level theory. Figure 3.1 indicates the relations within hierarchy-attenuating and within hierarchy-enhancing forces. In addition, there are relations between hierarchy-attenuating and hierarchy-enhancing forces. Thus, in understanding phenomena through the lens of SDT, one must consider the forces that explain these phenomena both within and across levels. For example, the previous example of gender differences in salary negotiations is not sufficient to explain the gender salary gap. Instead, this gap results from multiple forces not only at the group level, but also at the individual and institutional levels, as well as interactions between forces across levels.

Manifestations and consequences of social hierarchies

The existence of hierarchies with dominant and subordinate social groups in society, which have differential privileges and access to resources, is a proposition that is difficult to contest (see, e.g., Magee and Galinsky, 2008; Sidanius and Pratto, 1999). In fact, Pratto *et al.* (2006, p. 272) referred to it as a "human universal" (Tilly, 1998). Social hierarchies extend to the geopolitical sphere of conflict and are also evident in more local manifestations of prejudice and discrimination in communities and organizations. Prejudice and discrimination against subordinate groups are frequently observed characteristics of everyday life, as the following sample of recent stories from the national Canadian media attests:

- Discrimination [*against* minorities] common in Toronto rental market: study (www.cbc.ca/news, July 7, 2009).
- Immigrants more vulnerable to global recession, OECD says (www.cbc.ca/news, July 1, 2009).
- Gays and lesbians of Canada's ethnic minorities fight homophobia (www.cbc.ca/news, May 18, 2009).

Thus, the negative consequences of social hierarchies for members of subordinate groups are well documented. In addition to discrimination (i.e., less favorable outcomes for the same performance), hierarchies can also operate to reduce actual performance (Magee and Galinsky, 2008). On the positive side, status hierarchies can be a useful organizing device. In organizations, hierarchies are used to create clarity of work roles (who does what?) and to underscore coordination mechanisms (who works and reports to whom?). Because hierarchies are associated with status and power, they also create clarity around rewards (who gets what?). In light of these positive consequences, it is plausible to argue that status hierarchies *per se* are not bad. Instead, they are an inevitable feature of organizations and can indeed support efficient organizational functioning. Such reasoning implies that changing hierarchies may not be so much a matter of replacing them with a hierarchy-free alternative (e.g., an anarchy), but a matter of resolving and managing the inequities that are associated with them. Below, we briefly discuss what SDT has to say about attenuating social hierarchies.

Elements of hierarchy attenuation in SDT

Considering both the multiple manifestations and consequences of social hierarchies in society, as well as the multiple, reinforcing mechanisms through which these effects are produced, it is easy to reach the conclusion that some existing configuration of group-based social hierarchies represents a durable arrangement. SDT suggests that in a clash of social groups, dominant groups have a structural advantage that seems difficult to overcome.

Yet, as Figure 3.1 indicates, while the theory suggests forces that work toward maintenance, it also recognizes hierarchy-attenuating forces at the individual and institutional levels. To begin with, while SDT notes the existence of hierarchy-enhancing myths, it also explicitly acknowledges the existence of hierarchy-attenuating myths. The key hierarchy-attenuating myth is the value of egalitarianism. SDT can thus be viewed as a theory of opposing forces in which the balance is tilted in favor of hierarchy-enhancing forces. On the basis of SDT, the question arises of whether status hierarchies would continue to exist if there were not forces that keep in check the extent to which hierarchies cement inequality. Magee and Galinsky (2008) discuss a similar notion, observing that while status hierarchies pervade human life, few "the winner takes it all" hierarchies exist or have been sustainable over time.

At the individual level, SDT suggests that there are people who essentially dislike status hierarchies and do not endorse hierarchies (that is, who are low on SDO). Umphress *et al.* (2007), for example, showed that members of high-status groups (men and Caucasians) who are low on SDO prefer to work in diverse organizations that afford members of low-status groups access to positions of power.

Furthermore, SDT suggests that institutions can use their power and concentrated resources to resolve inequities in social hierarchies. We already mentioned the success of institutionally based diversity interventions in increasing the representation of minorities in higher levels of organizational hierarchies. Taking this example even further, in the USA, it was the Civil Rights Act of 1964, a piece of legislation that was passed by the institutions of the House of Representatives and the Senate, which triggered organizational concern with diversity in the first place. On many indicators, including the actual representation of members of subordinate groups in powerful positions as well as the change in public attitudes toward discrimination, the Civil Rights Act of 1964 has caused dramatic change in social hierarchies.

In summary, for forces of hierarchy change in SDT, the emphasis is on the existence of hierarchy-attenuating myths and the actions of equality-minded individuals and powerful institutions. The theory implies for organizations that the attenuation of social hierarchies actually may best start at the very top, where equality-conscious leaders have access to resources. More broadly, SDT suggests that organizations can be seen as arrangements of hierarchy-attenuating and hierarchy-enhancing forces that operate in tandem toward a common purpose. In organizations, one might argue that this duality of forces can be observed both in the coexistence of formal and informal social hierarchies in organizations as well as in the dynamics of labor and management representation of often competing interests.

Having reviewed the macro aspects of SDT, we now turn to its individual difference component, SDO.

Social Dominance Orientation (SDO)

Definition

The SDO construct has been described as "the psychological component of SDT" (Umphress *et al.*, 2007). SDO is an individual difference reflecting the strength of an individual's endorsement of group-based social hierarchies. It is theorized to affect the degree to which individuals may be susceptible to the underlying myths on which social hierarchies rest. In the words of Pratto *et al.* (1994), who developed the SDO construct, its definition is as follows:

We consider SDO to be a general attitudinal orientation towards intergroup relations, reflecting whether one generally prefers such relations to be equal, versus hierarchical, that is, ordered along a superior-inferior dimension. (p. 742)

This definition has also been formulated in stronger terms:

SDO is also thought to express a view of human existence as zero-sum and relentless competition between groups, the desire for generalized, hierarchical relationships between social groups, and the desire for ingroup dominance and superiority over outgroups. (Sidanius *et al.*, 1996, p. 148)

The characterization of SDO as a trait (i.e., a relatively stable, enduring property of an individual) or state (a more changeable, transitory characteristic) has been a matter of some dispute in the literature. Pratto *et al.* (2006) clarified that SDO is not a trait in a personality theory of prejudice, but a "general orientation" that is "sensitive to situational primes" (p. 292). In other words, it is stable in the relative sense and not in absolute terms, as SDO levels are affected by situations and contexts. Aquino, Stewart, and Reed (2005) reasoned that SDO might represent something more akin to a belief or an attitude than a relatively fixed and enduring trait (p. 737). Ekehammer and Akrami (2007) suggested that SDO was a surface trait rather than a core personality trait because of the responsiveness of SDO to characteristics of the situation. In some aspects this discussion of SDO as a trait versus a state is representative of the debate of prejudice as an individual difference versus a situational result of inter-group configurations. It is our impression that this debate is not entirely resolvable. In part, the positioning of SDO as a trait versus a state is a function of its theoretical positioning. For example, studies of SDO effects on inter-group behavior often treat it as a fairly stable individual difference, whereas those studies that examine the effects of inter-group behavior on SDO treat it as a state.

Related but distinct constructs: SDO and
right-wing authoritarianism (RWA)

Much of the psychometric research on SDO has focused on its relationship to RWA. Like SDO, RWA captures a perspective on intergroup relations. Altemeyer (1998, 2006) defined it as a composition of three attitudinal clusters: (1) submissiveness to seemingly legitimate and established authorities, (2) aggressiveness against deviants and out-group members, and (3) adherence to traditions and social norms that established authorities endorse. Both Altemeyer (1998) and Pratto *et al.* (2006) distinguished SDO and RWA through their underlying beliefs. RWA is grounded in a belief that "the world is a dangerous place" (p. 304), which motivates fearful deference to authority. SDO is based on the conception that "the world is a zero-sum game" (p. 304), which motivates acts of cruelty against members of subordinate groups.

It is not surprising that both SDO and RWA predict prejudice, and research by Duckitt, Sibley, and their colleagues (e.g., Duckitt, 2001; Duckitt and Sibley, 2006; Duckitt *et al.*, 2002; Sibley, Robertson, and Wilson, 2006) embeds SDO, RWA, and prejudice in a nomological network that is consistent with the above distinction between SDO and RWA on the basis of their underlying beliefs. These scientists suggest that prejudice can result from dual complementary processes: on the one hand, tough-mindedness associated with SDO and the belief that the world is a competitive jungle where some win and some lose and, on the other hand, social conformity associated with RWA and the belief in the world as a threatening place. As such, SDO is a manifestation of a proactive motivation for group-based dominance and superiority, while RWA reflects a more passive need for security and control.

The research on SDO and RWA also speaks to the above discussion of SDO as a trait versus a state. It is plausible to argue that describing out-groups as either threats to the social order or competitive threats may shape levels of SDO and RWA, while at the same time individuals vary in the extent to which they are prone to react to these characterizations of out-groups. On the basis of the above reviewed research on SDO and RWA, it is obvious that the simultaneous assessment of SDO and RWA is often advantageous (and even necessary), in particular in research on prejudice and discrimination in the workplace.

Measures of SDO

There are two versions of the SDO scale: SDO_5 (fourteen items), which taps SDO in general, and the more common form, SDO_6 (sixteen items), which "focuses on intergroup relations and group dominance" (Nicol, 2007). A major difference between these scales is the referent: SDO_5 mentions groups directly only once – Item 1 reads "Some groups of people are simply not the equals of others" – while SDO_6 mentions groups specifically in thirteen of sixteen items (Pratto *et al.*, 1994, Appendices A and C).

Pratto *et al.* (1994) reported the scale development and psychometric properties of SDO_5. They found adequate scale reliability (mean internal consistency reliability of 0.83 over thirteen samples: p. 747) and evidence of validity of the measure including evidence of construct validity based on measures of related (i.e., empathy, altruism, and communality) and unrelated constructs. The measure also predicted various social attitudes associated with authoritarianism, while it was uncorrelated or only weakly correlated with two measures of authoritarianism.

The psychometric properties of the SDO_6 scale are well supported by numerous studies, including those conducted by Umphress *et al.* (2007) and other organizational scientists described later in this chapter. Umphress *et al.*, for example, reported internal consistency reliabilities between 0.80 and 0.90 in three samples. We endorse the use of the SDO_6 measure for organizational research. It can be used as a unidimensional measure or a measure of two factors of SDO, as Jost and Thompson (2000) reported. These researchers reported that SDO_6 captured two separable factors: opposition to equality and support for group-based dominance. These alternate uses of the scale may represent more of an opportunity than a threat to construct validity, consistent with the literature on facets and higher-order factors in the personality domain. Despite our advice in support of the SDO_6 scale, we acknowledge that psychometric investigations into SDO scales are ongoing. For example, Nicol (2007) considered both SDO scales in relation to two measures of how individuals interpret and relate to their environments. On a final note, under conditions where it is not feasible to assess prejudice directly, SDO may be a useful proxy measure.

Summary: SDT as a basis for understanding effects of social hierarchies

Overall, SDT, including the attendant construct SDO, is a formidable basis for understanding the emergence and relative (but not absolute) durability of group-based social hierarchies in organizations, and in society generally. The theory is a complex and integrative blend of multiple social scientific sources and has been summarized as "an attempt to connect the worlds of individual personality and attitudes with the domains of institutional behavior and social structure" (Sidanius and Pratto, 1999, p. 31). The multi- and cross-level nature of SDT should make it attractive to scholars of organizational behavior, who often seek to investigate effects emerging out of interactions among levels of analysis. Yet, SDT has not made much of an entry into organizational behavior research to date, as we illustrate in the next section.

Organizational behavior research on SDT

To date, few organizational behavior scholars have employed SDT in their research. This research has largely utilized the construct of SDO, thus not fully taking advantage of the multi-level nature of SDT. It is our belief that the relative dearth of studies is a function of the youth of SDT. There is tremendous potential for students of organizational behavior to benefit from SDT in their research. In this section, we will review the existing research, organized by the themes of hierarchy enhancement and hierarchy attenuation, before we turn to recommendations to exploit more fully the potential of SDT in organizational behavior research. We acknowledge that the categorization into the themes of hierarchy enhancement and hierarchy attenuation is arbitrary for studies focusing on SDO. As noted earlier, low levels of SDO represent a hierarchy-attenuating force, whereas high levels of SDO are a hierarchy-enhancing force. As organizational scientists have typically framed their arguments around high levels of SDO, we present these studies in the following section.

Hierarchy-enhancement studies

Among these studies, two themes are prevalent: (1) inter-group relations and conflict in organizations and (2) leadership. In the first theme, one block of studies (Aquino *et al.*, 2005; McKay and Avery,

2006; Umphress *et al.*, 2007) has considered effects of SDO. A second block of studies has been concerned with SDO and its effects on leadership (Son Hing *et al.*, 2007; Nicol, 2009).

Inter-group relations and conflict in organizations

In a conceptual piece, McKay and Avery (2006) considered the issue of racioethnicity in explaining intent to accept job offers following site visits by job applicants. They argued that SDO moderates relationships among a job seeker's racioethnicity (minority member versus majority member), demographic diversity (minority representation), and interracioethnic interaction quality in predicting diversity climate perceptions. Specifically, minority applicants who are low in SDO are expected to be particularly positively affected in their diversity climate perceptions in the presence of demographic diversity and positive interracioethnic interactions. For whites, the effects are expected to be somewhat less pronounced. McKay and Avery argue that minority members who are high in SDO do not care too much about a lack of demographic diversity and interaction quality as they are tolerant of or even favor arrangements that indicate power and status inequalities among ethnic groups. Members who are low on SDO, however, do not tolerate such inequalities and will likely actively strive to reverse them.

Umphress *et al.*'s (2007) study can be viewed as an empirical test of McKay and Avery's (2006) arguments. Umphress *et al.* investigated the effects of job seekers' levels of SDO on the relationship between organizational diversity and an organization's attractiveness. Across three studies of gender and ethnic diversity, these scientists consistently found that job seekers low on SDO were turned off by a lack of organizational diversity, whereas those high on SDO were attracted to it. This pattern was observed for both members of dominant groups and members of subordinate groups. Thus, SDO reverses effects of demographic similarity for minority members who are high in SDO and for majority members who are low in SDO: high-SDO minority applicants prefer organizations with greater proportions of majority employees, while low-SDO majority applicants prefer organizations with greater proportions of minority employees. More importantly, as indicated earlier, this study documents the hierarchy-enhancing force of high SDO and the hierarchy-attenuating force of low SDO. Umphress *et al.* noted the threat to diversity that high-SDO individuals (be they members of dominant or subordinate groups) pose, while their research also shows how low-SDO individuals may embrace diversity, thus contributing to hierarchy attenuation. Furthermore, the study illustrates behavioral asymmetry such that high-SDO members of low-status groups exhibit out-group favoritism, while high-SDO members of high-status groups exhibit in-group favoritism.

Aquino *et al.* (2005) considered how observers evaluated an African-American worker who benefited from affirmative action (AA) legislation, which refers to public policy in the USA designed to redress historically disadvantaged groups, including women and racial and ethnic minorities. These researchers theorized SDO as a form of motivated social cognition, under which SDO motivates the use of stereotypes to rationalize the existence of group-based social hierarchies. They found a significant, negative association of SDO and both expected job performance and prognosticated career progression of an African-American employee. This association was moderated by AA policy, such that the race-based effect was more pronounced in the presence rather than the absence of such a policy. The authors interpreted the presence of an AA policy as a "social cue" for hierarchy-maintaining behavior among high-SDO individuals. The study hints at the use and perpetuation of stereotypes (or myths in the terminology of SDT). Stereotypes are used to devalue members of minority groups, and the devaluation may result in poorer careers perpetuating the stereotypes.

Leadership

A study by Son Hing *et al.* (2007) illustrated the negative effects of high SDO in leaders. Illustrating the earlier mentioned striving of high-SDO individuals for dominance, Son Hing *et al.* found that people high in SDO (1) were more likely to obtain leadership positions than subordinate positions after discussions of role assignments, and (2) as leaders made more unethical decisions than did leaders low on SDO. Extending the latter finding, Son Hing *et al.* also reported that dyads of high-SDO leaders and high-RWA followers were particularly likely to make unethical decisions. Research by Nicols (2009), who investigated associations between SDO and leadership styles, is helpful in interpreting Son Hing *et al.*'s findings. She found that SDO was related to an emphasis on production, less concern for the consideration of followers, a lower demand for reconciliation in the case of complex problems, and less tolerance of uncertainty. Jointly, these findings illustrate the dark side of striving for group dominance, in particular when counter-balancing forces (e.g., followers who are willing to resist) are missing. Hence, one might view the research of Son Hing *et al.* as illustrative of an SDT-inspired conceptualization of organizations as an equilibrium (albeit a tilted one) of hierarchy-attenuating and hierarchy-enhancing forces. On a side note, regarding the construct of SDO, Son Hing *et al.* acknowledged that it is likely that SDO does not only capture a favorable attitude toward group-based dominance, but also an egoistic concern for power and status.

Hierarchy-attenuation studies

In contrast with the set of hierarchy-perpetuating studies described above, the set of hierarchy-attenuating studies is comparatively small. The following two studies show how knowledge of the mechanisms of SDT, including considerations related to SDO, can be used to better understand how individual attitudes and actions toward group-based social hierarchies can change, as a function of education or possibly of the judicious exercise of authority.

Dambrun *et al.* (2009) considered how students' academic major moderated the effect of university education on levels of SDO. They found that social science students on average showed lower SDO scale scores over the course of their education in comparison with biology students. The authors attributed this effect to beliefs about the relative impact of environmental and genetic forces in shaping behavior. Social science explicitly considers the contribution of environmental factors in explaining behavior, these authors asserted, and beliefs along these lines are negatively associated with SDO. This study is important because it represents an illustration of the hierarchy-enhancing/attenuating role of institutions, perhaps encompassing but also going beyond the contributions of specific myths. At the same time it is difficult to frame this finding as a potential intervention, as students probably tend to self-select into these disciplines, at least in part in anticipation of studying alongside like-minded others.

Umphress *et al.* (2008) considered both the existence of SDO-based effects in a selection of applicants from subordinate groups (a white female and a black male) and the potential that among high-SDO individuals, directions from an authority figure might attenuate these effects. They found support for the moderating role of explicit direction on selection criteria (i.e., demonstrated ability) from an authority figure. This finding shows that strong situations can limit the effects of SDO on selection decisions. Of course, precision in the explicit formulation of selection criteria is important for many reasons beyond remediating the effects of attitude-related biases.

Summary observations on SDT in organizational behavior and the link to status

Considering the body of organizational behavior research utilizing SDT, it is not unreasonable to ask what we have learned from these studies. First, we have learned about the value of SDO, an individual difference construct representing both a predictor and a moderating variable with respect to various outcomes of interest at the organizational level. SDO seems particularly useful in helping us understand the complex and often counter-intuitive mechanisms of inter-group relationships at work, through the differential behaviors of individuals high and low on this characteristic. These findings suggest that concerns for status hierarchies represent an important alternative to concern for one's in-group in explaining inter-group relations.

At the level of leader–follower dyads, there is some evidence that mismatches on SDO/ RWA can contribute to unethical behavior, or at least a propensity for less ethical decision making (Son Hing et al., 2007). Whether this equally represents an opportunity in the sense that mere instructions from a leader to a high-SDO follower can efface these sorts of behaviors (Umphress et al., 2008) is perhaps best considered an open question. Changing levels of theory, there is also some evidence that institutions are well positioned to harness authority and access to resources in the interests of shaping individual beliefs concerning social hierarchy, through myths and by other, explicitly cross-level means. Opportunities afforded by institutions in this vein represent untapped potential for those seeking to redress the deleterious consequences of social hierarchies. It seems there is cause for some cautious optimism in this regard, notwithstanding the lag between the existing base of empirical evidence and the theoretical promise of SDT-informed thinking and action.

In short, SDT exposes channels through which status effects in organizations operate. Ascribed status, based on gender, age, and arbitrary-set social hierarchies, differentially allocates social power to groups in society and organizations. In the organizational case,

SDT shows how these social hierarchies, which may interfere or align with hierarchical arrangements that support the purposive functioning of the organization, are created and sustained, while also suggesting opportunities for changing hierarchical arrangements.

Recommendations for future research

We see numerous opportunities for future research in organizations that can be mutually beneficial to advancing knowledge about organizational behavior and extending SDT. Below, we present six ideas.

1. Organizations as multi-level equilibria of hierarchy enhancement and attenuation

SDT can serve as a model for conceptualizing organizations as multi-level equilibria of hierarchy enhancement and attenuation. Such a model, for example, explains the continuing underrepresentation of women and minorities in the upper echelons of management. It also highlights the Marxist roots of SDT, whereby members of different social classes (in SDT terminology, members of subordinate and dominant groups) struggle with each other over economic resources, yet dominant groups retain control and subordinate groups develop a "false consciousness" of accepting the existing social hierarchy as a natural and inevitable configuration. Hierarchies on the basis of age, gender, and arbitrary criteria can be seen as epiphenomena to social class hierarchies. As such, SDT reminds organizational scientists that they have neglected to study social class as a marker of diversity (cf. Jonsen, Maznevski, and Schneider, in press). The greater potential of SDT for organizational scientists, however, lies in its multi-level formulation. To date, for example, there are few multi-level models of diversity and even fewer studies along these lines (Jackson, Joshi, and Erhardt, 2003). Organizational scientists who are interested in a multi-level understanding of age, gender, and other demographically based hierarchies in their organizations can use SDT in two ways. First, SDT offers a tool to analyze the presence and relative strength of hierarchy-enhancing and hierarchy-attenuating forces in organizations. One might utilize SDT to describe and analyze the existence of opposing organizational myths (e.g., how does an organization resolve the duality of equality and freedom vs. merit-based access to opportunity?), organizational levels of SDO and its distribution, the enactment of behavioral asymmetry, etc. Returning to our opening example about the severity of female gatekeepers toward female play-wrights, SDT does not only explain that female gatekeepers engage in behavior that maintains the current status hierarchy (and hence is a disservice to women as a subordinate group). It also implies that insti-tutional discrimination may result in a disproportionately low rate of submissions by female playwrights in the first place. In addition, SDT inspires multi-level research questions, such as the following:

- How does the national context of equity legislation, labor–management relations (e.g., the strength of unions), and predominant cultural values affect the enactment of hierarchy-affecting behaviors by members of dominant and subordinate groups in organizations?
- Are the dynamics of hierarchy formation at the social–group and individual levels different in for-profit and not-for-profit organiza-tions as the institutional purpose of the latter is not to generate a surplus for members of dominant groups?
- Research indicates that SDO is not a random individual difference in organizations and occupations (e.g., Los Angeles police officers tended to have relatively high levels of SDO: Pratto *et al.*, 1994). Furthermore, levels of SDO seem to be affected by one's work and organizational environment, making it both an individual-level and organizational-level phenomenon. Does the similarity of SDO lev-els within organizations result from attraction, selection, and attri-tion processes, or do organizations shape their employees' levels of SDO, and if so, how?

2. Changing status hierarchies: SDT on diversity interventions

SDT offers provocative insights on the effectiveness of diversity inter-ventions. Returning to the opening example about diversity interven-tions, SDT not only explains the reasons for the relative success of institutionally anchored programs, but also the lack of success of pro-grams designed to reduce managers' biases. SDT explains that these biases are not only a product of managers' individual characteristics, but also of the asymmetrical behaviors of members of dominant and subordinate groups, and institutional patterns of discrimination in organizations. The roots of these effects are much deeper than the cognitions of individual managers.

Furthermore, SDT implies that diversity interventions that highlight the low status of a group may, contrary to their purpose, reinforce that group's low status. On the basis of SDT, we argue that making a low-status group the focus of preferential hiring, or extending particular opportunities for training or advancement to members of that group, signals that this group requires special attention and protection. Hence, such interventions, well intentioned and reasonable though they may be, could in effect serve as hierarchy-enhancing myths.

SDT also offers constructive advice for the design of diversity interventions in the form of hierarchy-attenuating forces, most notably hierarchy-attenuating myths. Sidanius *et al.* (2004, p. 276) assert that the strength of a myth is "the degree to which it is consensual, particularly across members of both subordinate and dominant groups." This theoretical insight suggests that the literature of persuasion (Cialdini, 2001), not to mention the arts of rhetoric and the *form* of prospective interventions, distinct from their *content*, are all in play. Both dominant and subordinate groups in organizations will interpret interventions that bear on the social hierarchy of the organization according to their own interests. When they can be led to agree on hierarchy-attenuating myths, the context for diversity interventions should be more positive (conversely, when organizational members agree on hierarchy-enhancing myths, diversity interventions do not have much of a chance). SDT suggests several questions for research on diversity interventions:

- What are the strategies that organizations can use to develop, support, and build consensus on hierarchy-attenuating myths?
- How does the relative mean level and distribution of SDO in an organization affect the traction that interventions aimed at addressing prejudice and discrimination are likely to obtain?
- SDT acknowledges the role that the behaviors of members of subordinate groups play in the perpetuation of social hierarchies. Hence, SDT lifts the lid on a taboo topic among advocates of diversity, namely the contribution that members of subordinate groups make to their low position in hierarchies. SDT implies that diversity interventions may require tough-minded, direct, and honest conversations with members of both dominant and subordinate groups

about their behaviors that perpetuate status hierarchies and their negative effects. How can organizations break the habit of inadvertently engaging in these behaviors?

- SDT is a multi-level theory that implies that, ultimately, interventions that are designed to increase the representation of members of subordinate groups at higher levels of organizational hierarchies require coordinated efforts across levels. How do organizations coordinate diversity interventions at the individual, group, and organizational levels?

3. The intersection of ascribed and earned hierarchical status

While status remains an understudied variable in the organizational sciences, researchers (see Magee and Galinsky, 2008 for a review) have recognized that lower ascribed status (e.g., on the basis of age and gender) results in poorer opportunities for earning status (e.g., on the basis of ability and performance). The earlier mentioned research on stereotype threat and stereotype lift, for example, illustrates this phenomenon. Furthermore, status expectations theory (e.g., Berger *et al.*, 1977) proposes higher performance expectations for people who have high ascribed status. Men, for example, are assumed to be better leaders. What organizational scientists to date have largely ignored is that SDT provides an encompassing explanation of the association between ascribed and achieved status. SDT posits that members of subordinate groups have lower economic and societal capital, suffer from individual and institutional discrimination, and engage in self-debilitating behaviors. SDT-inspired questions on links between ascribed and achieved status in organizations include the following:

- To what extent do hierarchy-enhancing behaviors (e.g., stereotype confirmation) of members of subordinate groups vary as a function of organizational values that emphasize equality and/or merit?
- Do levels of SDO affect the career progression of members of subordinate groups? SDT implies that low-SDO individuals should be less likely to engage in self-debilitating behaviors.
- Is an emphasis in personnel decisions on person–organization fit a hierarchy-enhancing myth that undermines selection on the basis of ability and competence? Person–organization fit has been

framed in demographic terms (Petersen and Dietz, 2005) and it has been shown that decision makers who are biased against members of low-status groups are particularly likely to buy into this demographic notion of person–organization fit (e.g., Brief *et al.*, 2000; Petersen and Dietz, 2000). Even if person–organization fit is framed in terms of values, it may be a code for maintaining things just the way they are (by referring to the values of members of dominant groups).

- Is mentoring another sort of organizational ruse (similar to person–organization fit), which allows members of dominant groups to create small initial advantages for similar others?

4. Ideological asymmetry in organizations

As indicated earlier, members of subordinate groups experience inconsistencies between beliefs that tend to favor their group (i.e., in-group bias) and beliefs that justify the system (or the social hierarchy) as a whole. When African-American employees, for example, feel positively about their ethnicity, and yet observe that there are few African Americans in leadership positions in their organization, they experience an inconsistency that can create a tension. This inconsistency would be particularly severe among members of subordinate groups who have high SDO. Yet the study of Umphress *et al.* (2007) showed that high-SDO women preferred male-dominated organizations, resulting in the question of whether high-SDO members of subordinate groups are willing to experience psychological tension in order to become members of hierarchy-enhancing organizations. Numerous questions arise, including the following:

- What is the impact of SDO, social group identification, and career aspirations on the work attitudes and general well-being of members of subordinate groups?
- As a follow-up to the above question, one might ask to what extent does working in an ethnic versus a non-ethnic business affect the relative impact of SDO, social group identification, and career aspirations on work attitudes and general well-being? This would require controlling for potentially systematic differences between ethnic and non-ethnic businesses.

- How can organizations manage the effects of ideological asymmetry? In this context, research by Ely and Thomas (2001) on diversity management perspectives is relevant. They found that concentrating employees from low-status groups in branches that serve mostly customers from low-status groups is not the answer, as it creates first- and second-class branches, which are associated with increased levels of dissatisfaction among the employees from low-status groups in the second-class branches.

5. Low-SDO individuals in organizations

We have already pointed out that low-SDO individuals represent hierarchy-attenuating forces. They prefer working in diverse organizations (Umphress *et al.*, 2007), are less prone to use stereotypes in evaluating employees (Aquino *et al.*, 2005), and as leaders are more ethical (Son Hing *et al.*, 2007) and more considerate of their followers (Nicol, 2009). Aquino *et al.* (2005, p. 737) alluded to the metacognitive abilities, stating "low SDO people ... may be better able to purge their minds of stereotypic thoughts when they encounter stereotyped others." Collectively, this research suggests that organizations might be well advised to support their low-SDO employees. Questions about low-SDO individuals include:

- In light of their awareness of stereotyping and their leadership style preferences, are low-SDO individuals particularly well suited to occupy roles as leaders or organizational change agents? Do situational factors (e.g., a crisis management situation versus a situation of proactive change; leading a diversity initiative versus a cost control initiative) moderate the effect of SDO on leadership success? Perhaps HR interventions with goals related to reducing prejudice and discrimination (or more broadly social hierarchies in organizations) would diffuse further and more rapidly when led by individuals or groups low in SDO.
- Does the SDO of leaders rub off on their subordinates? If so, how? Addressing this question provides insights into the ongoing debate of SDO as a trait versus a state. Our suspicion is that the SDO of leaders might in fact have contagious effects because of the sensitivity of SDO to situational influence and the power of models in processes of social learning.

6. *Acceptance of status hierarchy systems, homophily, or status threat/gain?*

What motivates organizational members, in particular, in their interactions with members of other social groups? The dominating perspective in the organizational sciences is that of homophily (i.e., favoring one's in-group). Social identity theory, social categorization theory, and the similarity-attraction paradigm are the most popular theoretical models in relational demography research. Recently, gaining status or protecting one's own status has also been mentioned as a force that motivates the behavior of members of both subordinate and dominant groups. For example, Pearce and Xu (2010) found that female and younger supervisors gave lower performance ratings to male and older subordinates while male supervisors did not differentially evaluate male and female subordinates, and older supervisors did not differentially evaluate younger and older subordinates. These researchers argued that female and younger supervisors needed to protect their status. Chatman and O'Reilly (2004), in a study of work groups, found that men were more likely to want to transfer out of work groups with greater proportions of women, supposedly to move into higher-status groups. Women, however, were less likely to desire transferring out of male-dominated groups relative to transferring out of mixed groups.

SDT proposes neither homophily nor status gain as primary motives. It suggests that people vary in the degree to which they endorse social hierarchies (i.e., levels of SDO vary). Hence, according to SDT, people are not just concerned about their status and their own social group, but also with accepting or resisting existing social hierarchies. However, the theory also suggests that generally the forces toward hierarchy maintenance are stronger. Despite differences in SDO, for example, both members of subordinate and dominant groups behave in ways that perpetuate existing arrangements of power and status. Organizations are a context that is well suited to sort out when which of these motives dominates and how they interact. Hence, organizational research can not only benefit from, but also inform SDT:

- Status inconsistency results when a person has high status on one criterion and low status on another criterion. Do status inconsistencies constitute a boundary condition for SDT, in particular when members of subordinate groups (ascribed low status) have earned status on the basis of their ability and competence (cf. Pearce and Xu, 2010)?

- Status threat is likely a stronger motivational force than status gain. The question then arises as to whether status threat can explain the weakness of hierarchy-attenuating and status-threatening myths (e.g., egalitarianism) relative to hierarchy-enhancing myths. It has been proposed that status, for example, might explain prejudicial attitudes among white liberals (who endorse egalitarian values) in the USA (Caditz, 1975).
- Under what conditions will members of subordinate groups strive for status gains? A key condition is the system legitimacy of status gains. We propose that members of subordinate groups will behave in a way that will maintain existing hierarchies when status gains are seemingly illegitimate under the terms of the existing system, but will strive for status gains when they are legitimate (e.g., seeking a career). As such, the system legitimacy of status gains can be seen as a boundary condition for SDT.

Conclusion

This chapter addresses SDT, which incorporates the individual-level construct SDO, in terms of its potential to illuminate status effects in organizations that emerge from group-based social hierarchies. The theory provides explanations for social hierarchies at the individual, social group, and institutional levels, and also demonstrates relationships across these levels. Emphasizing the coexistence of hierarchy-enhancing and hierarchy-attenuating forces, it advocates interesting and, at times, controversial positions. For example, it points out that social hierarchies are not only maintained by those who benefit from them, but also by those who suffer under them. Yet, investigations of SDT by organizational scientists have tended to favor SDO, which has resulted in a relative neglect of other aspects of SDT.

In the end, we are not surprised when we hear reports of negative effects of social hierarchies in organizations, but we are surprised that organizational scientists to date have not considered SDT more frequently and elaboratively. We have made numerous suggestions for future organizational research on the basis of SDT and sincerely hope that our chapter motivates organizational scientists to employ and extend SDT as a prime tool for understanding organizational hierarchies and, thereby, the role of status in organizations.

References

Adorno, T. W., Frenkel-Brunswick, E., Levinson, D. J., and Sanford, R. N. 1950. *The Authoritarian Personality*. New York: Norton.

Akrami, N. and Ekehammar, B. 2006. "Right-Wing Authoritarianism and Social Dominance Orientation: Their roots in Big-Five personality factors and facets." *Journal of Individual Differences* 27: 117–126.

Altemeyer, B. 1998. "The other 'authoritarian personality.'" *Advances in Experimental Social Psychology* 30: 47–92.
  2006. *The Authoritarians*. Winnipeg: Lulu.com.

Aquino, K., Stewart, M., and Reed, A., II. 2005. "How Social Dominance Orientation and job status affect perceptions of African-American affirmative action beneficiaries." *Personnel Psychology* 58: 703–744.

Berger, J. M., Fisek, H., Norman, R., and Zelditch, M. 1977. *Status Characteristics and Social Interaction: An Expectation States Approach*. New York: Elsevier.

Blumer, H. 1960. "Race prejudice as a sense of group position." *Pacific Sociological Review* 1: 3–5.

Brief, A. P., Dietz, J., Cohen, R. R., Pugh, S. D., and Vaslow, J. B. 2000. "Just doing business: Modern racism and obedience to authority as explanations for employment discrimination." *Organizational Behavior and Human Decision Processes* 81: 72–97.

Caditz, J. 1975. "Dilemmas over racial integration: Status consciousness vs. direct threat." *Sociological Inquiry* 45: 51–58.

Chatman, J. A. and O'Reilly, C. A. 2004. "Asymmetric reactions to work group sex diversity among men and women." *Academy of Management Journal* 47: 193–208.

Cialdini, B. 2001. *Influence: Science and Practice* (4th edn.). Boston, MA: Allyn and Bacon.

Cohen, Patricia. 2009. "Rethinking gender bias in theatre," *New York Times*, June 24, 2009: C1.

Correll, S. J., Benard, S., and Paik, I. 2007. "Getting a job: Is there a motherhood penalty?" *American Journal of Sociology* 112: 1297–1339.

Dambrun, M., Kamiejski, R., Haddadi, N., and Duarte, S. 2009. "Why does Social Dominance Orientation decrease with university exposure to the social sciences? The impact of institutional socialization and the mediating role of 'geneticism,'" *European Journal of Social Psychology* 39: 88–100.

Duckitt, J. 2001. "A cognitive-motivational theory of ideology and prejudice," in M. P. Zanna (ed.), *Advances in Experimental Social Psychology*, Vol. XXXIII. San Diego, CA: Academic Press, pp. 41–113.

Duckitt, J. and Sibley, C. 2006. "Right wing authoritarianism, Social Dominance Orientation, and the dimensions of generalized prejudice." *European Journal of Personality* 20: 1–18.

Duckitt, J., Wagner, C., du Plessis, I., and Birum, I. 2002. "The psychological bases of ideology and prejudice: Testing a dual process model." *Journal of Personality and Social Psychology* 83: 75–93.

Ekehammar, B. and Akrami, N. 2007. "Personality and prejudice: From Big Five personality factors to facets." *Journal of Personality* 75: 899–926.

Ely, R. and Thomas, D. 2001. "Cultural diversity at work: The effects of diversity perspectives on work group processes and outcomes." *Administrative Science Quarterly* 46: 229–273.

Jackson, S. E., Joshi, A., and Erhardt, N. L. 2003. "Recent research on team and organizational diversity: SWOT analysis and implications." *Journal of Management* 29: 801–830.

Jonsen, K., Maznevski, M. L., and Schneider, S. C. (in press). "Diversity and its not so diverse literature: An international perspective." *International Journal of Cross-Cultural Management*.

Jost, J. T. and Thompson, E. P. 2000. "Group-based dominance and opposition to equality as independent predictors of self-esteem, ethnocentrism, and social policy attitudes among African Americans and European Americans." *Journal of Experimental Social Psychology* 36: 209–232.

Kalev, A., Kelly, E., and Dobbin, F. 2006. "Corporate affirmative action and diversity policies." *American Sociological Review* 71: 589–617.

Magee, J. C. and Galinsky, A. D. 2008. "Social hierarchy: The self-reinforcing nature of power and status." *Academy of Management Annals* 2: 351–398.

McKay, P. F. and Avery, D. R. 2006. "What has race got to do with it? Unraveling the role of racioethnicity in job seekers' reactions to site visits." *Personnel Psychology* 59: 395–429.

Nicol, A. A. M. 2007. "Social Dominance Orientation, Right-Wing Authoritarianism, and their relation with alienation and spheres of control." *Personality and Individual Differences* 43: 891–899.

2009. "Social Dominance Orientation, Right-Wing Authoritarianism, and their relation with leadership styles." *Personality and Individual Differences* 47: 657–661.

Pareto, V. 1901/1979. *The Rise and Fall of the Elites*. New York: Arno.

Pearce, J. L. and Xu, Q. J. 2010. "Rating Performance or Contesting Status: A Test of a Social Dominance Theory of Supervisor Demographic Skew in Performance Ratings." Merage School Working Paper, University of California, Irvine.

Petersen, L. E. and Dietz, J. 2000. "Social discrimination in a person-nel selection context: The effects of an authority's instruction to dis-criminate and followers' authoritarianism." *Journal of Applied Social Psychology* 30: 206–220.

2005. "Prejudice and enforcement of workforce homogeneity as expla-nations for employment discrimination." *Journal of Applied Social Psychology* 35: 144–159.

Pratto, F., Sidanius, J., and Levin, S. 2006. "Social Dominance Theory and the dynamics of intergroup relations: Taking stock and looking for-ward." *European Review of Social Psychology* 17: 271–320.

Pratto, F., Sidanius, J., Stallworth, L. M., and Malle, B. F. 1994. "Social Dominance Orientation: A personality variable relevant to social roles and intergroup relations." *Journal of Personality and Social Psychology* 67: 741–763.

Rokeach, M. 1979. "The two-value model of political ideology and British politics," in M. Rokeach (ed.), *Understanding Human Values: Individual and Social*. New York: Free Press, pp. 192–196.

Rudman, L. A. and Glick, P. 1999. "Feminized management and back-lash toward agentic women: The hidden costs to women of a kinder, gentler image of middle-managers." *Journal of Personality and Social Psychology* 77: 1004–1010.

Sands, E. 2009. "Opening the curtain on playwright gender: An inte-grated economic analysis of discrimination in American theater." Princeton University Master's Thesis, available at www.nytimes. com/2009/06/24/theater/24play.html, last accessed August 4, 2009.

Sibley, C. G., Robertson, A., and Wilson, M. S. 2006. "Exploring the additive and interactive effects of Social Dominance Orientation and Right-Wing Authoritarianism on prejudice and related intergroup atti-tudes." *Political Psychology* 27: 755–768.

Sidanius, J., Liu, J. H., Shaw, J. S., and Pratto, F. 1994. "Social Dominance Orientation, hierarchy attenuators and hierarchy enhancers: Social Dominance Theory and the criminal justice system." *Journal of Applied Social Psychology* 24: 338–366.

Sidanius, J. and Pratto, F. 1999. *Social Dominance: An Intergroup Theory of Social Hierarchy and Oppression*. New York: Cambridge University Press.

Sidanius, J., Pratto, F., Sinclair, S., and van Laar, C. 1996. "Mother Teresa meets Genghis Khan: The dialectics of hierarchy-enhancing and hierarchy-attenuating career choices." *Social Justice Research* 9: 145–170.

Son Hing, L., Bobocel, D. R., Zanna, M. P., and McBride, M. V. 2007. "Authoritarian dynamics and unethical decision making: High Social Dominance Orientation leaders and high Right-Wing Authoritarianism leaders." *Journal of Personality and Social Psychology* 92: 67–81.

Stevens, C. K., Bavetta, A. G., and Gist, M. E. 1993. "Gender differences in the acquisition of salary negotiation skills: The role of goals, self-efficacy and perceived control." *Journal of Applied Psychology* 78: 723–735.

Tajfel, H. and Turner, J. C. 1986. "The social identity theory of intergroup behavior," in S. Worchel and L. Austin (eds.), *Psychology of Intergroup Relations*. Chicago, IL: Nelson-Hall.

Tilly, C. 1998. *Durable Inequality*. Berkeley, CA: University of California Press.

Umphress, E. E., Simmons, A. L., Boswell, W., and Triana, M. C. 2008. "Managing discrimination in selection: The impact of accountability and Social Dominance Orientation." *Journal of Applied Psychology* 93: 982–993.

Umphress, E. E., Smith-Crowe, K., Brief, A. P., Dietz, J., and Baskerville, M. 2007. "When birds of a feather flock together and when they do not: Status composition, Social Dominance Orientation, and organizational attractiveness." *Journal of Applied Psychology* 92: 396–409.

Walton, G. and Cohen, G. 2003. "Stereotype lift." *Journal of Experimental Social Psychology* 39: 456–467.

PART II

The influence of status on markets

4 | The importance of status in markets: A market identity perspective

MICHAEL JENSEN, BO KYUNG KIM,
AND HEEYON KIM

The importance of status in markets is well established. Since Podolny (1993) introduced his status-based model of market competition, more than 160 articles published in top management and sociology journals have explored this area. These articles show that market status affects a broad range of outcomes, including the perceived quality and legitimacy of organizations, the costs of producing a given level of quality, the prices that organizations can charge for specific products, their attractiveness as exchange partners, and their ability to exercise agency. Despite the widespread agreement that status plays an important role in markets, there is less agreement about how to define status. Status has traditionally been defined as a position in a social system that can be ranked among other positions based on relative prestige or social esteem (Weber, 1968; Linton, 1936; Merton, 1957). Following Podolny (1993), however, status has more recently been redefined simply as a signal of quality, thus removing status from its traditional anchoring in the social system. We argue that defining status as a signal of quality unnecessarily limits the explanatory power of status and confuses status with other signals of quality, most notably reputation. We develop instead a framework for studying status in markets that integrates work on status as social positions (Linton, 1936; Merton, 1957) and work on identity as social categories (Hannan, Pólos, and Carroll, 2007), thus providing a more comprehensive perspective on status in markets.

We seek to accomplish three specific objectives in this chapter. First, we develop a new conceptual framework that integrates theoretical research on status and identity to clarify what we understand by status in markets. Our status–identity framework builds on the definition of status as a position in a social system. However, we add that these positions entail identities that reside in the intersections of the horizontally and vertically differentiated social categories that define the social system. Our status–identity framework builds extensively on the existing research on status and identity because we seek to provide conceptual clarity to existing and future research on status and identity rather than distancing ourselves from that research. We emphasize that our framework must not only help distinguish status from other related theoretical concepts such as reputation and legitimacy, but must also be useful in empirical research by helping to develop theory-driven research agendas. Second, we use our status–identity framework to systematically review existing research on status in markets. Rather than reviewing all market status research, we use our framework to identify the most important theory-driven research questions, and then provide a selective review of how these questions have been addressed in empirical research. Third, having used the status–identity framework to identify important research questions and to evaluate how existing research addresses these questions, we then identify and discuss more systematically the most important areas for future research.

Before developing our status–identity framework, it is useful to briefly explain our philosophical and methodological approach. Philosophically, we view status simply as a theoretical construct and are therefore concerned less with the ontology of status and more with the epistemology of status. The epistemological value of status as a theoretical construct and therefore the value of our status–identity framework depends mainly on the specific insights obtained through its use in specific empirical research projects. Methodologically, we focus primarily on empirical research published in the *Academy of Management Journal, Academy of Management Review, Administrative Science Quarterly, American Journal of Sociology, American Sociological Review, Management Science, Organization Science,* and *Strategic Management Journal* from 1993 to 2008. We focus on these journals and the period from 1993 onward because the vast majority of research on market status appeared in these journals and because the interest in status before Podolny (1993) introduced his status-based model of market competition was more sporadic. We also limit our review to macro-research focusing on markets and organizations, and do not consider micro-research that focuses on individuals and small groups, an area covered by other chapters in this volume.

The status–identity framework

Our survey of status in markets research revealed that fifteen of the thirty-nine articles that provide an explicit definition of status define it simply as a signal of quality. Therefore, we begin by discussing the theoretical foundations for research that defines status as a market signal and show how it sets the stage for equating status and reputation. We then revisit early sociological work on status as positions in social systems and more recent work on identity as social categories to develop the theoretical foundation for our status–identity framework.

Status and signaling

Podolny (1993, p. 830) defined status as the perceived quality of an organization in relation to the perceived quality of other competing organizations and he noted that it is critical to view status as a signal of underlying product quality. Following Spence (1974), status can function as a signal of quality for two reasons: First, the status of an organization is partly decided by its previous actions, which means that an organization can exercise at least some control over its status. Second, the difficulty of acquiring high status is inversely related to the ability of organizations to actually deliver the corresponding product quality. Defining status as a signal of quality is not necessarily inconsistent with defining status as a position in a social system, but viewing status *only* as a signal of quality results in a narrower conceptualization of status. By viewing it in this way, status is ultimately dislocated from social structure, and turned into a resource that some organizations possess independently of other organizations. The conceptualization of status as a signal of quality dominates not only Podolny's own subsequent work on status, especially his early work (including Podolny, 1994, and Podolny and Stuart 1995), but also the work of other scholars including Baker, Faulkner, and Fisher (1998), Chung, Singh, and Lee (2000), Haas and Hansen (2007), and Chen, Hambrick, and Pollock (2008). Our main concern with defining status as a signal of quality is not that status does not function as a signal of quality – typically it does – but that it is not always a signal of quality and that it is often more than a signal of quality.

Status and reputation

By viewing status as a signal of quality, Podolny (1993) provided the theoretical foundation for equating status with reputation in subsequent research, including Stuart (2000), Geletkanycz, Boyd, and Finkelstein (2001), Gulati and Higgins (2003), Rao, Monin, and Durand (2003), and Rhee and Haunschild (2006). Equating status and reputation does not necessarily question the empirical results of these studies because both status and reputation function as signals of quality. However, status is not the same as reputation. Most economists define reputation as a prediction about future behavior that is derived from the history of previously observed actions (Wilson, 1985, pp. 27–28), thus emphasizing the importance of reputation as a market signal. Even if both status and reputation function as signals of quality, it is important to distinguish theoretically between status and reputation, a point we are not the first to make. Washington and Zajac (2005, p. 284) suggested that reputation refers to a summary categorization of historical differences in quality among actors, whereas status refers to a socially constructed ordering or ranking of actors in a social system. More uniquely, they emphasized that reputation captures differences in quality that generate earned, performance-based rewards but that status captures differences in social rank that generate unearned, non-performance-based privilege.

Jensen and Roy (2008) also agreed that it is important to distinguish between status and reputation. They defined status as the prestige accorded to organizations because of their positions in the social structure and reputation as the prestige accorded to organizations because of how they have carried out particular activities in the past. Jensen and Roy did not restrict status to the unearned ascription of social rank, however, but allowed, as did Weber (1968), privilege-granting status positions to be earned (achieved status) or unearned (ascribed status). They emphasized instead that status is an actor–level concept, whereas reputation is an attribute–level concept – a social actor occupies only one status in *a* social system (but can occupy different statuses in different social systems), which gives the actor one status with the *same* audience, whereas an actor may simultaneously have a positive reputation and a negative reputation on different attributes with the *same* audience. Although Jensen and Roy (2008) did not define status and reputation as signals of quality, their distinction between status and reputation also affects how they *function* as signals of quality – status provides an assessment of the quality of the organization as a whole, whereas reputation provides an assessment of the quality of individual organizational attributes. Finally, even if Podolny (1993) first provided the impetus for defining status as a market signal and using status and reputation interchangeably, he later noted that status is best defined as a position in a social system that determines opportunities and constraints, and that reputation is best defined as an expectation of some behaviors based on past demonstrations of these same behaviors (Podolny, 2005).

Status and identity

We agree with Washington and Zajac (2005), Jensen and Roy (2008), and Podolny (2005) that it is important to distinguish between status and reputation and that status is best defined as a position in a social system. However, we add that it is useful to refine the definition of status as a position in a social system in two ways. First, following Linton (1936) and Merton (1957), we distinguish between social status and social roles, and argue that both concepts reflect commonly shared cognitive categories. Linton (1936, p. 113) defined social status as a position in a social system that encompasses a collection of rights and duties, and social roles as the enactment of a status that puts rights and duties into effect. Linton (1936, p. 114) continued by stating that status and roles together represent "the minimum of attitudes and behavior" that individuals must assume to participate in a given social system. Or, as expressed by Merton (1957, p. 110), status and roles serve to connect "culturally defined expectations" with the patterned conducts and relationships that define social systems. We argue that the minimal attitudes and behaviors or cultural expectations identified by Linton (1936) and Merton (1957) form the core elements of market identities. The two dominant market identities in French gastronomy, classical and nouvelle cuisines, for example, represent different positions in that they embody different expectations about cooking methods, typical ingredients, chef roles, and menu organization (Rao, Monin, and Durand, 2005).

The market identity of an organization is its membership in a social category that is used to identify a social actor and specify what to expect from the social actor (Jensen and Kim, 2009). The minimal attitudes and behaviors and culturally defined expectations identified by Linton (1936) and Merton (1957) correspond to the social codes or schema defaults that Hannan, Pólos, and Carroll (2007, p. 102) argued constitute the core elements of identities. Market identities serve an important function as interfaces between organizations and their audiences. They prescribe the minimal expectations to claimants of a particular identity and they allow the audiences to compare and evaluate different claimants of a particular identity (Zuckerman, 1999). Just as Linton (1936) argued that some minimal attitudes and behaviors must be assumed to participate in a social system, Hannan, Pólos, and Carroll (2007) argued that violations of the social codes that define identity bring about sanctions. The stock-market illegitimacy discount experienced by diversified organizations whose complex business portfolios did not conform to the focused industry categories used by security analysts illustrates the sanctions that can follow violating identity codes (Zuckerman, 1999). The identity expectations associated with a status–role complement are therefore ultimately what circumscribe the actions of the occupants of a status position. This conclusion is, interestingly, not foreign to Podolny (1993, pp. 846–847), who viewed identity as a position in the status order and argued that actors with an advantageous identity avoid actions that threaten their identity. Nor is it foreign to early sociology: Hughes (1937, p. 404) noted, for example, that "status assigns individuals to various social categories; each category has its own rights and duties."

Second, following Sorokin (1959) and Jensen (2010), we argue that positions within a social system are usefully defined along a horizontal and a vertical dimension. The horizontal dimension divides the social system into different categories based on different properties and attributes, while the vertical dimension divides the social system into different categories based on a shared ranking of the members of a particular horizontal category. The horizontal dimension of the social system, for example, refers to an array of product categories and the vertical dimension refers to a ranking (whether based on size, quality, exchange partners, or something else) of the organizations within a

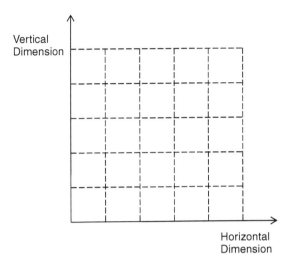

Figure 4.1 Status–identity framework

particular product category. When Linton (1936) and Merton (1957) defined status as positions in a social system, they referred mainly to the horizontal dimension, as evidenced by their examples of statuses such as male, physician, and professor. It is important to distinguish between horizontal and vertical dimensions, however, because the differences within a horizontal category may be as important or even more important than the differences between horizontal categories. The prestige granted to professors, for example, probably varies as much within an academic discipline (vertical) as does the prestige of different academic disciplines (horizontal). In summary, when we define status as a position in a social system, we therefore refer to a particular horizontal and vertical intersection, and when we define market identity as a social category, we refer to the schema that codifies the expectations to that particular intersection.

Figure 4.1 illustrates our status–identity framework. The horizontal axis arrays the social actors based on similarity in attributes and the vertical axis arrays the social actors based on similarity in rank, with the intersection defining a status market and its corresponding identity. A bank may, as shown in Figure 4.2, be categorized horizontally as an investment bank based on its business portfolio and vertically as highly ranked based on its market share or client portfolio, which together gives the bank its status market and identity as

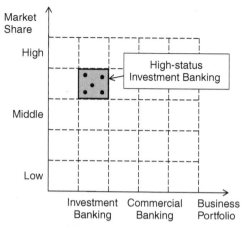

Figure 4.2 Market space of the banking industry

a "high-status investment bank." In other words, our status–identity framework suggests that the horizontal and vertical dimensions in isolation simply represent categories of similar organizations, but that their intersections represent a status position and its corresponding market identity. The minimal attitudes and cultural expectations (Linton, 1936; Merton, 1957) or social codes and schema defaults (Hannan, Pólos, and Carroll, 2007) are only fully specified in the intersections. Although most current research on status in markets focuses only on the vertical status differences between organizations within a horizontal category, we seek to clarify the relationship between status as positions and identity as categories by emphasizing *both* the horizontal *and* the vertical dimensions. Having outlined our status–identity framework, we next use it to review prior status research and identify promising new research areas.

Market status research

Regardless of the specific empirical context, our status–identity framework raises three different types of research questions. The first type of question focuses simply on the advantages and disadvantages of memberships in specific horizontal and vertical categories within the market space. The second type of question takes the horizontal and vertical categories for granted but allows mobility within the current configuration of categories. The third type of question treats the horizontal and vertical categories as endogenous structures and focuses on the creation and destruction of the horizontal and vertical categories themselves.

Market spaces without organizational mobility

The first type of research question takes the current configuration of horizontal and vertical categories as well as the positions organizations occupy within the market space for granted. With the configuration of the market space and the position of organizations within the market space fixed, the main focus becomes how the positions organizations occupy affect their behavior and performance. Although organizations differ in both the horizontal and the vertical positions they occupy, the common identification of status with vertical positions leads us to focus mainly on the advantages and disadvantages of vertical positions. The advantages and disadvantages of horizontal positions are the main focus in industrial organization (Caves, 1980; Porter, 1979), but this research is beyond the scope of our chapter.

Advantages of vertical positions

Based on our review of status research in markets, we found that most research focuses on how vertical positions affect quality, grant agency, and provide legitimacy.

Quality. Vertical positions affect perceived quality in two different ways. First, by functioning as signals of quality, vertical positions affect the perceived value of organizations, which ultimately increases their revenue streams and attractiveness as exchange partners. When the quality of the products is unobservable or otherwise difficult to determine *a priori*, customers depend instead on the observable status of the organizations behind the products to infer the actual quality of the products (Podolny, 1994). The products of organizations in higher vertical positions are therefore perceived to be higher quality and less risky than those of organizations in lower positions, which allow them to charge a premium for their products and to attract potential exchange partners. Several studies have tested different versions of this argument, including Podolny (1994), Eisenhardt and Schoonhoven (1996), Podolny, Stuart, and Hannan (1996), Stuart (2000), Gulati and Higgins (2003), Hoetker, Swaminathan, and

Mitchell (2007), and Rosenkopf and Padula (2008). Benjamin and Podolny (1999), for example, showed that a high-status winery could charge a higher price for a bottle of wine than other organizations, even after controlling for the quality of the wine and the cost of the grapes. In addition, Baker, Faulkner, and Fisher (1998) argued that client organizations used the status of advertisement agencies as an indicator of quality and that they therefore assigned more value to relationships with high-status advertisement agencies, which lowered the risk of dissolving their relationships with these agencies.

Second, vertical positions also affect the cost at which organizations can produce a given level of quality. The aforementioned advantages of higher vertical positions and their at least partial transferability through exchange relationships make organizations in these positions attractive exchange partners and allow them to form exchange relationships at a lower cost than other organizations. Several studies have tested different versions of this argument, including Podolny (1993), Stuart, Hoang, and Hybels (1999), Sine, Shane, and Di Gregorio (2003), and Uzzi and Lancaster (2004). Podolny (1993) found that high-status investment banks could underwrite bonds at a lower cost than low-status banks because they generally had lower transaction costs. Stuart, Hoang, and Hybels (1999) similarly reported that endorsements by prominent institutions enabled privately held biotech organizations to go to IPO faster and to earn better IPO valuations than those without endorsements because the prominent endorsements helped increase the perceived quality of the biotech organizations. Uzzi and Lancaster (2004) showed that corporate clients also preferred transactions with high-status law organizations. They reasoned that although high-status law organizations initially charged higher prices than other law organizations, the overall costs of legal services provided by high-status organizations were lower than those provided by low-status organizations because of their higher quality.

Agency. Vertical positions affect not only quality but also provide a source of agency that allows some organizations to exercise more control over their surroundings and act more independently than other organizations. A few studies have tested different versions of this argument, including Stuart (1998), Phillips and Zuckerman (2001), and Guler (2007). Stuart (1998) argued that high-status organizations are in a position where they have superior bargaining power over low-status organizations, which enables them to secure favorable contract terms. Phillips and Zuckerman (2001) focused on the middle-status conformity argument and found that middle-status law organizations were the least likely to deviate by beginning to practice family law compared to low- and high-status law organizations. According to their argument, high-status organizations have a secure membership in the given category, so they experience less pressure to conform to the norms of the category and avoid practicing family law. Low-status organizations also have the freedom to defy because they are not perceived as legitimate players in the category and audiences in general do not care much about their behavior. Middle-status organizations, however, may lose the opportunity to move upward in the status hierarchy or may even risk losing their position as legitimate players by not conforming to the norms. Guler (2007) argued similarly that high-status organizations can act independently of social pressures and showed that high-status venture capitals were more likely to terminate their investments in less promising organizations.

Legitimacy. In addition to quality and agency, vertical positions also provide organizations with legitimacy or social acceptability. The diffusion of new practices reflects an important legitimacy concern. Status-based imitation provides a solution to the problem of whether or not to adopt new practices or abandon established practices to earn legitimacy through direct or indirect affiliations. Some studies have tested different versions of this argument, including Davis and Greve (1997), Haunschild and Miner (1997), Rao, Monin, and Durand (2003), and Sanders and Tuschke (2007). Davis and Greve (1997) emphasized the positive effect of the participation of high-status organizations in the diffusion of the poison pill, a then new controversial corporate governance practice. Participants also imitate high-status organizations in order to claim indirect affiliations, if there exists no direct association with high-status organizations which increases their perception of legitimacy and visibility. Haunschild and Miner (1997) argued that organizations adopted an organizational practice of hiring an investment bank to obtain advice on acquisitions in an attempt to raise their status level by imitating high-status organizations. Rao, Monin, and Durand (2003) focused on the effects of high-status chefs on the institutional change from classical cuisine to nouvelle cuisine in the French restaurant industry. They argued that the high-status positions of early

defectors conferred legitimacy on the identity movement from classical cuisine to nouvelle cuisine, encouraging more chefs to abandon
the rules of classical cuisine to embrace nouvelle cuisine.

Disadvantages of vertical positions

A vertical position can also limit agency and therefore organizational
growth. Although organizations in higher vertical positions are able
to produce a given quality at a lower cost and generate higher revenue streams, they cannot necessarily expand their market to that
of organizations in lower vertical positions. Podolny (1993) argued
that when high-status organizations start expanding into markets
frequented by low-status organizations, they could lose the benefits
that come with their higher vertical positions. The reason is status
leakage (Podolny, 1994) – because status is transferred through affiliations, affiliating with low-status organizations could reduce the status of a high-status organization, thus threatening the organization's
own vertical position. Podolny (1994) showed empirically that high-
status investment banks did not totally dominate the primary securities market, despite the fact that they were able to issue a security of
a given quality at a lower cost. These high-status investment banks
were reluctant to enter the non-investment grade market which was
generally populated with low-status investment banks. Gould (2002)
approached the same phenomenon from a different angle and argued
that the limit of the number of ties that high-status organizations
can form circumscribe high-status organizations from entering into
low-status markets. Because high-status organizations use most of
their limited resources to form a relationship with other high-status
organizations or categories, they lack resources to expand beyond
their own high-status markets.

Vertical positions can also magnify negative consequences of failure, which is referred to as an inverse Matthew effect: the more you
have, the more that can be taken away (Jensen, 2006). As mentioned
above, high-status organizations have a secure membership in the
given category and thus can deviate from the prevailing norms more
easily (Phillips and Zuckerman, 2001). High-status organizations
may be punished more severely, however, if they deviate from core
aspects of their market identity (Hsu and Hannan, 2005). High-
status organizations are more conspicuous in the eyes of their audiences and the audiences tend to have higher expectations of these

organizations. As such, deviations from the core aspects of market identities are more easily noticed by the audiences and they may even regard these deviations as severe threats to the standing of the market identities, causing audiences to punish those deviated high-status organizations more severely (Jensen, 2006). Several studies have tested different versions of this argument, including Jensen (2006), Rhee and Haunschild (2006), and Durand, Rao, and Monin (2007). Jensen (2006) argued that Arthur Andersen, a high-status auditing firm, collapsed more dramatically after its association with accounting fraud following the collapse of Enron in 2001 because its clients valued it primarily for its uncompromised high-status position. Similarly, Durand, Rao, and Monin (2007) analyzed French haute cuisine restaurants to examine the inverse Matthew effect and found that the attempts of high-status restaurants to change social codes that defined the core aspects of the market identities tended to receive less positive evaluations from food critics.

Advantages and disadvantages of occupying multiple positions
In developing our status–identity framework, we focused on organizations that only occupy one position within the market space. However, some highly diversified organizations occupy more than one position within a horizontal category or across horizontal categories. Most research on status and identity concentrates on the disadvantages of occupying multiple positions. If organizations occupy more than one vertical position in the same horizontal category, status leakage suggests that they may lose some of the prestige accorded to the high-status position (Podolny, 1994). If organizations occupy more than one horizontal category, the multiple positions may attract a broader audience from different categories, but the fit of each position to the corresponding horizontal category expectation is worse than those of single-position organizations (Hsu, 2006; Hsu, Hannan, and Koçak, 2009). Therefore, in both cases, organizations experience negative consequences by occupying multiple positions. Moreover, multiple-position organizations may be understood less easily by their audiences who, in many cases, use one-category schema to recognize potential members of the category, which ultimately affects organizations negatively. For example, Zuckerman (1999) showed that security analysts tended not to cover diversified companies that spanned various industries

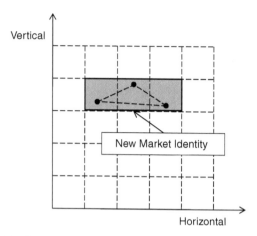

Figure 4.3 Multiple positions in the market space

which did not fit into the simple and traditional categories of securities analysts and caused the companies to experience the stock-market illegitimacy discount.

We suggest that occupying multiple positions need not always be disadvantageous if the organization can shift the audience's attention to a new category with different minimum attitudes and behaviors (Jensen, 2010), in other words, to a new market identity as presented in Figure 4.3. The conditions under which multiple positions affect organization positively are still relatively unexplored. A potentially important condition for successfully occupying multiple positions is that the multiple positions across different horizontal categories are within the same vertical status. When multiple horizontal positions are located within the same vertical status category, status leakage between the different positions is unlikely – all the business units are of approximately the same status. The US conglomerate GE provides an example. The business units of GE include financial service (GE Capital), technology (GE Technology Infrastructure), energy (GE Energy Infrastructure), and entertainment (NBC Universal). Although in different horizontal categories, GE's business units are all vertically ranked highly in their horizontal category. According to our framework, the company is not perceived as a high-status organization in any one industry, such as financial service or energy, or any combination of different industries, but as a high-status conglomerate with distinct attitudes and behaviors. There is little research on how spanning multiple positions can affect organizations positively and we suggest that future research on multiple-position organizations will help us develop a more nuanced understanding of our status-identity framework.

Future research on static market spaces without organizational mobility

In addition to the future research suggested above, there are other possibilities for future research on market status within the boundaries of static market spaces without organizational mobility. First, a closer examination of the origins of status has been proposed in several studies (D'Aveni, 1996; Chen, Hambrick, and Pollock, 2008). Chen, Hambrick, and Pollock (2008) pointed out that we still have a limited understanding of the initial forces that create the vertical status structure itself. D'Aveni (1996) also argued that more research on the inputs that create status can help us better understand how each organization initially comes to occupy a particular status position. Second, future research should examine questions related to the vertical distribution of organizations within a horizontal category. Some markets have a pyramid distribution with few high-status actors and many low-status actors, while other markets have actors distributed more evenly across vertical status levels. What are the factors that determine this distribution? What are the implications of different distributions or, in other words, how does the distribution of organizations within a horizontal category affect the advantages and disadvantages of occupying a certain position? Third, future studies should focus on providing a more nuanced understanding of how the perception of an organization is affected by its operations in other categories. While most research on organizations occupying multiple positions has been directed at organizations occupying multiple horizontal positions, future research should also examine organizations occupying multiple vertical positions.

Market spaces with organizational mobility

The second type of research question allows organizations to change positions within the market space but view the current configuration of horizontal and vertical categories as exogenously given. Organizational mobility can take two forms: organizations can move horizontally from one product category to another and vertically

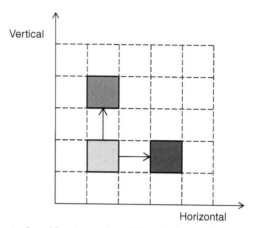

Figure 4.4 Vertical and horizontal mobility in the market space

from one status category to another, as shown in Figure 4.4. Again, given the common identification of a status position with a vertical position, we focus mainly on vertical mobility and examine only horizontal mobility to the extent that it relates to vertical position. Our review of market status research shows that there is considerably less research on vertical mobility within the market space than on the advantages and disadvantages of occupying particular vertical positions. This prioritization is not surprising given that the vertical distribution of organizations within the market space tends to be relatively stable over time, with more organizations staying in the same positions than moving from one position to another.

Vertical organizational mobility

An organization can move to a higher or a lower vertical position in two different ways. First, when organizations understand the dominant criterion for ranking organizations within a particular market space, they can make targeted investments to improve their ranking. For example, if product quality is an important criterion to rank organizations, organizations may decide to invest more resources in product quality both to improve actual quality and to maintain an already-established reputation for quality. Shapiro (1983) argued specifically that if an organization decides to enter the high-quality segment of a market in which product quality is difficult to observe, then it must initially invest in building a reputation for product quality by

actually producing quality products. The minimum cultural expectations for entering a particular vertical position therefore represent
not necessarily an insurmountable barrier to entry, but function more
like an entry cost. However, the entry cost could be high, because the
organizations that already occupy higher-ranked vertical positions
have several distinct position-based competitive advantages. As discussed above, the organizations in higher-ranked vertical positions
can make products at a given level of quality at a lower cost than
organizations occupying lower-ranked positions (Podolny, 1993) and
they earn a higher return on their investments in product quality
(Benjamin and Podolny, 1999).

Second, regardless of direct investments to improve their rankings,
organizations may also attempt to move to a higher vertical position
by affiliating with organizations in the desired vertical positions.
To highlight the difference between reputation and status, Podolny
(1994) argued that status, unlike reputation, which derives only from
past performance, also derives from the status of affiliations and
exchange partners. Podolny and Phillips (1996) developed a model
of status growth according to which organizational status grows not
only through their direct investments in reputation, but also through forming affiliations with high-status organizations. Similarly,
Higgins and Gulati (2003) argued that by affiliating with prominent
organizations, the focal organization can increase its status over time.
They showed that the organizations with a greater number of upper-
echelon members with prominent affiliations were able to attract a
high-status investment bank as their lead underwriter for their IPO.
However, obtaining the opportunities to affiliate with organizations
from higher vertical positions could be illusive, due to status homophily. The incentives for organizations in higher vertical positions to
affiliate with organizations from lower vertical positions are not clear,
given the potential threat that such affiliations pose to organizations
in higher-status positions (Podolny, 1994). As Burris (2004) showed
in his study of academic status hierarchies, status hierarchies are generally reproduced over time because organizations located in similar
positions have a tendency to form relationships with each other.

An important assumption in research on vertical organizational
mobility is that moving to a higher vertical position is always beneficial.
Despite the disadvantages of higher vertical positions discussed above,
it is reasonable to conclude that higher vertical positions generally

are more advantageous than lower vertical positions. However, this does not imply that moving from a lower to a higher vertical position cannot in itself have important negative consequences (Jensen and Kim, 2010). When organizations move from a lower vertical position to a higher position, they may gain access to more resources and opportunities, but they also risk cognitive and social dislocation. Because moving to a higher vertical position implies adopting a different market identity, upward mobility could result in transgressing the minimal expectations of an unfamiliar market identity, which could result in severe sanctions from important audiences. Similarly, to the extent that homophily pressures make it difficult to continue affiliating with organizations from lower vertical positions, moving to a higher vertical position could force the organization to rebuild its affiliation network, which could result in replacing trusted partners with unknown partners. The negative consequences of vertical organizational mobility have largely been neglected in market status research. We suggest that an initial research agenda should focus on the extent to which the size and suddenness of vertical dislocation affect its negative consequences.

Horizontal organizational mobility

The vertical position an organization occupies may also affect horizontal organizational mobility. Focusing on commercial banks entering the investment banking industry, Jensen (2003) reported that organizations were more likely to use commercial banks from high vertical positions in commercial banking as lead managers in investment banking. He argued that vertical positions can be leveraged across horizontal categories because they reduce the quality uncertainty associated with new entrants. Podolny and Scott Morton (1999) also examined the advantages of high-status organizations when entering new horizontal categories. Their empirical analysis indicated that entrants from high vertical positions were more easily accepted into British shipping cartels because incumbents viewed their status in the previous markets as a signal of future cooperation. However, when entering a horizontal category from a high vertical position in another horizontal category, the entering organizations may also experience discrimination from the incumbent organizations because they pose a particularly strong challenge to those organizations. Jensen (2008) found that incumbent investment banking organizations were indeed reluctant to partner with entering commercial banks from high vertical positions, which is consistent with the incumbent investment banks fearing that these entering commercial banks could more easily change the industry logics in ways that would favor commercial banks.

Given the ambivalent effects of vertical positions on horizontal organizational mobility, it is important to clarify under what conditions vertical positions affect horizontal mobility positively. We suggest that two factors are at work when vertical positions are beneficial for new entrants. First, vertical positions have positive effects when the market logics of the targeted new market are similar to those of the market from which entrants come. In the British merchant shipping industry, high-status entrants could enjoy the benefits of their vertical positions because of the similarity between the markets. The incumbents could understand how entrants earned their vertical positions in other markets and, in turn, believe that these entrants would uphold the moral community of the industry because of the similarity between the markets (Podolny and Scott Morton, 1999). On the contrary, the market logics of the commercial and investment banking industries were different, so high-status commercial banks could not fully enjoy the benefits of high status in the new investment banking industry. Second, vertical positions are advantageous for horizontal mobility when it is difficult for potential exchange partners to evaluate product quality *ex ante*. Podolny (2001) argued that occupying high vertical positions is most valuable for organizations when it is difficult for their audiences to evaluate the quality of their products, which implies that organizations in high vertical positions are more likely to focus on markets in which audiences face more uncertainty.

Future research on market spaces with organizational mobility

Whether vertical mobility is primarily due to targeted investments or targeted affiliations, or whether vertical positions have a positive or negative effect on horizontal organizational mobility, future research must consider the extent to which basic characteristics of the market space itself affect mobility. We propose three future research questions that address how the market space with different characteristics could affect vertical and horizontal mobility. First, because the distribution of organizations across vertical positions varies from market to market, it is important to examine whether organizational mobility is more likely in market spaces with continuous vertical positions or in spaces with discontinuous vertical positions. Second, some categories have clear and unambiguous boundaries, whereas others have fuzzy boundaries. Future studies should examine how the characteristics of the boundaries around vertical and horizontal categories affect vertical and horizontal organizational mobility. Third, future research should approach the status–identity framework from a dynamic market perspective and ask whether vertical status or horizontal organizational mobility is more likely in new market spaces with emerging vertical positions or in old market spaces with established vertical positions.

Dynamic market spaces

The third type of research question moves away from viewing the horizontal and vertical categories as exogenously fixed categories. By allowing the horizontal and vertical categories to change, the focus shifts from the positions organizations occupy in a market space to the market space itself and the boundaries that separate the categories that define the market space. Hannan and Freeman (1989) noted that it is important to identify and explain the segregating and blending processes that institutionalize and deinstitutionalize the boundaries that make it possible to distinguish between different categories. Our status–identity framework suggests focusing on identifying and explaining the segregating and blending processes that result in the creation and destruction of both horizontal and vertical categories.

Creating categories

A growing stream of research focuses on the emergence of new horizontal product categories, whereas hardly any research focuses on the emergence of new vertical status categories. The main emphasis in research on horizontal category creation is to identify and explain the segregation processes that ensure the emergence of a new category. We identified two different approaches to the segregation processes that ensure horizontal category emergence.

The first approach focuses on how nascent categories are populated. The main argument here is ecological density dependence (Hannan and Freeman, 1989; Carroll and Hannan, 2000). As the density (i.e., the number) of organizations in a nascent category increases, the nascent category gains constitutive legitimacy and becomes taken for granted as a category. Adopting this approach, Ruef (2000) first identified a comprehensive array of populated and unpopulated horizontal or market identities in the healthcare industry. Next he showed that the likelihood that an unpopulated category becomes populated depended partly on the density of healthcare organizations in similar neighboring horizontal categories. McKendrick *et al.* (2003) argued that horizontal organizational forms emanate from the density of producers that have a "perceptually focused identity" because they mainly operate within that particular horizontal category. They then showed that the density of focused disk array producers increased the entry rate into and decreased the exit rate from the horizontal disk array category, thus ensuring that the category was being populated. And Kennedy (2008) argued that the patterns of associations among market entrants found in the public discourse about the market provide an important basis for studying market formation. He found that another way to legitimate a new market is to enable a census of its entrants, which transforms the horizontal category into something that seems real to other market participants.

The second approach shifts the focus from how nascent categories are being populated to how the nascent categories emerged in the first place. Compared to the population of a category, there is less research on the actual emergence of categories. McKendrick and Carroll (2001) examined the creation of a market for disk arrays in order to understand when and where new organizational forms emerge. By tracing the early history of the disk array market, they concluded that the emerging category for disk array producers ultimately failed to cohere into a mature category because most disk array producers derived their primary market identities from other activities. Jensen (2010) examined the creation of a market for sex-comedy movies in 1970s Denmark to understand how market identities are used to legitimate new normatively illegitimate or socially unacceptable products. He traced how filmmakers created a new horizontal film genre by combining elements from pornography and comedy selectively in film posters to carve a new unique horizontal position for sex-comedies. Jensen also showed that the vertical positions actors occupied helped to ensure that film audiences actually viewed the new horizontal category as a normatively legitimate category. Middle-status actors were frequently used because they both provided legitimacy to the sex-comedies, unlike the low-status actors in illegitimate pornography, and had lower opportunity costs, unlike high-status actors.

Carroll and Swaminathan (2000) examined the emergence of the microbrewery category in the US brewing industry. They focused on the creation of a new market identity for the specialty beer segment that excluded major brewers from entering the specialty segment by emphasizing tradition and authenticity rooted in small organizations using craft brewing methods and natural ingredients. The microbrewery category raises an important question: is the microbrewery category a horizontal (product) category or a vertical (status) category? The microbrewery category is a new horizontal product category that encompasses different product characteristics including natural ingredients and traditional brewing methods, but it could also be viewed as a new vertical status category that positions microbreweries and specialty beers above the major breweries and mass-market beers. We view the microbrewery market identity as a combination: a new horizontal product category in which the distribution of members is skewed toward higher vertical positions. Even when the major breweries meet the quality standards set by microbreweries, many consumers are unwilling to accept them as members of the microbrewery category because they derive their core market identity from a product category with a lower vertical status distribution. It may therefore be easier for organizations from more distant product categories but with a higher vertical status distribution, such as wineries and restaurants, to enter the microbrewery category without concealing their core market identity.

Combining and splitting categories

Besides the creation of new horizontal or vertical categories, it is also important to examine how existing categories combine and split. Whereas research on the creation of new categories focuses mainly on the segregating processes that erect and protect the boundaries around new categories, research on combining and splitting categories focuses on the blending processes that erode existing category boundaries. Rao, Monin, and Durand (2003) examined first how nouvelle cuisine split off from classical cuisine as part of the broader 1960s anti-authoritarian social movements that also transformed other French cultural institutions including literature, theater, and film. They argued that activist chefs both exploited the foundations of classical cuisine, including its emphasis on simplicity, and celebrated their differences with its dominant orthodoxy, including the lack of autonomy for chefs in splitting off nouvelle from classical cuisine. Next Rao, Monin, and Durand (2005) examined how the categorical boundaries of classical and nouvelle cuisines weakened as the borrowing of elements from the rival category diffused broadly and resulted in the hybridization of the two cuisines. Although the authors (2005) focused on borrowing as a blending process that weakens the boundary between horizontal product categories, they also reported that the diffusion of borrowing was triggered by chefs in high vertical positions, which emphasizes that horizontal categories and vertical categories interact to shape market spaces.

Kim and Jensen (2010) adopted a different approach. Rather than focusing on actually changing the horizontal product categories, they argued that horizontal product categories are constitutive parts of market identity taxonomies, and focused on how the taxonomic level at which organizations are identified affects their perceived market identity. They argued specifically that even if individual product categories remain exogenously fixed, an organization can still influence the taxonomic level at which it is identified by its audiences. Toyota, for example, can emphasize that it belongs to the subcategory "Japanese auto manufacturer" in some situations and the basic category "auto manufacturer" in other situations. Market identity taxonomies thus provide organizations with a source of agency that enables them to shape their perceived appeal depending on the specific situation and the specific audience with whom they interact. Or, to use the distinction between segregating and blending processes, market identity taxonomies are *both* segregating *and* blending mechanisms: they allow organizations to split categories by moving from categories to subcategories and they allow organizations to combine categories by moving from subcategories to categories. Simple moves between category levels can in themselves affect the market appeal of an organization: Kim and Jensen (2010) showed that opera companies that interspersed modern operas in their repertoires to avoid the emergence of a negative subcategory sold more season tickets even if the operas in the repertoire remained the same.

Future research on dynamic market spaces

There are still many areas to be explored in the domain of dynamic market spaces. First, relating back to the disadvantages of occupying a highly ranked vertical position, future research can focus on what constrained high-status organizations from creating or redefining categories. Durand, Rao, and Monin (2007), for example, suggested a further examination of how broader cultural factors such as social movements can restrict high-status organizations from taking advantage of new technologies. Rao (2009) provided a partial answer to the question by showing that the anti-biotechnology movement in Germany prevented high-status organizations from commercializing new technology due to their high visibility, while low-status organizations remained largely unaffected. Building on this study, future research can provide more evidence regarding the liabilities of high-status positions in creating new categories or changing their identities. Second, while some studies examine the creation of new horizontal categories, few studies focus on the creation of new vertical categories within a horizontal category. Organizations can, however, vertically expand a category, for example, by creating high-end products. Third, future research can explore how different vertical positions affect the creation of new categories and how organizations of different vertical positions respond differently to the newly created categories. Which organizations will be the first to create new categories, for example, and which organizations will be the first to move into a new category?

Conclusion

In this chapter, we have developed a new status–identity framework by integrating work on status as positions in social systems and market identity as membership in social categories. According to this framework, status refers to a position in a social system or intersection of horizontally and vertically arrayed social categories, and market identity refers to the schema that codifies the minimal expectations of that particular intersection. We used the status–identity framework to systematically review status research in markets and, more importantly, to identify promising areas for future research. Most research focuses on the advantages and, to a lesser extent, the disadvantages of occupying a particular vertical position, and emphasizes how they affect quality perceptions and production, organizational agency, and legitimacy. Some research focuses on vertical and horizontal mobility in the market space, most of which emphasizes the difficulties of moving to higher vertical positions or how a vertical position produces the opportunity for horizontal mobility by leveraging status from one horizontal category to another. The least researched area focuses on the creation and destruction of the horizontal and vertical categories themselves, in particular, as this area of research relates to the actual creation of categories rather than the density-dependent legitimization of nascent categories. Finally, we identified specific new research opportunities in all the three main research areas identified by our status–identity framework, including the consequences of occupying multiple positions in the market space, the extent to which the fuzziness of category boundaries affect organizational mobility, and how new vertical positions emerge.

Although we believe that our status–identity framework both provides conceptual clarity to status research and a systematic approach to identifying future research opportunities, it is also clear that the status–identity framework has its own limitations that require further conceptual development. First, the status–identity framework represents a single social system with a *single* audience that agrees on a single ranking of products and organizations. However, organizations sometimes participate in multiple markets for the same product and therefore have *multiple* audiences that may rank the *same* products and organizations differently. GM's Buick is considered one of the high-status automobiles among Chinese consumers, for example, whereas American consumers do not rate Buick automobiles so highly. We are less concerned with situations in which the different audiences are clearly separated, such as American and Chinese consumers, because these situations simply call for applying the framework separately to each of the audience groups. It is more problematic when different audiences are not clearly separated, which could happen when mobility across cultural boundaries allows different audiences to merge, if non-separation allows different rankings to coexist permanently. However, we find the permanent coexistence of radically different rankings unlikely, because interactions among the audiences will eventually lead to a convergence in rankings due to simple status arbitrage between audiences with different rankings (or the abandonment of rankings that are perceived to be less valid).

Second, the status–identity framework represents a market space at a particular horizontal and vertical category level, but most categories are parts of a broader nested category system that are not easily represented in the basic framework. As mentioned before, Toyota is a member of a number of different nested categories including "manufacturer," "auto manufacturer," and "Japanese auto manufacturer," and Toyota may emphasize its membership in each of these nested horizontal categories in different situations. Moving between category levels changes the market space and the included audience groups, and therefore calls for applying the framework at each category level. As with the case of multiple markets with different audience groups, if we want to examine any relationships across different category levels, we need to take into consideration the different audiences associated with each category level. Third, we assumed in our framework that all actors can be mapped unambiguously onto a particular position. However, some category boundaries can be relatively unclear or fuzzy, making it difficult to map the status positions onto the given framework. In the case of newly established categories such as sex-comedies or microbreweries, for example, it may be difficult to position a particular organization as high status, middle status or low status on the vertical dimension. In addition, the boundaries between the horizontal categories themselves may not always be clear. The framework may therefore be more directly applicable to established market spaces than to emerging market spaces.

We have developed and used the status–identity framework in the context of markets and organizations, but we believe that it can be generalized to other contexts. We have already discussed how the status–identity framework can accommodate different markets at the same level of analysis, such as the American and Chinese auto markets, and how it can accommodate different markets at different levels of analysis, such as "auto manufacturers" and "Japanese auto manufacturers." The abstract nature of the status–identity framework allows it to be used in market as well as non-market contexts and to focus on organizations as well as individuals, groups, and other social actors. When moving from one context to another, the horizontal and vertical categories obviously change but the fundamental insight remains the same: a status is an intersection of horizontally and vertically arrayed social categories, and status is important because it provides an identity that facilitates and constrains the actions of the social actors in that particular intersection. Regardless of its flexibility and generalizability, the ultimate value of our status–identity framework is determined mainly by the actual insights it provides by being used in specific empirical research projects.

References

Baker, W. E., Faulkner, R. R., and Fisher, G. A. 1998. "Hazards of the market: The continuity and dissolution of interorganizational market relationships." *American Sociological Review* 63: 147–177.

Benjamin, B. A. and Podolny, J. M. 1999. "Status, quality, and social order in the California wine industry." *Administrative Science Quarterly* 44: 563–589.

Burris, V. 2004. "The academic caste system: Prestige hierarchies in PhD exchange networks." *American Sociological Review* 69: 239–264.

Carroll, G. R. and Hannan, M. T. 2000. *The Demography of Organizations and Industries*. Princeton University Press.

Carroll, G. R. and Swaminathan, A. 2000. "Why the microbrewery movement? Organizational dynamics of resource partitioning in the US brewing industry." *American Journal of Sociology* 106: 715–762.

Caves, R. E. 1980. "Industrial-organization, corporate-strategy and structure." *Journal of Economic Literature* 18: 64–92.

Chen, G., Hambrick, D. C., and Pollock, T. G. 2008. "Puttin' on the ritz: Pre-IPO enlistment of prestigious affiliates as deadline-induced remediation." *Academy of Management Journal* 51: 954–975.

Chung, S., Singh, H., and Lee, K. 2000. "Complementarity, status similarity and social capital as drivers of alliance formation." *Strategic Management Journal* 21: 1–22.

D'Aveni, R. A. 1996. "A multiple-constituency, status-based approach to interorganizational mobility of faculty and input-output competition among top business schools." *Organization Science* 7: 166–189.

Davis, G. F. and Greve, H. R. 1997. "Corporate elite networks and governance changes in the 1980s." *American Journal of Sociology* 103: 1–37.

Durand, R., Rao, H., and Monin, P. 2007. "Code and conduct in French cuisine: Impact of code changes on external evaluations." *Strategic Management Journal* 28: 455–472.

Eisenhardt, K. M. and Schoonhoven, C. B. 1996. "Resource-based view of strategic alliance formation: Strategic and social effects in entrepreneurial firms." *Organization Science* 7: 136–150.

Geletkanycz, M. A., Boyd, K., and Finkelstein, S. 2001. "The strategic value of CEO external directorate networks: Implications for CEO compensation." *Strategic Management Journal* 22: 889–898.

Gould, R. V. 2002. "The origins of status hierarchies: A formal theory and empirical test." *American Journal of Sociology* 107: 1143–1178.

Gulati, R. and Higgins, M. C. 2003. "Which ties matter? The contingent effects of interorganizational partnerships on IPO success." *Strategic Management Journal* 24: 127–144.

Guler, I. 2007. "Throwing good money after bad? Political and institutional influences on sequential decision making in the venture capital industry." *Administrative Science Quarterly* 52: 248–285.

Haas, M. R. and Hansen, M. T. 2007. "Different knowledge, different benefits: Toward a productivity perspective on knowledge sharing in organizations." *Strategic Management Journal* 28: 1133–1153.

Hannan, M. T. and Freeman, J. 1989. *Organizational Ecology*. Cambridge, MA: Harvard University Press.

Hannan, M. T., Pólos, L., and Carroll, G. R. 2007. *Logics of Organization Theory: Audiences, Codes, and Ecologies*. Princeton University Press.

Haunschild, P. R. and Miner, A. S. 1997. "Modes of interorganizational imitation: The effects of outcome salience and uncertainty." *Administrative Science Quarterly* 42: 472–500.

Higgins, M. C. and Gulati, R. 2003. "Getting off to a good start: The effects of upper echelon affiliations on underwriter prestige." *Organization Science* 14: 244–263.

Hoetker, G., Swaminathan, A., and Mitchell, W. 2007. "Modularity and the impact of buyer-supplier relationships on the survival of suppliers." *Management Science* 53: 178–191.

Hsu, G. 2006. "Jacks of all trades and masters of none: Audiences' reactions to spanning genres in feature film production." *Administrative Science Quarterly* 51: 420–450.

Hsu, G. and Hannan, M. T. 2005. "Identities, genres, and organizational forms." *Organization Science* 16: 474–490.

Hsu, G., Hannan, M. T., and Koçak, Ö. 2009. "Multiple category memberships in markets: An integrated theory and two empirical tests." *American Sociological Review* 74: 150–169.

Hughes, E. C. 1937. "Institutional office and the person." *American Journal of Sociology* 43: 404–413.

Jensen, M. 2003. "The role of network resources in market entry: Commercial banks' entry into investment banking, 1991–1997." *Administrative Science Quarterly* 48: 466–497.

2006. "Should we stay or should we go? Accountability, status anxiety, and client defections." *Administrative Science Quarterly* 51: 97–128.

2008. "The use of relational discrimination to manage market entry: When do social status and structural holes work against you?" *Academy of Management Journal* 51: 723–743.

2010. "Legitimizing illegitimacy: How creating market identity legitimizes illegitimate products." Working Paper, University of Michigan.

Jensen, M. and Kim, B. K. 2009. "Great, Madame Butterfly again! How robust market identity shapes opera repertoires." Working Paper, University of Michigan.

2010. "The real Oscar curse: The negative consequences of position status shifts." Working Paper, University of Michigan.

Jensen, M. and Roy, A. 2008. "Staging exchange partner choices: When do status and reputation matter?" *Academy of Management Journal* 51: 495–516.

Kennedy, M. T. 2008. "Getting counted: Markets, media, and reality." *American Sociological Review* 73: 270–295.

Kim, B. K. and Jensen, M. 2010. "It is not just what you have, but how you present it: How subcategorization affects opera market identity." Working Paper, University of Michigan.

Linton, R. 1936. *The Study of Man.* New York: D. Appleton-Century Co.

McKendrick, D. G. and Carroll, G. R. 2001. "On the genesis of organizational forms: Evidence from the market for disk arrays." *Organization Science* 12: 661–682.

McKendrick, D. G., Jaffee, J., Carroll, G. R., and Khessina, O. M. 2003. "In the bud? Disk array producers as a (possibly) emergent organizational form." *Administrative Science Quarterly* 48: 60–93.

Merton, R. K. 1957. *Social Theory and Social Structure.* Glencoe, IL: The Free Press.

Phillips, D. J. and Zuckerman, E. W. 2001. "Middle-status conformity: Theoretical restatement and empirical demonstration in two markets." *American Journal of Sociology* 107: 379–429.

Podolny, J. M. 1993. "A status-based model of market competition." *American Journal of Sociology* 98: 829–872.

1994. "Market uncertainty and the social character of economic exchange." *Administrative Science Quarterly* 39: 458–483.

2001. "Networks as the pipes and prisms of the market." *American Journal of Sociology* 107: 33–60.

2005. *Status Signals: A Sociological Study of Market Competition.* Princeton University Press.

Podolny, J. M. and Phillips, D. J. 1996. "The dynamics of organizational status." *Industrial and Corporate Change* 5: 453–471.

Podolny, J. M. and Scott Morton, F. M. 1999. "Social status, entry and predation: The case of British shipping cartels 1879–1929." *Journal of Industrial Economics* 47: 41–67.

Podolny, J. M. and Stuart, T. E. 1995. "A role-based ecology of technological change." *American Journal of Sociology* 100: 1224–1260.

Podolny, J. M., Stuart, T. E., and Hannan, M. T. 1996. "Networks, knowledge, and niches: Competition in the worldwide semiconductor industry, 1984–1991." *American Journal of Sociology* 102: 659–689.

Porter, M. E. 1979. "The structure within industries and companies' performance." *The Review of Economics and Statistics* 61: 214–227.

Rao, H. 2009. *Market Rebels: How Activists Make or Break Radical Innovations.* Princeton University Press.

Rao, H, Monin, P., and Durand, R. 2003. "Institutional change in Toque Ville: Nouvelle cuisine as an identity movement in French gastronomy." *American Journal of Sociology* 108: 795–843.

2005. "Border crossing: Bricolage and the erosion of categorical boundaries in French gastronomy." *American Sociological Review* 70: 968–991.

Rhee, M. and Haunschild, P. R. 2006. "The liability of good reputation: A study of product recalls in the US automobile industry." *Organization Science* 17: 101–117.

Rosenkopf, L. and Padula, G. 2008. "Investigating the microstructure of network evolution: Alliance formation in the mobile communications industry." *Organization Science* 19: 669–687.

Ruef, M. 2000. "The emergence of organizational forms: A community ecology approach." *American Journal of Sociology* 106: 658–714.

Sanders, W. and Tuschke, A. 2007. "The adoption of institutionally contested organizational practices: The emergence of stock option pay in Germany." *Academy of Management Journal* 50: 33–56.

Shapiro, C. 1983. "Premiums for high quality products as returns to reputations." *The Quarterly Journal of Economics* 98: 659–680.

Sine, W. D., Shane, S., and Di Gregorio, D. 2003. "The halo effect and technology licensing: The influence of institutional prestige on the licensing of university inventions." *Management Science* 49: 478–496.

Sorokin, P. A. 1959. *Social and Cultural Mobility.* Glencoe, IL: The Free Press.

Spence, M. 1974. *Market Signaling.* Cambridge, MA: Harvard University Press.

Stuart, T. E. 1998. "Network positions and propensities to collaborate: An investigation of strategic alliance formation in a high-technology industry." *Administrative Science Quarterly* 43: 668–698.

2000. "Interorganizational alliances and the performance of firms: A study of growth and innovation rates in a high-technology industry." *Strategic Management Journal* 21: 791–811.

Stuart, T. E., Hoang, H., and Hybels, R. C. 1999. "Interorganizational endorsements and the performance of entrepreneurial ventures." *Administrative Science Quarterly* 44: 315–349.

Uzzi, B. and Lancaster, R. 2004. "Embeddedness and price formation in the corporate law market." *American Sociological Review* 69: 319–344.

Washington, M. and Zajac, E. J. 2005. "Status evolution and competition: Theory and evidence." *Academy of Management Journal* 48: 282–296.

Weber, M. 1968. *Economy and Sociology: An Outline of Interpretive Sociology.* Translated and edited by G. Roth and C. Wittich. New York: Bedminister Press.

Wilson, R. 1985. "Reputations in games and markets," in A. E. Roth (ed.), *Game-theoretic Models of Bargaining.* Cambridge University Press, pp. 27–62.

Zuckerman, E. W. 1999. "The categorical imperative: Securities analysts and the illegitimacy discount." *American Journal of Sociology* 104: 1398–1438.

5 | On the need to extend tournament theory through insights from status research

MICHAEL NIPPA

Whatever organizational theory one considers, organization and management are viewed as means to motivate and coordinate individuals most efficiently so as to direct all their competences and efforts to the organization's goals. For instance, early concepts such as Scientific Management proposed selecting the best workers, assigning them to the most appropriate tasks, and using money as a predominant motivator (e.g., Locke, 1982). Despite fierce criticism, especially from advocates of the Human Relations movement, monetary incentives are still considered by scholars and practitioners alike as prime motivators of individual behavior and performance. Studies and publications focusing – on the one hand – on single problems and issues of motivating workers and managers by means of money to work hard, and rewarding them for their productive contribution, or – on the other hand – on developing the optimal compensation schemes are overwhelming.

Explaining existing compensation structures, analyzing normative properties of alternative compensation schemes, and determining efficient executive compensation systems are at the center of personnel and organizational economics (e.g., Lazear, 1999; Encinosa, Gaynorb, and Rebitzer, 2007; Lazear and Shaw, 2007). This literature analyzes the motivational effects of compensation and reward systems at the organizational level, and predominantly emphasizes the need to increase shareholder interests by defining and applying optimal employment contracts and efficient pay structures (e.g., Becker and Huselid, 1992). Of special interest among neoinstitutional economists and organizational theorists is the theory of tournaments, as it provides a rigorous formal model to explain the phenomenon of disproportionate executive compensation, for instance.

The basic ideas and the concept of tournament theory have been elaborated by Lazear and Rosen (1981). In order to overcome inherent problems of incentive contracts based upon *absolute* levels of individual performance, i.e., defining and monitoring precise performance measures at high cost regarding effort and output independent of external shocks (e.g., Baker, 1992), the authors propose using *relative* performance in rank-order tournaments. Under certain assumptions it is shown that competitive tournaments and respective prizes are frequently more efficient and superior to traditional pay-for-performance compensation schemes, as they not only motivate the targeted manager or management level, but all employees of subordinate levels that strive for promotion. Thus, it is proposed to substitute salaries contingent upon absolute output levels by predetermined prizes for winners and losers of periodic tournaments according to the rank-order of contestants (Lazear and Rosen, 1981; Lazear and Shaw, 2007, pp. 94ff.), similar to the medieval knight tournaments and today's sports tournaments (e.g., tennis or soccer cups). Tournament theory has found broad acceptance, particularly among economists, because of its formal rigidity and testability and has been further elaborated on (early contributions, e.g., by Green and Stokey, 1983; Nalebuff and Stiglitz, 1983; Rosen, 1986; and Bhattacharya and Guasch, 1988). Although a lack of tests has been initially acknowledged (e.g., O'Reilly, Main, and Crystal, 1988; Becker and Huselid, 1992; Main, O'Reilly, and Wade, 1993), tournament theory received at least some empirical support in various contexts – frequently sport events and experimental studies – over the years (e.g., Rosenbaum, 1979; Bull, Schotter, and Weigelt, 1987; Ehrenberg and Bognanno, 1990; Gibbs, 1994; Eriksson, 1999; Conyon and Sadler, 2001).

Tournament theory, embedded in neoinstitutional theory and principal–agent reasoning, has been predominantly applied to explain and to justify the grading of salaries and disproportionately high chief executive officer (CEO) compensation. As it provides a logical and to some extent empirically confirmed justification of salary differentials, tournament theory falls victim to a more general criticism of excessive executive compensation (e.g., Byrne and Bongiorno, 1995; McCall, 2004). Triggered by corporate scandals, mismanagement, and bankruptcies in the course of the recent economic crisis, corporate governance practices and especially compensation of CEOs and senior managers have been publicly disputed, and income caps have been called for (e.g., Solomon and Meckler, 2009). However, applying tournament theory to executive compensation is also criticized for its improper argumentation by analogy to sports tournaments (Rees, 1992) or due to inaccurate tests regarding its relevance (Gibbs, 1994). Moreover, from the beginning it has been fundamentally questioned with regard to its simplistic assumptions and models, which do not match reality. Interestingly, this questioning has emanated not only in behavioral sciences, but also from economists such as Baker, Jensen, and Murphy (1988, pp. 600ff.), whose concluding statement reads as follows:

Ultimately, it may be that psychologists, behaviorists, human resource consultants, and personnel executives understand something about human behavior and motivation that is not yet captured in our economic models. Alternatively, it could be that practitioners are adopting policies that sacrifice organizational efficiency for egalitarian pay systems. If one of these reasons explains the gap between economic theory and compensation practices, then either there are intellectual profits or organizational efficiencies to be gained by focusing attention on the compensation puzzles we have outlined. We believe both kinds of profit opportunities will materialize. (p. 615)

This – in principle – open view contrasts starkly with Lazear's perspective, who believes that "economics provides a rigorous and in many cases better way to think about these human resource questions than do the more sociological and psychological approaches" (1999, p. 200).

Most probably, one has to assume that there is no "either – or" rather than the opportunity to mutually advance different disciplines, research streams, and theories (Washington and Zajac, 2005). There is a great overlap regarding structural and conceptual foundations of tournament theory and status research. Central to both concepts are hierarchical orders and their impact on human behavior. Tournaments are based on relative performance assessments, and status is in any case the expression of relative esteem. Attempts to win a tournament are not only motivated by the monetary value of the prize, but also by the pure status effect (e.g., the Ashes in Cricket, the Sydney to Hobart Yacht Race, the Ironman Triathlon in Hawaii or the Nobel Prize). Winners of tournaments improve their status, which is sometimes more important (e.g., being engraved on a challenge cup) than the monetary prize that may come with it. The gained status may allow the winner to reap additional monetary profits (e.g., own fashion labels) or non-monetary benefits (e.g., exclusive club membership). Thus, one might ask to what extent research questions addressed and insights generated by status researchers from various disciplines are adopted by tournament theorists. In particular, it may be of interest to learn whether striving for status has been explicitly considered by tournament theory with regard to its possible substitutive or complementary effect on monetary incentives. In addition, to what extent do tournament theorists reflect and test their recommendations (i.e., an increase in number of contestants or an increase in organizational levels from tournaments) against practical limitations and reverse organizational developments such as downsizing? As status research has highlighted the motivational importance of procedural aspects such as the process of bestowing status, the question arises as to whether this has also been considered by tournament theorists. However, beyond such a stock-taking review it might have a stimulating effect for future research and corporate practice to emphasize insights from status research that may extend and advance our understanding of organizational tournaments.

The therefore, the main objective of this contribution is to show how and to what extent important insights derived from research on organizational status (a) have been applied by tournament theory, (b) may help to further develop and enrich tournament theory in order to better explain organizational practices, as well as (c) provide practitioners with more appropriate principles to design and efficiently implement competitive tournaments as a means of improving organizational effectiveness.

The chapter is structured as follows. First, the relevant literature that centers on tournament theory will be reviewed. Beyond simply repeating the main assumptions and basic models, important extensions, particularly with regard to integrating crucial factors such as emotions (Kräkel, 2008) or status (Moldovanu, Sela, and Shi, 2007), are reviewed, recommendations and empirical tests are summarized, and criticism is substantiated. Second, it will be shown how insights from interdisciplinary research on status may offer answers to relevant aspects of this criticism or may direct organizations that make use of tournaments toward important issues that improve its efficiency and effectiveness. Finally, results and implications for future research and management practice are summarized.

Tournament theory – stratification and competition

Rank-order tournaments and promotion-based compensation

Although some predecessors may be identified (e.g., Rosenbaum, 1979), tournament theory has its seeds in the seminal work of Lazear and Rosen (1981) and in extensions elaborated by Rosen (1986). In search of optimal labor contracts that ensure maximum effort by employees while minimizing non-marginal monitoring costs on the part of the employer, economists propose substituting traditional compensation schemes that link wages to input or output units (e.g., piece rates) for rank-order payment schemes, if monitoring is difficult or not reliable (Lazear and Rosen, 1981; Rosen, 1986; Anabtawi, 2005). In order to understand the underlying approach and rationale, it is necessary to emphasize that tournament theory has its roots in neoinstitutional economic thinking, especially agency theory (Holmström, 1979; Carmichael, 1983; Rees, 1985; Shapiro, 2005). Acknowledging bounded rationality, tournament theory assumes (a) the existence of economic actors that opportunistically try to maximize their individual utility, (b) money as a predominant motive, and (c) information asymmetry in favor of the agent. Under such premises, risk-averse employees, i.e., agents, will seize any opportunity to exploit risk-neutral supervisors and shareholders, i.e., principals, if they are not monitored, sanctioned, or aligned with the interests of the principal. If monitoring costs have to be accounted for, economic reasoning expects rational assessment and maximization of the principal's utility function, i.e., weighing monitoring benefits (e.g., well-performing employees) and monitoring costs. Given these assumptions, tournament theorists argue that compensating agents based on relative rank-order tournaments, i.e., promotion-based remuneration, is economically superior to other compensation schemes "in the presence of costly monitoring of workers' efforts and output" (Lazear and Rosen, 1981, pp. 841ff.), and in the presence of externalities such as technical breakdowns or economic cycles that affect their efforts and output (Gibbs, 1994).

Applying tournaments as a means of compensating and motivating employees in organizations implies the existence of some sort of hierarchy or ranks, i.e., promotion opportunities, and attractive prizes and rewards for winners. For a single period or tournament the motivation and effort of a contestant is mainly determined by two factors: the individual valuation of the promised reward (prize offer) and the individual expectation (probability) of winning the prize. The latter depends on the amount of skill and effort exerted (Anabtawi, 2005), the number and quality of competing contestants, and a random element of chance (Lazear and Rosen, 1981), which has been further elaborated as "noise" by Lazear (1998, pp. 231–236).

Rosen (1986) extended the original one-stage model into a model that accounts for *n* sequential elimination rounds, i.e., multiple promotions. His model and subsequent calculation refers to tennis tournaments as a proxy for career games in order to determine optimum prize or inter-rank spreads across organizational levels (e.g., Lambert, Larcker, and Weigelt, 1993). Under the conditions of sequential elimination tournaments it is formally demonstrated that for risk-neutral managers, prize spreads increase linearly until the final round, i.e., running for CEO, while for risk-averse managers, prize spreads have to follow a convex function (pp. 440f.).

Other important predictions derived from tournament reasoning are: (a) the larger the prize the more effort and performance are exerted, (b) motivation and effort reach a maximum if the chance of winning is uniformly distributed, while they decrease if the chance of winning declines (probability $\to$ 0) or improves (probability $\to$ 1), (c) due to an infinite horizon of future competitions, the prize of becoming a CEO has to be particularly large (Gibbs, 1994). As difficulties of monitoring absolute effort and outcomes are fundamental preconditions of applying tournament theory, empirical proof of the "tournament based compensation system"–"individual effort" link is characterized as anachronistic (Lazear, 1998, p. 241) or difficult (Gibbs, 1994). Nevertheless, there are some studies that prove predictions with regard to sports (e.g., Ehrenberg and Bognanno, 1990; Becker and Huselid, 1992), experimental settings (Bull *et al.*, 1987), and the corporate world (e.g., Conyon and Sadler, 2001).

Criticism and limitations

However, other studies report findings that contradict tournament theory predictions (e.g., O'Reilly, Main, and Crystal, 1988; Ariely *et al.*, 2009). These inconsistencies fuel criticism that refers to the irreconcilable differences between sports and executive compensation (e.g., Rees, 1992) and improper simplifications of organizational reality (e.g., Baker *et al.*, 1988; Gibbs, 1994). While any theory has to simplify reality to produce generalizable predictions, it has to withstand the assessment of its prediction quality and practical applicability. In other words, simplicity alone does not make a good theory – what does is a theory's explanatory and normative reliability with regard to the phenomena it pretends to predict. The following paragraphs detail major criticisms and respective limitations of tournament theories of executive compensation.

Basic criticism. Lazear and Rosen's tournament model (1981) and later extensions have been fundamentally criticized for their inherent tendency "to mask complexity" (Baker *et al.*, 1988, p. 600), which is a friendly glossing-over for the term "oversimplification," i.e., negligence of important variables and interdependencies, that leads to equivocal explanations and recommendations. However, as it is not possible to elaborate every aspect of criticism of tournament theory published in scholarly literature here, the following section will focus on issues that address stratification, competition, and prizes in order to clarify possible extensions based on the interdisciplinary research on status within organizations.

As briefly mentioned above, tournament theory stands in the tradition of neoinstitutional economics and its fundamental assumptions. Accordingly, most studies, like the seminal work by Lazear and Rosen (1981), follow a highly formalized approach to deriving general conclusions and recommendations with regard to optimum labor contracts, superior design of organizational incentive structures (e.g., Green and Stokey, 1983), or contract production (Knoeber, 1989; Knoeber and Thurman, 1994). Most economists do not criticize the basic model, its assumptions, and applicability within organizational contexts, but rather extend it by introducing, for instance, multiple agents (Green and Stokey, 1983), multiple elimination tournaments (Rosen, 1986; Leeds, 1988), or by modeling contests (O'Keeffe, Viscusi, and Zeckhauser, 1984), for example, to avoid "Yes-Men" behavior (Cummins and Nyman, 2007). More fundamental criticism comes from a few economists who challenge its advantageousness over other compensation schemes and/or its organizational applicability (e.g., Dye, 1984; Baker *et al.*, 1988; Rees, 1992; Gibbs 1994).

Moreover, originators and advocates of rank-order tournaments as a means of motivating managers to show an optimum level of effort and performance predominantly build an analogy with sports tournaments: "The theory is easily described using the metaphor of a tennis match. Consider a tennis match between Agassi and Sampras" (Lazear, 1998, p. 225). "For analytical tractability and simplicity, the ideas are best revealed by a paired-comparison structure, as in a tennis-ladder. The tournament begins with 2^N players and proceeds sequentially through N stages" (Rosen, 1986, p. 702). However, as pointed out by a few discerning economists, the analogy of promotion-based compensation schemes with sports tournaments falls short for several reasons (see Table 5.1).

While this criticism also empirically questions proofs that refer to sports tournaments, it is still rooted in economic reasoning (e.g., rationality, utility maximization, monetary rewards). Therefore, not surprisingly, alternative compensation schemes (e.g., Baker *et al.*, 1988) or alterations of the original models are proposed so as to overcome single tournament limitations. Examples of the latter approach are proposals to increase prize spreads in order to account for external entrants, i.e., inter-firm and inter-tournament mobility (Anabtawi, 2005), introducing handicaps to adjust for heterogeneous contestants (O'Keeffe *et al.*, 1984), preventing uncooperative behavior by decreasing chances of interference among contestants (Lazear, 1995, pp. 35ff.), or responding to the problem of abetting the Peter Principle (Lazear, 2004).

For whatever reason, there is – to my best knowledge – no comprehensive debate about or criticism of tournament theory among social scientists, especially from disciplines such as psychology, sociology, or organizational behavior. Apparently, personnel economics and behavioral science-based human resource management widely ignore each other and seem to predominantly cultivate two separate worlds. This comes as a surprise as both disciplines have the same research subject and objective, particularly to increase organizational efficiency by explaining human behavior and steering individual motivation. Tournament theory deals with prizes (i.e., monetary motivators), structures (i.e., multi-level elimination tournaments and rank-orders), and processes (i.e., competition among contestants) as means of maximizing individual effort and performance for the sake of the organization. Strikingly, status research within the context of

Table 5.1 *Important limitations to the analogy between sports and organizational compensation tournaments*

Feature	Sports tournaments	Organizational tournaments	Exemplary sources
Homogeneity of contestants with regard to abilities and skills	Rather homogeneous (e.g., invited PGA players) to ensure attractive competition (e.g., closer races have greater prizes)	Often rather heterogeneous (e.g., different age, gender, education, experience, firm-specific knowledge)	Dye (1984) Gibbs (1994) Rees (1992)
Structure and stability of tournament	Deterministic organization (e.g., number of rounds and stages, fixed slots, elimination rules, and prizes) As a rule no entrants at later stages of the tournament; in any case fixed number of contestants	Flexible organization (e.g., variation of career paths, random slots, ambiguous rules, no elimination except for up-or-out policies, partly negotiable prizes/salaries) Frequent openness to external contestants at different stages, i.e., variable number of contestants	Dye (1984) Gibbs (1994)
Quantification of utility function	Relatively easy	Very difficult or impossible	Rees (1992)
Rules and requirements on subsequent stages	Identical	Different (i.e., best performer at a lower level may not be the best candidate for the next stage)	Baker et al. (1988) Rees (1992)

Observability and measurability of effort and performance	Rather easy (e.g., unforced errors) and without delay	Rather difficult with long lags between effort and success or failure	Baker et al. (1988) Dye (1984)
Impact and observability of opportunism, cheating, and collusion	Low impact as long as attractive competition is not endangered Rather easy to monitor and to sanction	High impact as collaboration and team products supplement competition among employees Rather difficult to monitor and sanction (e.g., politicking, "yes-men")	Anabtawi (2005) Baker et al. (1988) Dye (1984) Main et al. (1993)
Success factor(s)	Primarily abilities, disposition, and effort of all competing contestants Competition	Contestants for an open position and non-contestants (e.g., blue-collar workers) Collaboration even among contestants	Rees (1992)
Need to motivate losers	No, as contestants may enter the soon-to-follow next tournament at the opening round	Yes, as most passed-over candidates are demotivated and stay within the organization or may take an external promotion option because of infrequent promotion opportunities	Anabtawi (2005) Baker et al. (1988) Dye (1984) Gibbs (1994) Rees (1992)

organizations is concerned with rather similar issues, for instance, the individual strive for status (e.g., Huberman, Loch, and Öncüler, 2003), the development and shaping of formal and informal status structures (e.g., Ridgeway and Walker, 1995), and the existence of status competition and its impact on group performance (e.g., Loch, Huberman, and Stout, 2000). A closer look reveals that there are some minor indications within the economic literature that status may have an impact on the design of organizational tournaments and that promotion-based compensation systems relying on status may supplement money as a relevant motive: "While few would dispute the importance of money, it is the status derived from it that may be most important, and this is known through a process of social comparison" (Main *et al.*, 1993, p. 624).

Assessing attempts to integrate status. A few economists have responded to calls for analyzing tournaments with prizes other than money by either treating status as part of the individual utility function (e.g., Fershtman and Weiss, 1993; Fershtman, Murphy, and Weiss, 1996) or – most recently – by modeling a pure status case, i.e., status as sole motive, and a case where status is a direct result of the monetary prize a contestant may win (Moldovanu *et al.*, 2007). While the first approach shows substitution effects between occupational status and wages as well as – to some extent economically negative – adverse selection problems, the second approach claims that the "model offers a convenient framework for the study of the various implications of concerns for social status on organizational design" (Moldovanu *et al.*, 2007, p. 355).

Moldovanu *et al.* formalize the decision problem of a principal who wants to maximize total output of his or her agents by designing an optimal status hierarchy based upon restrictive assumptions. For the chosen assumptions the authors show: (a) "that for any distribution of abilities, the top category in any optimal partition must contain a single agent," (b) "Given a partition in status classes, adding a new element to an arbitrary class may, in fact, reduce output," with the exception that homogeneous entrants at the lowest status class are beneficial, (c) "A proliferation of status classes is optimal if the distribution of abilities has an increasing failure (or hazard) rate," i.e., the more professional the contestants, the greater a proliferation of job titles and status, (d) "whenever there are transaction costs attached to finer partitions, the coarsest possible nontrivial partition may be ultimately optimal," and (e) for the case of status deriving purely from monetary prizes, the optimal structure is always two classes, of which "the top class consisting of the single most productive agent and the lower class containing all other agents who get paid just enough to keep them in the contest" (Moldovanu *et al.*, 2007, pp. 341f.).

While the fact that economics and tournament theory are aware of the impact of status is commendable, the explanatory power of the attempts mentioned above is rather limited due to two main reasons. First, the degree of simplification which is needed to derive formal equations for rational decision makers, be it individuals participating in a tournament or principals designing the optimal status classes. For instance, considering status as a discrete factor of an individual utility function appears not to be too enlightening because it may turn out to be a "fudge" factor that makes it possible to explain any possible phenomena (e.g., Leibenstein, 1986; Postlewaite, 1998). Similarly, assuming a deterministic and equal relation between effort and output, assuming simultaneously submitted efforts, or assuming abilities as private information of each candidate (e.g., Moldovanu *et al.*, 2007) facilitate formal equations and definite solutions, but do not match the real phenomenon that authors pretend to explain. Second, tournament theory is restricted to status as an end and to structuring rank-order systems, and neglects procedural aspects such as the importance of the process of awarding status, i.e., promotions (e.g., Ferris, Buckley, and Allen, 1992), temporal issues like the expected timeframe for receiving a promotion after being passed over, and contextual factors like labor markets and legal environments. Thus, one has to doubt that it is only the relative strengths of monetary incentives versus striving for status that determines optimal promotion and rank-order tournaments, and that this explains and justifies extremely high CEO salaries as stated by Moldovanu *et al.* (2007).

Conclusion. Explanations and recommendations based upon tournament theory are plausible and consequential within its system of a highly restrictive set of assumptions. While economists argue that these assumptions are beneficial and comply with "Godfrey Hardy's dictum whereby good science must, at least, provide some 'decent' distance between assumptions and results" (Moldovanu *et al.*, 2007, p. 344), the dark side, i.e., the danger of basing decisions on theories that differ from reality, is frequently concealed. For instance, tournament theory is predominantly used to justify and to perpetuate salary spreads and absurdly high CEO compensation packages, because it seems to explain the phenomenon, despite striking deviations from its underlying assumptions.

By applying insights from status research, the narrow perspective of tournament theory will be broadened with regard to four important issues that show the value of status in understanding organizational compensation. Within the following section, the extent to which non-monetary motives and incentives contribute to an actor's willingness to participate in organizational tournaments and to exert extra effort, in order to derive more efficient promotion-based compensation schemes, will be analyzed. The second section will highlight the fact that designing organizational hierarchies has to account for several organizational objectives, some of which may contradict recommendations derived from purely economic rank-order tournaments. The third section will examine the impact of the tournament process upon the tournament results and the organizational efficiency. Finally, in the fourth section the possible conflict that originates from the fact that tournament theory unilaterally builds upon individual competition, whereas many organizations are designed to foster interindividual collaboration, is highlighted.

Value of status in understanding organizational compensation

Beyond money – striving for status

The underlying assumption of tournament theory is that contestants, e.g., employees in any organization, are ultimately motivated by monetary incentives to increase their effort and performance or output. Accordingly, exerting oneself and competing for promotion, i.e., climbing the career ladder and achieving higher organizational status, should depend purely on the money that is linked to it (directly and indirectly by being further promoted). Consequently, striving for status is seen as being motivated by the monetary gains related to a higher status or its instrumentality in generating monetary advantages (e.g., being a celebrity). As such an assumption contradicts even the most basic motivation theories one finds in any textbook on organizational behavior or human resource management (e.g., McClelland's [1961] theory of needs), one has to elaborate the factors that motivate people to strive for status, i.e., try to win a rank-order tournament, in a more psychologically complete way.

Within the interdisciplinary research on status, two distinct individual motives for the aspiration to reach a certain status are distinguished. Human beings view status as a means to an end or as an end in itself. Status is instrumental, i.e., a means to achieve other ends, if employees strive for promotion, i.e., status, in order to receive a higher salary and other monetary benefits. However, money is just one end. Other ends are status symbols which are tied to a certain status and can be handed over at award ceremonies (Berger *et al.*, 1998; English, 2005) whether tangible like office location or company car (Zalesny and Farace, 1987) or intangible like the deference of co-workers and privileges (Weber, 1922, p. 305). Status symbols are an important motive for people to outperform others, because of their signaling power that leads to a favorable perception by others (Ridgeway, 1991) and boosts the self-esteem of their owners (Sachdev and Bourhis, 1987). Winning a tournament can produce – independently of the winner's prize – valuable signals that may put additional resources such as talents, customers, capital, or social networks at the disposal of the winner (see Chapter 1 for a long list of the benefits of having higher status). Another means to an end is the hierarchical authority organizations assign to management positions, not only because the position holder can exert power over subordinates, but also with regard to the discretion and freedom it provides. Brass (1984) has shown that there is a strong relationship between organizational positions and their influence regarding important decisions. Based upon their position within the organizational hierarchy, high-ranked employees are able to enforce their will on to lower-rank employees and to govern them, leading to an increase in their own discretion (Finkelstein, 1992). Notably, senior managers and CEOs can use their high status to control, for instance, strategic decisions of their company (*ibid.*) as well as their own severance packages (Wade, O'Reilly, and Chandratat, 1990). Table 5.2 provides an overview of selected studies that explain different issues and ways for status to become a means to an end.

While one may argue that many of the aforementioned examples prove that striving for status has only one reason, which is money, the variety of tangible and intangible motives impedes formalization and general solutions. If a person's motivation is dominated by the need

Table 5.2 *Studies emphasizing status as a means to an end*

Authors	Ends for which status may be exploited
Ahuja, Galletta, and Carley (2003)	High status improves – under certain circumstances – chances of scientists to publish
Aquino, Grover, Bradfield, and Allen (1999)	Individuals of high status less frequently fall prey to harassments than comparable individuals of low status
Ball and Eckel (1996)	Individuals of high status achieve better results in negotiations
Ball and Eckel (1998)	High-status individuals earn more, all else equal, than low-status individuals
Ball, Eckel, Grossman, and Zame (2001)	Actors of high status reach higher prices as sellers and pay less as buyers
Okamoto and Smith-Lovin (2001)	High status makes it possible to change the subject and consequently to exert influence within group discussions
Owens (2000)	Group members with high status are more likely to use dominating tactics such as interruptions and threatening gestures to control group participation and attention
Thye (2000)	As part of negotiations individuals of high status receive more resources, their own resources are perceived as more valuable, and they are privileged transaction partners

for power or by the wish to be a respected member of an exclusive club, he or she will demonstrate any necessary effort and performance to become a CEO, even if the compensation package is significantly lower than that pre-calculated by tournament theory. Furthermore, social recognition associated with status and status symbols such as job titles, desirable parking spaces, or office equipment are comparatively cheap motivation factors (Loch, Yaziji, and Langen, 2001; Stajkovic and Luthans, 2001). Taking this perspective, it is more than likely that firms and shareholders alike sustain substantial financial losses resulting from paying their executives irrational, i.e., needlessly high, salaries.

In addition, there is an ongoing discussion among researchers of organizational status as to whether status is an end in itself, i.e., that participating in and especially winning a tournament is an intrinsic value by itself that provides satisfaction and thus motivation for contestants (Waldron, 1998; Loch *et al.*, 2000). It might be argued that the human need for recognition, esteem, and positive differentiation from others supports the claim that status is an end in itself (Rijsman, 1983; Rege, 2008). Empirical studies show that people value relative ranking with regard to peers more than absolute income (e.g., Solnick and Hemenway, 1998; Huberman *et al.*, 2003). They waive potential income (e.g., a higher base salary, higher paying investors) in favor of reaching a higher status (e.g., belonging to a special group, being aligned with more prestigious venture capitalists) that wins them recognition and reputation among relevant judges (Hsu, 2004; Almenberg and Dreber, 2009). According to Frank (1985), employees have waived parts of their rightful monetary compensation in favor of lower-ranked group members in order to ensure their appreciation and in order to safeguard their higher status.

The fact that various motives determine striving for status and thus the willingness to participate in rank-order tournaments begs the question of how this may influence insights derived from tournament theory, which relies solely on monetary motives. However, scientific research has not come up with consolidated results regarding the motivational impact of different incentives, i.e., stimuli (Stajkovic and Luthans, 2001, p. 580). In particular, the relevance and interdependencies of status versus monetary incentives have not been researched sufficiently (Weiss and Fershtman, 1998). As a result, there are no basic insights as to whether absolute prizes, i.e., salary spreads, between two hierarchical levels, status symbols, or status in itself motivate employees. Instead, some scholars argue that the motivational impact of these motives depends on contingencies and especially on individual characteristics (e.g., Bandura, 1977; Goddeeris, 1988; Stajkovic and Luthans, 2001). This also applies for money. People have different attitudes and opinions regarding both money (Solnick and Hemenway, 1998; Mitchell and Mickel, 1999) and status (Huberman *et al.*, 2003), to say nothing of the variety of behavior induced by cultural and institutional differences (e.g., Zelizer, 1997). Yet, beyond the absolute value of tournament prizes, whether money or status, one may analyze trade-offs.

Money, status symbols, and privileges have a diminishing marginal utility like any other good that satisfies personal needs (e.g., Rabin, 2000). Additionally, we can assume substitutability between these incentives. Salaries of senior managers allow for consumption and for acquiring certain status symbols (e.g., sports cars, luxury villas). Similarly, they may use their organizational status and respective privileges to achieve things such as club memberships or admission to exclusive schools for their children – things that are less dependent on income than on belonging to a special class. The motivational power of money decreases for holders of highly ranked positions within an organization that have accumulated significant income while climbing the career ladder. According to recommendations derived from tournament theory, companies have to offer disproportionately larger increases in prize spreads in order to compensate for this loss of motivation to expend effort and to participate in future tournaments (Rosen, 1986). Assuming increasing marginal costs for the abovementioned incentives, it seems to be rational to substitute money with status, status symbols, and status-based privileges.

Rank-orders and hierarchies – more than motivational instruments

According to personnel economics and tournament theory, organizational hierarchies mainly serve to motivate employees – particularly managers at all organizational levels – to exert maximum effort and performance in the service of company objectives and shareholder interests. Consequently, relevant variables such as (a) the number and homogeneity of contestants, i.e., employees, (b) the number of tournaments, i.e., hierarchical levels, and (c) prizes, i.e., salary increases, are optimized with regard to maximize output at the lowest cost (e.g., monitoring). As a result, tournament theory recommends increasing homogeneity among contestants, reducing "noise," i.e., internal and external uncertainties, increasing salary spreads (particularly at the top of the firm's hierarchy), filling the highest rank with just one person, and proliferating stratification, i.e., to maintain as many organizational (or prize) levels as possible (e.g., Lazear, 1998; Moldovanu *et al.*, 2007). With regard to the optimal number of contestants, an appropriate probability to win the tournament has to be considered (Orrison, Schotter, and Weigelt, 2004). Apparently, applying these assumptions and recommendations results in a large and stable organization of many hierarchical levels that operates in a rather static environment, which allows the organization to continuously grow.[1] However, with rare and rather shallow exceptions (e.g., Lazear, 1998, pp. 238–241), interdependencies between different dimensions of organizational structures and normative recommendations derived from tournament theory, as well as their respective impact on organizational efficiency, have not been elaborated by these theorists. Instead of addressing business trends that run counter to the abovementioned requirements such as organizational downsizing or the uncertainty in turbulent markets, an overly simplistic compensation magic bullet is offered. Because these real markets and organizational trends ultimately increase noise and reduce the individual probability of winning the tournament, they are assumed to require a further increase in the prize, in the salary spreads, in order to further maximize the effort exerted by contestants (Bognanno, 1994; Lazear, 1998). In this regard, an empirical study provided some evidence that firms with low promotion rates and limited upward mobility have comparatively larger salary spreads (Leonard, 1990).

Apparently, tournament theory neglects other, partly conflicting objectives that determine an optimal organizational structure. Without repeating and reviewing the broad and rich literature about organizational theories, organizational design, and organizational behavior here, organizations are effective means to attract and pool scarce resources (e.g., the resource-based view – Wernerfelt, 1984) and an efficient alternative to markets with regard to coordinating specialized work (e.g., transaction cost theory – Williamson, 1981). From the perspective of resource dependency theory (Pfeffer and Salancik, 1978), an organization is mainly shaped by its competitive environment and hence by its effective control of strategic resources. If CEOs and senior managers are a strategic resource, i.e., scarce and difficult to substitute or copy, the need to pay competitive salaries may provide another explanation for significant spreads at the top levels of the firm. However, more importantly, the different theories elucidate the need to view hierarchies and organizational structure as means of fulfilling different purposes beyond purely motivating managers to exert effort. As a result, the rather simple formalization of rank-order tournaments has to give way to the challenge of a complex optimization problem.

How may research about organizational status contribute to extend tournament theory? First of all, it is necessary to note that status research suffers from similar problems, i.e., for status and status symbols to be effective motivational instruments, the number of hierarchical levels and rank-order tournaments has to be increased. Downsizing organizations and flattening hierarchies result in fewer promotion prospects and in fewer formal career opportunities – the probability of winning a tournament is shrinking because there are almost no tournaments. Consequently, promotion-based motivation becomes less effective, leading either to frustration induced by long waiting periods or to increased employee turnover, which may not be in the best interests of the firm. However, utilizing insights from status research may at least partially solve the motivation problem while avoiding a significant increase in salary spreads. Accordingly, additional formal status hierarchies besides the flattened management hierarchy may be established. Respective examples are the "100 Percent Club" (Norwest Corporation Financial Services) or the "Top Elite Club" (AGF Insurance) mentioned by Auriol and Renault (1999). Universities that have limited hierarchical levels from assistant professor to tenured professor make use of parallel status hierarchies and rankings based on individual achievements regarding research (e.g., publications, funds) and teaching. Combining these additional rank-orders with status symbols such as titles (e.g., Senator in the case of 3M), forms of recognition (e.g., displays, award ceremonies), or challenge trophies that cannot be bought but have to be awarded may motivate extra effort at much lower cost than increasing the salary spread (Greenberg and Ornstein, 1983). Additionally, such technical or specialist career tracks may better match both the specific needs of the organization and the variety of motives of different groups of employees. A fact often overlooked by economists is that people are not motivated solely by monetary or promotion, the prize they may gain at the end of a tournament, but also by the tournament itself and the circumstances of the award ceremony, i.e., procedural issues (e.g., Lambert *et al.*, 1993, p. 456). Accordingly, implementing different forms of intra-organizational tournaments may stimulate additional efforts (e.g., top researcher, top lecturer, top fundraiser of the year).

Tournament processes – who wins depends not only on who competes, but how

Research on status adds to our knowledge about organizational compensation beyond tournament theory by highlighting the relevance of processes as supplements of structure. Tournament theory – even extensions as provided by Moldovanu *et al.* (2007) – considers only the starting conditions of a tournament (e.g., number of contestants, stages, prizes) and its results. The process itself is rather neglected (Lambert *et al.* 1993, p. 456). Consequently, determinants and issues of the tournament process that may impact its efficiency are also neglected. While tournament theory assumes that all contestants play against an anonymous market and are not able to interact with and influence their opponents' chances to compete (Lazear and Rosen, 1981, p. 101), reality seems to be at odds with this assumption. Tennis and golf players and even (US) National Football League or National Basketball Association teams compete against each other using a limited set of clear rules in a highly monitored environment that leaves little room for hidden characteristics, action, or intention, such as doping and bribery. Apparently, organizational reality differs considerably from this kind of sports tournament. It is not noise, i.e., luck alone, that biases organizational tournaments and rank-order promotion systems, but rather it is the existence of multiple interdependencies. Management tasks are predominantly team products or at least dependent on the input of internal and external contributors. Team products, lack of transparency, ambiguous assessment criteria, interdependencies as well as externalities offer many opportunities to influence the chances of oneself and others to win the tournament.

Power, for instance, may be exploited to manipulate the outcome of organizational promotion tournaments (Bratton, 2005). Status is an important source of power and exercise of influence. Organizational members that hold a high status, e.g., senior managers, frequently have the legitimate authority to monitor, assist, or encourage organizational members with lower status regarding their motivation and effort to win a certain tournament, i.e., being promoted (Finkelstein, 1992, pp. 508f.). Empowerment related to achieved status provides its holder with additional sources of power such as budget, access to scarce resources, information, or participation in critical decision-making processes (Pfeffer, 1981). Graffin *et al.* (2008) found evidence for the fact that there are spill-over effects from high-status CEOs, so-called star CEOs, on their direct subordinates insofar as the latter receive higher average compensation and are more likely to become CEOs themselves. Assuming further that employees of a certain organizational level competing for a position on the next level are heterogeneous with regard to their informal status and their status of expertise, even if they are of equal capabilities and skills, there is ample reason to predict that high-status contestants will opportunistically exploit their status. On the one hand, they may openly or covertly enforce contestants of lower status to withdraw or to reduce their effort by threatening them in order to increase their own chances of winning. On the other hand, high-status contestants may even design the tournament in their own favor. High-status employees are able – due to interdependencies – to influence higher authorities in favor of their own promotion (Wade *et al.*, 1990). And even if one does not assume direct influence of high-status actors, there is evidence "that status makes a significant difference in the tournament selection process" (Washington and Zajac, 2005, p. 294), i.e., who is seen as eligible and who is not.

However, people with low status may attempt to impact promotion-related decisions by holders of high status through social influence tactics like collaboration and friendliness (Stahelski and Paynton, 1995). A good example is that of young scholars, who try to become part of high-status faculties or collaborate with high-status faculty members in order to increase their chances of publishing in reputed academic journals, which will subsequently increase their probability of being promoted and receiving tenure. Although their performance may be lower than that of contestants who try to publish innovative ideas on their own, the likelihood that they will win the competition for an academic position is enhanced. Furthermore, it could be argued that such behavior will impair the overall goals of the research community, as it frequently leads to perpetuating old paradigms rather than propelling scientific breakthroughs. Additionally, lower-status people like those with less capability may use unfair means, may cheat, and may use sabotage to increase their chances of winning a tournament based on relative performance (Chen, 2003). Especially in highly competitive contexts with tournament structures that have winner-take-all characteristics (Frank, 1995), these seem to spur attempts to circumvent existing rules, norms, and ethical standards and to make use of illegitimate means, as small relative differences lead to huge benefits for the winners (e.g., Lazear, 1989). Even scientific and research societies – though equipped with fundamental ethics of scientific rigor, incorruptibility, and honesty – are not free of misconduct. Highly publicized examples of this are fake reports of a scientific breakthrough that shocked the scientific community (e.g., Einhorn and Arnst, 2006; Jia, 2006). However, science in so-called developed countries is far from being less impacted from academic or scientific misconduct, as past studies have proved already (e.g., Armstrong, 1983). Hence, there is some evidence that rank-order tournaments and promotion-based incentive systems may produce dysfunctional behavior that runs counter to the intended objectives, especially in non-deterministic contexts (Nippa and Markoczy, 2007).

Instead of an overt competition among rather homogeneous contestants not influenced by non-contestants (e.g., tennis players), organizational promotion is most likely influenced by personal networks, affiliation, and cliques. Acknowledging gratitude for being promoted through the support of co-workers or knowing of their loyalty, promoted employees will frequently use their new status and respective power to get their supporters promoted as well. Additionally, status has an impact on negative affectivity and violence in the workplace which biases organizational tournaments, probabilities of being promoted, and hence individual performance (Aquino *et al.*, 1999).

Consequently, tournaments suffer from the fact that rather heterogeneous contestants entwined in several social networks of varying status fight with different weapons. Imagine the outcome of a medieval tournament where one knight who sits on a donkey but armed with a musket faces his opponent on a war-horse directing a lance on him while team members stroll around looking for opportunities to trick the rivals. As a result the tournament is neither efficient nor does it produce the right winner. On the one hand, influential, powerful, scheming, and cheating actors will not have to exert the expected effort and – more importantly – do not contribute to the objectives of the organization (Loch *et al.*, 2000). On the other hand, the chances that employees who stick to predetermined rules and perform independently will win diminish. If these employees perceive or believe that there is no fair competition, i.e., a fight with unequal weapons, they will either adjust, which turns out to be even more counter-productive for the organization ("cheating is infectious" – Ariely, 2009) or they will reduce their effort according to insights from equity theory (e.g., Adams, 1963) or expectancy theory (e.g., Vroom, 1964).

If power and the exercise of influence induced by status differences within an organization frequently lead to biases regarding the true ranking of contestants and subsequently demotivation among those who believe they are being treated unfairly, how can organizations counter these effects? First, like proposals based upon tournament theory, they may try to increase homogeneity among contestants, i.e., reduce status differences. While this might be possible with formal status, it appears to be rather difficult with various forms of informal status hierarchies. In any case, it presumes a positivistic belief that societies and organizations can be shaped and designed at will. Yet, as a result of interdependencies, complexity, and dynamism, many variables defy management control. The same is true with the second approach, which tries to suppress any irregular influence of contestants on the structure and process of the tournament. Organizational promotion tournaments in most cases require measures of performance other than probing whether the tennis ball was on or behind the line. While it may appear to be easy to determine the best salesperson based upon annual sales or profit, it is naïve to believe that promotions at the senior management level are free from contextual impacts and subjective appraisals (e.g., Judge and Ferris, 1993). In a study of factors influencing compensation systems authored by Encinosa *et al.* (2007, p. 204), only seventeen percent of all respondents reported having a formal policy or explicit guidelines on expected productivity of group members. Hence, rank-order tournaments and promotion-based motivation in complex organizations frequently suffer from ambiguity and manipulation.

The efficiency of tournament-based incentive schemes is not only impeded by status, power, influence, and fairness, but is also significantly influenced by another procedural aspect, i.e., performance feedback. While feedback on individual performance is commonly perceived as increasing work performance, the contrary is the case with tournament incentive schemes. Providing feedback on individual performance during the tournament "causes mean performance to deteriorate," for several reasons highlighted by Hannan, Krishnan, and Newman (2008, p. 911).

Competition versus collaboration – key mediator of performance impacts of status

Tournament theory implicitly assumes that organizations profit exclusively from competition among their employees. Therefore, fueling competition among contestants for a higher rank or position leads to an increase in individual effort, i.e., less shirking and laziness, which results in optimal performance for the employer. However, as mentioned above, competition among employees runs counter to teamwork, knowledge sharing, empowerment, and providing support for co-workers. As research on status has frequently analyzed the striving for the status–performance link, reviewing these studies may also add to our knowledge about organizational compensation and motivation.

However, there are no clear and consistent results so far. Studying the effect of high status on the performance of individuals, Ball and Eckel (1996) found that people with higher status gain significantly greater benefits within and from negotiation processes than their lower-status counterparts. These results are in line with findings of Ball *et al.* (2001), who examined the impact of status on market performance. Belliveau, O'Reilly, and Wade (1996) investigated the influence of status on the compensation of CEOs and showed that CEOs received significantly higher compensation if their status is higher than that of the compensation chair. Additionally, Okamoto and Smith-Lovin (2001) emphasize the advantage of superior status within negotiation processes, and report that discussants with relatively high status had a strong influence on the process and result of group discussions. However, contrary to these positive effects, Spataro (2002) reports a negative impact on the individual work performance for individuals possessing high status, especially if they have to work with someone of lower rank. Empirical studies regarding individuals possessing a low status basically report reverse findings (see Ball and Eckel, 1996; Belliveau *et al.*, 1996; and Ball *et al.*, 2001). Spataro's (2002) work on behavioral and performance changes of high- and low-status individuals within collaborative situations reports performance improvements for the low-status individuals and less effort from the high-status individuals.

In search of an explanation for these ambiguous results, the degree of competitiveness, i.e., the question of whether the organizational context is characterized by competitive or cooperative activities and behavior, appears to be a key mediator. The starting point here is to recall the perspective of status as an economic resource, i.e., as a means to an end (Berger *et al.*, 1977; Podolny, 1993; Ball *et al.*, 2001). Thus, status will be used in order to achieve its possessor's goals like any other resource. Assuming, in accordance with the main economic theories, that all economic actors act in their own interests, try to maximize their own utilities, and are opportunistic, it becomes an open question as to whether these actors will be competitive or collaborative. Applying this distinction to the findings regarding the behavior of high-status owners leads to the following explanations.

Competitive behavior. Two preconditions characterize an organizational context as competitive (versus collaborative): (1) high-ranking owners receive abnormal rents compared to low-status actors, and (2) there is an ongoing struggle for positions among group members. Under such assumptions, those of high status will not show signs of cooperative, collaborative behavior while interacting with counterparts that have lower status. This kind of competitive environment and behavior seems to match, for example, the studies of Ball and Eckel (1996), Ball *et al.* (2001), and the experimental setting of Podolny (1993). Even situations described by Belliveau *et al.* (1996) can be characterized as competitive, because CEOs and compensation chairs should not act cooperatively in compensation negotiations. Furthermore, the conditions described in the studies of Turner and Brown (1978), Sachdev and Bourhis (1987), and Cadinu and Reggiori (2002) also indicate a rather competitive situation.

Collaborative behavior. In cooperative or collaborative situations, those of high status do not receive significant rents compared to low-status actors and there is no struggle for positions. Thus, high-ranking owners regard the interests and objectives of lower-status subjects while interacting with them. Interestingly, such a condition of a "competition-free" environment seems only to be the case for the study of Spataro (2002), which basically analyzed people that worked together on a joint task.

Apparently, this distinction of whether an organization relies on and fosters competition or collaboration among its employees provides new insights regarding conflicting findings provided by status research. From this perspective, high status – respectively rank-order tournaments – enables individuals, groups, and organizations to increase their performance under competitive conditions. Under collaborative conditions, performance, which is highly dependent on cooperation, suffers; conversely, those of low status are able to enhance their performance under cooperative conditions, whereas competitive conditions create counter-productive forces leading to an erosion of performance.

Thus, applying insights from research on organizational status sheds light on the appropriateness of using rank-order tournaments within organizations. Organizations that rely on collaboration as well as on employee loyalty and retention should avoid or use rank-order tournaments with caution, while those with tasks that require independent effort from employees can benefit from highly competitive tournaments for distributions of promotions and monetary prizes. While, not surprisingly, professional service firms are frequent users of sophisticated tournament systems,[2] it turns out to be wise, i.e., efficient, for them to also find ways to maintain a minimum of collaborative behavior, for example, by integrating respective criteria into the individual assessment.

Conclusion

Despite the fact that tournaments and promotion-based incentive systems exert strong motivational effects on employees, one has to conclude that their impact on organizational efficiency is highly overstated. The optimism of major advocates of economic tournament theory, most prominently Edward Lazear, regarding its applicability and superiority in generating the optimal labor contracts finds no support after leaving the narrow world of thought-experiments with its restrictive assumptions and misleading analogy to sports tournaments. Inducing and maintaining motivation to perform and exert effort at a maximum level through implementation of rank-order tournaments within organizations grabs one's attention due to its affinity to well-known sports events and its utility for deducing unequivocal solutions based upon formalization and mathematical calculation. However, its implementation in organizations is at the very least risky, if not in many cases counter-productive. While the economic benefit of rank-order tournaments within organizational contexts, i.e., its motivational impact, has not been measured directly,[3] there are several indications of hidden costs and ineffectiveness.

First, research in the field of organizational status has shown that people strive for status even if it is not linked to monetary resources or if they have to waive a monetary advantage (Almenberg and Dreber, 2009). Additionally, offering status and status symbols frequently turns out to be of lower cost than raising salaries. In the light of a diminishing marginal utility of money – like any other motive – it seems completely irrational to focus on just one motive, i.e., money, and to offer disproportionately high management salaries.

Second, tournament theory requires a high degree of homogeneity and stability of contestants, organizational structures, and processes to be effective. Lazear (1998) points out that rank-order tournaments not only motivate senior managers competing for promotions to the executive suite or long-time faculty seeking tenure, but also motivate junior managers and faculty. Yet, it is important to emphasize important side conditions. Lower-level employees are only motivated by tournaments on the "champion league level" if they perceive a realistic chance of also becoming eligible. Within large organizations this may be the exception rather than the rule. It is difficult to determine all of the actual participants of any "executive board" tournament (O'Reilly, Main, and Crystal, 1988, p. 260). Instead of one clear-cut management rank-order tournament, organizations offer different career paths leading to the top (e.g., sales and marketing, research and development, auditing) that have different rules and requirements. Research in the field of organizational status highlights the fact that various rank-orders, formal and informal, exist within an organization, which may all be used to motivate employees.

Third, tournament theory assumes or proposes independence of contestants (Lazear 1989), i.e., promotion depends exclusively or predominantly on the individual performance in comparison to other individuals, as in tennis or golf tournaments or car racing. However, instead of lone fighters, most organizations are based upon teamwork and efficient production of team products (Main *et al.*, 1993). Motivating employees to focus on their own career and the next promotion may even fuel opportunistic behavior and erode the willingness to collaborate, such as exchanging important information, especially among executives (e.g., Dye, 1984; Siegel and Hambrick, 2005). This tendency may be countered by assessing collaborative behavior or including co-workers in performance evaluations; however, this opens the field to power and influence tactics that run contrary to the organizational objectives. Consequently, it must be assumed that many CEOs and executive board members are not those who possess the best competencies to run the firm or those who have been the best performers at each previous organizational rank in the best interests of the firm, but those that have shown Machiavellian behavior and are mainly driven by extrinsic motivators.

Thus, tournament theory creates adverse human behavior such as collusion (Bandiera, Barankay, and Rasul, 2005) rather than preventing it. Tournament theory may enjoy great popularity because it seems to explain on a rational basis incomprehensibly high management compensations that are increasingly perceived as unfair and unethical by members of society. However, there is some evidence that the theory is abused to legitimize a fact that has other causes because it is in the best interests of these highly paid actors. Status research sheds a different light on possible causes of such comparatively high executive compensation: interdependencies, formal and informal organizational processes, and the benefits of high status within organizations. Future research might profitably investigate how insights from status research may be even better translated into clear propositions and recommendations similar to the highly formal approach of economic tournament theory.

Notes

The author gratefully acknowledges essential preliminary work by his former Ph.D. student Andreas Ehrhardt as well as valuable comments and suggestions from the book editor Jone Pearce.

1 Baker *et al.* (1988) mention the need for organizational growth as an important precondition of tournaments to be effective. While the problem may be reduced by up-or-out rules that allow for recruiting new entrants on lower levels due to elimination of those who did not succeed, the practicability of other assumptions have not been debated explicitly. Yet, requiring low "noise" translates into internal and external certainty, i.e., organizational routines and stability, as well as the proliferation of hierarchical levels translates into "steep" organizational structures. Both requirements seem not be in line with interests of most organizations and their stakeholders.

2 It is noteworthy to add that professional service firms match other organizational requirements for efficiently applying rank-order tournaments such as rather steep hierarchies, comparatively clear performance measures, and also firm growth.

3 In the sense of asking employees how much they care for promotion, for money linked to a promotion, for further career chances and its monetary equivalent, or a willingness to participate in tournaments while controlling for other motives and theoretical explanations. Becker and Huselid (1988, p. 349) mention a more basic "Catch-22" problem, as tournament structures are proposed for contexts where measuring individual performance is difficult: "A test of tournament incentive effects thus requires that greater performance be elicited when the participant knows that he or she cannot be accurately evaluated at any particular point in time."

References

Adams, J. S. 1963. "Toward an understanding of inequity." *Journal of Abnormal and Social Psychology* 67: 422–436.

Ahuja, M. K., Galletta, D. F., and Carley, K. M. 2003. "Individual centrality and performance in virtual R&D groups: An empirical study." *Management Science* 49(1): 21–38.

Almenberg, J. and Dreber, A. 2009. "Lady and the Trump: Status and wealth in the marriage market." *Kyklos* 62(2): 161–181.

Anabtawi, I. 2005. "Explaining pay without performance: The tournament alternative." *Emory Law Journal* 54(4): 1557–1602.

Aquino, K., Grover, S. L., Bradfield, M., and Allen, D. G. 1999. "The effects of negative affectivity, hierarchical status, and self-determination on workplace victimization." *Academy of Management Journal* 42(3): 260–272.

Ariely, D. 2009. "The end of rational economics." *Harvard Business Review* 87(7/8): 78–84.

Ariely, D., Gneezy, U., Loewenstein, G., and Mazar, N. 2009. "Large stakes and big mistakes." *The Review of Economic Studies* 76(2): 451–469.

Armstrong, J. S. 1983. "The ombudsman: Cheating in management science." *Interfaces* 13(4): 20–27.

Auriol, E. and Renault, R. 1999. "The costs and benefits of symbolic differentiation in the work place." Working Paper, University of Toulouse. http://idei.fr/doc/wp/2002/thecosts.pdf.

Baker, G. P. 1992. "Incentive contracts and performance measurement." *Journal of Political Economy* 100(3): 598–614.

Baker, G. P., Jensen, M. C., and Murphy, K. J. 1988. "Compensation and incentives: Practice vs. theory." *Journal of Finance* 43: 593–616.

Ball, S. and Eckel, C. C. 1996. "Buying status: Experimental evidence on status in negotiation." *Psychology and Marketing* 13(4): 381–405.

1998. "The economic value of status." *Journal of Socio-Economics* 27(4): 495–514.

Cummins, J. G. and Nyman, I. 2007. "Yes-men in tournaments." Hunter College Department of Economics Working Papers 417.

Dye, R. A. 1984. "The trouble with tournaments." *Economic Inquiry* 22(1): 147–149.

Ehrenberg, R. G. and Bognanno, M. L. 1990. "The incentive effects of tournaments revisited: Evidence from the European PGA Tour." *Industrial & Labor Relations Review* 43(3): 74–88.

Einhorn, B. and Arnst, C. 2006. "Science friction." *BusinessWeek* (May 29, 2006), pp. 44–45.

Encinosa, W. E., III, Gaynorb, M., and Rebitzer, J. B. 2007. "The sociology of groups and the economics of incentives: Theory and evidence on compensation systems." *Journal of Economic Behavior & Organization* 62(2): 187–214.

English, J. F. 2005. *The Economy of Prestige: Prizes, Awards, and the Circulation of Cultural Value*. Cambridge, MA: Harvard University Press.

Eriksson, T. 1999. "Executive compensation and tournament theory: Empirical tests on Danish data." *Journal of Labor Economics* 17(2): 262–280.

Ferris, G. R., Buckley, M. R., and Allen, G. M. 1992. "Promotion systems in organizations." *Human Resource Planning* 15(3): 47–68.

Fershtman, C., Murphy, K. M., and Weiss, Y. 1996. "Social status, education, and growth." *Journal of Political Economy* 104(1): 108–132.

Fershtman, C. and Weiss, Y. 1993. "Social status, culture and economic performance." *The Economic Journal* 103(419): 946–959.

Finkelstein, S. 1992. "Power in top-management-teams: Dimensions, measurement, and validation." *Academy of Management Journal* 35(3): 505–538.

Frank, R. H. 1985. *Choosing the Right Pond: Human Behavior and the Quest for Status*. Oxford University Press.

1995. *The Winner-Take-All Society*. New York: Penguin Books.

Gibbs, M. 1994. "Testing tournaments? An appraisal of the theory and evidence." *Labor Law Journal* 45(8): 493–500.

Goddeeris, J. H. 1988. "Compensation differentials and self-selection: An application to lawyers." *Journal of Political Economy* 96(2): 411–428.

Graffin, S. D., Wade, J. B., Porac, J. F., and McNamee, R. C. 2008. "Impact of CEO status diffusion on the economic outcomes of other senior managers." *Organization Science* 19(3): 457–474.

Green, J. R. and Stokey, N. L. 1983. "A comparison of tournaments and contracts." *Journal of Political Economy* 91(3): 349–364.

Greenberg, J. and Ornstein, S. 1983. "High status job title as compensation for underpayment: A test of equity theory." *Journal of Applied Psychology* 68(2): 285–297.

Hannan, R. L., Krishnan, R., and Newman, A. H. 2008. "The effects of disseminating relative performance feedback in tournament and individual performance compensation plans." *Accounting Review* 83(4): 893–913.

Holmström, B. 1979. "Moral hazard and observability." *Bell Journal of Economics* 10(1): 74–91.

Hsu, D. H. 2004. "What do entrepreneurs pay for venture capital affiliation?" *Journal of Finance* 59(4): 1805–1844.

Huberman, B. A., Loch, C. H., and Öncüler, A. 2003. "Status as a valued resource." *Social Psychology Quarterly* 67(1): 103–114.

Jia, H. 2006. "Frequent cases force China to face up to scientific fraud." *Nature Medicine* 12(8): 867.

Judge, T. A. and Ferris, G. R. 1993. "Social context of performance evaluation decisions." *Academy of Management Journal* 36(1): 80–105.

Knoeber, C. R. 1989. "A real game of chicken: Contracts, tournaments, and the production of broilers." *Journal of Law, Economics, and Organization* 5(2): 271–292.

Knoeber, C. R. and Thurman, W. N. 1994. "Testing the theory of tournaments: An empirical analysis of broiler production." *Journal of Labor Economics* 12(2): 155–179.

Kräkel, M. 2008. "Emotions in tournaments." *Journal of Economic Behavior & Organization* 67(1): 204–214.

Lambert, R. A., Larcker, D. F., and Weigelt, K. 1993. "The structure of organizational incentives." *Administrative Science Quarterly* 38(3): 438–461.

Lazear, E. P. 1989. "Pay equality and industrial politics." *Journal of Political Economy* 97(3): 561–580.

1995. *Personnel Economics*. Cambridge, MA: MIT Press.

1998. *Personnel Economics for Managers*. New York: John Wiley & Sons.

1999. "Personnel economics: Past lessons and future directions." *Journal of Labor Economics* 17(2): 199–236.

2004. "The Peter Principle: A theory of decline." *Journal of Political Economy* 112(1): 141–163.

Lazear, E. P. and Rosen, S. 1981. "Rank order tournaments as optimum labor contracts." *Journal of Political Economy* 89(5): 841–864.

Lazear, E. P. and Shaw, K. L. 2007. "Personnel economics: The economist's view of human resources." *Journal of Economic Perspectives* 21(4): 91–114.

Leeds, M. 1988. "Rank-order tournaments and worker incentives." *Atlantic Economic Journal* 16(2): 74–77.

Leibenstein, H. 1986. "On relaxing the maximation postulate." *Journal of Behavioral Economics* 15(Winter): 3–63.

Leonard, J. S. 1990. "Executive pay and firm performance." *Industrial & Labor Relations Review* 43(3): 13–29.

Loch, C. H., Huberman, B. A., and Stout, S. 2000. "Status competition and performance in work groups." *Journal of Economic Behavior & Organization* 43(1): 35–55.

Loch, C. H., Yaziji, M., and Langen, C. 2001. "The fight for the alpha position: Channeling status competition in organizations." *European Management Journal* 19(1): 16–25.

Locke, E. A. 1982. "The ideas of Frederick W. Taylor: An evaluation." *Academy of Management Review* 7(1): 14–24.

Main, B. G. M., O'Reilly, C. A., III, and Wade, J. 1993. "Top executive pay: Tournament or teamwork?" *Journal of Labor Economics* 11(4): 606–628.

McCall, J. J. 2004. "Assessing American executive compensation: A cautionary tale for Europeans." *Business Ethics: A European Review* 13(4): 243–254.

McClelland, D. 1961. *The Achieving Society*. Princeton, NJ: Van Nostrand.

Mitchell, T. R. and Mickel, A. E. 1999. "The meaning of money: An individual-difference perspective." *Academy of Management Review* 24(3): 568–578.

Moldovanu, B., Sela, A., and Shi, X. 2007. "Contests for status." *Journal of Political Economy* 115(2): 338–363.

Nalebuff, B. and Stiglitz, J. 1983. "Prizes and incentives: Towards a general theory of compensation and competition." *Bell Journal of Economics* 14(1): 21–43.

Nippa, M. and Markoczy, L. 2007. "Economic pressure and the deterioration of research ethics." *Academy of Management Proceedings* Philadelphia, PA, August 5–9: 1–6.

Okamoto, D. G. and Smith-Lovin, L. 2001. "Changing the subject: Gender, status, and the dynamics of topic change." *American Sociological Review* 66(6): 852–873.

O'Keeffe, M., Viscusi, W. K., and Zeckhauser, R. J. 1984. "Economic contests: Comparative reward schemes." *Journal of Labor Economics* 2(1): 27–56.

O'Reilly, C. A., III, Main, B. G., and Crystal, G. S. 1988. "CEO compensation as tournament and social comparison: A tale of two theories." *Administrative Science Quarterly* 33(2): 257–274.

Orrison, A., Schotter, A., and Weigelt, K. 2004. "Multiperson tournaments: An experimental examination." *Management Science* 50(2): 268–279.

Owens, D. A. 2000. "Structure and status in design teams: Implications for design management." *Design Management Journal: Academic Review* 1(1): 55–63.

Pfeffer, J. 1981. *Power in Organizations*. Marshfield, MA: Pitman.

Pfeffer, J. and Salancik, G. R. 1978. *The External Control of Organizations: A Resource Dependency Perspective*. New York: Harper & Row.

Podolny, J. M. 1993. "A status-based model of market competition." *American Journal of Sociology* 98(4): 829–872.

Postlewaite, A. 1998. "The social basis of interdependent preferences." *European Economic Review* 42(3–5): 779–800.

Rabin, M. 2000. "Risk aversion and expected utility theory: A calibration theorem." *Econometrica* 68(5): 1281–1292.

Rees, A. 1992. "The tournament as a model for executive compensation." *Journal of Post Keynesian Economics* 14(4): 567–571.

Rees, R. 1985. "The theory of principal and agent – part I." *Bulletin of Economic Research* 37(1): 3–26.

Rege, M. 2008. "Why do people care about social status?" *Journal of Economic Behavior & Organization* 66(2): 233–242.

Ridgeway, C. 1991. "The social construction of status value: Gender and other nominal characteristics." *Social Forces* 70(2): 367–386.

Ridgeway, C. and Walker, H. A. 1995. "Status structures," in K. Cook, G. Fine, and J. House (eds.), *Sociological Perspectives on Social Psychology*, Boston, MA: Allyn & Bacon, pp. 281–310.

Rijsman, J. 1983. "The dynamics of social competition in personal and categorical comparison situations," in W. Doise and S. Moscovici (eds.), *Current Issues in European Social Psychology*, Vol. I. Cambridge University Press, pp. 279–312.

Rosen, S. 1986. "Prizes and incentives in elimination tournaments." *American Economic Review* 76(4): 701–715.

Rosenbaum, J. E. 1979. "Tournament mobility: Career patterns in a corporation." *Administrative Science Quarterly* 24(2): 220–241.

Sachdev, I. and Bourhis, R. Y. 1987. "Status differentials and intergroup behavior." *European Journal of Social Psychology* 17(3): 277–293.

Shapiro, S. P. 2005. "Agency theory." *Annual Review of Sociology* 31(1): 263–284.

Siegel, P. A. and Hambrick, D. C. 2005. "Pay disparities within top management groups: Evidence of harmful effects on performance of high-technology firms." *Organization Science* 16(3): 259–274.

Solnick, S. J. and Hemenway, D. 1998. "Is more always better? A survey on positional concerns." *Journal of Economic Behavior & Organization* 37(3): 373–383.

Solomon, D. and Meckler, L. 2009. "Strict executive-pay caps planned." *Wall Street Journal*, February 4, 2009, A3.

Spataro, S. E. 2002. "Not all differences are the same: The role of informal status in predicting reactions to demographic diversity in organizations." Working Paper Series OB No. 3, Yale School of Management.

Stahelski, A. J. and Paynton, C. F. 1995. "The effects of status cues on choices of social power and influence strategies." *Journal of Social Psychology* 135(5): 553–560.

Stajkovic, A. D. and Luthans, F. 2001. "Differential effects of incentive motivators on work performance." *Academy of Management Journal* 44(3): 580–590.

Thye, S. R. 2000. "A status value theory of power in exchange relations." *American Sociological Review* 65(3): 407–432.

Turner, J. C. and Brown, R. J. 1978. "Social status, cognitive alternatives, and intergroup relations," in H. Tajfel (ed.), *Differentiation Between Social Groups*. London: Academic Press, pp. 201–234.

Vroom, V. H. 1964. *Work and Motivation*. New York: Wiley.

Wade, J., O'Reilly, C. A., III, and Chandratat, I. 1990. "Golden parachutes: CEOs and the exercise of social influence." *Administrative Science Quarterly* 35(4): 587–603.

Waldron, D. A. 1998. "Status in organizations: Where evolutionary theory ranks." *Managerial and Decision Economics* 19(7/8): 505–520.

Washington, M. and Zajac, E. J. 2005. "Status evolution and competition: Theory and evidence." *Academy of Management Journal* 48(2): 282–296.

Weber, M. 1922. *Wirtschaft und Gesellschaft*. Tübingen: JCB Mohr.

Weiss, Y. and Fershtman, C. 1998. "Social status and economic performance: A survey." *European Economic Review* 42(3–5): 801–820.

Wernerfelt, B. 1984. "A resource-based view on the firm." *Strategic Management Journal* 5(2): 171–184.

Williamson, O. E. 1981. "The economics of organization: The transaction cost approach." *American Journal of Sociology* 87(3): 548–577.

Zalesny, M. D. and Farace, R. V. 1987. "Traditional versus open offices: A comparison of sociotechnical, social relations, and symbolic meaning perspectives." *Academy of Management Journal* 30(2): 240–259.

Zelizer, V. A. 1997. *The Social Meaning of Money: Pin Money, Paychecks, Poor Relief, and Other Currencies*. Princeton University Press.

PART III

The role of status in new
industries and ventures

6 The cultural context of status: Generating important knowledge in nanotechnology

TYLER WRY, MICHAEL LOUNSBURY,
AND ROYSTON GREENWOOD

Status is an important concept that is invoked widely across the social sciences. One common definitional starting point emphasizes how status enables an "effective claim to social esteem in terms of positive or negative privileges" (Weber, 1978, p. 305). In this way, status distributes esteem, deference, honor, and prestige within a social collective (Berger, Cohen, and Zelditch, 1972; Ridgeway, 1991) and, as such, stratifies its members (Knoke and Burt, 1983; Lounsbury, 2002; Podolny, 1993). Because status tracks closely with influence, prominent actors often have the ability to shape the development of fields and markets to their advantage (Fligstein, 1996, 2000) and challenge extant arrangements without facing the harsh penalties levied on other change agents (Greenwood and Suddaby, 2006; Lounsbury, 2007; Merton, 1968; Rao, Monin, and Durand, 2003). Prominent actors also receive more acclaim for performing the same practices than their low-status alters (Benjamin and Podolny, 1999; Merton, 1968). Moreover, high-status actors tend to be targets of imitation, with the result that their practices become widely adopted and highly valued (Haunschild and Miner, 1997; Kraatz and Zajac, 1996).

However, while extant literature has highlighted the many benefits related to high status, much less attention has been paid to the conditions, especially those related to cultural context, under which such benefits are realized. For instance, it is typically assumed that the value of a particular practice tracks closely with the status of its most prominent advocates. This is reinforced by the empirical emphasis on relatively settled fields where culture, status, and practice are well aligned and mutually constitutive (e.g., Bourdieu, 1984; Podolny, 1993). In addition, studies of institutional change suggest that the deference given to high-status actors allows them to foment and valorize new practices relatively unproblematically (e.g., Fligstein, 1996, 2001; Greenwood, Suddaby, and Hinings, 2002; Rao *et al.*, 2003). The resulting imagery is of culture as uniformly beneficial to prominent actors or something which they can act upon to their advantage. But this is not always the case, since marginal actors can also catalyze and facilitate the spread of novel practices and facilitate institutional change (e.g., Leblebici *et al.*, 1991).

Thus, in this chapter, we argue that status effects are not always as smooth and consistently advantageous as typically portrayed. More specifically, we suggest that attending to the cultural context of a field can help to cast light on how and when status matters. Unlike stable fields with settled cultural beliefs, a more contingent relationship between an actor's status and the valuation of their practices is apparent in nascent or unstable fields. In such situations, the influence of status on practice valuation is more malleable and can be more easily reconfigured, making the importance of the cultural context of status more visible. For instance, Lounsbury, Ventresca, and Hirsch (2003) showed how crisis conditions in the US solid waste field opened up space for activists to enhance the cultural acceptance (and status) of recycling while displacing previously valorized incineration practices endorsed by central authorities – the Department of Energy and the Environmental Protection Agency. Thus, the crux of our argument is that status matters a great deal when actors operate within a cultural milieu that valorizes their practices, but it is rather inconsequential when prominent actors pursue culturally discrepant practices.

In an effort to encourage more systematic research on the cultural conditioning of status, we rely on an illustrative case of how cultural elements shaped the effects of status in a nascent field. More specifically, we empirically analyze the role that status played in defining the emerging field of nanotube technology – a key area of nanotechnology that carries much commercial potential as well as solutions to many pressing social, medical, and environmental problems (e.g., Berube, 2006; Meyyappan, 2005). As a field emerging at the interface of science and technology, we focus on the relationship between the status of nanotube scientists, as well as inventing corporations, and the importance of the patents that they were issued.

In any field of technological advance, ideas and innovations compete with each other for the allocation of resources and attention. Inevitably, winners and losers emerge with highly cited (important) patents providing the foundation for future technological development (Katila, 2002; Nerkar, 2003; Podolny and Stuart, 1995). Thus, identifying where important patents come from is fundamental to understanding which streams of innovation are advanced and extended, and which become marginalized. This issue is particularly pressing in the nanotube field because of its potential to revolutionize applications in areas such as optics, computing, materials, drug delivery, robotics, and energy, as well as the concomitant investments that governments are making in the field worldwide (see Berube, 2006; Hoffman, 2006; Meyyappan, 2005). Thus, which patents become important (i.e., highly cited) is related to which application areas of a technology become culturally valorized as more fruitful or pressing than others.

Existing research on techno-scientific fields suggests that high-status actors, especially star scientists, play a crucial role in creating foundational knowledge that shapes the direction of a field (e.g., Zucker, Darby, and Brewer, 1998; Zucker and Darby, 2007). However, not everything that star scientists do is golden, and what corporations find potentially valuable in technological development may not articulate well with the problems that scientists focus on. This is not to say that high-status actors (star scientists and large corporations) do not matter; clearly they do. However, the effect of their activities is contingent upon broader cultural processes of field development that define which areas of technological development gain the attention of broader audiences and become valorized as fruitful areas for the investment of energy and resources. While there is undoubtedly a functional aspect to this, the process of achieving social agreement about what is, and is not, a germane area of technology development is fundamentally cultural.

In the case of nanotechnology patenting, we focus on how different domains of development – as reflected in the United States Patent and Trademark Office (USPTO) technology categories – became central in nanotube technology, and how this shaped status effects in the field. Categories are key cultural nodes that group similar items together in ways that simplify cognition while facilitating valuation and commensuration (Bowker and Star, 2000; Douglas, 1986; Zerubavel,

1997). Moreover, the potential exists for groups of categories to become linked together under higher-order cultural elements such as collective identities (Bourdieu, 1984), organization forms (Mohr and Duquenne, 1997), and institutional logics (Mohr, 1998). Building on this line of research, we show that patent categories linked to inorganic nanotube research clustered together in the center of the field, while those associated with alternate approaches of organic and polymer research became peripheral. Our results show that patents within central categories were more likely to emerge as important nodes of technological advance. This effect was particularly pronounced for patents issued to star scientists and large corporations. When these high-status actors patented in central categories, their patents were especially likely to be highly cited; however, their patents in more marginal categories failed to catalyze much further development. As such, we provide considerable evidence that status effects are culturally conditioned.

In the next section, we develop our theoretical perspective on status dynamics and generate hypotheses. After this, we present our case on the development of nanotube patenting, including a detailed discussion of the field's evolving cultural infrastructure as reflected in its category system. Drawing on negative binomial regression models of patent citation, we provide evidence to support our claims of how cultural context conditions the effects of status. We finish by discussing how a focus on culture points to germane opportunities for future research on status within fields.

Theory and hypotheses

The dominant approach to status in organization theory emphasizes that the practices or output of high-status actors are valued more highly. This approach is particularly prevalent in the literature on the functioning of markets and fields (Podolny, 1993; Rao *et al.*, 2003; Stuart, Hoang, and Hybels, 1999). In the context of patents, evidence suggests that the status of an inventor can lead to perceptions of higher patent quality and importance (Podolny and Stuart, 1995). One key measure of the status of inventors in this context is their standing in the scientific community. There is a consistent finding that innovations introduced by prominent scientists are viewed more favorably because their expertise is unquestioned (a phenomenon that Merton

[1968] termed the "Matthew effect"). Also, as with other high-status actors, prominent scientists are targets for imitation by others in their field (Stuart and Ding, 2006). As a result, their innovations tend to play a key role in shaping the trajectories of scientific and intellectual movements (Fujimura, 1987; Frickel and Gross, 2005). For example, Lynne Zucker and colleagues have shown the importance of star scientists in the development of bio- and nano-technologies (Zucker, Darby, and Brewer, 1998; Zucker and Darby, 2007).

Evidence also suggests that large corporations occupy high-status positions within many fields and markets. For instance, Haveman (1993) showed that new market categories attracted more new entrants when large, successful firms demonstrated the fruitfulness of opportunities in a new category. Mezias and Lant (1994) similarly argue that large organizations are more visible and provide role models for imitation by other actors in a field. Similar dynamics appear to play out in technological fields. For example, Podolny and Stuart (1995) found that semiconductor patents issued to large, prominent firms such as Intel and IBM were more likely to accrue citations than similar patents issued to small firms (see also Greenwood *et al.*, 2002). Thus:

H1: Patents associated with a star scientist inventor are more likely to be highly cited than patents associated with other inventors.

H2: Patents associated with a large corporation inventor are more likely to be highly cited than patents associated with other inventors.

While actor status may help to enhance the valuation of a patent, the processes by which patents become valued are embedded in a broader cultural milieu where technological paths are developed. Path creation is a complicated and contingent process that involves a disparate array of actors that contribute to the emergence of shared beliefs about the value and appropriateness of specific lines of technological advance (Garud and Karnoe, 1999). And, even within particular technological paths, there are a wide variety of possible developments whose ultimate utility is hard to discern *a priori* (Podolny and Stuart, 1995). To highlight the importance of this broader cultural context of path creation as a determinant of status effects in the field of nanotube technology, we focus on the categorization of patents.

Classification is abundant in the construction of markets (see Hsu, 2006; Lounsbury and Rao, 2004). As with other categorization processes which provide the cultural material that shapes identities, behavior, and status positions, market categories differentiate and stratify products, services, and firms (e.g., Bowker and Star, 2000; Mohr and Duquenne, 1997). In the context of patenting, USPTO categories are designed to segregate different types of technologies based on their attributes and functional purpose. For instance, category 257 is for inventions related to transistors, while category 427 is for coating processes. Each patent application contains a set of claims that describe the focal invention. A series of expert examiners review these claims to determine whether or not a patent should be granted and, if so, which technology category the invention fits best within (USPTO, 2009). As such, categorization in nanotube technology follows a process, much like feature film classification (Hsu, 2006), where producers are aware of the category system and develop "products" that are targeted for specific categories, but classification is ultimately determined by an external audience. In this way, USPTO categories are cultural elements that simplify reality and provide widely shared understandings about the similarity and distinctiveness of various types of inventions (e.g., Douglas 1986; Zerubavel 1997).

Looking at USPTO patent categories, we expect that patents situated in categories with high levels of activity will be more likely to amass citations than those in categories with lower activity levels. A number of studies have argued that categories gain legitimacy and are perceived more favorably when they emerge as sites of manifold activity (Aldrich, 1999; Aldrich and Fiol, 1994; Hannan and Freeman, 1989). Moreover, learning theory suggests that as the number of patents increases in a knowledge category, so too should the number of new patents that are formed to exploit these opportunities (March, 1991). As such, a high level of activity is likely to draw positive attention to a category and lead to further patenting. And, since patent categories roughly distinguish between different domains of knowledge and technology development, patents in a category are more likely to build on prior patents in the same category (Wry *et al.*, 2010). Thus:

H3: Patents that are positioned within categories that have many other patents are more likely to be highly cited than patents positioned in sparsely populated categories.

Beyond basic density effects, scholars have argued that the relational structure of categories in a field also plays a key role in how the contents of categories are understood (Breiger, 1974). For instance, Mohr and Duquenne (1997) showed how the logic of social relief was ushered in as social workers altered the meaning of poverty relief categories by changing the nature of practices linking different categories. In a similar vein, Bourdieu (e.g., 1984) has shown that the meaning and status of categories are defined by the practices that link them together in a broader classification structure.

This general orientation is echoed by research on knowledge dynamics (Powell and Snellman, 2004) which suggests that the overall features of the knowledge system itself should affect the creation process within it (Gavetti and Levinthal, 2000; Owen-Smith and Powell, 2004; Powell, Koput, and Smith-Doerr, 1996). All knowledge systems contain implicit grouping, hierarchies, and comparisons (Espeland and Stevens, 1998). In science, knowledge is particularly hierarchical (Merton, 1968), with broader disciplinary subjects like physics dominating narrower subjects like chemical engineering (Pfeffer and Langton, 1993). This research suggests that in the context of patent categories, a great deal of cross-citation between categories will reveal categories that are more central to the development of the field of knowledge (Powell *et al.*, 1996; Wasserman and Faust, 1997). This hierarchy may be extended and deepened over time, resulting in a distinct core–periphery structure (Fligstein, 2001). In it, patent categories that build on each other will more likely form technology cliques that generate ever more citations among their incumbent patents. Categories that contain patents having a narrower appeal will tend not to emerge as central categories in the system; they will become marginalized and the patents within will tend not to stimulate further development (see also Podolny and Stuart, 1995; Sorenson and Fleming, 2004).

As we will discuss in some detail later, and summarize in Table 6.3, a clear pattern of category linkages emerged in nanotube technology. In particular, a group of star scientists began to patent processes for synthesizing carbon nanotubes in USPTO categories related to inorganic chemistry (204 and 423). These scientists and a handful of large corporations subsequently began to extend patents in these foundational categories to take out patents related to rudimentary applications of carbon nanotubes in categories such as compositions (252) and coatings (427) – a basic pattern which was repeated over time as disparate categories linked to the application of carbon nanotubes became linked together through heavy and patterned cross-citations. These categories formed an expanding cluster positioned at the center of the category system. We anticipate that patents in these central categories will be more likely to amass citations than patents in more distant categories. Hence:

H4: Patents that are positioned in a central category are more likely to be highly cited than patents in peripheral categories.

Finally, we expect that the cultural context that defines which categories are focal points for patenting will condition the effect of an actor's status on the importance of their patents. Thus, patents in central categories will be particularly likely to become important nodes of technological advance when they are associated with a prominent inventor. We expect this because high-status actors are especially likely to be rewarded when their practices align closely with the categories at a field's core (Bourdieu, 1984; Rao *et al.*, 2003). When positioned in this way, prominent actors serve as the highly visible exemplars of a field's core activities and are accorded concomitant attention and deference. As such, they provide a template for others to draw on and imitate (Haunschild and Miner, 1997; Scott, 2008; Wry *et al.*, 2010). Thus:

H5: Patents associated with a star scientist inventor are more likely to be highly cited when they are positioned in a central category.

H6: Patents associated with a large firm inventor are more likely to be highly cited when they are positioned in a central category.

Data and method

Empirically, we explore one key area of nanotechnology, nanotubes, the most common of which are carbon-based. The development of nanotube technology can be traced back to 1985 when a team at Rice University led by Richard Smalley and Harold Kroto published an article in *Nature* detailing the discovery and synthesis of buckminister fullerenes, or Carbon60 (C60)[1] (Kroto *et al.*, 1985). C60 was a new carbon allotrope and the first fundamental advance in carbon science since the discovery of two diamond derivatives (chait and carbon VI) in the early 1970s. Accordingly, the discovery generated a great deal of research interest and, reflecting its importance to scientific advances, was awarded the 1996 Nobel Prize in Chemistry (Berube, 2006).

After Smalley and Kroto's discovery, fullerene research blossomed in many directions. One stream based on inorganic carbon science focused on developing fullerene structures with different shapes, sizes, and openings, such as C70, C76, and ultimately carbon nanotubes (CNTs) (Dresselhaus, Dresselhaus, and Eklund, 1996). While they are only a few nanometers in diameter, CNTs are extremely strong and have unique thermo and electrical conductivity properties (Meyyeppan, 2005).

Alternate paths based on organic and polymer science also took root. Activity in these areas focused on developing nanotubes from materials other than carbon and creating fullerene derivatives through bonding with other elements (DaRos *et al.*, 2001). While non-carbon nanotubes are not as strong as CNTs, they can be filled with conductive material to form nanowires and many are water-soluble, which enables their use in biological systems. Techniques from organic and polymer science can also be used to coat nanotubes and to create derivative structures with chemical properties that allow bonding to different molecules (Ghadiri *et al.*, 1993).

As with related studies that have examined the underlying niches and families that form among related patents (e.g., Podonly and Stuart, 1995; Harhoff, Scherer, and Vopel, 2003; Wartburg, Teichart, and Rost, 2005), we view patenting activity as importantly embedded in the USPTO classification system. The USPTO provides an extremely detailed way of segregating technological developments, encompassing more than 400 categories which cover all subject matter that is patentable under US law (USPTO, 2005). Each category is mutually exclusive, contains a title and description that detail its boundaries, as well as a number of more nuanced subcategories. For example, class 427 is for "Chemical processing technologies: Coating processes," class 438 is for "Chemical processing: Semiconductor device manufacturing," and class 534 is for "Organic compounds: Radioactive or rare earth metal compounds." Based on the claims that a patent makes, USPTO examiners place it within a primary category that reflects its most prominent area of technological application. If a patent contains a broad set of claims, it may also be assigned into secondary categories as necessary to reflect its more ancillary applications; this may include placement into multiple subcategories within the primary category or into different categories apart from the primary one (see USPTO, 2009 for a detailed discussion of the classification process).

Our data includes all USPTO-issued nanotube patents that are included in Nanobank, an exhaustive database tracking all patents, grants, and academic articles in the broader field of nanotechnology (see Zucker and Darby, 2007). To identify nanotube patents from this larger dataset, we searched for the terms "nanotube," "C60," "C70," "buckeyball," and fullerene" in the title, abstract, and claims section of each patent. The search yielded 1,128 patents from 1992 through to the end of 2005 when the Nanobank data stops. For each patent, we recorded its title, issue year, abstract, primary classification, secondary classifications (where applicable), inventor names, and scientific standing (as reflected in academic citations), as well as the organization a patent was assigned to and its geographic location. Based on Nanobank citation data, we also created a related database recording the number of times a patent was cited each year post-issue. As the number of patents in 1992 was trivial (n=3) and our independent variables are lagged by a year, our analysis runs from 1994 to 2005.

Dependent variable

Our dependent variable is the number of citations received by a focal patent each calendar year after it was issued. As a count variable, it is truncated at the upper end (in this case 27) and bounded at the lower end by zero, with an average of about 1.5 citations per patent/year.

Independent variables

At the patent level, *star scientist* is a dummy variable that reflects the scientific standing of a patent's inventor. To determine which scientists were stars, we examined their publication records up until the year in which they were issued a focal patent. Based on citation data reported in the Web of Science database, we coded inventors with +1,000 citations to their scholarly articles as stars, a figure that corresponds roughly to the top twenty percent of inventors across the years of our analysis. Association with a *large corporation* is also a dummy variable that reflects whether a patent was assigned to a firm with +$500 million in sales in the prior year. At the category level, the *density* of patents in a category is measured as the cumulative number of nanotube patents issued in a category before a focal patent was issued.

Our approach to the analysis of centrality and the overall structure of patent categories is consistent with other approaches based on co-citation analysis (Henderson *et al.*, 1998; Wagner and Leydesdorff, 2005). The impact of the position of a category in the knowledge structure is captured using *closeness centrality* scores (Borgatti *et al.*, 1999) based on prior art citations. Each patent application includes a detailed inventory of related patents, or "prior art," which patent researchers consider to be the stocks of knowledge that a focal patent builds on (see Katila, 2002; Nerkar, 2003; Rosenkopf and Nerkar, 2001). We extend this basic logic and examine prior art citations at the category level. We began by constructing yearly two-mode matrices of *primary patent classes* by *cited patent classes* with cells in each matrix containing the number of citations from patents with primary classification in a given class going to patents in a receiving class. This enabled us to draw on network analytic techniques to analyze what network analysts refer to as joint involvement or affiliation data (e.g., Breiger, 1974). Next, unlike many studies using affiliation data, which conventionally include data on director interlocks or cross-citations, we examined the extent to which categories share similar citation patterns. As such, even though centrality and patent citation counts are calculated with the same data, they are fundamentally different variables – a fact reflected in the weak correlation between the two (0.146). Finally, we used UCINET to calculate closeness centrality scores for each patent class (Borgatti *et al.*, 1999). Closeness centrality is the most appropriate spatial distance measure when direct actor ties are not being analyzed – such as with affiliation data (see Wasserman and Faust, 1997).

Control variables

We include several controls in our models. The *founding patent* category is a binary variable set to "1'" when a patent is the first to receive primary classification in a given USPTO class. This type of opening of new categories signals market opportunities and is associated with the rise of new entrants that take up related positions in order to take advantage of new resource spaces (Aldrich, 1999). Patent *age* counts the number of years since a patent was issued and is included to control for life-course effects. *Age squared* is the square of patent age and is used to account for the fact that citations to a patent tend to wane over time. We also include *post-NNI* as a dummy variable set to "1" after 2001 to account for the field-wide bump in citations we expect with the passage of the US National Nanotechnology Initiative (NNI) – legislation that earmarked +$1 billion per year for nanotechnology funding.

We also control for patent *breadth* and *cross-categorization*. The former is a measure of the number of secondary classifications assigned to a patent regardless of whether these are to subcategories within a patent's primary category or to other categories. It is included to account for the potential for patents that make broad claims to inform developments across multiple domains and generate more citations accordingly (see Grindley and Teece, 1997). *Cross-categorization* is a subset of breadth that reflects the number of secondary categories to which a patent is assigned outside of its primary category. Evidence suggests that the most powerful innovations are those that locate themselves within particular categories, but are uniquely differentiated within them (Glynn, 2008; Lounsbury and Glynn, 2001). Thus, patents which encompass diverse secondary categories may be more resonant because they are both novel within a specific technology category, but also make linkages to external categories, drawing attention from actors innovating in these areas as well.

In addition, we controlled for geographic effects (Marquis and Lounsbury, 2007; Marquis, Glynn, and Davis, 2007). We included dummy variables for patents issued to organizations in the US and Japan, two countries which have made considerable investments in nanotube research (Hoffman, 2006) and have emerged as the most prominent in nanotube patenting. In addition, based on evidence that some geographic regions evolve high-technology clusters linked to specific areas of technological advance (Owen-Smith and Powell, 2004; Saxenian, 1994), we also controlled for *regional cluster*. To construct this variable, we followed previous research which suggests that Boston, Houston, and the San Francisco Bay area are particularly prominent centers of nanotube research and have a propensity to produce highly cited patents (see Wry *et al.*, 2010). Patents assigned to an organization located in one of these regions were assigned a "1."

For the sake of completeness, we also included a *density squared* variable which is simply the square of density of patents in a patent category. Akin to conventional organizational ecology logic, some learning theorists suggest that overcrowding can diminish the value or learning activity in a domain (March *et al.*, 2000; Szulanski, 1996). However, we do not hypothesize this formally because it is unclear whether there are any scale limits in knowledge development arenas such as patenting. All independent and control variables were lagged by one year and updated annually.

Method of analysis

Patent citations is a non-negative count variable which represents an arrival process (Hausman, 1978). The parameter of interest in this process is the arrival rate, defined as the instantaneous probability of arriving at state (y + 1) at time (t + Δt), as given in the following:

$$\lambda_y(t) = \lim_{\Delta t \to 0} \frac{Pr\{Y(t + \Delta t) - Y(t) = 1 \mid Y(t) = y\}}{\Delta t} \quad [1]$$

where Y(t) is the cumulative number of entries up to time t. The baseline model formulation assumes that $\lambda_y(t) = \lambda$ and that the conditional probability of Y_t arrivals in any time interval is governed by the probability law:

$$Pr(Y_t = y_t x_t) = \frac{[e^{-\lambda(xt)} \lambda(X_t)^{yt}]}{Yt!} \quad [2]$$

where the expected number of entries in each period $E(Y_t) = \lambda_t$ equals the variance. This is the procedure for a normal Poisson regression where λt is the deterministic function of the covariates. In cases of overdispersion, such as ours, when the conditional variance of the entry process exceeds the conditional mean, a stochastic component is needed in the entry rate. To address this issue, negative binomial regressions are conventionally used (see Carroll and Hannan, 2000). Accordingly, our models are analyzed using the *xtnbreg* command in STATA 9. Further, because our theory argues for variation in citations among patents over years, our data provides repeat observations

Ball, S., Eckel, C. C., Grossman, P. J., and Zame, W. 2001. "Status in markets." *Quarterly Journal of Economics* 116(1): 161–188.

Bandiera, O., Barankay, I., and Rasul, I. 2005. "Social preferences and the response to incentives: Evidence from personnel data." *Quarterly Journal of Economics* 120(3): 917–962.

Bandura, A. 1977. *Social Learning Theory.* Englewood Cliffs, NJ: Prentice Hall.

Becker, B. E. and Huselid, M. A. 1992. "The incentive effects of tournament compensation effects." *Administrative Science Quarterly* 37(2): 336–350.

Belliveau, M. A., O'Reilly, C. A., III, and Wade, J. B. 1996. "Social capital at the top: Effects of social similarity and status on CEO compensation." *Academy of Management Journal* 39(6): 1568–1593.

Berger, J., Fisek, H., Norman, R. Z., and Zelditch, M. 1977. *Status Characteristics and Social Interaction: An Expectation States Approach.* New York: Elsevier.

Berger, J., Fisek, M. H., Ridgeway, C. L., and Norman, R. Z. 1998. "The legitimation and delegitimation of power and prestige orders." *American Sociological Review* 63(3): 379–405.

Bhattacharya, S. and Guasch, J. L. 1988. "Heterogeneity, tournaments, and hierarchies." *Journal of Political Economy* 96(4): 867–881.

Bognanno, M. L. 1994. "CEO pay as a tournament prize." *Labor Law Journal* 45(8): 485–492.

Brass, D. J. 1984. "Being in the right place: A structural analysis of individual influence in an organization." *Administrative Science Quarterly* 29(4): 518–539.

Bratton, W. W. 2005. "The academic tournament over executive compensation." *California Law Review* 93(5): 1557–1584.

Bull, C., Schotter, A., and Weigelt, K. 1987. "Tournaments and piece rates: An experimental study." *Journal of Political Economy* 95(1): 1–32.

Byrne, J. A. and Bongiorno, L. 1995. "CEO pay: Ready for takeoff." *BusinessWeek* (April 24, 1995), pp. 88–110.

Cadinu, M. and Reggiori, C. 2002. "Discrimination of low-status outgroup: The role of ingroup threat." *European Journal of Social Psychology* 32(4): 501–515.

Carmichael, L. H. 1983. "The agent-agents problem: Payment by relative output." *Journal of Labor Economics* 1(1): 50–65.

Chen, K. P. 2003. "Sabotage in promotion tournament." *Journal of Law, Economics and Organization* 19(1): 119–140.

Conyon, M. J. and Sadler, G. V. 2001. "Executive pay, tournaments and corporate performance in UK firms." *International Journal of Management Reviews* 3(2): 141–168.

of individual patents over time. To control for unobserved endogenous effects associated with different patents, we estimated random effects models with *patent number* as the grouping variable. Since the random effects model treats group effects as uncorrelated with the other regressors, a Hausman's test for orthogonality of the random effects and the regressors was needed. As we did not reject the null hypothesis (group effects are uncorrelated with the other regressors), the random effects model was the appropriate choice for our analysis. Fixed effect and robust cluster models showed similar results.

Results

Table 6.1 provides the means, standard deviations, and correlations for the variables used in our analysis, and shows that there were no correlation problems. Table 6.2 reports results from our negative binomial analysis of patent citation rates. Model 1 provides a baseline including only control variables. Model 2 adds our hypothesized variables and Model 3 includes all interaction terms. The models with hypothesized variables show significant improvement in fit over the baseline model.

Among control variables, we find that patent *age* is positive and significant across all of our models while *age squared* is significant and negative, suggesting that patents amass citations as they age, but that this falls off as time goes on. Neither patent breadth nor cross-categorization had a significant effect, suggesting that the more technical aspects of a patent had little effect on its propensity to accrue citations.

We also find that patents issued to firms located in the US are more likely to amass citations, while those issued in Japan are not. Moreover, within the US, the regional clusters of Boston, Houston, and San Francisco have a positive independent effect, providing further evidence of generative and self-reinforcing nanotube knowledge creation communities in these regions (Wry *et al.*, 2009). We also see the expected bump in citation rates after passage of the NNI. Category founding patents have no significant effect in any model.

Turning to our hypothesized variables, hypotheses 1 and 2 argued that a patent was more likely to be highly cited if it was associated with a star scientist or large corporation inventor. As Table 6.2 shows,

Table 6.1 *Means, standard deviations, correlations of variables*

Variables	Mean	St. Dev.	2	3	4	5	6	7	8	9	10	11	12	13	14
1 Age	3.95	2.76	.963	.062	.074	.177	.173	-.112	-.011	-.507	.004	.009	.069	.053	.114
2 Age^2	23.22	29.97	—	.058	.066	.175	.175	-.116	-.003	-.443	-.001	.010	.076	.065	.128
3 Breadth	2.92	4.62		—	.472	.056	.053	-.116	-.087	-.110	.017	.063	-.120	-.102	-.080
4 Cross-category	1.11	1.13			—	.103	.043	-.081	-.110	-.114	.104	-.025	-.140	-.107	-.143
5 Category founding	0.26	0.44				—	.128	-.144	.001	-.201	.002	-.014	-.355	-.234	-.343
6 US	0.65	0.48					—	-.636	.312	-.180	.228	-.261	-.112	-.082	-.098
7 Japan	0.18	0.38						—	-.198	.108	-.113	.238	.134	.099	.129
8 Regional cluster	0.15	0.36							—	.017	.106	-.274	.074	.072	.069
9 Post-NNI	0.35	0.48								—	-.059	.039	.193	.167	.365
10 Star scientist	0.56	0.49									—	-.607	.082	.095	.011
11 Large corp.	0.63	0.48										—	-.111	-.129	-.013
12 Density	17.02	19.13											—	.939	.415
13 Density^2	655.75	1390.27												—	.298
14 Centrality	68.02	33.10													—

Table 6.2 *Random effect negative binomial analysis of nanotube patent citations, 1994–2005*

Variables	Models		
	1	2	3
Constant	–.327	–.868***	–.307
	(.241)	(.299)	(.390)
Age	.530***	.454***	.451***
	(.037)	(.038)	(.038)
Age^2	–.038***	–.037***	–.037***
	(.003)	(.003)	(.003)
Breadth	.006	.003	.003
	(.013)	(.013)	(.013)
Cross-categorization	.021	.066	.069
	(.061)	(.061)	(.060)
Category founding	–.203	.085	.061
	(.148)	(.158)	(.157)
US	.525***	.525***	.523***
	(.161)	(.161)	(.161)
Japan	.337*	.196	.199
	(.184)	(.188)	(.188)
Regional cluster	.304**	.293*	.300*
	(.157)	(.160)	(.160)
Post-NNI	.575***	.259*	.258*
	(.126)	(.135)	(.136)
Star scientist		.448***	.185
		(.158)	(.291)
Large corporation		.451***	.131
		(.171)	(.290)
Density		.011**	.011**
		(.006)	(.006)
Density$^2 \times 100$		.003	.003
		(.005)	(.006)
Centrality		.034***	.037
		(.014)	(.035)
Star scientists $\times$ Centrality			.008***
			(.003)
Large corps. $\times$ Centrality			.004*
			(.003)

Table 6.2 (*cont.*)

Variables	Models		
	1	2	3
Log pseudolikelihood	−3194.98	−3166.11	−3162.41
Wald R2	.000***	.000***	.000***

* p < .10; ** p < .05; *** p < .01.
Standard errors in parentheses; one tailed tests for hypothesized variables.

our models support both hypotheses and find that these variables have considerable power for explaining patent citations. This finding is consistent with previous work that has argued that high-profile scientists are key drivers of technological developments (e.g., Zucker *et al.*, 1998) and that the prominence of large corporations draws increased attention and deference to their patent activities under certain conditions (e.g., Podolny and Stuart, 1995).

Turning to category level (cultural context) variables, we find that the density of patents in a category has a positive and significant effect on citations to resident patents. This suggests that, as we argued in hypothesis 3, patents positioned in classes with more innovative activity are likely to accrue citations. Note that there is no effect for overcrowding (the squared density term).

In hypothesis 4, we argued that patents in more central categories would be more likely to amass citations. As Model 2 shows, patents in classes with higher centrality scores were significantly more likely to accrue citations than patents in less central categories. Further, it is important to note that centrality effects supersede other explanatory factors related to density, breadth, and patent age which are predominant in patenting and entrepreneurship literatures. Thus, we find strong support for hypothesis 4.

Also, in line with hypotheses 5 and 6, Model 3 shows that the interaction between star scientists and centrality is positive and highly significant, and the interaction between large corporations and centrality is also significant, but at a lower level. Thus, we find strong support for our argument that star scientist patents in central categories are more likely to become important and somewhat weaker support for the influence of large corporations in central classes. In addition, it is important to note that in the full model, the marginal effect of high status on patent importance is not significant; that is, the output of high-status actors is only valued more highly when their patents are positioned within central categories. Thus, in the field of nanotube technology, we find that the effect of status on patent importance is culturally conditioned.

A more qualitative exploration helps to illuminate how the construction of the cultural context conditioned the ways that actor status mattered in this field. In the early development of nanotube technology, prominent research programs crystallized around *inorganic, organic,* and *polymer* approaches to creating nanotubes, fullerenes, and their derivatives (see Meyyappan, 2005). While the boundaries between the three technological paths were not always sharp, patent activity was segregated in different patent categories. From 1992 to 1995 categories 204 and 423 (chemistry/inorganic chemistry), 523–528 (polymer compounds), and 532–570 (organic compounds) accounted for over seventy percent of nanotube patent activity despite representing less than thirty percent of the overall classes where nanotube patents were issued. During these years, the three paths looked fairly similar; patent density was comparable, star scientists and large corporations were present in each, and citation rates were about the same (organic classes actually had a slight edge). However, only inorganic patent categories became central, bringing a commensurate bump in the citations to resident patents.

While there are various functional reasons why patenting in inorganic chemistry categories has accelerated in contrast to polymer and organic approaches, in the early years it appeared as if all three approaches had utility. Our point is that even if inorganic approaches were proven to have more potential, at least during the time of the study, a great deal of cultural work is required to gain field-wide agreement about that potential, especially in the early phases of technological development, where there is heightened uncertainty and ambiguity. While a complete explanation of how some patent categories became more central in the nanotube field is beyond the scope of this chapter, we highlight some aspects of this process. We suggest that at the core of this process is the work of star scientists who seek to construct a broader infrastructure around their research and patenting activity that will ultimately lead their work to be deemed important and highly cited. However, while we stress the cultural work of star scientists, they are not in complete control of such institutional design, and so the effect of high-status actors on creating an institutional infrastructure that valorizes their work is fraught with the potential for failure, and can be at best considered as an indirect effect of status. As we discuss at the end of the chapter, how status relates to the construction of cultural contexts is an important focus for future research.

From science to technology. Mirroring our quantitative findings, qualitative analysis suggests that the activities of a handful of star scientists played a key role in enabling some patent categories to become central in the field's development. While not an exhaustive list, this group included Richard Smalley from Rice, Dieter Gruen at the Argonne National Laboratory, Sumio Iijima at NEC, Charles Lieber from Harvard, Chad Mirkin at Northwestern, Jack Howard at MIT, and Richard Haddon from the University of Kentucky, who were all among the most highly cited scientists over the duration of our analysis. Conducting research with the potential for commercial application was pursued vigorously by these scientists (Harris, 1999). For example, in his Nobel Lecture, Smalley stated that the discovery of fullerenes resulted from "research that at nearly every stage was justified by its relevance to real world technological problems" (Smalley, 1996, p. 101). And Lieber similarly stated that "I think my goal is to try to push this science in ways that will ultimately turn it into a working technology" (Lieber, 2003, p. 4). Accordingly, the initial flourish of inorganic nanotube patenting reflected the efforts of star scientists to translate their academic findings into patents. In particular, there was a wave of patenting related to the production of carbon-based nanostructures: categories 204 and 423. Moreover, the activity of these scientists was very focused: over eighty percent of their patents were in these two categories and they collectively comprised over seventy-five percent of the patent activity in the area from 1992 to 1995.

Different dynamics were evident in organic and polymer research. Unlike the inorganic categories, patenting in these classes was dominated by a handful of large corporations: DuPont, Shell, and Exxon. Though these are prominent organizations and many of their patents were assigned to star scientists on their staffs, these failed to catalyze broader efforts. A key differentiating factor appears to be that these firms were not heavily invested in catalyzing organic and polymer patenting. Large firms typically have diverse intellectual property portfolios that span multiple technological domains (Grindley and Teece, 1997); DuPont, Exxon, and Shell were no different. In sum, only about two percent of the patents issued to these firms between 1992 and 1995 related to nanotube technology. Their efforts were more akin to technological hedging than a concerted effort to catalyze a stream of technological innovation around organic or polymer nanotube technologies. In fact, after the initial flourish of activity between 1992 and 1997, each firm exited the nanotube technology field altogether.

Creating a knowledge hub. In addition to transposing their scientific findings into patents, star scientists actively acted as cultural brokers (Hargadon and Sutton, 1997; Obstfeld, 2005), knitting these innovations together into a coherent and meaningful knowledge core for inorganic nanotube technology. Analysis of the "prior art" sections of early patents taken out by star scientists yields a consistent and extensive pattern of linkages among patent categories and the development of a clearly identifiable knowledge core. As we have noted, early inorganic patents clustered in categories related to chemistry (204) and inorganic chemistry (423). In their patents in the area, star scientists engaged in heavy cross-citation between these categories, creating a meaningful knowledge core that bridged categories with a shared focus on the creation of carbon nanostructures. Though the field had not yet evolved a clear core-periphery structure, by 1998 categories 204 and 423 were among the most central in the field and began to include patents from progressively diverse sets of actors. The pattern of prior art citations in these patents mirrored those made by the early star scientists, reinforcing the emerging knowledge core. Moreover, the original star scientist patents linking the classes were very highly cited among these new entrants. For example, Smalley's patents (#5227038, #5300203) were the two most highly cited in category 204, and patents from Gruen (#5209916) and MIT's Jack Howard (#5273729) were the most highly cited in category 423.

Conversely, early patents in organic and polymer categories failed to develop a dense relational network that could provide a meaningful foundation for further development which, as Figure 6.1 suggests, put downward pressure on citation rates in contrast to inorganic

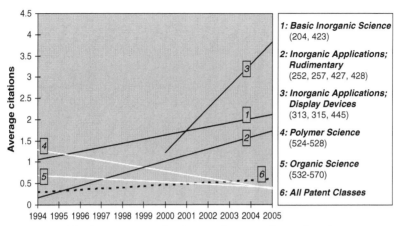

Figure 6.1 Citation patterns for inorganic, organic, and polymer patent categories, 1994–2005

patents. Still, there were some highly cited patents in these categories. For example, one of Exxon's organic nanotube patents (#5292813) was among the most highly cited of all nanotube patents in the early 1990s. However, unlike inorganic science, the majority of these citations came from patents outside of the nanotube field. In fact, only about half of the organic and polymer patents from 1992 to 1997 cited any prior art, and those that did only made sporadic links to each other. Thus, a consistent pattern of links among patent categories failed to emerge in these areas, with the result that neither established a cohesive or generative knowledge core to catalyze a path of technology development within the field.

Expanding the core. Further, as the field developed, we observe star inorganic scientists making links to categories beyond the initial knowledge core, drawing them into a central cluster of inorganic patent classes. More specifically, star scientists cited prior art from disparate areas of technical application, patented across categories, and actively promoted the applications of carbon nanostructures in areas such as display devices. In the years following the initial flourish of patent activity in the inorganic chemistry categories (204 and 423), significant activity emerged around rudimentary applications for carbon nanotubes. From 1997 to 2005, four of the fastest growing patent classes in the nanotube field were compositions (252), solid state devices (257), coatings (427), and stock materials (428). Significantly, activity in these categories was foreshadowed in the prior art citation patterns among early star scientist patents. For example, the initial nanotube production patents by Smalley and Iijima made numerous linkages to categories 427 and 428, as well as 252 to a somewhat lower extent. Gruen and Lieber's early patents in the inorganic chemistry categories also featured dense references to categories 257, 427, and 428.

While star scientists worked to signal the relevance of inorganic nanotechnology to broader audiences and applications, a different pattern emerged among organic and polymer patents. Examining the patents taken out by DuPont, Exxon, and Shell from 1992 to 1997, there is no consistent pattern of linkages to other patent categories. While there were sporadic references to categories 44 (fuel and related compositions), 106 (compositions: coating or plastic), and 508 (solid anti-friction devices), none of these generated meaningful activity. As such, the firms who were at the forefront of organic and polymer nanotube technology failed to signal the utility of their patents for a broader array of associated applications.

In addition to cross-category citations that reached out from the knowledge core to diverse patent categories, star inorganic scientists helped shape the emerging knowledge structure by patenting in novel categories and linking these patents to central classes through prior art citations. While some like Smalley dedicated themselves exclusively to the production and purification of carbon nanostructures, other stars worked to integrate these new materials into other technical domains. Charles Lieber, Richard Haddon, and Dieter Gruen provide a good illustration of star scientists who reached out to link diverse categories into the knowledge core through their patent activity.

Before developing ways to synthesize nanotubes, Charles Lieber had already gained considerable acclaim for his work in high temperature semiconductors. In a 2003 interview, Lieber detailed his entry into nanotube research:

With my work (in the early 1990s) on high temperature semiconductors, I had been studying quasi-two-dimensional planar structures ... Also, at the same time, interesting work was going on with fullerenes and carbon nanotubes ... (one dimensional) nanowires were going to be absolutely essential and I figured I might as well go for it. (Lieber, 2003, p. 2)

In addition to taking out patents related to nanotube production, Lieber engaged in cross-category patenting that reflected the semiconductor expertise in his scientific repertoire. Specifically, he branched out into categories related to electronics and semiconductors, and began to seek intellectual property protection for his work on carbon-based nanowires while making links back to patents in categories 204, 423, 257, and 427. For example, his patents #5196396 and #6781166 were issued for "a superconducting fullerene composition" and "nanoscopic wire-based devices and arrays," respectively.

The basic pattern found in Lieber's patenting was mirrored by Robert Haddon and Dieter Gruen. Haddon, like Lieber, had received considerable acclaim for work in superconductivity before starting his nanotube research. Consistent with this repertoire of scientific understanding, Haddon engaged in fairly extensive patenting related to nanotube production, as well as in categories related to the application of nanotubes in conductive structures (categories 252 and 257). Dieter Gruen at the Argonne National Lab also came to nanotube research from a distinguished background. Unlike Haddon and Lieber, however, Gruen's expertise was in the composition of chemical films (Gruen, 2008). Reflecting this, Gruen took out patents in categories 117 (single crystal films) and 427 (coating processes) which cited considerable prior art from classes 204 and 423.

Moreover, in making these linkages, star scientists signaled the utility of these patent categories. Indeed, each of the basic inorganic science and rudimentary application classes emerged as among the most active domains of nanotube patenting. Mirroring the dense linkages that formed between the basic inorganic categories (204, 423), new entrants into rudimentary application classes created dense linkages back to these categories, as well as among the emerging application categories. As Table 6.3 shows, the result was a thick pattern of citations among these categories, drawing them together as central nodes in the field-level knowledge structure. Not surprisingly, the most highly cited patents in these categories were those issued to the star scientists who did the initial work of knitting the classes together. For instance, the most highly cited patents in category 257 were issued to Haddon (#5693977) and Robert Sarciffici at the University of California (#5331183), while Gruen (#6447851) and Iijima (#5747161) were among the most highly cited in categories 427 and 428, respectively.

Table 6.3 *Within field "prior art" citations; inorganic classes, 1992–2005*

	Patents	Total cites	% to inorganic classes	Citations to inorganic classes								
				204	423	252	257	427	428	313	315	445
Basic inorganic science	**126**	**728**	**63%**	**43**	**238**	**15**	**26**	**35**	**65**	**14**	**5**	**16**
204	31	219	67%	25	71	4	14	13	17	2	0	0
423	95	509	61%	18	167	11	12	22	48	12	5	16
Rudimentary inorganic applications	**149**	**450**	**58%**	**25**	**68**	**4**	**38**	**43**	**60**	**9**	**3**	**11**
252	19	19	84%	3	7	2	0	2	2	0	0	0
257	43	103	63%	8	11	0	19	2	13	5	1	6
427	36	134	58%	6	19	1	8	20	18	3	1	2
428	51	194	53%	8	31	1	11	19	27	1	1	3
Inorganic display applications	**100**	**613**	**75%**	**19**	**45**	**2**	**14**	**20**	**39**	**211**	**22**	**88**
313	58	376	79%	10	17	2	10	12	19	155	13	60
315	16	55	89%	2	6	0	0	4	9	20	3	5
445	26	182	62%	7	22	0	4	4	11	36	6	23

Another way that scientists drew diverse application classes into the core of the knowledge structure was to theorize the applications of carbon nanotubes through the formal organizations which they formed to sell them. In 1998, Haddon, together with fellow high-profile University of Kentucky researcher Peter Eklund, opened Carbolex. Two years later Smalley founded Carbon Nanotechnologies (now Unidym), and in 2001 Lieber founded Nanosys and Mirkin formed NanoInk. In each case, the patent profiles of these firms mirrored that of the inorganic nanotube knowledge structure and, from this base, each firm actively theorized the uses of carbon nanostructures in electronics and display devices. For example, a 2001 press release from Nanosys claimed that "the Lieber group (has) constructed nano-scale logic gates … which can be combined to perform any of the functions needed in a (nano)computer" (Nanosys, 2003). NanoInk and Carbon Nanotechnologies also made a number of claims about the uses of CNTs in flat panel displays (see NanoInk, 2008; Unidym, 2008). Conversely, the press releases from DuPont, Exxon, and Shell from 1992 to 1997 (when each stopped patenting in inorganic and polymer categories) show no evidence of attempts to promote their organic nanotubes or polymer-fullerene derivatives for use in specific technological applications.

While identifying the discrete influence of this theorization in cata-lyzing knowledge structure expansion is not possible, these claims coincided closely with the proliferation of patent activity in cognate categories associated with flat panel display devices (313, 315, 445) and computing (365, 369, 438). Beginning in 2001, a number of large electronics firms such as AMD (11 patents), Intel (8 patents), Samsung (26 patents), and Sony (12 patents) became very active in these categories.

As Table 6.3 shows, in taking out these patents, firms made fre-quent linkages to both basic inorganic and rudimentary application categories, linking them to core areas of the knowledge structure. As a result, by 2004, categories pertaining to flat panel displays and computing had moved toward the core, forming a clearly distinguish-able subcluster. Reflecting the centrality and quantity of activity in the area, patents in these classes were the most highly cited of all classes post-2001. Further, reflecting our marginally significant find-ing for the interaction between large corporations and centrality, we observe that while there were few very highly cited corporate patents in the basic inorganic and rudimentary application categories, large corporations were clearly the dominant actors in display and computing categories. Indeed, early patents from Motorola (#6891319), Samsung (#6339281), and Sharp (#6650001) were most highly cited patents in these categories.

Overall, we observe a consistent pattern in comparing inorganic, organic, and polymer nanotube patent categories. The inorganic categories moved to the center of the knowledge structure, anchored by the category linking patents taken out by star scientists (and large corporations for display devices), while organic and polymer categories sat on the periphery. Figure 6.1 maps the citation trajectories of these streams. As the knowledge structure formed and inorganic classes knit together a central and cohesive path of innovative activity, citations to patents in the area rose markedly, especially among star scientist patents. In counter distinction, citations to organic and polymer categories dropped as the classes fell to the periphery of the field.

Discussion

In this chapter, we sought to highlight the importance of studying the cultural context within which the status of actors has effects. To do so, we provided an illustrative case of an emergent technological field and showed how the direct effects of high-status actors on the importance of patents was conditional on whether the categories within which they patented were central to the field's development. Our results show that the direct effects of high-status actors dissipated when interaction terms between category centrality and high-status actors were included. These results indicate that high-status actors engage in a wide variety of activities, only some of which turn out to be important. Thus, our emphasis on the cultural embeddedness of status suggests a slight corrective to dominant approaches in organization theory that treat status effects as smooth and universal (Podolny, 1993; Uzzi and Lancaster, 2004). Status appears to matter when the practices of prominent actors align with a field's cultural infrastructure, but it has little effect when their practices are considerably discrepant. Moreover, to the extent that the nebulous cultural infrastructure of an emerging field results in some types of high status being rewarded and others not, our findings suggest that not all types of status can transfer easily between fields and that status effects become uncertain when actors wade into institutional voids (Aldrich and Fiol, 1994).

By emphasizing how the effects of status are culturally conditioned and contingent, our study raises important questions about the role of status in the shaping of a field's culture infrastructure over the course of its emergence. Much of the extant literature in this milieu has focused on the ways in which high-status actors are able to cultivate favorable cultural arrangements (e.g., Fligstein, 1996, 2001; Rao *et al.*, 2003). While this certainly appeared to be the case with the star inorganic scientists in our investigation, it is equally clear that prominent actors fomenting organic and polymer nanotubes failed to catalyze development in these areas, with the result that citations to their patents waned. Thus, while status may allow actors to advantageously shape cultural arrangements, their success in this pursuit is by no means guaranteed. Moreover, studies drawing on the social movements literature have shown that marginalized groups are capable of opening new fields and introducing novel types of organizations despite their low status – successful cultural projects are not the exclusive purview of high-status actors (Clemens, 1997; Lounsbury, Ventresca, and Hirsch, 2003; Mische and Pattison, 2000). Thus, while it is not a particularly novel finding, our study makes clear that a focus on status alone provides an incomplete explanation for field and market emergence. As such, our results point to the importance of studying both successful and unsuccessful cultural projects undertaken by high-status actors, as well as the factors that allow one group of high-status actors to prevail over others (see also Rao, 1998). Future research examining the effects of status on organization, mobilization, and advocacy – as well as emerging regulatory and normative structures – has considerable potential to aid understanding in this area.

The contingent relationship between status and culture that we have highlighted also highlights a general problem within the institutional analysis of organizations. In addition to pointing to a need for further research on field emergence, we cast light on issues of institutional change. While some have argued that marginal actors are more likely to challenge prevailing cultural arrangements because incumbents are oriented toward the status quo (Leblebici *et al.*, 1991), others have suggested that high-status actors can efficaciously alter a field's cultural composition under certain circumstances (Frickel and Gross, 2005; Greenwood and Suddaby, 2006; Stuart and Ding,

2006). Accordingly, much more research is needed to understand how and under what conditions high-status actors can create or alter cultural contexts. As recent work on distributed entrepreneurship has noted, such changes are often highly complex and emergent, and while high-status actors play a role, their role may be much more subtle than is typically theorized (Lounsbury and Crumley, 2007; Wry *et al.*, 2010).

Our study also has implications for the literature on categorization. Looking within fields, industries, and markets, a growing body of literature explores the influence of category positioning on the status of incumbent actors and practices (Hsu, 2006; Hsu and Hannan, 2005; Zuckerman, 1999). The general argument is that categories are discrete entities which audiences associate with specific actors and practices. Conformity results in higher standing, while divergence and category spanning are punished (see especially Hsu, 2006). Our findings expose limitations in line of thinking while pointing to opportunities for novel lines of research.

We find that actors and practices compete for status not only within categories, but within the system of categories itself. As such, conformance with the tenets of a category might bring relatively higher status among category members, but comparatively low status within a broader field or market. Moreover, by emphasizing the relational nature of categories, we suggest that not all fields are comprised of discrete and segregated category sets. In this way, our conception of categories is closer to work in relational sociology (Breiger, 1974; Mohr and Duqenne, 1997) and cognitive psychology (Rosch, 1975; Lakoff, 1987), which emphasize that categories exist at multiple levels and that combinations among them can be as generative of status dynamics as the processes within them. Most significantly, we suggest that category spanning by actors may actually bring higher returns to status by altering the position of a category within the dynamically shifting field-level category structure.

Our results also suggest the need for more work on the dynamic and agentic processes that underpin status dynamics, adding texture to extant arguments about the emergence of stable status orders within fields. Reflecting early conceptualizations about the diffusion and institutionalization of dominant practices within a field (e.g., Tolbert and Zucker, 1983), institutionalists have tended to argue that fields settle on stable patterns of domination and coalition, with high-status actors imposing their preferred practices (DiMaggio and Powell, 1983; Fligstein, 1996). While recent literature has turned to processes of institutional entrepreneurship and change which can alter the status ordering of practices, the dominant imagery has been of punctuated episodes of change which book-end eras of stable practice stratification (e.g., Lounsbury and Rao, 2004; Greenwood and Suddaby, 2006). However, while arrangements may appear stable on the surface level, our findings are consistent with studies which argue that innovation and creative action persist at lower levels of analysis (Orlikowski, 2000; Rosa *et al.*, 1999). Thus, by illuminating the role of star scientists in knitting together a progressively broader array of categories of practice over time, we provide further evidence for the endogenous and ongoing evolution of status orderings within fields (Clemens and Cook, 1999) while illuminating a novel set of micro-processes that underlie it. Further, by showing the ongoing structuration of the field-level category structure, we help cast light on the micro-processes of field formation, one of the most underdeveloped lines of research in institutional theory (Greenwood *et al.*, 2008; Hirsch and Lounsbury, 1997).

In conclusion, we believe that a focus on the cultural context within which status operates addresses a key gap in the literature, directing attention to both the influence of broader cultural frameworks on the effects of status as well as the genesis of these arrangements. Such a focus has important implications for our understanding of status dynamics at a macro level, as well as for the ways in which scholars understand the role of categories and institutional dynamics in these processes. Moreover, by casting light on the micro-processes that are generative of the structures which embed categories of practice, we find that a focus on status can usefully direct attention to understudied dynamics of endogenous change and structuration within fields.

Note

1 The names "buckminister fullerene" and "C60" reflect the inclusion of sixty carbon atoms in the allotrope arranged in a pattern similar to the geodesic dome popularized by noted architect Richard Buckminister Fuller.

References

Aldrich, H. 1999. *Organizations Evolving*. London: Sage.

Aldrich, H. and Fiol, C. 1994. "Fools rush in? The institutional context of industry creation." *Academy of Management Review* 19: 645–670.

Benjamin, B. and Podolny, J. 1999. "Status, quality, and social order in the California wine industry." *Administrative Science Quarterly* 44: 563–589.

Berger, J., Cohen, B., and Zelditch, M. 1972. "Status characteristics and social interaction." *American Sociological Review* 37: 241–255.

Berube, D. 2006. *Nanohype: The Truth Behind the Nanotechnology Buzz*. Amherst, NY: Prometheus Books.

Borgatti, S. P., Everett, M. G., and Freeman, L. C. 1999. *UCINET 5 for Windows: Software for Social Network Analysis*. Natick, MA: Analytic Technologies.

Bourdieu, P. 1984. *Distinction: A Social Critique of the Judgment of Taste*. Cambridge, MA: Harvard University Press.

Bowker, G. C. and Star, S. L. 2000. *Sorting Things Out: Classification and its Consequences*. Cambridge, MA: MIT Press.

Breiger, R. 1974. "The duality of persons and groups." *Social Forces* 53: 181–190

2000. "A tool kit for practice theory." *Poetics* 27: 91–115.

Carroll, G. and Hannan, M. 2000. *The Demography of Corporations and Industries*. Princeton University Press.

Clemens, E. 1997. *The People's Lobby: Organizational Innovation and the Rise of Interest Group Politics in the United States, 1890–1925*. University of Chicago Press.

Clemens, E. and Cook, J. 1999. "Politics and institutionalism: Explaining durability and change." *Annual Review of Sociology* 25: 441–466.

DaRos, T., Spalluto, G., and Prato, M. 2001. "Biological applications of fullerene derivatives: A brief overview." *CCA* 74: 743–755.

DiMaggio, P. and Powell, W. 1983. "The iron cage revisited: Institutional isomorphism and collective rationality in organizational fields." *American Sociological Review* 48: 147–160.

Douglas, M. 1986. *Purity and Danger: An Analysis of the Concepts of Pollution and Taboo*. London: Routledge & Kegan Paul.

Dresselhaus, M., Dresselhaus, G., and Eklund, P. (eds.). 1996. *Science of Fullerenes and Carbon Nanotubes*. San Diego, CA: Academic Press.

Espeland, W. and Stevens, M., 1998. "Commensuration as a social process." *Annual Review of Sociology* 24: 313–343.

Fligstein, N. 1996. "Markets as politics: A political-cultural approach to market institutions." *American Sociological Review* 61: 656–673.

2001. "Social skill and a theory of fields." *Sociological Theory* 19: 105–125.

Frickel, S. and Gross, N. 2005. "A general theory of scientific/intellectual movements." *American Sociological Review* 70: 204–232.

Fujimura, J. 1987. "Constructing doable problems in cancer research: Articulating alignment." *Social Studies of Science* 17: 257–293.

Garud, R. and Karnoe, P. 1999. *Path Dependence and Creation.* Princeton, NJ: Lawrence Erlbaum and Associates.

Gavetti, G. and Levinthal, D. 2000. "Looking forward and looking backward: Cognitive and experiential search." *Administrative Science Quarterly* 45: 113–137.

Ghadiri, M., Granja, J., Milligan, R., McRee, D., and Khazanovich, N. 1993. "Self-assembling organic nanotubes based on a cyclic peptide architecture." *Nature* 366: 324–327.

Glynn, M.A. 2008. "Beyond constraint: How institutions enable identities," in R. Greenwood, C. Oliver, K. Sahlin-Andersson, and R. Suddaby (eds.), *The SAGE Handbook of Organizational Institutionalism.* Thousand Oaks, CA: Sage Publications.

Greenwood, R., Oliver, C., Sahlin, K., and Suddaby, R. 2008. "Introduction," in R. Greenwood, C. Oliver, K. Sahlin-Andersson, and R. Suddaby (eds.), *The SAGE Handbook of Organizational Institutionalism.* Thousand Oaks, CA: Sage Publications.

Greenwood, R and Suddaby, R. 2006. "Institutional entrepreneurship in mature fields: The Big Five accounting firms." *Academy of Management Journal* 49: 27–48.

Greenwood, R., Suddaby, R., and Hinings, C. R. 2002. "Theorizing change: The role of professional associations in the transformation of institutionalized fields." *Academy of Management Journal* 45: 58–80.

Grindley, P. and Teece, D. 1997. "Managing intellectual property: Licensing and cross-liscencing in semiconductors and electronics." *California Management Review* 39: 8–41.

Gruen, D. 2008. Dieter Gruen overview. Accessed from www.anl.gov/Science and_Technology/Distinguished_Fellows/gruen.html, March 2008.

Hannan, M. and Freeman, J. 1989. *Organizational Ecology.* Cambridge, MA: Harvard University Press.

Hargadon, A. and Sutton, R. 1997. "Technology brokering and innovation in a product development firm." *Administrative Science Quarterly* 42: 716–749.

Harhoff, D., Scherer, F., and Vopel, K. 2003. "Citations, family size, opposition and the value of patent rights." *Research Policy* 32: 1343–1363.

Harris, P. 1999. *Carbon Nanotubes and Related Structures: New Materials for the 21st Century.* Cambridge University Press.

Haunschild, P. and Miner, A. 1997. "Modes of interorganizational imitation: The effects of outcome salience and uncertainty." *Administrative Science Quarterly* 42: 427–500.

Hausman, J. 1978. "Specification tests in econometrics." *Econometrica* 46: 1251–1271.

Haveman, H. 1993. "Follow the leader: Mimetic isomorphism and entry into new markets." *Administrative Science Quarterly* 38: 593–627.

Henderson, R., Jaffe, A., and Trajtenberg, M. 1998. "Universities as a source of commercial tech: A detailed analysis of university patenting, 1965–1988." *Review of Economic Statistics* 80: 119–127.

Hirsch, P. M. and Lounsbury, M. 1997. "Ending the family quarrel: Towards a reconciliation of 'old' and 'new' institutionalism." *American Behavioral Scientist* 40: 406–418.

Hoffman, M. 2006. *The Nanotech Report: Investment Overview and Market Research for Nanotechnology,* 4th edn. New York: Lux Research.

Hsu, G. 2006. "Jack of all trades and masters of none: Audience responses to spanning genres in feature film production." *Administrative Science Quarterly* 51: 420–450.

Hsu, G. and Hannan, M. 2005. "Identities, genres and organizational forms." *Organization Science* 16: 474–490.

Katila, R. 2002. "New product search over time: Past ideas in their prime." *Academy of Management Journal* 45: 995–1010.

Knoke, D. and Burt, R. S. 1983. "Prominence," in R. S. Burt and M. J. Minor (eds.), *Applied Network Analysis.* Beverly Hills, CA: Sage, pp. 195–222.

Kraatz, M. and Zajac, E. 1996. "Exploring the limits of the new institutionalism: The causes and consequences of illegitimate organizational change." *American Sociological Review* 61: 812–836.

Kroto, H., Heath, J., O'Brien, S., Curl, R., and Smalley, R. 1985. "C60: Buckminster fullerene." *Nature* 318: 162–163.

Lakoff, G. 1987. *Women, Fire, and Dangerous Things: What Categories Reveal about the Mind.* University of Chicago Press.

Leblebici, H., Salancik, G., Copay, A., and King, T. 1991. "Institutional change and the transformation of interorganizational fields: An organizational history of the U.S. radio broadcasting industry." *Administrative Science Quarterly* 36: 333–363.

Lieber, C. 2003. "Harvard's Charles M. Lieber: An inside line on nanowires." *Science Watch* 14: 1–5.

Lounsbury, M. 2002. "Institutional transformation and status mobility: The professionalization of the field of finance." *Academy of Management Journal* 45: 255–266.

2007. "A tale of two cities: Competing logics and practice variation in the professionalizing of mutual funds." *Academy of Management Journal* 50: 289–307.

Lounsbury, M. and Crumley, E. 2007. "New practice creation: An institutional perspective on innovation." *Organization Studies* 28: 993–1012.

Lounsbury, M. and Glynn, M. A. 2001 "Cultural entrepreneurship: Stories, legitimacy, and the acquisition of resources." *Strategic Management Journal* 22: 545–564.

Lounsbury, M. and Rao, H. 2004. "Sources of durability and change in market classifications: A study of the reconstitution of product categories in the American mutual fund industry, 1944–1985." *Social Forces* 82: 969–999.

Lounsbury, M., Ventresca, M., and Hirsch, P. 2003. "Social movements, field frames and industry emergence: A cultural-political perspective on U.S. recycling." *Socio-Economic Review* 1: 71–104.

March, J. 1991. "Exploration and exploitation in organizational learning." *Organization Science* 2: 71–87.

March, J., Schulz, M., and Zhou, X. 2000. *The Dynamics of Rules: Change in Written Organizational Codes*. Stanford University Press.

Marquis, C., Glynn, M. A., and Davis, G. 2007. "Community isomorphism and corporate social action." *Academy of Management Review* 32: 925–945.

Marquis, C. and Lounsbury, M. 2007. "Vive la Résistance: Competing logics in the consolidation of community banking." *Academy of Management Journal* 50: 799–820.

Merton, R. 1968. "The Matthew effect in science." *Science* 159: 56–63.

Meyyappan, M. (ed.). 2005. *Carbon Nanotubes: Science and Applications*. New York: CRC Press.

Mezias, S. and Lant, T. 1994. "Mimetic learning and the evolution of organizational populations," in J. Baum and J. Singh (eds.), *Evolutionary Dynamics of Organizations*. New York: Oxford University Press, pp. 179–193.

Mische, A. and Pattison, P. 2000. "Composing a civic arena: Publics, projects, and social settings." *Poetics* 27: 163–194.

Mohr, J. 1998. "Measuring meaning structures." *Annual Review of Sociology* 24: 345–370.

Mohr, J. and Duquenne, V. 1997. "The duality of culture and practice: Poverty relief in New York City, 1888–1917." *Theory and Society* 26: 305–356.

NanoInk. 2002. "NanoInk founder and Northwestern University professor Chad Mirkin wins the Feynman Prize in nanotechnology." Accessed from www.easyir.com/easy, March 2008.

2008. Press releases. Accessed from www.easyir.com/easyir/prss. do?easyirid=0FB7E2B1EA672290&version=live, March 2008.

Nanosys. 2003. "Advances by Nanosys scientific founders honored as the breakthrough of the year by Science magazine." Accessed from www. nanosysinc.com, March 2008.

Nerkar, A. 2003. "Old is gold? The value of temporal exploration in the creation of new knowledge." *Management Science* 49: 211–229.

Obstfeld, D. 2005. "Social networks, the tertius iungens orientation, and involvement in innovation." *Administrative Science Quarterly* 50: 100–130.

Orlikowski, W. 2000. "Using technology and constituting structure: A practice lens for studying technology in organizations." *Organization Science* 12: 404–428.

Owen-Smith, J. and Powell, W. 2004. "The expanding role of university patenting in the life sciences: Assessing the importance of experience and connectivity." *Research Policy* 32: 1695–1711.

Pfeffer, J. and Langton, N. 1993. "The effect of wage dispersion on satisfaction, productivity, and working collaboratively: Evidence from college and university faculty." *Administrative Science Quarterly* 38: 382–407.

Podolny, J. 1993. "A status-based model of market competition." *American Journal of Sociology* 98: 829–872.

Podolny, J. and Stuart, T. 1995. "A role-based ecology of technological change." *American Journal of Sociology* 100: 1224–1260.

Powell, W., Koput, K., and Smith-Doerr, L. 1996. "Interorganizational collaboration and the locus of innovation: Networks of learning in biotechnology." *Administrative Science Quarterly* 41: 116–145.

Powell, W. and Snellman, K. 2004. "The knowledge economy." *Annual Review of Sociology* 30: 199–220.

Rao, H. 1998. "Caveat emptor: The construction of non-profit watchdog organizations." *American Journal of Sociology* 103: 912–961.

Rao, H., Monin, P., and Durand, R. 2003. "Institutional change in Toque Ville: Nouvelle cuisine as an identity movement in French gastronomy." *American Journal of Sociology* 108: 795–843.

Ridgeway, C. L. (1991). "The social construction of status value: Gender and other nominal characteristics." *Social Forces* 70: 367–386.

Rosa, J., Porac, J., Runser-Spanjol, J., and Saxon, M. 1999. "Sociocognitive dynamics in a product market." *Journal of Marketing* 63: 64–77.

Rosch, E. 1975. "Cognitive representations of semantic categories." *Journal of Experimental Psychology* 104: 192–233.

Rosenkopf, L. and Nerkar, A. 2001. "Beyond local search: Boundary spanning. Exploration, and impact in the optical disk industry." *Strategic Management Journal* 22: 287–306.

Saxenian, A. 1994. "Silicon Valley versus Route 128." *Inc* 16: 25.

Scott, W. 2008. *Institutions and Organizations*, 3rd edn. Thousand Oaks, CA: Sage Publications.

Smalley, R. 1996. "Discovering the fullerenes: Nobel lecture, December 7, 1996." *Chemistry* 89–103.

Sorenson, O. and Fleming, L. 2004. "Science and the diffusion of knowledge." *Research Policy* 33: 1615–1634.

Stuart, T. and Ding, W. 2006. "When do scientists become entrepreneurs? The social structural antecedents of commercial activity in the life sciences." *American Journal of Sociology* 112: 97–144.

Stuart, T., Hoang, H., and Hybels, R. 1999. "Interorganizational endorsements and the performance of entrepreneurial ventures." *Administrative Science Quarterly* 44: 315–349.

Szulanski, G. 1996. "Exploring internal stickiness: Impediments to the transfer of best practice within the firm." *Strategic Management Journal* 17: 27–43.

Tolbert, P. and Zucker, L. 1983. "Institutional sources of change in the formal structure of organizations: The diffusion of civil service reform, 1880–1935." *Administrative Science Quarterly* 28: 22–39.

Unidym. 2008. Press room. Accessed from www.unidym.com/company/pressroom.html, March 2008.

USPTO. 2005. *Overview of the Classification System*. Washington, D.C.: United States Patent and Trademark Office.

2009. Handbook of classification. Accessed from www.uspto.gov/web/offices/opc/documents/handbook.pdf, June 2009.

Uzzi, B. and Lancaster, R. 2004. "Embeddedness and price formation in corporate law markets." *American Sociological Review* 69: 319–344.

Wagner, C. and Leydesdorff, L. 2005. "Network structure, self-organization, and the growth of international collaboration in science." *Research Policy* 34: 1608–1618.

Wartburg, I., Teichert, T., and Rost, K., 2005. "Inventive progress measured by multi-stage patent citation analysis." *Research Policy* 34: 1591–1607.

Wasserman, S. and Faust, K. 1997. *Social Networks Analysis: Methods and Applications*. New York: Cambridge University Press.

Weber, M. 1978. *Economy and Society: An Outline of Interpretive Sociology*. Berkeley, CA: University of California Press.

Wry, T., Greenwood, R., Jennings, P. D., and Lounsbury, M. 2010. "Institutional sources of technology innovation: A community perspective on nanotechnology emergence," in N. Phillips (ed.), *Research in the Sociology of Organizations: Special Issue on Technology and Organization*, forthcoming

Wry, T., Lounsbury, M., and Glynn, M. 2009. "Collective identity mobilization: Prototype framing, boundary expansion, and cultural recognition." Working Paper, University of Alberta.

Zerubavel, E. 1997. *Social Mindscapes: An Invitation to Cognitive Sociology*. Cambridge, MA: Harvard University Press.

Zucker, L. and Darby, M., 2007. *Nanobank Data Description, Release 1.0 (Beta Test)*. Los Angeles, CA: UCLA Center for International Science, Technology, and Cultural Policy and Nanobank.

Zucker, L., Darby, M., and Brewer, M. 1998. "Intellectual human capital and the birth of U.S. biotechnology enterprises." *American Economic Review*: 88, 290–306.

Zuckerman, E. 1999. "The categorical imperative: Securities analysts and the illegitimacy discount." *American Journal of Sociology* 104: 1398–1438.

7 | Venture launch and growth as a status-building process

M. KIM SAXTON AND TODD SAXTON

"Nobody ever got fired for buying IBM." This old adage sums up the advantage large established firms have in securing customers and sustaining their business. As a prototypical institution, IBM epitomizes the established organization that through longevity, size, and reputation is beyond reproach. New firms, in contrast, are status-challenged. They have no history, little name recognition, an unknown brand, and a lack of established resources to leverage. So how do new firms go about establishing legitimacy and securing status to go from being an unknown to a viable, growing entity?

New ventures face intimidating odds in the development phase. New venture research consistently documents high venture failure rates, even approaching eighty percent (Baum, Locke, and Smith, 2001; Cooper, Dunkelberg, and Woo, 1988). Founders often struggle with scarce resources including time, human capital, the physical and strategic resources required to turn ideas into commercialized products, and financial capital to develop and launch the emerging enterprise (Acs and Audretsch, 2003).

Indeed, researchers have shown that new ventures suffer from a "liability of newness" (Aldrich and Auster, 1986; Bruderl and Schussler, 1990; Hannan and Freeman, 1989; Singh, Tucker, and House, 1986; Stinchcombe, 1965). The lack of an established reputation, limited legitimacy, and a paucity of external network resources are some of the major reasons why the liability of newness plagues these ventures. Internal resource constraints and lack of experience are also challenges associated with the liability of newness. Why, when, and how entrepreneurs overcome these barriers to successfully exploit opportunities are some of the central questions in entrepreneurship research (Acs and Audretsch, 2003; Venkataraman, 1997).

Over time, new ventures gain experience as they acquire resources to leverage, establish a position in the market, and build an organization. Engaging in a status-building process can help new ventures secure the resources they need to move from a founder with a product concept that is self-funded to a fully-fledged company with employees and paying customers supported by equity funding (e.g., angel or venture capital). More successful new ventures are able to build status with a variety of stakeholder groups by leveraging a wide variety of mechanisms. This chapter describes the evolution of new firms from unknown entities to viable businesses as a status-building process.

Theoretical background

Institutional theory attributes much of organizational and individual action and outcomes to the larger context in which all firms function (Heugens and Lander, 2009; Scott, 2001). The environment, as a socially constructed context, shapes the decisions and evolution of firms; economic theories that attribute organizational birth and growth to rational choices and venture resource configurations alone risk undersocializing the very complex and chaotic process of venture development (Granovetter, 1985). While the venture literature recognizes the liability of newness and lack of institutional legitimacy that entrepreneurs face, the interplay between social processes and status building in the broader environmental context has been underdeveloped in the literature.

In addition to the liability of newness, some researchers have suggested that new ventures will continue to experience the liability of adolescence even after emerging from the "entrepreneurial honeymoon" at their launch (Fichman and Levinthal, 1991). The resource-based view suggests that new ventures start with a stock of assets or resources that provide for survival through the early years, even in the face of disappointing outcomes. The initial funding, employee base, and set of relationships a founder establishes upon launch may carry the new enterprise through the turbulent early years, and in fact reduce the likelihood of failure for this initial honeymoon period. However, during the adolescent phase, the initial resource endowments from birth, including network relationships, initial employee base, capital investment, and other assets, can lead in two directions – success and growth, or failure. We argue that it is the social processes that accompany and help build further resources that separate the successful venture from the failure. The status gained through interaction with key stakeholders during the initial few years can help the adolescent firm continue on the path to success.

Before we delve into the status-building process of new ventures in more detail, we need to clearly define the terms we are discussing. Already in these introductory paragraphs, we have used the terms "status," "reputation," and "legitimacy" to describe intangible resources that new ventures build to ensure their success. It is helpful to consider these constructs on a continuum. At the very least, new ventures need to gain legitimacy. By legitimacy, we mean that these new ventures are recognized as abiding by well-accepted standards of behavior (King and Whetten, 2008). New ventures lack legitimacy due to their newness – it is unknown whether or not they will abide by these standards. So, at the very least, the status-building process for new ventures must create the legitimacy that allows them to continue to exist (Singh, Tucker, and House, 1986).

A positive reputation is a step higher than legitimacy, in that it accrues from being distinctively good at something. Reputable firms not only meet acceptable standards, but have also shown that they can be trusted to do something better than other firms (Deephouse and Carter, 2005; Rindova and Fombrun, 1999). A firm's reputation acts as a signal of the quality of the organization on a variety of dimensions (Jensen, Kim, and Kim, 2009; Podolny, 1993). Status building for new ventures helps them to build perceptions that they are in fact good at something notable, that is, that they do something notable in a high-quality manner. Establishing an initial reputation is a critical step in the evolution beyond legitimacy. Being seen as good at something is far more desirable than simply being acceptable.

Finally, status refers to "position or standing with reference to a particular grouping" (Pearce, Ramirez, and Branyiczki, 2001, p. 157). High status suggests that people or firms are deserving of respect, honor, and prestige. Being of high status means that others in a social grouping both recognize the positive reputation of the new venture and evaluate it as being honorworthy among other new ventures or other firms in the local geographic area. Status, then, is a higher-level signal than reputation, in that it implies how the venture as a whole can be distinguished from other organizations (Jensen, Kim, and Kim, 2009). Thus, there is a hierarchy whereby an emergent firm must establish legitimacy, earn a positive reputation, and ideally achieve a position of relatively high status within a group of other new and/or ongoing ventures.

Most researchers of new venture growth suggest a somewhat linear or iterative model of growth whereby firms start, accumulate resources, develop specific strategies, and grow sales, employees, and/or market share over time. Some researchers do recognize that the growth process can iterate through a number of stages (see Churchill and Lewis, 1983; Greiner, 1972) with reduction in size and/or failure a viable outcome at each stage. Thus, new ventures either get bigger as they get older or struggle to survive and eventually fail. As a result, new ventures are sometimes described as having an emergent phase whereby they are not yet "in business" but are transitioning from concept to viable commercial entities (Gartner and Carter, 2003). The key indicator of emerging as a viable commercial entity comes with an ongoing revenue stream (Churchill and Lewis, 1983). Prior to having an ongoing revenue stream, the venture is still figuring what products and services to offer, how to produce them in a high-quality manner, and how to offer them to the market.

We are addressing here the *de novo* independent venture; corporate ventures such as spin-offs may have some similar resource and evolutionary challenges, but face a different set of circumstances we do not address. Status-building initiatives in this emergent phase may make the difference between success and failure for new ventures. Since they do not already have a track record of achievement, they are dependent on having a wide variety of stakeholders believing that they have what it takes to emerge as a viable company. In the remainder of this chapter, we will discuss the stages that an emerging venture goes through, which stakeholders are critical to each stage, and how status building in each stage can increase the likelihood of the new venture's success.

Stages of growth for emerging ventures

For emerging ventures, we are focused on firm growth *from inception of the idea through the establishment of the viable enterprise and early growth*. Of course, this process can vary dramatically by industry; software firms, for example, may take only months to launch, while biotech firms require ten to fifteen years to navigate US Food and Drug Administration (FDA) regulations and testing.

Typically, though, this process may last from three to five years (Allen *et al.*, 2009).

The launching trajectories of ventures can be divided into stages as new ventures bring together the critical components of ideas, people, and funding. These emergent ventures progress through development stages via the co-evolution of the human, financial, and product components. Furthermore, different skills and combinations of tangible and intangible resources affect this progression. The individual founder may have a good idea and a credit card or second mortgage to fund early iterations of the venture; a founding team with a more fully developed plan and seed funding may require a different combination of assets to secure their first customer. For most of these emerging ventures, the evolutionary process has three components that need to grow simultaneously: the people involved, the product/service idea itself, and the money required to launch. The initial idea of one individual with limited associated funds typically progresses to a founding team and a more developed product or service concept with early stage or seed funding. Finally, for a business model or even a fully articulated business plan and venture funding, it is normally necessary to launch the product as a company with employees and legal status. These concentric rings of growth along these three dimensions are captured in Figure 7.1.

We offer a couple of venture exemplars to highlight the difficulty emerging ventures encounter in evolving all three sets of resources simultaneously, while trying to build their own status. These two prototypes are based on real ventures. The names and specifics of the situation have been slightly changed to protect the identity of the ventures and founders:

> *Example 1: Aptus.* The core idea for Aptus was developed by a consultant in the outplacement service industry. He identified an opportunity created by the convergence of broadband internet access and digital video capture combined with high recruitment costs and inefficiencies in the typical face-to-face interview process. He connected with an information technology (IT) professional with entrepreneurial experience to further develop the product idea. They spent six months to a year developing the software to create video resumes that could be quickly uploaded, downloaded, and stored. Then, they added an accountant and

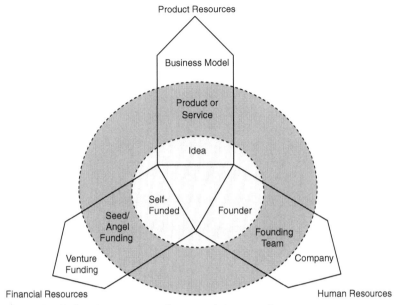

Figure 7.1 Balancing resources for growth in emerging ventures

business consultant with experience in business development and strategic alliance formation to the founding team. Over the next two years, the team invested $50,000 of their own money, undertook significant market research, developed a business plan, and built a prototype kiosk as the key node in capturing digital video of job candidates. Based on early promise, Aptus secured office space at a reduced cost in a local business incubator. Aptus wanted to work with a retail copy store where job seekers traditionally have gone to reproduce their resumes. Aptus struggled to engage in discussions with any regional or national chain because the venture was too new and untested. Likewise, none of the principals were well known on their own. Instead, Aptus began looking for an angel investor who would also be the CEO and help accomplish these goals. It found an ideal partner with the right credentials and funding. Unfortunately, he decided to join a different venture that had more customer proof of concept and a higher status founding team. Since that time, Aptus has foundered and been unable to raise funds or secure customers to achieve commercial viability. Despite establishing initial legitimacy, Aptus was unable to build a distinctive reputation, secure customers, and achieve status in the venture world.

Example 2: QuickMine. QuickMine was started by two software developers who already had significant experience with well-known software companies. Like Aptus, they identified a service gap in the market and engineered a way to allow online retailers to more quickly and insightfully mine their existing customer behavior data. Given their experience and knowledge, they were able to develop a marketable service in approximately six months. At that time, they needed additional funding to develop value-added features to their basic product offering and sell their services to customers. They connected with a local serial entrepreneur who was also an angel investor. This entrepreneur/ investor had high status in the technology sector and local venture community given his prior and current success. He not only funded QuickMine, but also brought them a CEO with significant sales experience in their target market. Within two months, QuickMine secured its first three customers – customers whose revenue stream would allow them to actually complete their product/service development plans. Thus, the legitimacy and status of the QuickMine founders, combined with the status of their major investor, gave them access to the human and financial resources that enabled the successful development of their service to a fully-fledged venture in less than one year from the initial idea.

These two vignettes were chosen to demonstrate the difference that legitimacy, reputation, and status can make as emergent ventures co-develop the three sets of resources they need to succeed. This co-development task is indeed a difficult one, where the relative emphasis between human, product/service, and financial resources constantly shifts and changes as emergent ventures move through different stages of growth. So, we need to look at the stages of growth for emergent firms in more detail. As Figure 7.2 highlights, emergent ventures typically move through key steps or stages on their way to becoming viable, ongoing ventures. While other researchers have recognized larger, more holistic stages like existence, survival, success, etc. (Churchill and Lewis, 1983), we further explain the process to show that within existence there are several stages that today's

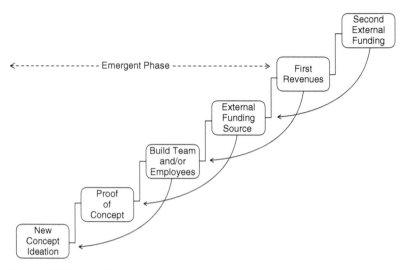

Figure 7.2 Stages of venture growth

emergent ventures must move through. These stages are akin to the stage-gate product development process (Cooper, 1983, 1990) and incorporate the ideas of punctuated equilibrium (Gersick, 1991); that is, emergent firms iterate through periods of upheaval as they approach one of the stage-gates. But, once through a specific stage-gate, relative stability follows as the emergent venture again marshals resources on its way to the next stage. Of course, with emergent ventures, the periods of upheaval and stability can occur over a period of months rather than years, as the QuickMine example above demonstrates.

We suggest that the status-building process of emergent ventures must vary by the stage of growth because different sets of resources are critical to successfully moving through each stage. These different sets of resources naturally call for a focus on different sets of stakeholders and social processes. As we have described before, an emergent venture often starts with a single founder who has an idea that he or she can self-fund, the first-level concentric circle shown in Figure 7.1. This founder's first task is to understand the market need for this product/service idea – is there an unmet need? Who needs it? What are they willing to pay? How big is this market? The focus in this stage is primarily external and in the product/service arena as the founder tries to determine what product/service to offer and where the revenues in the business model can be generated. Here, the founder needs to prove that his or her concept has market potential and can generate income. Accomplishing "proof of concept" legitimizes that the new venture indeed has a marketable idea that has the possibility of generating revenue.

Once the product/service idea has an established "proof of concept," the founder's focus shifts to creating and developing the actual product/service offering itself. Now, the focus shifts internally to building the team that can create and consistently deliver this product/service offering. With a product/service offering and founding team to create it in place, the focus once again shifts outward to funding the development effort and beginning selling. A legitimate product/service helps a new venture attract the people and funds that will allow it to fully develop this market offering. For the typical emergent venture, it takes the combination of a well-honed product/service offering, the team, and/or employees to deliver that product/service offering and the financial resources to pay for this development to garner the first customer. We should note that the growth of emergent ventures is not always linear and, in fact, some emergent ventures will skip a stage but cycle back through it later. Some will even pass through a stage and still not be successful, such that they drop back and repeat a stage two or more times. Still, most emergent ventures that become ongoing viable ventures have amassed all three sets of resources in a somewhat concurrent manner.

Mapping the status-building process on the three stages as we have done in Figure 7.3, we see the emerging venture initially struggle with legitimacy. Once it has achieved a baseline of legitimacy with the founder, product idea, and self-financing, the venture must begin to establish a reputation for something differentiable. Finally, as the business model is refined, the founding team solidified, and the funding secured, the venture begins to achieve high status as a viable commercial entity. In each stage, the stakeholder of importance varies, such that social processes and feedback focus on different elements of the underlying three resources. Still, in order to emerge as a viable entity, new ventures must gain legitimacy and status across all three resource elements in a relatively simultaneous fashion. It would be a mistake for a new venture to spend too much time perfecting its product/service offering through internal development without at least some legitimization from outside customers. Moreover, gaining high status in one dimension can play a helpful role in building reputation

Figure 7.3 New venture development as a status-building process

and status in the other dimensions. In particular, high-status funding can often be an attractive draw for potential employees – people are willing to risk investing their time in a venture that other successful people have invested in. Likewise, gaining the commitment of high-status customers signals that the venture is worthy of time and/or monetary investments. In the subsequent sections, we will describe the stakeholders and their respective roles as the venture strives for status. Successful founders must balance the external relationships and social processes with internal resource building for the venture to progress through these stages.

Stakeholders and mechanisms for building status

While the emergent venture's internal focus may be on product, funding, and the initial human resources or founding team, the external relationships for each component are no less important. A successful product or service does not exist independently of a customer or user; funding does not happen without investors; and founders do not build teams without interacting with external constituents who may or may not choose to "climb on board" with the new venture. Each stakeholder may look for different cues for legitimacy, reputation, and then status as the venture evolves. However, these judgments are not independent – in the absence of an established reputation, stakeholders may look for a variety of physical markers such as directory listings, awards, and grants (Singh, Tucker, and House, 1986), behavioral cues such as the founder's experience and business plan presentations, and relational cues such as a network of advisors and investors (Elsbach and Kramer, 2003) to assess the fledgling firm.

Establishing legitimacy. The first task of a founder must be to overcome the liability of newness and lack of legitimacy with potential constituents (Baum and Oliver, 1991). Until some baseline of social acceptability is earned, the venture will be unable to accrue the resources necessary to launch (Dowling and Pfeffer, 1975; Lin, Yang, and Arya, 2009). With customers, the initial question will revolve around the product concept itself – does the product address a recognized need? Does the founder understand the market's "point of pain" and offer a solution? Founder experience in the industry will help on both fronts – it enables the founder to "speak the language" of the customer and position the product in the appropriate social context for the customer to understand. Founder experience has strong empirical support as a predictor of venture survival and success (Lyles, Saxton, and Watson, 2004; Zacharakis and Meyer, 2000) as well as venture funding by venture capital firms (Zhang *et al.*, 2008). To many of these stakeholders, the founder's experience is the only real signal of his or her credibility and competence. At this stage, there may be no tangible product offering. Thus, the founder's credibility, as implied by his or her experience and industry knowledge, are even more important in customers' initial assessments.

While customers may focus on the product in assessing the initial legitimacy of the venture, potential investors and other advocates for the venture will be more concerned with the founder's history, the possible viability of the business model, and the network of relationships of the founder. This primarily involves a social judgment process – without a history of financial performance and established business model, these stakeholders are likely to categorize the founder as having legitimacy or not based on behavioral and physical cues displayed in meetings and pitch sessions (Elsbach and Kramer, 2003). Empirical research has established occupational status, venture experience, and personal skills as key drivers of this initial assessment (Byrne, 2000; MacMillan, Zemann, and Subbanarasimha, 1987; Zacharakis and Meyer, 2000; Zhang *et al.*, 2008). In addition, the perceived quality of business plan presentations is a predictor of investor funding (Chen, Yao, and Kotha, 2009; Kirsch, Goldfarb, and Gera, 2009). The founder at this point is not necessarily looking for money or employees, but the ability to interact with members of the venture community and establish legitimacy will be necessary for building a network of advocates (Saxton and Saxton, 2009) to help secure these resources in subsequent stages of development. In our exemplar firms, both Aptus and QuickMine were able to establish initial legitimacy by virtue of their familiarity with the market and technology, and apparent innovation in an emerging market space.

Building a reputation. As the venture moves into stage two, the firm must begin to build a reputation that further establishes the venture as viable and allows the founder to secure additional resources to grow. As a valuable intangible resource (Hall, 1992), a positive reputation must precede or at least coincide with the accumulation of tangible assets that allow the venture to launch. Reputation is a multi-dimensional construct (Fryxell and Wang, 1994; Saxton, 1997). Dimensions often include product, management, and financial soundness (Dollinger, Golden, and Saxton, 1997; Saxton, 1997), factors that nicely parallel our venture evolution model with product, founding team, and funding aspects. However, the emergent venture has no basis of past interaction or performance on which to base its reputation. It is in uncertain circumstances like this that reputation has significant value as a proxy for quality and expected behavior (Milgrom and Roberts, 1986).

The salience of specific dimensions of reputation may vary depending on the stakeholder. Customers, for example, will look for specific evidence that the product or service meets expectations and delivers on the promise suggested by the founder in initial discussions. During this stage, ventures will often establish close working relationships with their first or initial customers to decrease the uncertainty associated with a new product. Meeting milestones in development and continuing to refine the technology to establish "proof of concept" with a working prototype is the best way to begin to establish a reputation with the market and move from simple legitimacy to a positive reputation. Patents may also serve as additional validation that the venture's ideas are original and worthy of a positive reputation (Podolny, Stuart, and Hannan, 1996).

Investors, meanwhile, are unlikely to see (or expect) financial performance in the form of profit or returns in this stage – and even the viability of the business model remains in question until broader market acceptance is established. But the early customer reaction and relationship can serve as a proxy for market potential – thus, investors will look for positive signaling from the initial customer to validate the potential of the firm's initial market position. Research has shown that grant funding at this stage can also serve as an external stamp of approval and signal of a venture's emerging reputation (Elston and Audretsch, 2009). Likewise, reputation-building initiatives like forming advisory boards and seeking awards of recognition help to establish the venture's distinctiveness, even if they do not generate financial capital (Singh, Tucker, and House, 1986).

Investors and potential additional members of the founding team will also look for other external signals of venture reputation at this stage. While they may rely on their own counsel in the first stage to determine legitimacy of a venture, as the relationship develops and they approach commitment of resources (time or money), these stakeholders will seek reassurance from trusted others in their network. These stakeholders will engage in additional exploration and information sharing with the founder and others to verify or refute the initial legitimacy and emerging reputation of the emerging enterprise. Investors, for example, often form consortia (such as angel networks) or jointly explore investment in ventures at this stage, to help reduce the risk and gain broader reputational assessment from colleagues. In combination, securing a close customer relationship, validation by investment partners, and other external cues such as grants, patents, and even being listed in directories and forming an advisory board (Singh, Tucker, and House, 1986) help the emergent venture establish a reputation or "buzz" that serves as a platform to proceed to the next stage of growth.

For our exemplar firms, Aptus was unable to move from legitimacy to building a reputation. Though investors showed some initial interest, the additional cues that confer a positive reputation – patents, grants, and particularly a close customer relationship – did not materialize, and the venture stalled. QuickMine, meanwhile, was able to find a lead investor and leverage that into the additional funding

interest, which enabled it to quickly build a viable service model and
initial customer enthusiasm. These ingredients helped QuickMine
land a CEO and establish a reputation with the local venture community as a start-up to watch.

Achieving status. If a venture is able to clear the initial hurdles of
legitimacy and reputation building, the next step is converting hopes
and expectations into the resources that ensure viability. At this stage,
the founder must be able to translate his or her initial customer relationships and business model into a business plan that attracts investment, but more importantly serves as a communication vehicle that
translates a positive reputation into high status with key stakeholders.
Now, it is not merely enough to signal that the venture has the possibility of success. Instead, potential investors, employees, and customers have options to choose from. Deciding to invest/work for/buy
from one venture explicitly means not investing/working for/buying
from another organization. Achieving high status may provide the
momentum that allows investors/employees/customers to move from
consideration to commitment. These social actors naturally want to
align themselves with the venture they perceive has the best chance
for success. High status distinguishes a venture as the one most likely
to succeed. Stage three also involves moving from informal or arm's-
length agreements with stakeholders to more formal sales agreements (customers), employment contracts (founding team and initial
employees), and term sheets (investors) that codify relationships and
formalize expectations.

While reaching stage three is certainly not a guarantee of success,
the step function achieved by securing paying customers, a full-time
workforce, and investment is transformational. Customers will look
for assurance that the prototype product can be replicated reliably
and that the venture has a team capable of not only producing but
also servicing a stream of products. Employees will look for enough
financial stability to "make the leap" of working for a start-up –
though it may additionally take some equity in pay to encourage
early organization members to enter the uncertain world of a recently
established venture. Investors will look for the business plan and performance according to key milestones as an ongoing demonstration of
the founding team's ability to deliver on expectations – and hopefully
demonstrate a handsome return on investment as their reward. If the
venture is able to meet the objectives of these respective stakeholders,

it will be well on its way to achieving high status in the venture community. The accomplishment of goals and objectives is a signal that the venture is deserving of respect.

Order effects. One of the interesting elements to note in the progression above is how the "leading stakeholder" can and must shift in the evolution of the venture. Without the early interest in the product/service by a customer, it is virtually impossible for the founder to establish a reputation with investors. But the ability of the founder to convince the customer of its long-term ability to deliver reliable quality and quantity will be hard to establish without outside investment and an employee base. In each phase, the leading stakeholder may vary, but the venture will not be able to advance through all stages to high status without progress on all three dimensions.

Discussion and conclusion

It is interesting to note how many organizations have recently created awards to help signal the status of new ventures both nationally and regionally. *Inc.* magazine publishes an annual list of the fastest growing firms nationally. Organizations like the Edward Lowe Foundation have started state-based programs to identify the fifty "Companies to Watch"[SM] – their argument being that small firms have difficulty gaining the attention they deserve as they struggle to survive. Finally, city-based periodicals and organizations (for example, the *Indianapolis Business Journal* and TechPoint) also conduct annual awards to help identify young companies that are fast-growing, technology innovators, or notable in some other dimension. Most of these awards note that their goal is to help firms gain recognition for the resources that they have created. Apparently, these advocacy organizations realize just how difficult it is for new ventures to progress from legitimacy to high status.

Anecdotally, ventures tend to see a snowball effect among these various signals of high status. Once a firm is recognized as one of these award winners, they tend to see the number of resumes from potential employees increase. Rather than being seen as a small firm that is too risky to work for, these award winners are seen as up-and-coming organizations where there is a high potential payoff for "getting in on the ground floor." Frequently, these award winners try to maximize the value of their awards by displaying them prominently at their facilities, noting them in marketing materials, and frequently raising awareness of their high status conversationally. Further, it is not unusual to see a new venture win multiple awards in a fairly short period of time – once they have been recognized for their distinctiveness, it is easier for others to see this distinctiveness. Often, they even pursue these awards to accelerate their accomplishment of a high-status position.

At the beginning of this chapter, we suggested that emerging ventures are status-challenged. They are relative unknowns that must engage in the process of establishing legitimacy, building a reputation, and obtaining the status that makes them a viable firm customers want to engage with, employees want to work for, and investors seek to fund. Status building for emergent ventures leads to the accumulation of intangible resources that will help them overcome the liability of newness that can hamper their survival. Further, we suggest that status building is a hierarchical process whereby legitimacy is needed first, followed by a positive reputation, and ultimately the status that makes a new venture desirable to stakeholders. While legitimacy allows a venture to continue to survive, high status more broadly signals that this venture has a high likelihood of success. Most investors, employees, and customers want to align themselves with the firms they perceive as having the highest likelihood of success. So, high status signals that the venture is worthy of an investment.

However, building status is not a linear, straightforward process. Rather, emergent ventures cycle through a number of growth stages whereby the most critical stakeholders vary over time. We suggest that emergent ventures must balance an internal and an external focus as they accumulate resources across three dimensions simultaneously – the product/service offering, human resources, and financial capital. Interestingly, most ventures spend more time on internal coordination, although research has shown that establishing external legitimacy is an important predictor of survival (Singh, Tucker, and House, 1986). These three types of resources are linked to three different stakeholders: customers, employees, and investors. We suggest that there is an interactive relationship in building status across these stakeholders. Early legitimization by customers helps to build a positive reputation and establish status with employees and investors. Likewise, a perception of high status from investors helps attract employees. Thus, the status-building process for emergent ventures is complex, requiring both an internal and external focus, across multiple stakeholders that is both interactive across stakeholders and iterative over time.

In terms of research, the implications of this perspective suggest that the entrepreneurship literature needs to better reconcile the economic and social processes that shape venture creation. Studies need to examine not only the strategies and resources associated with success, but also the social processes that enable the founder to progress through "Death Valley." Such research questions call for longitudinal and hybrid study designs that follow firms over time with both qualitative and quantitative elements. Researchers could, for example, collect perceptual measures from key stakeholders as the venture evolves about the viability of the fledgling firm. It would be interesting to see how the resources developed as the firm moves through stages of evolution both follow and in turn enable further relationships and support. Such relationships are rarely captured in archival records, so fieldwork in this arena would be necessary. It might be possible, however, to capture key pieces of this evolution through experiments with qualified respondents; for example, a panel of venture capitalists could rate a series of ventures using a conjoint design to compare effects of varying levels of status and reputation on the willingness to invest or provide referrals.

For founders, our ideas suggest that entrepreneurs need to focus as much on external legitimacy and establishing a reputation with key stakeholders as on the product, technology, and business plan that guides internal resource development and deployment. Finally, from a teaching perspective, our chapter does call into question the model of teaching tomorrow's entrepreneurs strictly by classroom learning with a focus on business plan development. By treating the venture-creation process as endogenous, we are undertraining our students in the critical social processes that interactively and iteratively shape the successful venture through exchanges with stakeholders.

In summary, our chapter highlights the social elements of venture evolution, with a focus on venture creation as a status-building process. As the venture evolves, it must establish legitimacy, build a reputation, and achieve high status in order to secure resources for growth. Understanding entrepreneurial processes in this way has significant implications for research, the practice of venture creation, and teaching in the entrepreneurship domain.

Deephouse, D. L. and Carter, S. M. 2005. "An examination of differences between organizational legitimacy and organizational reputation." *Journal of Management Studies* 42(2): 329–360.

Dollinger, M. J., Golden, P. A., and Saxton, T. 1997. "The effect of reputation on the decision to joint venture." *Strategic Management Journal* 18: 127–140.

Dowling, J. and Pfeffer, J. 1975. "Organisational legitimacy: Social values and organisational behavior." *Pacific Sociological Review* 18: 122–136.

Elsbach, K. D. and Kramer, R. M. 2003. "Assessing creativity in Hollywood pitch meetings: Evidence for a dual-process model of creativity judgments." *Academy of Management Journal* 46(3): 283–301.

Elston, J. A. and Audretsch, D. B. 2009. "Financing entrepreneurship: Using experimental data on risk attitudes." Presented at the 2009 Annual Max Planck Institute Ringberg Conference on Entrepreneurship, Tegernsee, Germany.

Fichman, M. and Levinthal, D. A. 1991. "Honeymoons and the liability of adolescence: A new perspective on duration dependence in social and organizational relationships." *Academy of Management Review* 16: 442–468.

Fryxell, G. and Wang, J. 1994. "The Fortune corporate 'reputation' index: Reputation for what?" *Journal of Management* 20: 1–14.

Gartner, W. B. and Carter, N. M. 2003. "Entrepreneurial behavior and firm organizing processes," in Z. J. Acs and D. B. Audretsch (eds.), *Handbook of Entrepreneurship Research: An Interdisciplinary Survey and Introduction.* New York: Springer, pp. 195–222.

Gersick, C. 1991. "Revolutionary change theories: A multilevel exploration of the punctuated equilibrium paradigm." *Academy of Management Review* 16: 10–36.

Granovetter, M. 1985. "Economic action and social structure: The problem of embeddedness." *American Journal of Sociology* 91: 481–510.

Greiner, L. E. 1972. "Evolution and revolution as organizations grow." *Harvard Business Review* 50: 37–46.

Hall, R. 1992. "The strategic analysis of intangible resources." *Strategic Management Journal* 13: 135–144.

Hannan, M. T. and Freeman, J. 1989. "Structural inertia and organizational change." *American Sociological Review* 49: 149–164.

Heugens, P. P. M. A. R. and Lander, M. W. 2009. "Structure! Agency! (and other quarrels): A meta-analysis of institutional theories of organization." *Academy of Management Journal* 52: 61–85.

Jensen, M., Kim B. K., and Kim, H. 2009. "The importance of status in markets: A market identity perspective." Working Paper, University of Michigan.

King, B. G. and Whetten, D. A. 2008. "Rethinking the relationship between reputation and legitimacy: A social actor conceptualization." *Corporate Reputation Review* 11: 192–207.

Kirsch, D., Goldfarb, B., and Gera, A. 2009. "Form or substance: The role of business plans in venture capital decision making." *Strategic Management Journal* 30: 487–515.

Lin, Z., Yang, H., and Arya, B. 2009. "Alliance partners and firm performance: Resource complementarity and status association." *Strategic Management Journal* 30: 921–940.

Lyles, M. A., Saxton, T., and Watson, K. 2004. "Venture survival in a transitional economy." *Journal of Management* 30: 351–375.

MacMillan, I. C., Zemann, L., and Subbanarasimha, P. 1987. "Criteria distinguishing successful ventures in the venture screening process." *Journal of Business Venturing* 2: 123–137.

Milgrom, P. and Roberts, J. 1986. "Relying on the information of interested parties." *Rand Journal of Economics* 17: 18–32.

Pearce, J. L., Ramirez, R. R., and Branyiczki, I. 2001. "Leadership and the pursuit of status: Effects of globalization and economic transformation," in W. S. Mobley and M. McCall (eds.), *Advances in Global Leadership*, Vol. II. Greenwich, CT: JAI Press, pp. 153–178.

Podolony, J. M. 1993. "A status-based model of market competition." *American Journal of Sociology* 98: 829–872.

Podolny, J. M., Stuart, T. E., and Hannan, M. T. 1996. "Networks, knowledge, and niches: Competition in the worldwide semiconductor industry, 1984–1991." *American Journal of Sociology* 102: 659–689.

Rindova, V. P. and Fombrun, C. J. 1999. "Constructing competitive advantage: The role of firm-constituent interactions." *Strategic Management Journal* 20: 691–710.

Saxton, T. 1997. "The effects of partner and relationship characteristics on alliance outcomes." *Academy of Management Journal* 40: 443–461.

Saxton, T. and Saxton, M. K. 2009. "Staying on the path to launch: Factors that encourage venture advocate behaviors." Presented at Babson College Entrepreneurship Research Conference, Boston.

Scott, W. R. 2001. *Institutions and Organizations*, 2nd edn. Thousand Oaks, CA: Sage.

Singh, J. V., Tucker, D. J., and House, R. J. 1986. "Organizational legitimacy and the liability of newness." *Administrative Science Quarterly* 31: 171–193.

Stinchcombe, A. 1965. "Social structure and organizations," in J. March (ed.), *Handbook of Organizations*. Chicago: Rand McNally, pp. 142–193.

Venkataraman, S. 1997. "The distinctive domain of entrepreneurship research: An editor's perspective," in J. Katz and J. Brockhaus (eds.), *Advances in Entrepreneurship, Firm Emergence, and Growth.* Greenwich, CT: JAI Press.

Zacharakis, A. L. and Meyer, G. D. 2000. "The potential of actuarial decision models: Can they improve the venture capital investment decision?" *Journal of Business Venturing* 15: 323–346.

Zhang, J., Souitaris, V., Soh, P., and Wong, P. 2008. "A contingent model of network utilization in early financing of technology ventures." *Entrepreneurship: Theory & Practice* 32: 593–613.

PART IV

When ascriptive status trumps achieved status in teams

8 Status cues and expertise assessment in groups: How group members size one another up ... and why it matters

J. STUART BUNDERSON AND
MICHELLE A. BARTON

As contemporary organizations increasingly rely on task groups to perform complex, knowledge-intensive work, the ability of these groups to effectively leverage the knowledge and expertise of individual members has become ever more important. It is almost invariably the case that groups operating in real-world task environments will be composed of members who differ in the task-relevant knowledge and expertise that they bring to the group. These differences typically correlate with differences in education, experience, training, or natural ability, and can emerge naturally or as the result of intentional design decisions that place individuals with greater expertise in groups with less-expert individuals. Yet, regardless of the origin of expertise differences, a key challenge facing groups with expertise diversity is to ensure that members know who their more expert teammates are so that superior expertise is leveraged in decision making and problem solving. A growing body of research evidence suggests that task groups perform better when members are able to accurately identify and then defer to their more expert members (Bunderson, 2003a; Bottger, 1984; Libby, Trotman, and Zimmer, 1987; Littlepage et al., 1995; Littlepage, Robison, and Reddington, 1997; Stewart and Stasser, 1995).

However, the research evidence also suggests that the identification of member expertise is not a simple or straightforward problem (Miner, 1984; Littlepage et al., 1995; Littlepage and Mueller, 1997; Littlepage, Robison, and Reddington, 1997; Trotman, Yetton, and Zimmer, 1983). Expertise is not a visible or observable characteristic. As a result, group members must rely on those characteristics that are visible and observable in drawing inferences about the relative expertise of group members. But these manifest characteristics are not equally valid (i.e., accurate) or reliable (i.e., consistent and dependable) as indicators of actual expertise differences. Consequently, groups can, and often do, make attribution errors by deferring to members who "seem" like they should be experts but are not, or by overlooking members who do possess valuable expertise but do not give that impression. The result is squandered human capital and underperforming groups.

In order to understand, and ultimately manage, this group dynamic, we need a better understanding of the different cues that individuals rely on in assessing relative expertise in groups and the conditions under which they are likely to rely on cues that are more reliable and/or valid. Past research in several areas has laid a foundation for pursuing this understanding, although we lack an integrative conceptual framework. Our goal in this chapter is to outline such a framework. We begin with the observation that expertise recognition and utilization in groups is fundamentally a status-organizing process (Bunderson, 2003a). We then draw on and extend the rich literature in status characteristics theory (e.g., Berger *et al.*, 1977) to propose a typology of the "expert status cues" that drive expertise and status attributions in interdependent task groups, status cues that differ in their reliability and validity. We then identify specific factors in the group setting that can help to explain why and under what conditions group members might be more likely to rely on certain types of cues more than others. Our discussion concludes with some directions for future research on expertise, status, and influence in groups.

Expertise, status, and expert status cues

Expertise assessment as status organizing

Our analysis is grounded in the observation that expertise assessment in groups is fundamentally a status-organizing process (Bunderson, 2003a); that is, expertise assessment within a group is concerned with assigning each member to a position within the intra-group status hierarchy such that those members who are seen as more competent have higher status (i.e., higher prestige and esteem) and those members who are seen as less competent have lower status. Once developed, this status hierarchy plays a critical and pervasive role in group interaction by suggesting that the opinions, suggestions, and contributions of some members should be more actively solicited and more heavily weighted than those of others. Patterns of participation, deference, and influence in groups are therefore a direct function of the intra-group status hierarchies that result from expertise assessment (Berger, Cohen, and Zelditch, 1972; Berger *et al.*, 1977; Balkwell, 1991; Driskell and Mullen, 1990).

This is, in a nutshell, the motivating premise of status characteristics theory. Status characteristics theory builds on the notion that in interdependent task groups, where members have a shared and vested interest in accomplishing some collective task, hierarchies of participation and influence will be based on shared expectations of each member's ability to contribute to the accomplishment of that collective task, i.e., on expectations of relative member competence and expertise. Therefore, in order to understand which members of a group will have more influence over collective decisions and actions, we need to understand how groups form these expectations for relative member expertise. Status characteristics theory proposes that because expertise is a latent characteristic and therefore not directly observable, group members form these expectations by drawing inferences about relative expertise based on a consideration of those manifest member characteristics they have come to associate with expertise differences. How these associations develop and inform status perceptions and deference behavior within groups is therefore the principal agenda of status characteristics theory (see Balkwell, 1994; Berger, Cohen, and Zelditch, 1972; Berger *et al.*, 1977; Berger, Rosenholtz, and Zelditch, 1980; Ridgeway, 2001).

Member characteristics that have become associated with presumed expertise differences are referred to as status characteristics or *status cues*. Status characteristics theory articulates two conceptual categories of status cues: specific and diffuse (Hembroff and Myers, 1984; Humphreys and Berger, 1981). Specific status cues are characteristics that group members have come to associate with competence and expertise within a specific task domain, e.g., task experience or advanced task certifications. Diffuse status cues, in contrast, are characteristics that group members have come to associate with general capability and aptitude across a range of task domains including, but not limited to, the domain of tasks performed by the group. Examples might include age, gender, or physical attractiveness.

Empirical research in the status characteristics tradition has generated an impressive ability to predict intra-group status and influence based on a consideration of specific and diffuse status cues. Results suggest that members do consult both specific and diffuse status cues in assessing one another's ability to contribute to a group, that these assessments tend to converge within a group, and that members combine information from multiple cues in forming these assessments (Berger *et al.*, 1977; Bunderson, 2003a; Cohen and Zhou, 1991). In combining cues, individuals consider all status-relevant information, including both positively and negatively valued status cues, although additional pieces of consistent information have attenuated effects (Berger *et al.*, 1992). Moreover, expectations of member ability or expertise strongly mediate the relationship between status cues and opportunities for involvement and influence in interdependent task groups (Balkwell, 1991; Berger, Cohen, and Zelditch, 1972; Berger *et al.*, 1977; Bunderson, 2003a; Driskell and Mullen, 1990).

A typology of expert status cues

We build on the theoretical foundation provided by status characteristics theory to propose an integrative typology of the different status cues that members draw on in assessing relative member competence and assigning relative member status. Our typology results from recognizing two separate dimensions along which status cues can be differentiated. Our first dimension is the well-established distinction between *specific* and *diffuse* status cues described above. Our second dimension highlights an important distinction between member *attributes* (i.e., characteristics that can be described using demographic indicators such as age, race, educational background, experience, etc.) and member *behaviors* (i.e., observable actions taken by members during task interaction such as language, assertiveness, task confidence, etc.) as sources of information about relative expertise and status. Past research clearly suggests that group members consult both attributes and behaviors in assessing status and expertise and, moreover, that behavioral cues are evaluated differently from member attributes (Bottger, 1984; Rashotte and Smith-Lovin, 1997; Ridgeway, Berger, and Smith, 1985; Tiedens, 2001).

The combination of these two dimensions results in a typology that includes four distinct categories of expert status cues: diffuse attributes, diffuse behaviors, specific attributes, and specific behaviors (see Figure 8.1). Diffuse attributes include social category cues such as race and gender, physiognomic cues such as height and physical

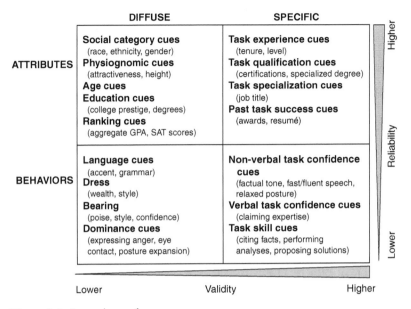

Figure 8.1 A typology of expert status cues

attractiveness, age cues, education cues, and ranking cues such as general test scores. Diffuse behaviors include language cues such as accent and grammar, dress and bearing cues that indicate wealth, class, and confidence, and dominance cues such as expressing anger or eye contact. Specific attributes include task experience and qualification cues such as tenure, level, and certification, task specialization cues such as job title, and past task success cues such as awards and formal recognition. Finally, specific behaviors include behavioral cues that demonstrate skill and/or confidence with the task. These might include non-verbal cues such as a factual tone or relaxed posture, verbal cues such as actual expertise claims, or behavioral cues such as citing facts, performing analyses, or proposing solutions.

We would expect, and past research would confirm (as noted above), that member differences within each of the four categories described in Figure 8.1 can predict attributions of expertise and status in groups. Nevertheless, we would also expect that these four categories differ in the validity and reliability of the expertise-related information they provide. So, for example, specific cues should be more *valid* indicators of actual expertise on a group's tasks than diffuse cues, since specific cues are more proximal indicators of expertise within a group's actual task domain (Humphreys and Berger, 1981; Dovidio *et al.*, 1988; Hembroff and Myers, 1984). Diffuse cues tend to be grounded in broad stereotypes about the superiority of particular social categories and social institutions, as well as in questionable assumptions about the extent to which general ability predicts specific task performance.

Moreover, we expect that attributes will be more *reliable* indicators of member expertise than behaviors. In measurement theory, the reliability of a measure is a function of its consistency and dependability in signaling some latent construct (Carmines and Zeller, 1979). We would expect that member behaviors will be less consistent and dependable indicators of actual differences in member expertise than member attributes for at least two reasons. First, behaviors are more susceptible to conscious impression management – i.e., attempts to appear knowledgeable, capable, and competent – than are attributes. So, whereas one can fake task confidence, it is harder to fake years of experience or a specialized degree. Second, even without conscious impression management, behavioral status cues may only be loosely coupled with actual member expertise. It is not always the case, for example, that the most confident and assertive group member actually possesses the greatest expertise. Moreover, even actual demonstrations of task skill can be unreliable since one cannot be certain that demonstrated ability is generalizable and replicable. As an example, the novice musician who has truly mastered one piece may be difficult to distinguish from the accomplished musician based on the performance of that one piece. Knowledge of years of musical training and experience, however, provide a more reliable basis for drawing generalizations about musical virtuosity.

In summary, we would suggest that expert status cues differ in their validity and reliability. It follows that assessments of expertise that are based on more valid and reliable status cues should correspond more closely to actual levels of expertise. And since opportunities for participation and influence within a group are significantly predicted by these expert status assessments (as noted above), reliance on more valid and reliable cues increases the likelihood that those members who possess superior competence are able to influence the behavior and decisions of the group. This should result in better-informed decisions and fewer missteps as groups benefit from the expertise of their members. In short, we would expect that groups will perform better to the extent that they rely on more valid and reliable cues in assessing relative member expertise (see Bunderson, 2003a):

Proposition 1: Groups will perform better when assessments of relative member expertise are based on more valid and reliable status cues.

When do different status cues matter?

The above proposition implies that we need a better understanding of when and why group members will rely on more versus less valid and reliable status cues in assessing relative member expertise so that we can understand when and whether groups are able to leverage the expertise of their members. But perhaps the more fundamental question is why group members do not always rely on valid and reliable cues given that reliance on less diagnostic cues has real performance implications. We suggest that the answer to this question hinges on the fact that status cues can vary in *salience*. The concept of salience is central within status characteristics theory (Balkwell, 1994; Berger, Cohen, and Zelditch, 1972; Humphreys and Berger, 1981). A given status cue will be more salient when group members a) truly differ on the characteristic in question, b) are aware of their differences on the characteristic in question, and c) associate differences on the characteristic in question with expertise differences. When any one of these three conditions is not met, a given status cue will have no bearing on relative expertise assessments within a group.

In this section, we consider the effect of cue salience on expertise assessment in groups. We begin by considering the status cues that will matter more under conditions of equal salience. We then move to a consideration of group factors that can affect the salience of different status cues.

Under conditions of equal salience

The case of equally salient status cues is the prototypical case under consideration within status characteristics theory; that is, status characteristics theory begins with a given set of equally salient cues and proceeds to theorize about the extent to which these different cues will factor into the status assessments that take place within a group.

As a result, we know quite a bit about status assessments under conditions of equal salience.

Past research has suggested, for example, that specific cues will be more heavily weighted than diffuse cues. Status characteristics theory would argue that the "path of task relevance" (Berger *et al.*, 1977) is longer for a diffuse status cue since diffuse cues are more distally related to actual task competence. So, whereas a specific status cue like task experience can be presumed to be associated directly with task competence, a diffuse status cue like gender is presumed to be associated with aptitude in some general skill domain (e.g., analytic reasoning) which is then presumed to predict performance on tasks that require related skills (e.g., engineering). As a result, when specific and diffuse status cues are equally salient, specific status cues will "take precedence" (Dovidio *et al.*, 1988, p. 234) over diffuse status cues in shaping assessments of relative competence and status. In the words of Hembroff and Myers (1984, p. 337), "differentiating characteristics explicitly relevant to the task will produce greater differentiation between actors ... than will characteristics not explicitly relevant." Past research has strongly supported this basic assertion for both attributes (e.g., Humphreys and Berger, 1981; Bunderson, 2003a) and behaviors (Ridgeway, 1987). We can therefore be fairly confident in the following proposition:

Proposition 2: Under conditions of equal salience, expert status will be more strongly determined by differences in specific cues than by differences in diffuse cues.

Moreover, there is also evidence to suggest that expert status is more strongly and reliably determined by salient member attributes than by salient member behaviors. For example, Ridgeway, Johnson, and Diekema (1994) found that dominance behaviors from a group member with a status-disadvantaged attribute (female gender) were viewed as less legitimate than the same behaviors from a group member with an advantaged attribute (male gender) (see also Bianchi and Lancianese, 2007; Rashotte and Smith-Lovin, 1997; Thomas-Hunt and Phillips, 2004). Moreover, Ridgeway, Berger, and Smith (1985) found that differences in the display of behavioral status cues (specifically, verbal latency and initial gaze) were a direct function of the status advantage created by differences in member attributes (gender). In other words, differences in member attributes – even diffuse attributes (Rashotte and Smith-Lovin, 1997; Ridgeway, Berger, and Smith, 1985) – appear to anchor status expectations in groups and constrain the range of status-relevant behavior that will be accepted as legitimate (Lovaglia and Houser, 1996). Therefore, when both attributes and behaviors are salient in a group setting, we would expect that attributes would have a stronger effect on expert status assessments than behaviors, regardless of whether those attributes are specific or diffuse. Stated formally:

Proposition 3: Under conditions of equal salience, expert status will be more strongly determined by differences in member attributes than by differences in member behaviors, regardless of whether those attributes are specific or diffuse.

Together, Propositions 2 and 3 suggest that in assessing expert status under conditions of equal salience, groups will rely most on specific attributes (high validity and reliability), then on diffuse attributes (high reliability, low validity), then on specific behaviors (high validity, low reliability), and finally on diffuse behaviors (low validity and reliability). In other words, groups will rely first on more valid and reliable cues and, if those cues are not available, will favor reliability over validity (i.e., diffuse attributes over specific behaviors). This is perhaps not surprising since a given indicator cannot be accepted as valid if it is not first accepted as reliable. This hierarchy of cue importance sets the stage for the following discussion of expert status assessment under conditions of unequal salience.

Under conditions of unequal salience

As noted above, a given status cue will be salient within a particular group setting when all three of the following conditions are met: a) members truly differ on the characteristic in question, b) members are aware of their differences on the characteristic in question, and c) members associate differences on the characteristic in question with expertise differences. In this section, we explore factors within a group setting that can affect these three conditions and thereby influence the extent to which a given set of status cues will have a bearing on expert status assessments within a group. We focus specifically on the following five factors: group diversity, group tenure, task novelty, face-to-face interaction, and motivation to be accurate.

Group diversity. The argument for a relationship between group diversity and expert status assessments is straightforward and follows naturally from the above definition of cue salience. Specifically, if a cue is salient only when members truly differ on the characteristic in question, it follows that a particular status cue or category of status cues will become irrelevant for expert status assessments in more homogeneous groups. In forming assessments of relative expertise, members will therefore default to the next category on which there are meaningful differences across members according to the hierarchy of cue importance described above. So, in a group where all members are encountering a particular task for the first time, there will likely be no meaningful differences across members in specific attributes like experience or certifications. We would therefore expect that members will rely first on diffuse attributes like age or gender in forming expertise assessments. So, for example, in a team of first-year medical students tasked with diagnosing a complex case for which they have no real experience, members might initially defer to the oldest member, to members with more prestigious undergraduate degrees, or to male members. If, however, members are homogeneous (or essentially homogeneous) on diffuse attributes, they would then turn to specific behaviors (e.g., if members of the medical student team were the same age, all male, and had similar undergraduate backgrounds, they might then defer to the member who spoke up most forcefully). Stated formally:

Proposition 4: When group members are more homogeneous on a particular category of status cue, that category becomes less relevant in determining expert status and members will turn to the next category on which meaningful differences exist (according to the hierarchy of importance implied by Propositions 2 and 3).

One implication of the above proposition is that researchers attempting to examine the importance of a particular category of status cue (e.g., demography, behavioral dominance, etc.) for status and influence in groups should consider whether members are homogeneous on cues that rank higher in importance. So, for example, the effects of gender on status and influence will be more clearly and unambiguously evident in groups where members have equivalent levels of task experience (e.g., on completely novel or artificial tasks). At the same time, we should be careful not to assume that patterns observed in groups that are homogeneous on higher-order status cues will replicate in more diverse groups. So, for example, behavioral status cues are likely to be more predictive of status and influence in studies involving undergraduate students (having a low diversity in some diffuse attributes like age) performing artificial tasks (having a low diversity in specific attributes) than they would be in groups with greater demographic and experiential diversity.

Group tenure. In comparison with specific status cues, diffuse status cues have an "observability" advantage; that is, differences in age, race, gender, dress, and bearing become apparent and can therefore begin to shape expert status assessments from the very first moments of interaction (McCann *et al.*, 1985). In contrast, specific status cues (and especially specific behaviors) become more apparent once members have the opportunity to interact around the group's task, to observe one another's behavior, and to explore and compare one another's task-relevant experience and credentials. As a result, we would expect that initial expectations about expert status will be more heavily based on a consideration of diffuse status cues and that these expectations will only be revised and updated once group members have had the opportunity to work together.

Past research supports this expectation. For example, in a study of manufacturing teams, Bunderson (2003a) found that specific status cues (i.e., technical certification and industry experience) mattered more and diffuse status cues (i.e., gender and ethnicity) mattered less as group tenure increased. However, it took at least ten months before expert status assessments were more strongly determined by specific status cues rather than diffuse status cues in his sample. In a study of dyads, Hembroff and Myers (1984) found that task-relevant cues became more important in determining status and influence over time, whereas non-task-relevant cues became less important. Moreover, a number of studies support the notion that expertise assessments become more accurate over time (Hollenbeck *et al.*, 1995; Liang, Moreland, and Argote, 1995; Littlepage, Robison, and Reddington, 1997). The following proposition therefore seems reasonable:

Proposition 5: Diffuse cues will more strongly determine expert status in the early stages of group interaction and specific cues in later stages.

Task novelty. When the tasks performed by a group are familiar or well established, group members are likely to have clear and agreed-upon criteria for what a task expert "looks like," i.e., what sort of experience they have, what credentials they have, how they behave in relation to the task, etc. Some of these criteria may have been imported from broader institutions (e.g., occupations, educational institutions, etc.) whereas others may be organization- or even group-specific. But regardless of their origin, shared expectations regarding the characteristics of task experts make it possible for group members to size one another up quickly and efficiently based on a focused consideration of task-relevant (i.e., specific) status cues.

When a group encounters novel or unfamiliar tasks, however, it is no longer clear what expertise on that task looks like or, consequently, what an expert on that task should look like. In other words, there are no agreed-upon specific status cues for a novel or unfamiliar task since shared expectations about task-relevant cues have not been developed. As a result, we would expect that in such cases, group members will default to diffuse status cues in assessing expert status, since diffuse status cues are at least presumed to indicate general aptitude and ability. For example, while it is clear that a team should defer to its Product X marketing people for advice about how to expand Product X into new markets, it is not at all clear that those individuals will have the most relevant expertise when it comes to introducing a completely new product in a different market. As a result, the team may instead defer to members with longer overall tenure, an MBA degree from a top university, or experience at a prestigious consulting firm. Stated formally:

Proposition 6: Diffuse cues will more strongly determine expert status for novel or unfamiliar tasks than will specific cues.

Face-to-face interaction. In contemporary organizations, members of the same work team do not always interact face-to-face. Members of distributed work teams, virtual work teams, and asynchronous teaming arrangements, for example, may seldom if ever coordinate their efforts through face-to-face interaction, relying instead on information and communication technologies such as email or voicemail (Malhotra, Majchrzak, and Rosen, 2007; Schiller and Mandviwalla, 2007). As a result, the range of status cues that members of these non-traditional work teams are able to carefully and consistently consult in forming expert status judgments will tend to be less varied. Specifically, we would expect that many of the behavioral cues described in Figure 8.1 are unlikely to be readily observable in most electronically mediated interactions. Consequently, members will be forced to rely instead on bios, resumés, and demographic profiles – data sources that communicate information about member attributes (both specific and diffuse) rather than member behaviors. In other words, we would expect that where face-to-face interaction is limited, expert status judgments will tend to rely more heavily on member attributes than on member behaviors:

Proposition 7: Behaviors will be weaker determinants of expert status than attributes in groups where there are fewer opportunities for face-to-face member interaction.

Motivation to be accurate. Finally, we would suggest that the status cues that group members rely on in assessing expertise will be influenced by the extent to which members are motivated to be accurate in their assessments. Past research on social cognition clearly suggests that human beings are not mechanical processors of social information but, rather, are purposeful and goal-directed as they sift through the complexity of social information they encounter (Fiske and Taylor, 1991). Moreover, goals and motivation will affect the extent to which an individual is effortful and discriminating in forming impressions of others (Neuberg and Fiske, 1987; Swann, 1984). So, for example, we know that individuals are more careful and discriminating in forming perceptions of another person when they are dependent on that person for valued outcomes (Berscheid *et al.*, 1976; Erber and Fiske, 1984; Fiske and Taylor, 1991). We also know that individuals are more careful in assessing another person when they know that they will be held accountable for the consequences of their assessments (Fiske and Taylor, 1991; Lerner and Tetlock, 1999). However, when careful assessment of another person has no bearing on one's goals and interests, individuals are content to rely on superficial or stereotyped attributions.

We made the point earlier that diffuse status cues are more easily and readily observable than specific status cues. Diffuse status cues involve physical characteristics that are immediately visible and are typically associated with widely held stereotypes. In contrast, specific status cues may not be visible or immediately apparent. As a result, some degree of investigation and focused observation may be required to ascertain the specific status cues of one's fellow group members and to appreciate how members compare on those cues. In other words, more effort is required to assess expert status from specific status cues than from diffuse status cues. It follows that group members who lack the motivation to be accurate in their assessments of relative expertise will be content to rely on diffuse status cues rather than exert the effort necessary to draw more valid inferences (see Neuberg and Fiske, 1987). So, for example, we would expect that a team of salespeople who are compensated based on their individual performance will have less motivation to be careful and discriminating in evaluating the expertise of other team members than will a team of production employees whose collective output requires interdependent contributions from each member. We therefore propose the following:

Proposition 8: As their motivation to be accurate increases, group members will rely more heavily on specific status cues and less heavily on diffuse status cues in assessing expert status.

Implications and directions for future research

Our analysis advances understanding of expertise recognition and utilization in groups in several ways. First, we propose an integrative typology of expert status cues to help focus and organize discussions of the member characteristics that signal expert status in groups, something that has been lacking in past research on expert status assessment in groups. Our typology highlights the fact that member characteristics differ in their reliability and validity as indicators of expert status. Second, we draw from past work on status and influence in groups to develop propositions about the relative importance of the different categories in our typology for expertise assessment under conditions of equal salience. Third, we elaborate the idea that status cues can differ in salience based on characteristics of a group and we identify specific group characteristics that can affect cue salience. In short, our analysis provides a more systematic framework for evaluating the cues that group members rely on in assessing expert status and for understanding when they will rely on more versus fewer reliable cues.

What, then, do we learn from this analysis about the extent to which groups are able to consistently and accurately identify their more expert members? In a nutshell, the above analysis underscores the fact that human information processors are intendedly but boundedly rational. When status cues are equally salient, we expect that group members will seek to base expert status on more valid and reliable cues. However, in the complexity of group life, where member differences on expertise-relevant cues are not always existent, apparent, or recognized as relevant, group members will often default to less valid and reliable cues. This is particularly likely in groups where members are homogeneous on task-relevant cues, have been together a short period of time, are engaged in novel or unfamiliar tasks, lack the motivation to be accurate, or lack the opportunity to observe task-relevant cues. In other words, we suggest that there are a variety of commonly occurring group situations under which those members with the most relevant expertise will go unrecognized and unleveraged.

Boundary conditions of the theory

It is important to be clear about the conceptual boundaries within which we expect the theoretical arguments advanced in this chapter to hold. Specifically, our theory is explicitly positioned within the context of interdependent task groups where all group members have a shared and vested interest in accomplishing some collective task. This boundary condition is fundamental to our theory because it leads to three important implications. First, it implies that group members have a clear and present interest in identifying their more expert members and deferring to those experts in decision making and problem solving, since doing so improves the likelihood that the group will achieve goals valued by all members. Second, it implies that shared perceptions of member expertise will form the basis for status within the group (Berger, Cohen, and Zelditch, 1972; Berger *et al.*, 1977). Third, it implies that some degree of coordination is required in order for members to achieve their goals and therefore that group members must communicate and interact.

In other words, the theory developed here assumes that members are motivated by an interest in collective task accomplishment. However, this is not to suggest that altruistic members with a purely collective motivation are a necessary precondition for our theory. Status striving is a fundamental human motivation and we would

References

Acs, Z. and Audretsch, D. 2003. *Handbook of Entrepreneurship Research: An Interdisciplinary Survey and Introduction.* New York: Springer.

2003. "Innovation, market structure and firm size." *Review of Economics and Statistics* 71: 567–574.

Aldrich, H. and Auster, E. R. 1986. "Even dwarfs started small: Liabilities of age and size and their strategic implications." *Research in Organizational Behaviour* 8: 165–198.

Allen, M., Davis, J., Saxton, M. K., and Saxton, T. 2009. "In search of a meaningful classification scheme: Towards a typology of 'small' and 'new' firms." Working Paper, Indiana University.

Baum, J. R., Locke, E. A., and Smith, K. G. 2001. "A multidimensional model of venture growth." *Academy of Management Journal* 44: 292–303.

Baum, J., and Oliver, C. 1991. "Institutional linkages and organizational mortality." *Administrative Science Quarterly* 36: 187–218.

Bromiley, P. and Flemming, L. 2002. "The resource-based view of strategy: A behaviorist critique," in M. Augier and J. G. March (eds.), *The Economics of Choice, Change and Organization: Essays in Honour of Richard M. Cyert.* Cheltenham: Edward Elgar.

Bruderl, J. and Schussler, R. 1990. "Organizational mortality: The liabilities of newness and adolescence." *Administrative Science Quarterly* 35: 530–547.

Byrne, J. A. 2000. "How a VC does it; Bob Davoli is a hands-on investor, and so far he hasn't picked a loser. Can he keep it up?" *BusinessWeek* (July 24): 96.

Chen, X. P., Yao, X., and Kotha, S. 2009. "Entrepreneur passion and preparedness in business plan presentation: A persuasion analysis of venture capitalists' funding decisions." *Academy of Management Journal* 52: 199–214.

Churchill, N. C. and Lewis, V. L. 1983. "The five stages of small business growth." *Harvard Business Review* (May–June): 30–50.

Cooper, A. C., Dunkelberg, W. C., and Woo, C. Y. 1988. "Survival and failure: A longitudinal study," in B. A. Kirchoff, W. A. Long, W. E. McMullen, K. H. Vesper, and W. E. Wetzel Jr. (eds.), *Frontiers of Entrepreneurship Research.* Wellesley, MA: Babson College, pp. 225–237.

Cooper, R. G. 1983. "The new product process: An empirically-based classification scheme." *R&D Management* 13: 1–14.

1990. "Stage-gate systems: A new tool for managing new products." *Business Horizons*, 33, 44–53.

therefore expect that group members who have an interest in achieving collective goals are also seeking to enhance their intra-group status whenever possible. Nevertheless, past research clearly suggests that in interdependent groups with a shared goal, attempts to gain status without legitimate expertise will be unsuccessful and, in fact, will be sanctioned. As a result, group members tend to have a very accurate sense of where they stand in the intra-group status hierarchy and typically avoid acting in status-inconsistent ways (Anderson *et al.*, 2006; Anderson, Ames, and Gosling, 2008). Research also suggests that group members who are perceived to be competent achieve higher status when they are also perceived to have a group-oriented motivation (Ridgeway, 1982; Keltner *et al.*, 2008; De Waal, 1998). In other words, the evidence suggests that in interdependent task groups, attempts to enhance one's status will be bounded by the demonstration of both superior competence (evident through status cues) and a group-oriented motivation.

Questions for future research

Our analysis of expertise and status in groups raised a number of important questions that we could not adequately address in this chapter but that represent promising directions for future research. This section articulates those questions and offers some suggestions for pursuing them.

Expert status in multi-disciplinary teams. Our theory assumes that groups seek to identify their more and less expert group members in terms of a specific task. But in many groups, members specialize in different expertise domains and therefore have different and perhaps even non-overlapping areas of expertise. Examples include cross-functional teams, multi-disciplinary teams, and many management teams. In such teams, the question of who are the more and less expert group members becomes more complicated, since the answer may depend on which domain of expertise is in question. On the one hand, such teams may have multiple expert status hierarchies, each with its own set of status cues that signal expertise within that domain. On the other hand, we know from past research that even in teams of task specialists, some team members are seen as better able to help the team achieve its broader goals, either because their specialized expertise is assumed to be particularly critical or because they possess "meta-expertise" that is ultimately a more important basis for intra-group status in multi-disciplinary teams (see Bunderson, 2003b). Sorting out how groups assign expert status in teams of task specialists therefore presents one very interesting and important direction for future research. Elsbach's chapter (Chapter 11 in this volume) begins to address a related set of conflicts.

Expert status and formal authority. The theoretical arguments advanced in this chapter are principally concerned with understanding *expert* status in groups. However, it is important to note that status and influence in groups may also be based on other influences, most prominently, formal authority. In other words, whereas our theory focuses on bottom-up processes of status emergence, status and influence in groups can also be based on the top-down assignment of group members to positions of formal authority. And since the top-down assignment of formal authority may not always align with the bottom-up assignment of expert status, it is possible that individuals who occupy a higher position in the intra-group influence hierarchy will occupy a lower position in the expert status hierarchy. The resulting tension between status based on formal authority and status based on perceived expertise has important and far-reaching implications for both our understanding of status and influence in groups, as well as for our understanding of group functioning and effectiveness. An examination of the relationship between formal authority and expert status is therefore another promising direction for future research.

In exploring this relationship, it is important to acknowledge that authority and expertise are not always at odds with one another and, perhaps more importantly, are often assumed to be aligned. For example, Bunderson (2003a) found that formal authority (a team coordinator role) in a sample of manufacturing teams was associated with perceptions of expertise even after accounting for the effects of specific and diffuse status cues. Moreover, Humphrey (1985) found that subjects who were aware that they had been randomly assigned to a clerk role as opposed to a manager role in an organizational simulation nevertheless rated managers as more competent than fellow clerks. Similarly, Sande, Ellard, and Ross (1986) found that subjects who were assigned to observe randomly assigned "supervisors" and "workers" rated supervisors as more competent even before any actual interaction had taken place. In other words, formal authority appears to serve as a specific status cue in groups such that individuals in positions of formal authority are perceived to be more expert, regardless of whether that authority is viewed as legitimate.

Task expert status versus relational expert status. Our arguments build on the implicit assumption that expert status in groups is primarily a function of technical expertise – information and knowledge related to the technical performance of a task. However, it is also possible that a group member could be viewed as an expert not in terms of technical task expertise but, rather, in terms of helping a group work together efficiently and effectively. This "relational expertise" can also play a critical role in facilitating task performance apart from task expertise. And yet, we would expect that the cues that members associate with relational expertise are different from the cues they associate with task expertise. Moreover, it is not clear whether or under what conditions members do pay attention to relational expertise or how they weigh the importance of relational expertise relative to task expertise. An investigation of the predictors of relational expert status and the effects of relational expert status on intra-group influence apart from or in combination with task expert status therefore represents another important direction for future research on expertise and status in groups.

Status inconsistency and subsets combining. Our theory did not explicitly address the situation in which a given group member has inconsistent status cues, e.g., some characteristics that would indicate high expert status and others that would indicate low expert status. Nevertheless, the question of how group members resolve status inconsistencies has received considerable attention within the status characteristics research tradition. A study by Berger *et al.* (1992) compared different theories of how individuals resolve these inconsistencies and found that only a "subsets combining principle" was supported by their data. The subsets combining principle posits that in resolving inconsistent status information, individuals first aggregate all positively and all negatively valued status information, with each additional piece of sign-consistent information having an additional but attenuated effect. The final status assessment then simply subtracts negatively valued expectations from positively valued expectations.

The idea that perceivers group related information into subsets before combining that information helps to address the question of status inconsistency. At the same time, it raises questions about whether there might be analogous grouping that occurs as perceivers evaluate information across the categories described in Figure 8.1. So, for example, could it be that perceivers consider behavioral information separately from information garnered from member attributes? Consider, for example, the highly experienced and award-winning scientist (positively valued attributes) who is socially awkward and therefore comes across as tentative or uncertain (negatively valued behaviors). It may be that in cases such as this, *attributes* are considered as a group and then compared against *behaviors* (which would receive a lower weight given our earlier arguments). An exploration of this possibility and of the broader question of whether information from different categories is considered as a group represents yet another promising direction for future research.

Implications for the management of groups

The theoretical framework presented in this chapter suggests a number of actions that might be taken by managers or team leaders to increase the probability that expert status assessments in groups will be based on more valid and reliable cues. For example, leaving teams together for longer periods of time rather than shuffling team membership should increase reliance on more valid and reliable cues. Measures that increase the motivation of team members to be accurate in their expertise assessments should also increase reliance on valid and reliable cues. These measures might include increasing task and outcome interdependence through shared incentives and task redesign or decentralizing decision-making authority so that each member feels more accountable and more interdependent (Bunderson, 2003a). And interventions designed to disseminate information about member background, experience, and achievements or to allow members to observe one another's actual task performance should also increase reliance on more valid and reliable cues. By increasing reliance on valid and reliable cues, these measures should, in turn, increase the likelihood that those members with greater levels of task expertise will have higher status within the group and therefore a greater opportunity to influence team decisions and actions in ways that contribute to superior task performance.

References

Anderson, C., Ames, D. R., and Gosling, S. D. 2008. "Punishing hubris: The perils of overestimating one's status in a group." *Personality and Social Psychology Bulletin* 34: 90–101.

Anderson, C., Srivastava, S., Beer, J., Spataro, S., and Chatman, J. 2006. "Knowing your place: Self-perceptions of status in face-to-face groups." *Journal of Personality and Social Psychology* 91: 1094–1110.

Balkwell, J. W. 1991. "From expectations to behavior: An improved postulate for expectation states theory." *American Sociological Review* 56: 355–369.

1994. "Status," in M. Foschi and E. J. Lawler (eds.), *Group Processes: Sociological Analyses*. Chicago: Nelson-Hall, pp. 119–148.

Berger, J., Cohen, B. P., and Zelditch, M., Jr. 1972. "Status characteristics and social interaction." *American Sociological Review* 37: 241–255.

Berger, J., Fisek, M. H., Norman, R. Z., and Zelditch, M., Jr. 1977. *Status Characteristics and Social Interaction: An Expectation-States Approach*. New York: Elsevier.

Berger, J., Norman, R. Z., Balkwell, J. W., and Smith, R. F. 1992. "Status inconsistency in task situations: A test of four status processing principles." *American Sociological Review* 57: 843–855.

Berger, J., Rosenholtz, S. J., and Zelditch, M., Jr. 1980. "Status organizing processes." *Annual Review of Sociology* 6: 479–508.

Berscheid, E., Graziano, W., Monson, T., and Dermer, M. 1976. "Outcome dependency: Attention, attribution, and attraction." *Journal of Personality and Social Psychology* 34: 978–989.

Bianchi, A. J. and Lancianese, D. A. 2007. "Accentuate the positive: Positive sentiments find status in task groups." *Social Psychology Quarterly* 70: 7–26.

Bottger, P. 1984. "Expertise and air time as bases of actual and perceived influence in problem-solving groups." *Journal of Applied Psychology* 69: 214–221.

Bunderson, J. S. 2003a. "Recognizing and utilizing expertise in work groups: A status characteristics perspective." *Administrative Science Quarterly* 48: 557–591.

2003b. "Team member functional background and involvement in management teams: Direct effects and the moderating role of power centralization." *Academy of Management Journal* 46: 458–474.

Carmines, E. G. and Zeller, R. A. 1979. *Reliability and Validity Assessment*. Beverly Hills, CA: Sage.

Cohen, B. P. and Zhou, X. 1991. "Status processes in enduring work groups." *American Sociological Review* 56: 179–188.

De Waal, F. B. M. 1998. *Chimpanzee Politics: Power and Sex Among Apes*. Baltimore: Johns Hopkins University Press.

Dovidio, J. F., Ellyson, S. L., Keating, C. F., Heltman, K., and Brown, C. E. 1988. "The relationship of social power to visual displays of dominance between men and women." *Journal of Personality and Social Psychology* 54: 233–242.

Driskell, J. E. and Mullen, B. 1990. "Status, expectations, and behavior: A meta-analytic review and test of the theory." *Personality and Social Psychology Bulletin* 16: 541–553.

Erber, R. and Fiske, S. T. 1984. "Outcome dependency and attention to inconsistent information." *Journal of Personality and Social Psychology* 47: 709–726.

Fiske, S. T. and Taylor, S. E. 1991. *Social Cognition*. New York: McGraw-Hill.

Hembroff, L. A. and Myers, D. E. 1984. "Status characteristics: Degrees of task relevance and decision processes." *Social Psychology Quarterly* 47: 337–346.

Hollenbeck, J. R., Ilgen, D. R., Sego, D. J., Hedlund, J., Major, D. A., and Philips, J. 1995. "Multilevel theory of team decision making: Decision performance in teams incorporating distributed expertise." *Journal of Applied Psychology* 80: 292–316.

Humphreys, P. and Berger, J. 1981. "Theoretical consequences of the status characteristics formulation." *American Journal of Sociology*, 86: 953–983.

Humphrey, R. 1985. "How work roles influence perception: Structural-cognitive processes and organizational behavior." *American Sociological Review* 50: 242–252.

Keltner, D., Van Kleef, G. A., Chen, S., and Kraus, M. W. 2008. "A reciprocal influence model of social power: Emerging principles and lines of inquiry." *Advances in Experimental Social Psychology* 40: 151–192.

Lerner, J. S. and Tetlock, P. E. 1999. "Accounting for the effects of accountability." *Psychological Bulletin* 125: 255–275.

Liang, D. W., Moreland, R. L., and Argote, L. 1995. "Group versus individual training and group performance: The mediating role of transactive memory." *Personality and Social Psychology Bulletin* 21: 384–393.

Libby, R., Trotman, K. T., and Zimmer, I. 1987. "Member variation, recognition of expertise, and group performance." *Journal of Applied Psychology* 72: 81–87.

Littlepage, G. E. and Mueller, A. L. 1997. "Recognition and utilization of expertise in problem-solving groups: Expert characteristics and behavior." *Group Dynamics: Theory, Research, and Practice* 1: 324–328.

Littlepage, G., Robison, W., and Reddington, K. 1997. "Effects of task experience and group experience on group performance, member ability, and recognition of expertise." *Organizational Behavior and Human Decision Processes* 69: 133–147.

Littlepage, G. E., Schmidt, G. W., Whisler, E. W., and Frost, A. G. 1995. "An input-process-output analysis of influence and performance in problem-solving groups." *Journal of Personality and Social Psychology* 69: 877–889.

Lovaglia, M. J. and Houser, J. A. 1996. "Emotional reactions and status in groups." *American Sociological Review* 61: 867–883.

Malhotra, A., Majchrzak, A., and Rosen, B. 2007. "Leading virtual teams." *Academy of Management Perspectives* 21: 60–70.

McCann, C. D., Tyner, L. K., Ostrom, T. M., and Mitchell, M. L. 1985. "Person perception in heterogeneous groups." *Journal of Personality and Social Psychology* 49: 1449–1459.

Miner, C. F. 1984. "Group versus individual decision making: An investigation of performance measures, decision strategies, and process losses/gains." *Organizational Behavior and Human Performance* 33: 112–124.

Neuberg, S. L. and Fiske, S. T. 1987. "Motivational influences on impression-formation: Outcome dependency, accuracy-driven attention, and individuating processes." *Journal of Personality and Social Psychology* 53: 431–444.

Rashotte, L. S. and Smith-Lovin, L. 1997. "Who benefits from being bold: The interactive effects of task cues and status characteristics on influence in mock jury groups," in B. Markovsky, M. J. Lovaglia, and L. Troyer (eds.), *Advances in Group Processes*, Vol. XIV. New York: Elsevier Science/JAI Press, pp. 235–255.

Ridgeway, C. L. 1982. "Status in groups: The importance of motivation." *American Sociological Review* 47: 76–88.

1987. "Nonverbal behavior, dominance, and the basis of status in task groups." *American Sociological Review* 52: 683–694.

2001. "Social status and group structure," in M. A. Hogg and R. S. Tindale (eds.), *Blackwell Handbook of Social Psychology: Group Processes*. Malden, MA: Blackwell, pp. 352–375.

Ridgeway, C. L., Berger, J., and Smith, L. 1985. "Nonverbal cues and status: An expectation states approach." *American Journal of Sociology* 90: 955–978.

Ridgeway, C. L., Johnson, C., and Diekema, D. 1994. "External status, legitimacy, and compliance in male and female groups." *Social Forces* 72: 1051–1077.

Sande, G. N., Ellard, J. H., and Ross, M. 1986. "Effect of arbitrarily assigned status labels on self-perceptions and social perceptions: The mere position effect." *Journal of Personality and Social Psychology* 50: 684–689.

Schiller, S. Z. and Mandviwalla, M. 2007. "Virtual team research: An analysis of theory use and a framework for theory appropriation." *Small Group Research* 38: 12–59.

Stewart, D. D. and Stasser, G. 1995. "Expert role assignment and information sampling during collective recall and decision making." *Journal of Personality and Social Psychology* 69: 619–628.

Swann, W. B. 1984. "Quest for accuracy in person perception – a matter of pragmatics." *Psychological Review* 91: 457–477.

Thomas-Hunt, M. C. and Phillips, K. W. 2004. "When what you know is not enough: Expertise and gender dynamics in task groups." *Personality and Social Psychology Bulletin* 30: 1585–1598.

Tiedens, L. Z. 2001. "Anger and advancement versus sadness and subjugation: The effect of negative emotion expressions on social status conferral." *Journal of Personality and Social Psychology* 80: 86–94.

Trotman, K. T., Yetton, P. W., and Zimmer, I. R. 1983. "Individual and group judgments of internal control systems." *Journal of Accounting Research* 21: 286–292.

9 | The malleability of race in organizational teams: A theory of racial status activation

MELISSA C. THOMAS-HUNT
AND KATHERINE W. PHILLIPS

In recent years, the heightened centrality of teams to the work of organizations has highlighted the critical importance of effectively and efficiently leveraging the human capital which resides within these organizational entities. However, the misspecification and underutilization of talent within teams remains widespread (Olivera and Argote, 1999; Wittenbaum and Stasser, 1996). These challenges to team functioning seem to be even more prevalent when demographic diversity is present (Mannix and Neale, 2005; Williams and O'Reilly, 1998). However, the increasing interdependence of demographically distinct individuals in the workplace necessitates that attention be devoted to understanding the specific ways in which demographic diversity impacts the ability of teams to leverage that knowledge which is collectively possessed across members. Specifically, we consider the circumstances under which the race/ethnicity of team members creates expectations about their ability to contribute to a group and become socially integrated. We focus specifically on those demographically distinct team members who already possess an existing reputation of achievement.

Drawing upon recent work that acknowledges the role status hierarchies play in obscuring the expertise possessed by team members (Bunderson, 2003; Thomas-Hunt and Phillips, 2004; Wittenbaum, 2000), diversity scholars have begun to apply a status lens as they consider the impact of demographic diversity on team dynamics. Such conceptualizations of demographic diversity argue that demographic characteristics are differentially valued and afford different levels of status to individuals within a team's hierarchy (Sauer, Thomas-Hunt, and Morris, 2010). Status is the degree to which an individual or group is respected or admired by others (e.g., Ridgeway and Walker, 1995; Magee and Galinsky, 2008). Status tends to be derived from two types of characteristics: those that are ascribed and those that are achieved (Linton, 1936; Merton, 1968; Parsons, 1951).

Sometimes an individual has no control over his or her possessed characteristics (race, gender, family lineage, socioeconomic circumstances at birth, religion at birth, etc.). Status derived from such characteristics is said to be ascribed. Throughout the course of one's life, however, there are also opportunities to exert individual effort toward the acquisition of certain characteristics (education, occupation, income, etc.). The status derived from such characteristics is said to be achieved (Merton, 1968; Parsons, 1951). In reality, individuals within teams possess multiple characteristics that may conflict in terms of the status they afford. For example, one may possess low ascribed characteristics which may conflict with the status afforded by one's high achieved characteristics.

Despite the fact that the US is a country which ideologically embraces achieved status over ascribed status (Griffin and Kalleberg, 1981; Rosette and Thompson, 2005), achieved status is often interpreted within the context of one's ascribed status. One often hears "She is such an accomplished Asian American" or "We thought he would do so much more given his family background." Only recently have researchers systematically begun to consider the implications of the interaction of multiple status cues (e.g., gender, race, education, position in the organization) on individuals' interactions within teams and organizations (Phillips, Rothbard, and Dumas, 2009; Rosette, Leonardelli, and Phillips, 2008; Thomas-Hunt and Phillips, 2004; Sauer, Thomas-Hunt, and Morris, 2010). Whereas this burgeoning research begins to suggest that positive effects of achieved status are constrained by ascribed status, the emergence of some women and underrepresented racial/ethnic minorities, for example, at the helm of US corporations and governmental structures suggests that under some circumstances low ascribed status characteristics can be overcome by achieved status.

In keeping with the status in organizations theme of this volume, we consider status but take a step back from previous examinations of the impact of status on knowledge exchange and influence within teams. Instead, we attempt to identify the circumstances under which low ascribed status characteristics (i.e., race/ethnicity) overwhelm high achieved status characteristics and drive the status determinations made about individuals within team contexts. In particular, we consider the circumstances under which individuals with high achieved status have their race-based status (i.e., Asian, Latino, black) activated in heterogeneous groups and teams. When does race impact expectations of performance, influence, and likeability within the team? We argue that the race of demographically distinctive individuals is most likely to be activated and used as a status characteristic when the behaviors and associations of individuals are either (1) consistent with the societal stereotypes of their racial/ethnic category, or (2) when those individuals' behaviors deviate from that which has been established as normative behavior within the *work* groups in which they hold membership. It is important that we acknowledge the work of many social psychologists that find that racial stereotypes are easily activated (Bargh, Chen, and Burrows, 1996; Lepore and Brown, 1997; Gilbert and Hixon, 1991). We do not challenge their assertions but, instead, consider how stereotypes become associated with particular individuals within teams and drive the status expectations held about them.

We begin by providing a backdrop for our investigation by describing a particular work team context in which racial diversity exists and racial characteristics may or may not be used to guide expectations about team members. We then draw upon research on demographic diversity in teams to suggest what outcomes such a team might experience. Using a status lens we elucidate the impact that the race of team members might have in shaping expectations about individuals, and the subsequent ways in which their contributions are solicited, valued, and integrated in team processes. Next, we consider the conditions under which race gets activated as a dominant driver of their status, specifically considering the role of racially distinctive team members' exhibition of stereotype-consistent behaviors and associations. Throughout we constantly refer to our team context to provide a mechanism for considering the interplay between behaviors and racial status activation, and end with a set of propositions designed to predict the use of race as a driver of status in our specified team context.

A team context

We begin by considering the case of a six-person cross-functional team that has been assembled at a consumer foods company for the purpose of developing and launching a new low-calorie sports drink. Included in the team are representatives from product strategy, marketing, R&D, finance, production, and sales. Imagine that the team happens to be entirely composed of men and that the individuals from marketing and finance are quite accomplished. The two of them have been an integral part of a previous successful product development and launch team, making critical contributions from their respective well-respected functions. Furthermore, they have attended prestigious MBA programs and are generally considered to be team players by those with whom they have interacted at the company. Ideally, the expertise of each member of the team will be recognized and leveraged to maximize the success of the development and launch of the new low-calorie sports drink. However, research on knowledge exchange within teams suggests that even under these circumstances, realizing this team's potential output will be challenging. Now consider that the team has some limited racial diversity with two non-white members, each from different race/ethnic categories. In fact, imagine that it is the same accomplished team members from finance and marketing, respectively, that contribute this racial diversity with the finance member being black and the marketing member Asian American. It is quite likely that the racial diversity present has the potential to further complicate the team's interaction and ability to perform. We start by considering the potential challenges to this racially diverse team.

Key concepts and theoretical background

The challenge of demographic diversity

As organizations have come to expect that the use of demographically diverse teams can improve organizational effectiveness (McLeod, Lobel, and Cox, 1996), researchers have directed a considerable amount of attention toward understanding the effects of age, race, sex, and other types of diversity on team performance (see Mannix and Neale, 2005; Van Knippenberg and Schippers, 2007; and Williams and O'Reilly, 1998 for reviews). While there is evidence that diversity can generate positive team processes and outcomes (Cox, Lobel, and McLeod, 1991; Phillips, Northcraft, and Neale, 2006; Sommers, 2006), the broader conclusions drawn from this vast body of research reveal that, in general, demographic diversity in a work group often negatively affects group processes and performance. Specifically, Milliken and Martins (1996), in their review of the literature on the effects of diversity in organizational groups, concluded that demographic diversity negatively affects outcomes such as turnover and performance through its impact on affective, cognitive, communication, and symbolic processes. Tsui, Egan, and O'Reilly (1992) found that individuals working in racially diverse groups had lower levels of psychological commitment, less intent to stay, and higher levels of absence. Pelled, Eisenhardt, and Xin (1999) found that racial diversity heightened emotional conflict. More recently, Chatman and Flynn (2001) found that the greater the demographic heterogeneity within a group, the less that group norms emphasized cooperation among teams of MBA students and financial services business officers alike. Furthermore, within diverse teams, those team members who contribute to the diversity bear the brunt of its negative effects. Studies have revealed that individuals who are demographically different from the rest of their group members are less integrated into the social fabric of their team (Tsui, Egan, and O'Reilly, 1992), receive lower performance evaluations (Sackett and Dubois, 1991; Lefkowitz, 1994), and are viewed more negatively (Flynn, Chatman, and Spataro, 2001). Even those in leadership roles seem to be susceptible to the negative effects of being demographically distinct (Rosette, Leonardelli, and Phillips, 2008; Kirkman, Tesluk, and Rosen, 2004). From these investigations, diversity researchers have begun to conclude that, in large part, the anticipated benefits of demographic diversity have not been realized (Mannix and Neale, 2005). So, it is quite possible that our new product development team will exhibit fewer cooperative norms and lower levels of performance than a comparable but racially homogeneous team. Furthermore, the possibility exists that the finance and marketing professionals on the team who contribute the racial diversity may bear the brunt of its negative impact, but why?

Part of the difficulty in identifying the effects of demographic diversity in teams is a function of the many different types of diversity that coexist in teams and their potentially opposing and synergistic effects (Harrison and Klein, 2007). Perhaps the least well-understood dimension of demographic diversity is race/ethnicity. Despite growing investigation, the effects of race/ethnic diversity on team performance and processes still remain murky. In a recent examination of thirty-one studies in which the impact of race and ethnicity on team performance was measured, Joshi and Roh (2009) found that sixty-one percent yielded null results and the remainder was evenly divided with respect to whether performance was enhanced or diminished.

Stepping back from a singular focus on performance outcomes and answering Lawrence's (1997) call for greater specification of the mechanisms by which diversity impacts performance, researchers have attempted to gain a better understanding of the impact of racial diversity in teams by describing the mechanism by which race/ethnicity may impact team processes. Van Knippenberg, De Dreu, and Homan (2004) have suggested that race/ethnicity impact teams through categorization processes in which in-group and out-group distinctions breed conflict. This conflict in turn inhibits the elaboration processes needed to ensure the effective integration of team member knowledge. Moreover, when these conflicts arise, they undermine effective group process and make it difficult to effectively capitalize on the contributions of those who are truly most knowledgeable. Nevertheless, even those empirical investigations that have followed suit have failed to yield consistent results for race/ethnicity on categorization and elaboration processes (Joshi and Roh, 2009).

The demographic configuration of most workplaces and the sensitivity associated with investigations of race/ethnicity contribute to the inability of researchers to make concrete advances in knowledge in this arena. Furthermore, racial/ethnic diversity takes many forms and not all types of racial/ethnic diversity have the same impact (Leslie, 2009). Nevertheless, until recently, much of this work focused on categorization processes without considering the actual nature of the difference. Consequently, attempts to examine the effects of racial diversity broadly, without attention to the particular nuances associated with the different ways in which racial/ethnic groups are perceived, lead to conclusions that are at best ambiguous (O'Reilly, Williams, and Barsade, 1998). More recently, researchers of groups and teams have begun to draw from the long history of status research in sociology and consider the value associated with members' different characteristics (Bunderson, 2003; Sauer, Thomas-Hunt, and Morris, 2010; Thomas-Hunt and Phillips, 2004). This recognition has enabled researchers to consider the particular role that status hierarchies play in thwarting expertise identification and integration in teams (e.g., Bunderson, 2003; Thomas-Hunt and Phillips, 2004; see also Bunderson and Barton, Chapter 8, this volume).

Past research has suggested that status hierarchies may thwart the appropriate weighting given to team member contributions, facilitating the influence of those with higher status but less knowledge over those with more knowledge but lower status (Thomas-Hunt and Phillips, 2004). This has proven to be a fruitful approach for those interested in the impact of race/ethnicity in teams. However, what has become clear is that the impact of race/ethnic diversity in teams is complex. Rarely is race/ethnicity the only characteristic recognized by teams. It would be absurd to assume that established reputation and achieved status of the racially distinctive members in our new product team would have no impact. Nevertheless, it is plausible that despite the many characteristics that could signal that an individual should be afforded high status for their achievements, under some circumstances race may emerge as the dominant status cue, generate lower performance expectations (e.g., Cancio, Evans, and Maume, 1996; Ridgeway, 1987; Roberson and Block, 2001), and impact the way in which the group engages with racially distinct individuals.

The significance of race

November 2008 saw the election of the first black man to be President of the United States. This occurrence was heralded as a momentous event in which hard work and personal achievement triumphed over the diminished status historically associated with being black. Despite empirical evidence to the contrary, much of the ensuing discourse in the popular press posited that racial discrimination might be a phenomenon of the past. Nevertheless, in July 2009, nearly six months after the inauguration of Barack Obama, another highly accomplished black man, Henry Louis Gates, a Harvard University professor, distinguished scholar, and public intellectual, was questioned in his own home about his identity after a passer-by reported that two black males were breaking and entering. The facts of this interaction remain murky, yet an onslaught of discussion resulted, highlighting the continued controversy over whether achieved status can ever truly dominate the ascribed low status of being black. In one instance, racial status failed to supplant demonstrated competence and achievement, allowing a black man to rise to the highest elected office in the

US, and in another it delegitimized achievement and earned stature, and resulted in a demeaning and dubious arrest of an individual who had committed no apparent crime. These examples are simplified and reflect the experiences of two prominent individuals whose experiences are not exactly comparable. Nevertheless, one might ask "What is it about the combination of achieved status, ascribed status and individual actions that framed the status assessments in these situations and how do they generalize to more ordinary organizational contexts?" Might it be that race becomes activated as a status characteristic when the behaviors of individuals are consistent with the stereotypes held concerning their racial category?

What is clear is that such debates over the prevalence of race as a driver of status in the US are not solely limited to a focus on blacks. The recent Supreme Court nomination of Sonia Sotomayor and earlier appointments of Elaine Chao as Secretary of Labor under George W. Bush, and Norman Mineta as Secretary of Commerce under Bill Clinton and Secretary of Transportation under George W. Bush have also represented significant advances in the representation of high-ranking racial/ethnic minorities in the public sector. Nevertheless, there remains a backdrop of numerous examples of the underrepresentation of racial/ethnic minorities in upper echelon positions within federal agencies and the private sector (Corporate Board Initiative, 2006; Fortune, 2006; McCoy, 2007; The Alliance for Board Diversity, 2005; Thomas and Gabarro, 1999). Even in contexts where blacks regularly achieve, such as sports, the complication of race cannot be escaped. Tiger Woods, a world-renowned golfer, is a prime example of a very high achieved status individual. However, this achieved status did not protect him from being categorized as black when his promiscuous and adulterous behavior was revealed. Prior to these incidents, his ascribed status was touted as "caublasian" because of his mixed heritage. However, when his behaviors were revealed to be negative and in accordance with stereotypes of black male athletes, his "blackness" arguably became more prominent and he was characterized as black by many in the media and society. As a result of his behaviors he lost several endorsements, even though other prominent figures (including several prominent politicians) remained relatively unscathed in the face of similar adulterous actions. Whether race played a role in the downfall of Tiger Woods cannot be known for certain, but it is the case that under some circumstances race-based status does not thwart the advancement of accomplished individuals, whereas in others it does. In the following section we draw upon status characteristics theory to help elucidate the way in which race, an ascribed characteristic, along with achieved status markers interact to affect individuals' experiences within teams and the evaluations that are made of those individuals.

Status characteristics theory

In attempting to understand the factors that increase and diminish the salience of race as a status indicator within teams, we draw upon expectation states and status characteristics theories. Expectation states theory tells us that interacting task groups form power and prestige orders based on the performance expectations held of individual members (Berger and Fisek, 1970; Berger, Cohen, and Zelditch, 1972). Furthermore, status characteristics theory, which is an extension of expectation states theory, suggests that these performance expectations are initiated based on the societal status of group members' personal characteristics that, over time, have become associated with certain levels of perceived task competence (Berger *et al.*, 1985; Ridgeway and Erickson, 2000; Bunderson, 2003).

Within organizational groups, status characteristics have a large impact on interpersonal dynamics because individuals defer to those members for whom the highest performance expectations are held. Researchers have found that individuals who possess characteristics associated with lower status (e.g., women, racial/ethnic minorities) are given fewer opportunities to participate (Meeker and Weitzel-O'Neill, 1977) and experience a diminished ability to exert influence on other group members (Thomas-Hunt and Phillips, 2004). The increase in demographic diversity within organizations results in situations in which the same characteristics that make some individuals demographically distinct (i.e., gender, race) may also ascribe them lower status, so it is unclear whether the difference itself or the value associated with a particular difference drives the effects of being demographically distinctive.

Classic sociological researchers have divided status characteristics into two categories: those that are *achieved* and those that are *ascribed* (Merton, 1968; Parsons, 1951). A more recent distinction used by status characteristics theorists distinguishing *specific* status cues (i.e., relevant for the particular task being worked on) from *diffuse* cues (i.e., used more broadly as a cue in many contexts) (see, e.g., Ridgeway, 1987) can be directly linked to the classic distinction. Thus, achieved characteristics typically provide more specific cues or information about one's demonstrated task competence or accomplishments (e.g., job title, occupation, educational level), whereas ascribed characteristics are used to provide more diffuse cues or generalized information about ability or performance across a wide range of activities based on the societal value that they command (e.g., race, gender, or age). In reality, individuals simultaneously possess multiple characteristics, both ascribed and achieved (e.g., black male and Stanford-educated), which can conflict in the status cues that they send.

The inappropriate use of status cues to solicit and weight contributions may be quite detrimental to teams that need to utilize the expertise of all of its members. So, returning to our new sports drink development team, the inappropriate weighting of certain status cues may undermine the collaborative efforts of the team, including their ability to leverage the knowledge possessed by all members of the assembled team. Remember that at the outset we established that two members of the new sports drink development team are particularly accomplished, possessing past experience with successful product development and launch efforts, prestigious MBAs, and solid reputations as team players within the firm. For the moment, let us ignore that they also contribute racial diversity to the team (i.e., one is black and the other is Asian American) and focus on how their accomplishments or achieved status would impact their influence on the team.

Achieved status characteristics. There has been a considerable amount of attention given to the effects of achieved status on the behaviors directed toward individuals. Sociologists have broadly construed achieved status as a state earned by effort or performance. More often, however, empirical considerations of the effects of achieved status have focused on the effects of acknowledged expertise or task experience on the ability of inidividuals to influence or gain opinion agreement. Those with high expertise can elevate the consideration given to outsiders' knowledge contributions (Thomas-Hunt, Ogden, and Neale, 2003) and elicit more conformity than low-expertise individuals (O'Hara, Netemeyer, and Burtin, 1991; Schouten, 2008). Additionally, those with task experience are able to exert influence with less effort than those not possessing task experience (Wittenbaum, 1998). Such investigations have also revealed that it is the perception of possessing expertise and not actual expertise that affords influence (Horai, Naccari, and Fattoullah, 1974; Hovland, Janis, and Kelley, 1953; Littlepage *et al.*, 1995; Loyd *et al.*, 2010; Tedeschi, 1972; Yoder, Schleicher, and McDonald, 1998). However, demonstrations of task experience can impact perceptions of expertise and subsequent influence, particularly when doubt exists about individuals' abilities (Hollingshead and Fraidin, 2003; Pugh and Wahrman, 1983; Wittenbaum, 2000).

Despite an empirical focus on experience and expertise on influence exertion, sociologists' construal of achieved status has not been limited to expertise or demonstrated task experience (Linton, 1939). Nevertheless, acknowledgement of educational attainment and occupational attainment as additional sources of achieved status has only resulted in minimal research that has focused on their effects on behavioral reactions to individuals. A notable exception is research that finds that educational credentials impact the prestige of institutions into which individuals are hired (Merritt and Reskin, 1997). Additionally, research examining occupational attainment on influence in groups is confined to studies that find that leaders who are elected (i.e., achieved status) are able to exert more influence than those who are appointed (Lucas, 2003; Anderson, Karuza, and Blanchard, 1977). Based on the described research, we expect that achieved status will impact the influence exerted within teams:

Proposition 1: Individuals with higher achieved status will exert more influence within their teams than those with lower achieved status

Thus far we have discussed the effects of status perceived to have been acquired by individual effort or demonstrated performance. We know that individuals within teams also possess status characteristics over which they have no control because they were assigned without regard to effort or performance. In fact, in our new product development team, two individuals have ascribed racial/ethnic characteristics that deviate from those of the other team members and each other's. These racial characteristics are said to afford ascribed status. In the following section we consider the effects of ascribed characteristics on the perceptions and behaviors directed toward individuals. We first give consideration to ascribed characteristics alone and then discuss the achieved status backdrop in which the ascribed characteristics are situated in our particular team.

Ascribed status characteristics. Status differences within groups may be based on characteristics beyond the control of individuals (e.g., race, ethnicity, gender) which prompt group members to make assessments based not on actual performance or accomplishment, but on preconceived societal notions of prestige and worth (Berger *et al.*, 1977; Linton, 1939). Surprisingly, despite the increased consideration given to the effects of racial diversity in groups and a significant focus on gender, little empirical research on groups has explicitly focused on the impact of race on the way in which individuals are valued and exert influence within groups (Hunt, 2000). However, a considerable amount of research has documented the differential outcomes of individuals by race. Most of this work has focused on the diminished outcomes of blacks. In a study of job applicant bias, Dovidio and Gaertner (2000) found that when applicants were clearly qualified or unqualified, evaluators' ratings were not influenced by race, but when qualifications were ambiguous, evaluators exhibited a bias against black applicants. Similarly, in a field study of the effects of race on callback rates for job interviews, Bertrand and Mullainathan (2004) found that applicants with black-sounding names received significantly fewer callbacks than applicants with white-sounding names. The bias against blacks continues after they are admitted into organizations as well; in their research on job placement decisions, Braddock *et al.* found that personnel officers often assign blacks to lower paying positions than their Caucasian counterparts (Braddock *et al.*, 1986). Additionally, a long tradition of research on performance appraisal indicates that blacks receive lower performance ratings than their Caucasian colleagues (Kraiger and Ford, 1985; Pulakos *et al.*, 1989; Sackett and Dubois, 1991; Elvira and Town, 2001; Stauffer and Buckley, 2005). These differential evaluations frequently translate into a divergence in the ratings of perceived promotability received by blacks and Caucasians (Greenhaus, Parasuraman, and Wormley, 1990). Even when performance evaluations are comparable, blacks and other underrepresented minorities receive lower bonuses and salary increases than their Caucasian peers in the same organization (Castilla, 2008). While the research on the effect of other racially ascribed characteristics is not extensive, there is evidence that other Latinos and Asians in certain contexts are disadvantaged by their racial characteristics as well (Ho and Jackson, 2001; Maddux *et al.*, 2008):

Proposition 2: Racial characteristics will affect the influence that individuals are afforded within teams

Despite the use of racial characteristics to assign value within organizations, we return to our premise that individuals possess multiple characteristics, some achieved and some ascribed. Given the positive effects of achieved status on influence within groups, our hope would be that achieved status would overshadow ascribed status. Research yields mixed support for this supposition. When gender is the ascribed characteristic, there is evidence that highly salient achieved status can overcome the diminished influence often exerted by women (Lucas, 2003; Hollingshead and Fraidin, 2003; Pugh and Wahrman, 1983). Within the realm of racial characteristics, there is less empirical evidence of the ability of achieved status to outweigh ascribed racial status. In fact, those black executives who do make it to the upper echelons of organizations may not be immune to biased evaluation. In their study of leadership evaluation, Rosette and her colleagues found that black CEOs are more likely to be personally blamed for organizational failures and receive less personal credit for organizational successes than similarly situated Caucasian executives (Rosette, Leonardelli, and Phillips, 2008). Furthermore, recent research demonstrates that blacks from high-prestige educational institutions are less able than their white counterparts to positively leverage their educational background in assessments made by those external to the firm (Sauer, Thomas-Hunt, and Morris, 2010).

Within our sports drink product development team, the hope would be that racially ascribed status cues are pre-empted by achieved status cues that suggest what members are really able to contribute. The evidence suggests that, at best, racially ascribed characteristics will often dominate or provide a context in which achieved characteristics are interpreted. The mitigation of gender effects suggests that there may also be circumstances under which racial characteristics are subordinated to achieved status characteristics. Those circumstances remain largely unexamined and little is known about the factors that cause race/ethnicity to emerge as the salient characteristic that drives status hierarchies and influence within groups.

Under what circumstances might race, rather than achieved status cues such as educational background, be used to guide expectations of the performance and perceptions of the racially distinctive members of our product development team? Imagine, for example, if in an early meeting the Asian-American team member from marketing was very quiet and did not contribute much to the conversation; or presented a very quantitative analysis; or was seen gathering with other Asian employees; or mentioned that his parents were first-generation immigrants? Would that not heighten the salience of his racial characteristic relative to the salience of his prestigious MBA or strong reputation for delivering? Imagine what would happen if the highly accomplished black team member from finance in an early meeting had a temper flare-up in a heated conversation; or if he asked for help on something he had been assumed to know; or if one of his early assertions proved incorrect? Alternatively, what if he was discovered playing basketball one lunch hour or revealed in a casual conversation that he came from a family with limited means? The consistency of these sets of behaviors or associations with stereotypes held of the team members' racial categories may be sufficient to activate their respective racial status and allow it to guide the degree to which they are able to exert influence within the group. Furthermore, separate from stereotype-consistent behaviors, any non-normative team behavior exhibited might cause team members to search for additional information in an effort to make sense of the behaviors. An easy attribution for the deviation from accepted behaviors might be a team member's distinctive and visibly salient characteristic, in this case, their race, thus triggering race as a status characteristic that guides influence acceptance.

In the next section we posit that there are three primary mechanisms by which racial status becomes activated within a team despite the presence of observable achieved status characteristics. First, we suggest that the degree to which racially distinctive team members are observed engaging in behaviors or associations that are consistent with their racial group's dominant stereotypes will impact racial status activation. Second, we argue that even in the absence of firsthand observations, team members' disclosures of their racial stereotype-consistent behaviors and associations will activate their racial status. Finally, we posit that displays of non-normative team behaviors, even those unrelated to or inconsistent with racial stereotypes, will evoke a sense-making process that will lead to attributions of the behavior to racial category membership and will activate racial status.

Racial status activation

Stereotype-consistent behaviors. Despite the advances made by individuals from racially underrepresented groups in the US, considerable evidence exists that racial stereotypes are still pervasive (Taylor, Lee, and Stern, 1995). For example, blacks continue to be perceived as uninitiated (Sniderman and Piazza, 1993), associated with high crime rates (Quillian and Pager, 2001), economically disadvantaged (Brezina and Winder, 2003), rhythmic, hostile, lazy, and athletic (Devine, 1989; Dovidio, Evans, and Tyler, 1986; Gaertner and McLaughlin, 1983; Henderson-King and Nisbett, 1996; Weitz and Gordon, 1993). Furthermore, research has shown that the same behaviors exhibited by whites are more likely to be categorized as violent when exhibited by blacks (Duncan, 1976; Sagar and Schofeld, 1980). Similarly, Latinos are frequently stereotyped as uneducated (Czepiec and Kelly, 1983) as well as possessing large families (Faber, 1987). However, stereotyping is not confined to generalizations made about blacks and Latinos. Asian stereotypes persist despite diverging significantly from those held of blacks and Latinos. Often thought of as the model minority (Fong, 2002; Tuan, 1998), Asians are stereotyped and categorized as studious, shy, and mathematically inclined, among other things (Shih, Pittinsky, and Trahan, 2006).

The continued prevalence of racial stereotypes has led researchers to investigate the circumstances under which they become activated. For quite some time, researchers asserted that stereotypes are automatically activated in response to exposure to a particular stimulus associated with a social group (Bargh, 1994, 1999; Brewer, 1988). More recently, such assertions have been qualified by research indicating stereotype activation is dependent upon features of the context in which exposure occurs (Blair and Banaji, 1996; Macrae *et al.*, 1997; Spencer, Steele, and Quinn, 1999) as well as characteristics of the perceiver (Gilbert and Hixon, 1991). Wittenbrink, Judd, and Park (2001) argue and find that the activation of racial stereotypes depends upon the additional contextual cues present. Specifically, exposure to positive racial stereotypes diminished participants' display of spontaneous prejudice more than when they were exposed to negative racial stereotypes. Even if the mere presence of a racial characteristic activates stereotypes, in the presence of salient achieved characteristics, racial status may not be the dominant status cue used to guide influence processes within a team. Research on stereotype maintenance suggests that stereotypic behaviors are processed more easily as they are in line with expectations (Hamilton and Rose, 1980). Consequently, when behaviors or associations consistent with the stereotypes of the exhibitors' racial category are observed, it is more likely that they will be crystallized and used to guide behavior within the team.

Recent research that examines the effects of socioeconomic status on evaluations of white and black MBA job applicants finds that blacks are evaluated less favorably than whites when they are also perceived to be of low socioeconomic status, suggesting that consistency of socioeconomic status with racial stereotypes heightens the use of race as a status characteristic (Duguid and Thomas-Hunt, 2009). This same negative assessment of blacks does not occur when they are of high socioeconomic status. Given that negative stereotypes are easier to confirm than positive stereotypes, it is likely that racial status is more likely to be activated when behaviors are consistent with negative stereotypes (Rothbart and Park, 1986). Our argument does not assume that stereotype-consistent behavior will always result in diminished influence. Instead, we argue that racial status will be activated and will guide expectations within that context. So, in our new product development team, if the team member from marketing who is Asian gives a highly quantitative analysis of market segments, his racial status will be activated and will guide influence. If the team task is quantitative, the team may overrely on the marketing person's input. If the team task is coded as strategic, the marketing member's contribution may be devalued in this context:

Proposition 3: When an individual's observable behaviors and associations are consistent with racial stereotypes, racial status will be activated and used to guide influence in teams

Stereotype-consistent disclosures. Despite the fact that many characteristics of organizational individuals are readily observable, many remain obscured – particularly those that involve behaviors or associations that are enacted away from work. The focus of many organizations on fostering authentic engagement between individuals (e.g., Fleming and Spicer, 2004; Pratt and Rosa, 2003) as well as individuals' own needs for self-verification (e.g., Swann, Milton, and Polzer, 2000) creates situations in which individuals (in their attempts to foster relations with co-workers and also feel valued for who they are) share information that might otherwise remain hidden. Past research has documented the positive benefits of personal disclosure (see, e.g., Collins and Miller, 1994 for a review and meta-analysis; Cozby, 1973; Jourard, 1959; Jourard and Lasakow, 1958; Worthy, Gary, and Kahn, 1969). However, such research has given minimal consideration to disclosures that occur within heterogeneous environments and, in particular, racially heterogeneous environments.

Phillips, Rothbard, and Dumas (2009), in their seminal piece on the impact of status distance on personal disclosure, suggest that individuals may strategically disclose status confirming or disconfirming information in an effort to manage the status distance between themselves and others. They argue that greater status distance hinders the development of high-quality relationships, so individuals should be motivated to strategically disclose information believed to diminish this status distance. This means that some individuals, especially those who are racially distinct, may be particularly aware of whether their disclosures are consistent or inconsistent with the stereotypes of the racial group to which they belong. Disclosures that are consistent with racial stereotypes (positive or negative) serve to crystallize the salience of an individual's racial characteristics. These types of disclosures are likely to activate race as a status characteristic that drives influence within a team. As such, the black team member from finance who discloses his humble beginnings may knowingly or unknowingly be reinforcing perceptions of blacks as economically disadvantaged. The activation of his race may lead him to exert less influence when the team is engaged in tasks in which low expectations of performance are held for blacks:

Proposition 4: The more racial stereotype-consistent information is disclosed by racially distinct individuals, the more likely that their racial status will be activated

Non-normative behavior. Within teams, strong norms of behavior are established relatively quickly (Bettenhausen and Murnighan, 1991). One can imagine that even though our new product development team is at its inception, members have expectations about how one should behave in this type of team in this organization. As the team interacts, other norms will emerge and become crystallized. They may always meet in the same location, begin their meetings in the same way, and establish patterns of interaction that are repeated over time. When one of the members engages in a non-normative behavior (e.g., leaving early, arriving late, or missing a meeting with no notice), the expectations of other members may be violated and attempts will be made to interpret the behavior (Burgoon, 1978; Burgoon and Hale, 1988; Burgoon, LePoire, and Rosenthal, 1995; Hale and Burgoon, 1984). In the presence of differentiating characteristics, the possibility exists that possession of distinctive racial characteristics may be used to make attributions about the non-normative behavior, further heightening the salience of race. When the non-normative behaviors are perceived to be extreme, individuals may be labeled as "deviants," an event which elicits negative reactions and causes others in the group to perceive the violators as threatening their shared identity (Menon and Blount, 2003). The already-heightened salience of race may be further exacerbated if deviant behavior is consistent with racial stereotypes. Potentially, if the finance team member who is black misses a meeting, the non-normative behavior will be seen as consistent with stereotypes of blacks as lazy and irresponsible, leading to the activation of race as a status characteristic:

Proposition 5: The more non-normative team behaviors exhibited by racially distinct individuals, the more likely that their racial status will be activated

Conclusions

We began by noting that researchers have been unable to identify the factors that determine when race will be used to guide influence within teams. In particular, we set out to identify circumstances under which racial status may become activated within a team and overwhelm achieved status. We focused on a six-person, all-male new product development team, two of whom were highly accomplished and Asian American and black, respectively. Through a review of status characteristics theory and discussion of the known impact of ascribed and achieved status, we considered three processes that may activate racial status. First, we discussed the impact of observable behaviors or associations that are consistent with racial stereotypes.

Second, we considered the role of disclosures of stereotype-consistent activities, and finally, we discussed the more generalized impact that norm-violating behavior has on the activation of the racial status of racially distinctive violators.

It is important to note that we do not assume that racial status activation diminishes influence within a team. Instead, we argue that the impact of activated racial status will depend upon what performance expectations are held for those racial characteristics in a particular context, for example, if knowledge that the finance man grew up economically disadvantaged activates his racial status. At an organizational retreat where a basketball competition is scheduled to take place, it may actually raise performance expectations for him because he is black. In this case the team may rely on the finance guy disproportionately because of his race even if he has demonstrated no basketball skill.

The need for more empirical research on how multiple status cues come together to affect influence in organizational teams is clearly warranted. As organizations embrace the changing diversity of the workforce and more women and minorities gain access to coveted positions of achievement in organizations, it will become even more important to understand the combination of ascribed and achieved status characteristics. Past research has shown that low ascribed status individuals must work harder than high ascribed status individuals to prove that their performance achievements are based on their abilities (Biernat and Kobrynowicz, 1997). This means that even the same achieved status exhibited by a low ascribed status individual may not garner the same level of influence as those same achievements exhibited by a high ascribed status individual (Sauer, Thomas-Hunt, and Morris, 2010). Managing this dilemma will be one of the greatest challenges faced by low ascribed status individuals as they strive to raise their status and have influence on others in organizations. We provide no prescriptions as to whether these racially distinctive individuals in teams should allow their stereotype-consistent activities to be observed or whether they should disclose that which is not readily observable. Likewise, we acknowledge that in some cases non-normative behaviors may serve the best interests of the organization or individual and should not necessarily be avoided. Our hope though is that the three mechanisms we discussed will be a starting point for recognizing when and how race becomes activated and dominates as a predictor of status within teams.

References

The Alliance for Board Diversity. 2005. Women and minorities on Fortune 100 boards. Washington, D.C., accessed March 1, 2007 from www. catalystwomen.org/files/full/ABD%20report.pdf.

Anderson, L. R., Karuza, J., and Blanchard, P. N. 1977. "Enhancement of leader power after election or appointment to undesirable leader roles." *Journal of Psychology* 97: 59–70.

Bargh, J. A. 1994. "The four horsemen of automaticity: Awareness, intention, efficiency, and control in social cognition," in R. S. Wyer and T. K. Srull (eds.), *Handbook of Social Cognition*, Vol. I. Hillsdale, NJ: Erlbaum, pp. 1–40.

1999. "The cognitive monster: The case against the controllability of automatic stereotype effects," in S. Chaiken and Y. Trope (eds.), *Dual-process Theories in Social Psychology*. New York: Guilford Press, pp. 361–382.

Bargh, J. A., Chen, M., and Burrows, L. 1996. "Automaticity of social behavior: Direct effects of trait construct and stereotype activation on action." *Journal of Personality and Social Psychology* 71: 230–244.

Berger, J., Cohen, B. P., and Zelditch, M., Jr. 1972. "Status characteristics and social interaction." *American Sociological Review* 37(3): 241–255.

Berger, J. and Fisek, M. H. 1970. "Consistent and inconsistent status characteristics and the determination of power and prestige orders." *Sociometry* 33: 287–304.

Berger, J., Fisek, M. H., Norman, R. Z., and Wagner, D. G. 1985. "Formation of reward expectations in status situations," in J. Berger and M. Zelditch (eds.), *Status, Rewards, and Influence*. San Francisco: Jossey-Bass, pp. 215–261.

Berger, J., Fisek, M. H., Norman, R. Z., and Zelditch, M., Jr. 1977. *Status Characteristics and Social Interaction: An Expectation-states Approach*. New York: Elsevier.

Bertrand, M. and Mullainathan, S. 2004. "Are Emily and Greg more employable than Lakisha and Jamal? A field experiment on labor market discrimination." *American Economic Review* 94(4): 991–1013.

Bettenhausen, K. and Murnighan, J. K. 1991. "The development of an intragroup norm and the effects of interpersonal and structural challenges." *Administrative Science Quarterly* 36: 20–35.

Biernat, M. and Kobrynowicz, D. 1997. "Gender- and race-based standards of competence: Lower minimum standards but higher ability standards for devalued groups." *Journal of Personality and Social Psychology* 72: 544–557.

Blair, I. V. and Banaji, M. R. 1996. "Automatic and controlled processes in stereotype priming." *Journal of Personality and Social Psychology* 70: 1142–1163.

Braddock, J., Crain, R., McPartland, J., and Dawkins, R. 1986. "Applicant race and job placement decisions: A national survey experiment." *International Journal of Sociology and Social Policy* 6: 3–24.

Brewer, M. B. 1988. "A dual process model of impression formation," in T. K. Srull and R. S. Wyer, Jr. (eds.), *Advances in Social Cognition*, Vol. I. Hillsdale, NJ: Erlbaum, pp. 1–36.

Brezina, T. and Winder, K. 2003. "Economic disadvantage, status generalization, and negative racial stereotyping by white Americans." *Social Psychology Quarterly* 66: 402–418.

Bunderson, J. S. 2003. "Recognizing and utilizing expertise in work groups: A status characteristics perspective." *Administrative Science Quarterly* 48: 557–591.

Burgoon, J. K. 1978. "A communication model of personal space violations: Explication and an initial test." *Human Communication Research* 4: 129–142.

Burgoon, J. K. and Hale, J. L. 1988. "Nonverbal expectancy violations: Model elaboration and application to immediacy behaviors." *Communication Monographs* 55: 58–79.

Burgoon, J. K., LePoire, B. A., and Rosenthal, R. 1995. "Effects of preinteraction expectancies and target communication on perceiver reciprocity and compensation in dyadic interaction." *Journal of Experimental Social Psychology* 31: 287–321.

Cancio, A. S., Evans, T. D., and Maume, D. J. 1996. "Reconsidering the declining significance of race: Racial differences in early career wages." *American Sociological Review* 61: 541–556.

Castilla, E. J. 2008. "Gender, race, and meritocracy in organizational careers." *American Journal of Sociology* 113: 1479–1526.

Chatman, J. A. and Flynn, F. 2001. "The influence of demographic heterogeneity on the emergence and consequences of cooperative norms in work teams." *Academy of Management Journal* 44: 956–974.

Collins, N. L. and Miller, L. C. 1994. "Self-disclosure and liking: A meta-analytic review." *Psychological Bulletin* 116: 457–475.

Corporate Board Initiative. 2006. 2005 update on the Committee of 100's Asian & Asian Pacific American (APA) Corporate Board report card. Accessed March 2, 2007 from www.committee100.org/initiatives/corporate_board/C-100_Corporate_Board_Update.pdf.

Cox, T. H., Lobel, S. A., and McLeod, P. L. 1991. "Effects of ethnic-group cultural differences on cooperative and competitive behavior on a group task." *Academy of Management Journal* 34: 827–847.

Cozby, P. C. 1972. "Self-disclosure, reciprocity, and liking." *Sociometry* 35: 151–160.

1973. "Self-disclosure: A literature review." *Psychological Bulletin* 79: 73–91.

Czepiec, H. and Kelly, J. S. 1983. "Analyzing Hispanic roles in advertising: A portrait of an emerging subculture." *Current Issues & Research in Advertising* 5: 219–240.

Devine, P. G. 1989. "Stereotypes and prejudice: Their automatic and controlled components." *Journal of Personality and Social Psychology* 56: 5–18.

Dovidio, J. F., Evans, N., and Tyler, R. B. 1986. "Racial stereotypes: The contents of their cognitive representations." *Journal of Experimental Social Psychology* 22: 22–37.

Dovidio, J. F. and Gaertner, S. L. 2000. "Aversive racism and selection decisions: 1989 and 1999." *Psychological Science* 11: 315–319.

Duguid, M. M. and Thomas-Hunt, M. C. 2009. "The impact of race and socio-economic status on social judgment." Working Paper, Olin School of Business, Washington University.

Duncan, B. L. 1976. "Differential social perception and attribution of intergroup violence: Testing the lower limits of stereotyping of blacks." *Journal of Personality and Social Psychology* 34: 590–598.

Elvira, M. and Town, R. 2001. "The effects of race and worker productivity on performance evaluations." *Industrial Relations* 40: 571–590.

Faber, R. J., O'Guinn, T. C., and Meyer, T. P. 1987. "Televised portrayals of Hispanics: A comparison of ethnic perceptions." *International Journal of Intercultural Relations* 11: 155–169.

Fleming, P. and Spicer, A. 2004. "You can checkout anytime, but you can never leave: Spatial boundaries in a high commitment organization." *Human Relations* 57: 75–94.

Flynn, F., Chatman, J. A., and Spataro, S. E. 2001. "Getting to know you: The influence of personality on the alignment of self-other evaluations of demographically different people." *Administrative Science Quarterly* 46(3): 414–442.

Fong, T. P. 2002. *The Contemporary Asian American Experience: Beyond the Model Minority*, 2nd edn. Upper Saddle River, NJ: Prentice Hall.

Fortune. 2006. Key Fortune 500 findings. Accessed March 1, 2007 from www.timeinc.net/fortune/information/presscenter/fortune/press_releases/20060403_fortune500.html.

Gaertner, S. L. and McLaughlin, J. P. 1983. "Racial stereotypes: Associations and ascriptions of positive and negative characteristics." *Social Psychology Quarterly* 46: 23–30.

Gilbert, D. T. and Hixon, J. G. 1991. "The trouble of thinking: Activation and application of stereotypic beliefs." *Journal of Personality and Social Psychology* 60: 509–517.

Greenhaus, J., Parasuraman, S., and Wormley, W. 1990. "Effects of race on organizational experiences, job performance evaluations, and career outcomes." *Academy of Management Journal* 33: 64–87.

Griffin, L. J. and Kalleberg, A. L. 1981. "Stratification and meritocracy in the United States: Class and occupational recruitment patterns." *British Journal of Sociology* 32: 1–31.

Hale, J. L. and Burgoon, J. K. 1984. "Model of reactions to changes in nonverbal immediacy." *Journal of Nonverbal Behavior* 8: 287–314.

Hamilton, D. L. and Rose, T. L. 1980. "Illusory correlation and the maintenance of stereotypical beliefs." *Journal of Personality and Social Psychology* 39: 832–845.

Harrison, D. A. and Klein, K. J. 2007. "What's the difference? Diversity constructs as separation, variety, or disparity in organizations." *Academy of Management Review* 32: 1199–1228.

Henderson-King, E. I. and Nisbett, R. 1996. "Anti-black prejudice as a function of exposure to the negative behavior of a single black person." *Journal of Personality and Social Psychology* 71: 654–664.

Ho, C. and Jackson, J. W. 2001. "Attitude toward Asian Americans: Theory and measurement." *Journal of Applied Social Psychology* 31: 1553–1581.

Hollingshead, A. B. and Fraidin, S. N. 2003. "Gender stereotypes and assumptions about expertise in transactive memory." *Journal of Experimental Social Psychology* 39(4): 355–363.

Horai, J., Naccari, N., and Fattoullah, E. 1974. "The effects of expertise and physical attractiveness on opinion agreement and liking." *Sociometry* 37: 601–606.

Hovland, C. I., Janis, I. L., and Kelley, H. H. 1953. *Communication and Persuasion: Psychological Studies of Opinion Change*. New Haven, CT: Yale University Press.

Hunt, M. O. 1996. "The individual, society or both? A comparison of black, Latino, and white beliefs about the causes of poverty." *Social Forces* 75: 293–332.

  2000. "Status, religion, and the 'belief in a just world': Comparisons of African Americans, Latinos, and whites." *Social Science Quarterly* 81: 325–343.

Jehn, K. A., Northcraft, G. B., and Neale, M. A. 1999. "Why differences make a difference: A field study of diversity, conflict, and performance of workgroups." *Administrative Science Quarterly* 44: 741–763.

Joshi, A. and Roh, H. 2009. "The role of context in work team diversity research: A metaanalytic review." *Academy of Management Journal* 52: 599–628.

Jourard, S. M. 1959. "Self-disclosure and other-cathexis." *Journal of Abnormal and Social Psychology* 59(3): 428–431.

Jourard, S. M. and Lasakow, P. 1958. "Some factors in self-disclosure." *Journal of Abnormal and Social Psychology* 56: 91–98.

Kirkman, B. L., Tesluk, P. E., and Rosen, B. 2004. "The impact of demographic heterogeneity and team leader-team member demographic fit on team empowerment and effectiveness." *Group & Organization Management* 29(3): 334–368.

Kraiger, K., and Ford, J. K. 1985. "A meta-analysis of ratee race effects in performance ratings." *Journal of Applied Psychology* 70: 56–65.

Lawrence, B. S. 1997. "The black box of organizational demography." *Organization Science* 8: 1–22.

Lefkowitz, J. 1994. "Sex-related differences in job attitudes and dispositional variables: Now you see them ..." *Academy of Management Journal* 37: 323–349.

Lepore, L. and Brown, R. 1997. "Category and stereotype activation: Is prejudice inevitable?" *Journal of Personality and Social Psychology* 72: 275–287.

Leslie, L. 2008. *Ethnic Diversity and Workgroup Effectiveness: An Intergroup Contact Perspective.* Unpublished manuscript, Carlson School of Management, University of Minnesota.

2009. "A question of status or power? Social hierarchy and the experiences of ethnic minorities." Presented at the annual meeting of the Academy of Management, Chicago, IL, August.

Linton, R. 1936. *The Study of Man: An Introduction.* New York: Appleton-Century-Crofts.

1939. *The Individual and his Society.* New York: Columbia University Press.

Littlepage, G. E., Schmidt, G. W., Whisler, E. W., and Frost, A. G. 1995. "An input-process-output analysis of influence and performance in problem-solving groups." *Journal of Personality and Social Psychology* 69: 877–889.

Loyd, D. L., Phillips, K. W., Whitson, J., and Thomas-Hunt, M. C. 2010. "Expertise in your midst: How congruence between status and speech style affects reactions to unique knowledge." *Group Processes and Intergroup Relations* 13: 379–395.

Lucas, J. W. 2003. "Status processes and the institutionalization of women as leaders." *American Sociological Review* 68: 464–480.

Macrae, C. N., Bodenhausen, G. V., Milne, A. B., Thorn, T. M. J., and Castelli, L. 1997. "On the activation of social stereotypes: The moderating role of processing objectives." *Journal of Experimental Social Psychology* 33: 471–489.

Maddux, W. W., Galinsky, A. D., Cuddy, A. J. C., and Polifroni, M. 2008. "When being a model minority is good ... and bad: Realistic threat explains negativity toward Asian Americans." *Personality and Social Psychology Bulletin* 34: 74–78.

Magee, J. C. and Galinsky, A. D. 2008. "Chapter 8: Social hierarchy: The self-reinforcing nature of power and status." *The Academy of Management Annals* 2: 351–398.

Mannix, E. A. and Neale, M. A. 2005. "What differences make a difference? The promise and reality of diverse teams in organizations." *Psychological Science in the Public Interest* 6: 31–55.

McCoy, F. 2007. Kings of the mountain, *HispanicBusiness.com*. Accessed March 1, 2007 from www.hispanicbusiness.com/news/newsbyid. asp?id=54516&cat=Today's+Most+Popular+Stories&more=/news/ newspopular.asp.

McLeod, P. L., Lobel, S. A., and Cox, T. H. 1996. "Ethnic diversity and creativity in small groups." *Small Group Research* 27: 248–264.

Meeker, B. F. and Weitzel-O'Neill, P. A. 1977. "Sex roles and interpersonal behavior in task-oriented groups." *American Sociological Review* 42: 91–105.

Menon, T. and Blount, S. 2003. "The messenger bias: How social relationships affect the valuation of knowledge," in R. M. Kramer and B. Staw (eds.), *Research in Organizational Behavior*, Vol. XXV. Greenwich, CT: JAI Press, pp. 137–187.

Merritt, D. J. and Reskin, B. F. 1997. "Sex, race, and credentials: The truth about affirmative action in law faculty hiring." *Columbia Law Review* 97(2): 199–311.

Merton, R. K. 1968. *Social Theory and Social Structure*. New York: Free Press.

Milliken, F. J. and Martins, L. L. 1996. "Searching for common threads: Understanding the multiple effects of diversity in organizational groups." *Academy of Management Review* 21: 402–433.

O'Hara, B., Netemeyer, R. G., and Burtin, S. 1991. "An examination of the relative effectiveness of source expertise, trustworthiness, and likeability." *Social Behavior and Personality* 19: 305–314.

Olivera, F. and Argote, L. 1999. "Organizational learning and new product development: CORE processes," in L. L. Thompson, J. M. Levine, and D. M. Messick (eds.), *Shared Cognition in Organizations: The Management of Knowledge*. Mahwah, NJ: Lawrence Erlbaum, pp. 297–325.

O'Reilly, C. A., Williams, K. Y., and Barsade, S. 1998. "Group demography and innovation: Does diversity help?" in D. Gruenfeld and M. A. Neale (eds.), *Research on Managing Groups and Teams*, Vol. I. Greenwich, CT: JAI Press, pp. 183–207.

Parsons, T. 1951. *The Social System*. Glencoe, IL: Free Press.

Pelled, L. H., Eisenhardt, K. M., and Xin, K. R. 1999. "Exploring the black box: An analysis of work group diversity, conflict, and performance." *Administrative Science Quarterly* 44(1): 1–28.

Phillips, K. W., Northcraft, G., and Neale, M. 2006. "Surface-level diversity and information sharing: When does deep-level similarity help?" *Group Processes and Intergroup Relations* 9: 467–482.

Phillips, K. W., Rothbard, N. P., and Dumas, T. L. 2009. "To disclose or not to disclose? Status distance and self-disclosure in diverse environments." *Academy of Management Review* 34: 710–732.

Pratt, M. G. and Rosa, J. A. 2003. "Transforming work-family conflict into commitment in network marketing organizations." *Academy of Management Journal* 46: 395–418.

Pugh, M. D. and Wahrman, R. 1983. "Neutralizing sexism in mixed-sex groups: Do women have to be better than men?" *American Journal of Sociology* 88: 746–762.

Pulakos, E. D., White, L. A., Oppler, S. L., and Borman, W. C. 1989. "Examination of race and sex effects on performance ratings." *Journal of Applied Psychology* 74: 770–780.

Quillian, L. and Pager, D. 2001. "Black neighbors, higher crime? The role of racial stereotypes in evaluations of neighborhood crime." *American Journal of Sociology* 107(3): 717–767.

Ridgeway, C. L. 1987. "Nonverbal behavior, dominance, and the basis of status in task groups." *American Sociological Review* 52: 683–694.

Ridgeway, C. L. 1991. "The social construction of status value: Gender and other nominal characteristics." *Social Forces* 70: 367–386.

Ridgeway, C. L. and Block, K. G. 2000. "Creating and spreading status beliefs." *American Journal of Sociology* 106: 579–615.

Ridgeway, C. L. and Erickson, K. G. 2000. "Creating and spreading status beliefs." *American Journal of Sociology* 106: 579–615.

Ridgeway, C. L. and Walker, H. 1995. "Status structures," in K. Cook, G. Fine, and J. House (eds.), *Sociological Perspectives on Social Psychology*. New York: Allyn & Bacon, pp. 281–310.

Roberson, L. and Block, C. J. 2001. "Racioethnicity and job performance: A review and critique of theoretical perspectives on the causes of group differences," in B. Staw and R. Sutton (eds.), *Research in Organizational Behavior*, Vol. XXIII. Greenwich, CT: JAI Press, pp. 247–325.

Rosette, A. S., Leonardelli, G., and Phillips, K. W. 2008. "The white standard: Racial bias in leader categorization." *Journal of Applied Psychology* 93: 758–777.

Rosette, A. S. and Thompson, L. 2005. "The camouflage effect: Separating achieved status and unearned privilege," in E. A Mannix, M. A Neale, and M. C. Thomas-Hunt (eds.), *Research on Managing Groups and Teams: Status and Groups*, Vol. VII. Oxford: Elsevier, pp. 259–282.

Rothbart, M. and Park, B. 1986. "On the confirmability and disconfirmability of trait concepts." *Journal of Personality and Social Psychology* 50: 131–142.

Sackett, P. R. and DuBois, C. L. Z. 1991. "Rater-ratee race effects on performance evaluation: Challenging meta-analytic conclusions." *Journal of Applied Psychology* 76: 873–877.

Sagar, H. A. and Schofeld, J. W. 1980. "Racial and behavioral cues in black and white children's perceptions of ambiguously aggressive acts." *Journal of Personality and Social Psychology* 39: 590–598.

Sauer, S. J., Thomas-Hunt, M. C., and Morris, P. A. 2010. "Too good to be true? The unintended signaling effects of educational prestige on external expectations of team performance." *Organization Science*. Retrieved from Articles in Advance, March 25, 2010. http://orgsci.journal.informs.org/cgi/content/abstract/orsc.1090.0523v1.

Schouten, B. C. 2008. "Compliance behavior and the role of ethnic background, source expertise, self-construals and values." *International Journal of Intercultural Relations* 32: 515–523.

Shih, M., Pittinsky, T. L., and Trahan, A. 2006. "Domain-specific effects of stereotypes on performance." *Self and Identity* 5: 1–14.

Sniderman, P. and Piazza, T. 1993. *The Scar of Race*. Cambridge, MA: Harvard University Press.

Sommers, S. R. 2006. "On racial diversity and group decision-making: Identifying multiple effects of racial diversity on jury deliberations." *Journal of Personality and Social Psychology* 90: 597–612.

Spencer, S. J., Steele, C. M., and Quinn, D. M. 1999. "Stereotype threat and women's math performance." *Journal of Experimental Social Psychology* 35: 4–28.

Stauffer, J. M. and Buckley, M. R. 2005. "The existence and nature of racial bias in supervisory ratings." *Journal of Applied Psychology* 90: 586–591.

Swann, W. B., Milton, L. P., and Polzer, J. T. 2000. "Should we create a niche or fall in line? Identity negotiation and small group effectiveness." *Journal of Personality and Social Psychology* 79: 238–250.

Taylor, C. R., Lee, J. Y., and Stern, B. B. 1995. "Portrayal of African, Hispanic, and Asian Americans in magazine advertising." *American Behavioral Scientist* 38: 608–621.

Tedeschi, J. 1972. *The Social Influence Processes*. Oxford: Aldine-Atherton.

Thomas, D. A. and Gabarro, J. J. 1999. *Breaking Through: The Making of Minority Executives in Corporate America*. Boston, MA: Harvard Business School Press.

Thomas-Hunt, M. C., Ogden, T. Y., and Neale, M. A. 2003. "Who's really sharing? Effects of social and expert status on knowledge exchange within groups." *Management Science* 49: 464–477.

Thomas-Hunt, M. C. and Phillips, K. W. 2004. "When what you know is not enough: Expertise and gender dynamics in task groups." *Personality and Social Psychology Bulletin* 30: 1585–1598.

Tsui, A. S., Egan, T. D., and O'Reilly, C. A., III. 1992. "Being different: Relational demography and organizational attachment." *Administrative Science Quarterly* 37: 549–579.

Tuan, M. 1998. *Forever Foreigners or Honorary White?* New Brunswick, NJ: Rutgers University Press.

Van Knippenberg, D., De Dreu, C. K. W., and Homan, A. C. 2004. "Work group diversity and group performance: An integrative model and research agenda." *Journal of Applied Psychology* 89: 1008–1022.

Van Knippenberg, D. and Schippers, M. C. 2007. "Work group diversity." *Annual Review of Psychology* 58: 515–541.

Weitz, R. and Gordon, L. 1993. "Images of black women among anglo college students." *Sex Roles* 28: 19–45.

Williams, K. Y. and O'Reilly, C. A. 1998. "Demography and diversity in organizations: A review of 40 years of research," in B. Staw and R. Sutton (eds.), *Research in Organizational Behavior*. Greenwich, CT: JAI Press, pp. 77–140.

Wittenbaum, G. M. 1998. "Information sampling in decision-making groups: The impact of members' task-relevant status." *Small Group Research* 29: 57–84.

2000. "The bias toward discussing shared information: Why are high status members immune?" *Communication Research* 27: 379–401.

Wittenbaum, G. M. and Stasser, G. 1996. "Management of information in small groups," in J. L. Nye and A. M. Brower (eds.), *What's Social About Social Cognition? Research on Socially Shared Cognition in Small Groups*. Thousand Oaks, CA: Sage, pp. 3–28.

Wittenbrink, B., Judd, C. M., and Park, B. 2001. "Spontaneous prejudice in context: Variability in automatically activated attitudes." *Journal of Personality and Social Psychology* 81: 815–827.

Worthy, M., Gary, A. L., and Kahn, G. M. 1969. "Self disclosure as an exchange process." *Journal of Personality and Social Psychology* 13: 59–63.

Yoder, J. D., Schleicher, T. L., and McDonald, T. W. 1998. "Empowering token women leaders: The importance of organizationally legitimated credibility." *Psychology of Women Quarterly* 22: 209–222.

PART V

Status in the workplace

10 Organizational justice and status: Theoretical perspectives and promising directions

JERALD GREENBERG AND
DESHANI B. GANEGODA

I really bust my butt now that I'm District Manager. I'm doing the same stuff that I did as Assistant District Manager – but that title, you know, I gotta work harder now that people look up to me.

District manager of a retail chain

If she were another manager around here, I would have asked her about the hours she wanted. But Trish is only a waitress, so I just scheduled her however I wanted. There's nothing wrong with that.

Restaurant manager

I explained the problem thoroughly and respectfully to my General Manager but not the technicians. There's no reason to involve any of the techs in making decisions. It's okay just to tell them what to do.

Service manager at auto dealership

The above comments, culled from the senior author's notes from workplace interviews over the years, suggest that managers are implicitly aware of a connection between justice and status. The district manager suggested that he was attuned to distributive justice when expressing the need to be deserving of his prestigious title. The restaurant manager did not think she was violating procedural justice by failing to give voice in the scheduling process to a lower status person, although she would have given voice to a higher status person. Finally, the service manager was sensitive to satisfying interactional justice by explaining outcomes to his superiors but not to his subordinates.

Not surprisingly, scholars are also familiar with connections between justice (or fairness) perceptions and status.[1] This is particularly evident among sociologists (e.g., McClendon, 1976), who have studied how positions in occupational status hierarchies dictate the shares of rewards to which individuals feel fairly entitled, and psychologists (e.g., Van Prooijen, Van den Bos, and Wilke, 2002), who have examined how people's thoughts about status led them to be concerned with following fair procedures. Despite such disciplinary links – and in keeping with the general observation that "status occupies a rather minor place in the … organizational behavior literature" (Pearce, Ramirez, and Branyiczki, 2001, p. 155) – connections between justice and status noted in the literature are not fully developed. However, scattered studies suggest that justice and status are interrelated in complex ways. Based on the belief that there is much to be learned about both justice and status by developing a rapprochement between them, we review their interrelationship in the present chapter. To this end, we juxtapose the various theoretical perspectives that shed light on the psychological processes underlying these connections and we also examine several of the most promising research directions stemming from them.

Defining terms

Before we can hope to clarify the connection between organizational justice and status, it is essential to make clear what we mean by these terms. To this definitional task we now turn.

Organizational justice

Quite simply, *organizational justice* refers to people's perceptions of fairness in organizations and their resulting reactions (Greenberg, 1987). As we alluded in our opening paragraph and as used in the literature (for an overview, see Greenberg, 2010a), organizational justice takes three major forms, each of which will be the focus of a separate section in the present chapter. These are as follows.

- *Distributive justice* – the perceived fairness of the distribution of outcomes, such as rewards or resources (Homans, 1961). For example, in Western society, people generally believe that pay is distributively fair to the extent that it reflects people's relative contributions to their jobs.
- *Procedural justice* – the perceived fairness of the manner in which outcomes are determined – that is, the processes or procedures used. For example, people consider procedures fair to the extent that they

are applied consistently and in an unbiased manner, are capable of being corrected if inaccurate (Leventhal, 1980), and give those who are affected a voice in determining those procedures (Thibaut and Walker, 1975).

- *Interactional justice* – the perceived fairness of the manner in which procedures are explained (Bies and Moag, 1986). For example, people believe that they have been treated in an interactionally fair manner to the extent that they are given thorough information about how decisions are made in a manner that shows dignity and respect (Greenberg, 1993a; Colquitt, 2001).

It is important to note that there is conceptual overlap between these forms of justice. This is understandable insofar as they are nested, with interactional justice referencing procedures and procedural just-ice referencing distributions. Despite this, researchers find it useful to distinguish between them in practice because the various forms of justice are predictive of different variables (Colquitt *et al.*, 2001). We follow this tradition in the present chapter.

Status

Because the term *status* is used in many different ways, it is import-ant for us to identify the particular perspective we have in mind when linking it to organizational justice. Specifically, following Pearce, Ramirez, and Branyiczki (2001), we define status as "position or standing with reference to a particular grouping" (p. 157).

Inherent in this definition is the notion that status is not a fixed characteristic of an individual, but rather a quality bestowed upon individuals by virtue of their relative standing in a grouping of people.[2] This suggests, for example, that within an organization a person occupying a high organizational level – that is, someone with a high degree of formal power – may have high status in that setting.[3] However, when this same individual plays in a softball league, status is likely to be defined by one's skills and contributions to the team. The high status the person enjoys in the corporate setting by virtue of his standing there is unlikely to be related to his status on the soft-ball team. Rather, to have high status in that setting, the executive would have to be one of the better players (e.g., a home-run slugger). This is not to say that an individual's status may not generalize across settings (e.g., Webster and Hysom, 1998), as is illustrated by the high degree of respect and deference shown to former US Presidents when interacting in social settings. However, status generalization cannot be assumed, suggesting that status must be earned in each setting within which an individual interacts.

Another point to note about status is that it connotes respect and dignity. As suggested by our example about former US Presidents, high-status individuals are accorded high levels of respect and dignity. Analogously, it is considered normatively acceptable for people of lower status to be shown lower levels of respect and dignity (although not below some minimum floor considered appropriate for all people regardless of their status). Put differently, being accorded high levels of respect and dignity is an indication of high status.

Distributive justice

At the heart of the role of status in distributive justice are people's perceptions of entitlement (Feather, 1994). Essentially, people consider outcomes to be fair to the extent that they are distributed in accordance with what they believe they are entitled, which in great part is determined by status. Thus, people of higher status are considered to be entitled to higher levels of reward than people of lower status. This phenomenon is explained by social exchange theory (Homans, 1961), equity theory (Adams, 1965), and role schema theory (Fiske, 1993), three conceptualizations that have inspired research on the role of status in distributive justice. As we indicate below, these theories do not make differential predictions about the connection between status and distributive justice, but they do call attention to the importance of different variables and posit different explanatory mechanisms.

Social exchange theory

Classical theories of social exchange, such as those advanced by Thibaut and Kelley (1959) and Gouldner (1960), conceive of social interaction in economic terms, wherein individuals analyze their relationships using subjective cost–benefit analyses. These approaches emphasize the notion that people maximize their long-term self-interests by adhering to a norm of reciprocity, which enhances the stability and predictability of relationships between people (Homans, 1961).

Contemporary theorists have extended the notion of social exchange to refer to a type of relationship between two or more interacting parties. These parties may have exchange relationships that range from primarily economically oriented, which tend to be relatively brief in duration (e.g., merchants and customers exchanging goods or services for money), to primarily social in orientation, which tend to be relatively long in duration (e.g., friends exchanging favors or social esteem). Research has established that both types of relationships are governed by principles of organizational justice (e.g., Aryee, Budwar, and Chen, 2002; Masterson *et al.*, 2000). For example, people interacting with one another distribute rewards between them in ways they believe to be distributively just (e.g., Lavelle, Rupp, and Brockner, 2007).

Incorporating status into our understanding of justice from a social exchange perspective, Schminke, Cropanzano, and Rupp (2002) conducted a survey study examining the relationship between a person's position in their organization's hierarchy (a proxy for status in this research) and their perceptions of distributive justice. The researchers reasoned that the benefits people believe they receive in exchange for working in their organizations will vary as a function of their organizational ranks. Specifically, the high levels of status associated with occupying a high place in an organization's hierarchy were believed to put such individuals in a position where they legitimately can command rewards commensurate with their standing. Thus, they expected that people at higher organizational levels (relative to those at lower levels) would perceive that they experienced higher levels of distributive justice. Indeed, this is precisely what they found.

Elaborating upon this significant main effect, Schminke and his associates also examined the possibility that organizational level would moderate the relationship between organizational structure and justice perceptions (a link established in earlier research by Schminke, Ambrose, and Cropanzano, 2000). They based this on the tenet of social exchange theory that people who have less of some valued asset (e.g., money) will place a higher value on each additional unit of that asset than people who already have a great deal of it (Homans, 1961). Consistent with this notion, Schminke, Cropanzano, and Rupp (2002) found that the distributive justice perceptions of people at lower organizational levels were affected more strongly by organizational structure than were those of people at higher organizational levels.

Specifically, several dimensions of organizational structure (e.g., participation, concentration of decision-making power) proved to be stronger predictors of organizational justice for lower level employees than for higher level employees.

These findings suggest that social exchange theory is a potentially useful conceptualization for understanding the role of status in distributive justice. These findings are also noteworthy because of their important implication that what is fair to people at lower levels might not appear to be fair to their superiors. Obviously, this can prove to be a problem when executives make strategic decisions to promote distributive justice (e.g., by designing a compensation system). For this to be successful, every effort should be made to take into account the justice perceptions of those individuals who will be affected by such policies.

Equity theory

Equity theory (Adams, 1965) is widely considered to be a special case of the broader social exchange theory. Specifically, in equity theory, Adams claims that people seek to maintain a balance between their work outcomes (i.e., the rewards received from working, such as pay and fringe benefits) and their work inputs (i.e., their work contributions, such as effort and experience). People who believe that the ratio of their own inputs to outcomes is greater than the corresponding ratio of a comparison other are said to experience overpayment inequity, resulting in feelings of guilt. However, people who believe that these ratios are less than the corresponding ratio of a comparison other are said to experience underpayment inequity, resulting in feelings of anger. Equity theory specifies that people are motivated to alleviate these negative emotional states by behaviorally or cognitively altering their perceptions of their own or another's inputs or outcomes such that they are believed to be equivalent. This creates a state of equity, resulting in feelings of satisfaction.

Status as an outcome. The esteem associated with status suggests that it functions as an outcome in the equity equation. This is apparent in the case of "status symbols," physical symbols that reflect the organizational status of job incumbents (Goodsell, 1977). For example, as noted by Steele (1973), large offices, carpeting, and windows are rewards symbolizing one's high position in an organizational status hierarchy (Konar and Sundstrom, 1985), reinforcing the social order of organizations (Edelman, 1978). However, when environmental features are not aligned with the status of job incumbents, status inconsistency results (Stryker and Macke, 1978), manifesting itself in the form of behavior and attitudes predicted by equity theory (Adams, 1965). This can take the form of overpayment inequity (if the recognition value of the physical symbols exceed one's attained organizational status) or underpayment inequity (if the recognition value of the physical symbols falls short of one's attained organizational status). According to equity theory, people find these inequitable states undesirable, leading them to compensate for them behaviorally or cognitively.

Greenberg (1988) examined people's behavioral reactions to inequities in status symbols in a naturalistic field experiment. Specifically, he examined how the job performance of insurance underwriters of differing levels varied as a function of the match or mismatch between their own organizational status and the status associated with offices to which they were assigned temporarily while their own offices were being refurbished. Within their unit, the status of underwriters was considered high, the status of underwriter trainees was considered low, and the status of associate underwriters was considered intermediate. All three groups performed the same kind of actuarial work but the high-status individuals (underwriters) were allowed to underwrite policies with higher limits, while low-status individuals (underwriter trainees) wrote policies with lower limits, and medium-status individuals (associate underwriters) wrote policies with intermediate level limits. Before and after the study period, these employees worked in offices that differed in ways that matched their status as recognized throughout the company. For example, underwriters worked in relatively spacious private offices with doors and large desks; underwriter trainees worked in more cramped, open cubicles in offices shared by six; and associate underwriters worked in conditions that fell between these two extremes.

Conceiving of the status associated with office features as outcomes, Greenberg (1988) examined job performance (inputs) in three two-week periods – before, during, and after assignment to temporary offices – to see if it varied in the manner predicted by equity theory. Consistent with equity theory, it was found that workers who were temporarily underpaid by being assigned to offices of lower status colleagues lowered their performance relative to baseline levels (i.e., while in their usual offices prior to reassignment). In contrast, workers who were temporarily overpaid by being assigned to offices of higher status colleagues raised their performance relative to baseline levels (it should be noted that people in each condition had the capacity to work at their usual levels). Finally, control group employees – those who either remained in their own offices or who were reassigned to the offices of equal-status colleagues – performed at levels that were not significantly different from the baseline.

Two additional findings also support equity theory. First, the changes in performance noted while working in temporary offices disappeared when employees returned to their permanent offices. In other words, reactions to status-based inequities lasted only as long as the inequities themselves. Second, reactions to status-based inequities were proportionate to the magnitude of the inequities experienced. Thus, underwriters who worked in the offices of underwriter trainees (two levels below them) were more underpaid than those underwriters who worked in the offices of associate underwriters (one level below them) and their performance declined more as a result. Analogously, the performance increases found among workers while they were being overpaid were greater among those assigned to offices of others two steps above them than those who were one step above them. These findings are in keeping with equity theory's proposition that the magnitude of responses to inequity is proportionate to the magnitude of the inequity experienced (Adams and Freedman, 1976).

With respect to establishing a link between distributive justice and status, the Greenberg (1988) study makes it clear that status is a determinant of entitlement. People who are accorded either more status or less status than they deserve by virtue of their positions (as communicated by their office surroundings) respond in ways that express their feelings of inequity. Moreover, this is the case both for individuals who are overpaid and underpaid.

Status as an input. Greenberg (1988) found that status functions as an outcome in the equity equation but it also may function as an input. For example, individuals considered to have high status (e.g., high-ranking executives) are expected to make greater contributions to their jobs than those who have low status (e.g., laborers). In other words, with status comes responsibility. In keeping with equity theory, this in turn is likely to be associated with the belief that one is worth more (greater outcomes to match the greater inputs), and when greater outcomes are not forthcoming, this creates a state of inequity.

This process is illustrated in two laboratory experiments by Greenberg and Ornstein (1983). These researchers had college students perform a proofreading task in exchange for what was pre-established in pilot testing to be a fair hourly wage. After performing a practice task, the work of a randomly selected group of participants was examined carefully by the experimenter, who told them that their task performance was so superior that they would be "senior proofreaders." This required them to work an extra hour in which they helped the experimenter score the work of others, but for which they would not be paid extra. In other words, they earned a high level of status with which came extra responsibilities. The researchers reasoned that to the extent participants believed the status gains associated with their title was adequate compensation for the extra work, they would feel equitably paid. Accordingly, they were not expected to show changes in performance relative to baseline levels (i.e., before status was bestowed). This is precisely what happened. In contrast, another group of randomly selected participants was told that they would be named senior proofreaders, but the experimenter failed to identify any basis for bestowing this title. In this case the high-status title was unearned, leading participants to feel that they were rewarded by the title more than was appropriate. As such, they were overrewarded and, as anticipated by equity theory, their task performance rose as they worked hard to become deserving of the unearned reward (i.e., to earn their high-status job title). Finally, a control group of participants who received no title and who were told that they would be paid for their work performed at unchanged levels throughout the study period.

Taken together, the studies by Greenberg and Ornstein (1983) and Greenberg (1988) make it clear that status plays a key role in the equity equation. These investigations reveal that overpayment results when people are given the unearned accoutrements of higher status individuals, be they more lavish offices or more prestigious job titles. It is important to note, however, that these effects are only temporary in nature. Both studies revealed that the effects were greater immediately and then weakened. As such, it is important to caution that it would be unwise to attempt to induce high performance by showing people indications of inappropriately high status. Not only would the effects be very short-lived, but they would be likely to backfire as workers came to believe that they had been manipulated.

Role schema theory

Unlike equity theory, which was developed for the purposes of explaining reactions to organizational injustice, role schema theory has been applied after the fact to shed light on the role of status in distributive justice. As conceived by Fiske (1993), role schemata reflect the accumulated knowledge about behavior that is expected of individuals in particular social positions. According to the theory, as people learn to differentiate the roles played by people in social interaction, they come to internalize various expectations associated with incumbents of various roles (Benne and Sheats, 1948). So, when people assume roles, it automatically activates (i.e., without cognitive effort) schemata associated with them, leading individuals to behave in ways consistent with those roles. Prevalent among these are expectations about what role incumbents should do to fulfill their positions and to what rights and privileges they are entitled by virtue of those positions. When roles are well defined and well established, role schemata are shared by leaders (who strive to act in accordance with their role expectations) and their followers (who may evaluate leaders in terms of the degree to which they fulfill their own expectations of how leaders should behave).

For example, the general expectations of organizational leaders may be considered role schemas because, by virtue of their positions, there are consensual expectations for leaders to behave in certain ways. Among these are expectations to make decisions regarding the allocation of reward (Yukl, 2009) and to do so in a fair and responsible manner (Lord, Foti, and De Vader, 1984). At the same time, part of the role schemata of leaders is that they are entitled to certain benefits associated with their positions. The various "status symbols" described earlier are good examples of such benefits. Such symbols legitimize people's positions in a hierarchy, activating schemata and leading people to act upon them.

With this in mind, leaders would be expected to consider it fair to assert their privileges by allocating shares of rewards to themselves that exceed those given to followers. Here, fairness is defined in a manner similar to equity theory (albeit less formally) in terms of consistency or inconsistency with norms. This phenomenon was demonstrated in a series of studies by De Cremer (2003). In three interrelated experiments, the researcher had undergraduate students play the roles of either leaders or followers in simulated managerial situations. In these capacities participants were required to distribute shares of reward between themselves and others. Supporting the notion that leaders believe their position entitles them to more reward than their followers, De Cremer (2003) found that leaders allocated significantly higher amounts to themselves than did followers who also were allowed to allocate rewards. This finding follows from the idea that assuming a leadership role entitles one to greater rewards than assuming a follower role. In terms of role schema theory, "occupying the role of a leader activates cognitive schemas that communicate that due to their position of responsibility, leaders deserve certain privileges" (De Cremer, 2003, p. 296). This would explain why high-status people respond negatively when their specialness is ignored or violated – that is, because it is unfair.

De Cremer (2003) also found that another factor beside one's role influenced participants' allocation decisions – their accountability for decisions. Specifically, participants were led to believe that their allocation decisions either would or would not be made known to everyone in the simulation (accountable or not accountable, respectively). It was found that the general tendency for leaders to take more for themselves than to give to others was moderated by accountability. Specifically, leaders took less for themselves when they were accountable for their decisions than when they were not accountable.

Although De Cremer (2003) does not mention it, this finding may also be explained in terms of the role schemata adopted by leaders. Specifically, one of the typical role requirements of leaders is to maintain group harmony and to avoid conflict. Several classic studies (see reviews by Deutsch, 1975; and Leventhal, 1976) have shown that leaders do this by refraining from differentiating between themselves and others. In other words, they follow an equality norm (in which they fail to differentiate based on performance) rather than an equity norm (in which they differentiate based on performance). We see this, for example, when people are asked to allocate rewards between themselves and others with whom they are close, such as friends and spouses (Greenberg, 1982). In this regard, the equal allocations may be considered status-neutralizing, whereas the equitable allocations (those differentiating rewards based on contributions) are considered status-asserting. Clearly, claiming superior status by allocating higher rewards to oneself based on greater contributions is likely to be antagonistic to the maintenance of close relationships. At the same time, however, it is considered normative in work situations, where hierarchical status relationships are expected and endorsed.

Support for role schema theory may also be found in a line of research showing that how people perceive their outcomes depends on what they believe they deserve, which is determined largely by status (Feather, 1994; Major, 1994). Thus, to the extent that people acknowledge a role schema linking higher status to higher rewards, it follows that members of lower status groups will believe that fairness makes them deserving of less reward than members of higher status groups. Consistent with this notion, research has found that high-status people believe they are more deserving of high outcomes than their lower status counterparts (e.g., Jost, 1997; Major, 1994; Pelham and Hetts, 2001) and that generally they are treated more fairly than low-status people (Fiddick and Cummins, 2001). As a result, high-status people respond more negatively when they fail to receive the rewards they deserve (Diekmann, Sondak, and Bearsness, 2007). Major, McFarlin, and Gagnon (1989) have found that people behave in precisely this manner. Specifically, these researchers reported that members of lower status groups who made the same contributions as their high-status counterparts took lower levels of reward for themselves in addition to working longer and harder to become deserving of those rewards. Likewise, it has been reported that people employed in low-status jobs feel less entitled to reward than those in high-status jobs (Pelham and Hetts, 2001).

By way of concluding this section, we cannot help but note the interconnections between the three perspectives on distributive justice outlined here. First, it is clear that role schemata influence the manner in which status contributes to justice perceptions. Second, schemata regarding status are also involved in people's judgments of equity and inequity, which are based on beliefs about what constitutes appropriate compensation for one's efforts. Third, such judgments derive from norms governing social exchange (particularly between people of different status). As a whole, what we know about the role of status in distributive justice can be explained using the various perspectives, but these essentially focus on different parts of the same story. With this in mind, it is important not to characterize social exchange theory, equity theory, and role schema theory as competing approaches, but rather as complementary approaches to the study of status in distributive justice.

Procedural justice

When conceived initially, procedural justice was considered desirable because fair procedures help promote predictable situations in which people have control over outcomes, thereby enhancing the probability of long-term gains (Leventhal, 1980; Thibaut and Walker, 1975). In a later formulation, Lind and Tyler (1988) supplemented this instrumental orientation by noting that people also seek fair procedures for interpersonal reasons – that is, even when ostensible connections to economic self-interest are not apparent. Research examining connections between procedural justice and status embraces the interpersonal approach. Under this rubric two particular theories have inspired research – group value theory (Lind and Tyler, 1988) and social identity theory (Tajfel and Turner, 1979). Here we describe both.

Group value theory

Suggesting that procedural justice is desirable for non-instrumental reasons, Lind and Tyler (1988) proposed the *group value theory* of procedural justice. This conceptualization suggests that by using fair procedures, authority figures send signals to subordinates about the status they are accorded in their organizations. Thus, people granted a voice in decision making and who are treated in a consistent, unbiased and respectful fashion are inclined to feel fairly treated – not because of any impending financial benefits, but rather because they are led to feel accepted and valued.

Specifying this notion in greater detail, Tyler (1989) identified three relational criteria that promote perceptions of procedural justice:

- *Neutrality* – the belief that a decision maker uses unbiased procedures.
- *Trust* – the belief that a decision maker is acting in accord with one's best interests.

- *Standing* – the belief that a decision maker uses decisions (e.g., granting voice) that confer status on an individual by recognizing his or her value to the group.

Validating this notion, Tyler (1989) found that citizens' perceptions of the fairness of legal authorities (i.e., police and judges) were related to the extent to which they believed those authorities behaved in accordance with each of these criteria. Importantly, these findings resulted even after controlling for the favorability of citizens' outcomes (e.g., fines levied).

Drawing on group value theory, several studies have examined the connection between status and procedural justice. Among the earliest such efforts were experiments by Van Prooijen, Van den Bos, and Wilke (2002) that directly examined the causal effects of status on people's reactions to fair and unfair procedures. In these studies the researchers conceived of status differently from previous researchers. Instead of focusing on the regard in which people are held, as is typical, participants in their experiments focused on their own conceptualizations of status. Specifically, they reasoned that by making the general concept of status cognitively accessible (e.g., by receiving feedback about the status of their position), participants would become concerned about their approval by others, leading them to seek cues about status when interacting with others. Drawing from the group value model, they claim that this may be found in procedural justice information.

Thus, the researchers proposed that people will be concerned more about procedural justice when status is made cognitively accessible than when it is not cognitively accessible. Specifically, they argued that "people have mental representations of the concepts of status and fairness and that there is a cognitive link, or mental association between these representations, such that representations of status affect representations of fairness" (Van Prooijen, Van den Bos, and Wilke, 2002, p. 1355). Accordingly, they expected that cognitively activating the concept of status would exacerbate people's reactions to fair and unfair procedures.

Testing this notion, they conducted an experiment manipulating status salience by asking participants to complete a questionnaire regarding the concept of status, while members of a control group were asked about issues unrelated to status. They also manipulated procedural justice by giving participants an opportunity to voice their opinions about a decision-making context or by denying such an opportunity. As expected, Van Prooijen, Van den Bos, and Wilke (2002) found that participants' judgments of how fairly they were treated were affected more strongly by the procedure when status was made salient than when it was not made salient. Revealing their robustness, the researchers replicated these findings in a second experiment in which procedural justice was operationally defined in a different manner. Here, too, they observed that status salience amplified reactions to procedures. Taken together, these findings are important because they suggest a causal relationship – status salience affects perceptions of procedural justice – that could not be established in cross-sectional survey research examining correlations between these variables (e.g., Tyler, 1984, 1997).

In a subsequent study, these same researchers (Van Prooijen, Van den Bos, and Wilke, 2005, Experiment 2) extended these earlier findings by manipulating the status of individuals (instead of status salience) directly in a laboratory experiment. Specifically, by informing participants about their relative task performance levels, the researchers were able to differentiate them with respect to a status dimension germane to their setting (i.e., people gain higher status from their superior task performance). In keeping with the notion of status salience examined in their earlier study (Van Prooijen, Van den Bos, and Wilke, 2002), the researchers found that simply being advised of their high status led to stronger negative responses to procedural injustice (i.e., absence of voice).

Yet, contrary to expectations, the researchers also found that different levels of status had no significant effects on such responses: low-status people responded equally strongly to procedural injustice as high-status people. We suspect that these null findings reflect artifacts of the research, however, as opposed to shortcomings of the group value theory. Specifically, manipulating status in terms of feedback about relative task performance confounds these two variables. In view of the artificial, short-term, low-involvement laboratory situation created in the research, it is unlikely that participants felt that meaningful differences in status resulted (despite results of manipulation checks, which may have provided cues as to the desired responses: Greenberg and Folger, 1988). With this in mind, it would be advisable for future researchers to assess predictions from group value theory by conducting research that manipulates status in a manner that has greater internal validity. To this end, we advise researchers to consider using situated experiments (Greenberg and Tomlinson, 2004) that capitalize on real differences in organizational status (as was done, for example, by Chen, Brockner, and Greenberg, 2003, Study 3).

Social identity theory

Tajfel and Turner (1979) developed social identity theory to understand the psychological bases for inter-group discrimination. A key element of their conceptualization is *identification*, which refers to association with certain groups for the purposes of bolstering self-esteem. The theory asserts that as social beings, people define themselves in terms of their group memberships and when these groups are held in high regard (i.e., they are high-status groups), it reflects positively on their members, boosting their self-esteem. The same dynamic also applies in organizations (Tyler, 1999) – that is, an individual's status in an organization is central to self-identity because it suggests how he or she is perceived by others. And, as suggested by group value theory (Lind and Tyler, 1988), positive social identities are likely to result when people believe that the procedures used with respect to them are fair – that is, the people who are treated with high levels of procedural justice are considered to have higher status than those treated with low levels of procedural justice.

Moderating effects of organizational levels. Building on this notion, Begley, Lee, and Hui (2006) argued that such findings are obtained in studies (such as in tests of group value theory) in which participants are at lower organizational levels. Indeed, in their survey study of Chinese employees they found that among lower level individuals, the more visibly outward signs of procedural justice were taken as indications of status. In contrast, senior employees focused more on what was most visible to them – that is, the fairness of the distribution of outcomes (i.e., distributive justice). They put it as follows:

At senior levels, resource generation and distribution often takes place in a widely visible "tournament" (e.g., Orrison, Schotter, and Weigelt, 2004) where winners and losers can readily be recognized. Failure deals a serious blow to self-esteem. The subjective nature of many resource allocation decisions, including promotions and pay, lends itself to different interpretations; thus, authorities that suffer from the decisions have ample room to conclude that they were unfairly victimized. The identity-related implications of such decisions are even more serious at higher levels because those in charge tend to commit more strongly to the organization than those at lower levels (Wiesenfeld, Brockner, and Thibaut, 2000). (Begley, Lee, and Hui, 2006, p. 707)

Based on this, Begley, Lee, and Hui (2006) argue that high-level individuals attend to distributive justice as an indicator of their organizational status. In addition, corroborating established findings from group value theory, they found that procedural justice contributed to the status (and thus the self-esteem) of lower level employees.

Curiously, additional research has reported opposite results for procedural justice. Specifically, in their study of Turkish bank employees, Erdogan, Kraimer, and Liden (2001) reported that individuals who had attained higher organizational levels believed strongly that their organizations had systems in place to ensure fairness. This, the authors explained, was a result of the efforts of participants to boost their self-esteem by convincing themselves that their high organizational levels could be taken as a valid indication of their worth to their organizations. That is, to the extent they believe they deserved their promotions because these followed from the use of fair procedures, they could feel good about themselves. This would also support the belief that the world is just as suggested by just world theory (Lerner and Miller, 1978).

Despite the seemingly contradictory findings of Begley, Lee, and Hui (2006), that status is related negatively to procedural justice, and Erdogan, Kraimer, and Liden (2001), that status is related positively to procedural justice, the differences are not difficult to reconcile. Although they interpret their findings through different theoretical lenses (social identity theory for Begley, Lee, and Hui, 2006, and just world theory for Erdogan, Kraimer, and Liden, 2001), both sets of researchers agree that efforts to enhance self-esteem lie at the heart of perceptions of procedural justice. Where they differ, however, is in assuming that people at different organizational levels have access to differential information about procedures. Yet, the way they use that information is presumed to be identical: to enhance self-esteem. The question then becomes a structural one – do people at higher organizational levels have access to different procedural information than people at lower organizational levels? Absent large-scale studies on this topic, the answer is not readily apparent. For now, it seems safe to suggest that the answer is likely to be based on the unique contextual differences of various settings (in this regard, see our discussion of possible cross-national differences later in this chapter).

Taken together, both these studies suggest that procedural justice judgments are not simply reflections of various structural factors as originally conceived (Leventhal, 1980; Thibaut and Walker, 1975) but the result of cognitions designed to enhance self-esteem. This notion was tested directly by Chen, Brockner, and Greenberg (2003), who posited that procedural justice serves different self-esteem functions for people at different status levels. Specifically, low-status employees desire not to be exploited by others and must assume that these others are trustworthy. To do this, they rely upon procedural justice information, assuming that people who use fair procedures are trustworthy. Low-status individuals also look to procedural justice because they are insecure about how well they are respected by others in their organizations (De Cremer, 2002) and take procedural justice as a cue (Tyler, 1988). In contrast, high-status employees desire to maintain their existing status and to reinforce it when interacting with others.

These differential motives led to different findings regarding the desire to have future interaction with others. Lower status employees least desired to interact with higher status colleagues when in the past the higher status person had granted them low levels of reward following unfair procedures. Under such conditions, the higher status person was considered untrustworthy and an undesirable partner for future interaction. In contrast, higher status employees most desired to interact with lower status colleagues when in the past the lower status person granted them high levels of reward following fair procedures. Under such conditions it was possible for high-level employees to receive the boosts to their status that they sought.

Expanding upon the notion that procedural justice can be ego-affirming, Diekmann, Sondak, and Bearsness (2007) found that high-status people were more satisfied with their jobs than low-status people when fair procedures were followed. Under fair procedural conditions, people are able to assume that there is a valid basis for their status differences, resulting in greater satisfaction for high-status people (whose high status boosts their self-esteem) than low-status people (whose low status threatens their self-esteem). Conversely, no such differences were found when unfair procedures were used because they offer no valid basis for people to learn anything about their own status. Job satisfaction (in part, a reflection on the organization that treated them unfairly) was equally low in both cases.

Leader prototypicality. As we have already described, justice is important because it reveals information about one's status. Specifically, fair treatment is an indication of the extent to which an individual is respected as a member of an in-group and can take pride in this association (Lind and Tyler, 1988; Tyler and Lind, 1992). In this connection, in-groups may be conceived as possessing consistent sets of attitudes, values, and beliefs that reliably differentiate them from out-groups. When people identify strongly with the in-groups to which they belong, they evaluate leaders positively to the extent that those leaders are considered prototypical members of those groups (i.e., they have the greatest degree of whatever attitudes, values, and beliefs are believed to define the group) (Lord, 1977). Also, individuals who are most likely to emerge as a group's leader are those who are considered the most highly prototypical of the group (Hogg and Van Knippenberg, 2003).

Following this line of reasoning, researchers have proposed that the relationship between procedural justice and status within a group would be moderated by the extent to which its leader is considered prototypical of that group. Specifically, this relationship was expected to be stronger within groups whose leaders were considered highly prototypical than those who were not. The underlying idea is that groups with prototypical leaders, because they are regarded to have more of what the group is all about, would be able to bestow higher status than groups whose leaders are not prototypical. In the first study to test this notion, Lipponen, Koivisto, and Olkkonen (2005) administered questionnaires to employees of Finnish banks. Their key dependent variable was judgments of the status of the groups to which the employees belonged. As expected, they found that justice had a greater impact on status among members of groups with highly prototypical leaders than those with less prototypical leaders.

These findings suggest that when it comes to using groups to define one's status, all groups are not created equal. Ones with prototypical leaders are particularly influential referents. It is noteworthy that Lipponen, Koivisto, and Olkkonen (2005) used an early measure of justice that confounds procedural justice and interactional justice (Moorman, 1991), making it difficult to determine the extent to which the effects are due uniquely to judgments of procedural justice. In a more recent study, however, Van Dijke and De Cremer (2008) replicated these findings using a carefully validated measure of procedural justice (Colquitt, 2001). Specifically, they found that compared to less prototypical leaders, highly prototypical leaders were perceived as being more procedurally fair and had a greater influence on self-perceived status. As expected, these effects were stronger among individuals who identified strongly with their organizations.

By way of concluding this section, we wish to emphasize that group value theory and social identity theory do not make different predictions about the role of status. Indeed, a key reason why people rely on procedural justice as a means of assessing their status is because of the information about their social identities that is revealed by the use of fair procedures. Thus, as in the case of the interrelated nature of the theories connecting status and distributive justice, the theories used to explain the role of status in procedural justice differ more in terms of their particular focus than their direction. Each approach uses different terminology and has a different focus, but the basic underlying mechanisms they propose are more alike than different.

Interactional justice

Given that the majority of contemporary studies of organizational justice focus on interactional justice (Greenberg, 2010a), it is curious that research linking status to interactional justice has been extremely limited. This absence is also underscored by the fact that descriptions of status make reference to qualities of interactional justice. For example, Pearce, Ramirez, and Branyiczki (2001) indicate that "Status connotes respect and integrity" (p. 157). Thus, satisfying interactional justice would require treating individuals with the levels of respect and integrity befitting their relative status. High-status people would likely consider it unfair of others to not show them the level of respect accorded to someone in their positions. Acknowledging this, it is considered customary to display higher levels of interactional justice to individuals at higher levels than to those at lower levels. As an illustration, consider the quotation from the service manager that opens this chapter. He differentiated between the status of a higher ranking person and a lower ranking person in terms of his willingness to share information. The high-status person (the general manager) was shown respect by deeming him worthy of an explanation, whereas lower status people (technicians) were not.

Key findings. The study by Schminke, Cropanzano, and Rupp (2002) that we described in our earlier discussion of distributive justice also included a measure of interactional justice. That investigation revealed that the effects of organizational structure on distributive justice judgments were moderated by organizational level (stronger effects among lower level employees and weaker effects among higher level employees). However, in the case of interactional justice judgments, most such moderating effects of organizational level failed to reach a conventional level of statistical significance. Although the exact reason for this is not apparent from the study, it is tempting to speculate that the difference is the result of restricted variance from a floor effect – that is, although higher status people may demand higher levels of interactional justice, this goes only so far. People are likely to believe that everyone, regardless of organizational position, is deserving of a certain level of dignity and respect. Just because people who have attained high-level positions in their organizations are shown respect, it does not mean that lower level employees do not also deserve a modicum of respect simply because they are human beings. This possibility, although untested here, is in keeping with the notion that the need for interactional justice is universal in nature (Bies, 2001). It would be useful for future researchers to examine this idea by exploring the possibility that the naturally occurring range of variance in interactional justice is more restricted than that for other forms of justice.

In one of the few studies linking status and interactional justice, Aquino, Galperin, and Bennett (2004) focused on deviant workplace behavior (i.e., voluntary violations of organizational norms that harm organizations and/or their members; see also Bennett and Robinson, 2000; and Greenberg, 2010b). Corroborating upon earlier findings (e.g., Greenberg. 1990, 1993; Greenberg and Alge, 1998), these investigators found that people respond to violations of interactional justice by engaging in deviant behavior. Of particular interest, this significant main effect was moderated by employees' status levels. Specifically, this relationship was greater among employees with lower levels of status in their organizations than those with higher levels of status.

Although Aquino, Galperin, and Bennett (2004) fail to report additional data to account for these findings, we suggest an explanation.

Specifically, compared to low-status employees, high-status individuals, guided by norms of professional decorum, are more inclined to consider it inappropriate to express dissatisfaction by engaging in the acts of physical aggression assessed in the study. Executives are generally expected to adopt a genteel and professional style that inhibits succumbing to physical aggression, leading them to channel their aggressive tendencies covertly. However, by normative standards, lower level employees are less inclined to be so inhibited, freeing them to express their feelings of injustice by engaging in aggressive behavior.

Future research. Although there have not been many studies linking status and interactional justice to date, there is a potentially important line of research on this topic that promises to inspire future research on this topic. In particular, we believe it would be worthwhile to introduce status as a moderator of the finding that high levels of interactional justice mitigate negative reactions to undesirable outcomes. Specifically, several studies have shown that people respond negatively to unfavorable outcomes, but that the degree to which this occurs varies as a function of the extent to which negative outcomes are explained using high levels of information and interpersonal sensitivity (for a review, see Greenberg, 2010a).

We see this, for example, in the case of authorities' explanations of temporary pay cuts, which mitigate reactions taking the form of theft (Greenberg, 1990, 1993b) and insomnia (Greenberg, 2006). In these cases, the interactional justice came at the hands of higher status individuals who appear to have assuaged feelings by offering assurance that things are going to be OK in the future. Such comfort and reassurance from superiors apparently makes distributive injustices (which result from pay cuts) seem less unfair. However, it is possible that people of equal and lower organizational status levels (i.e., peers and subordinates) may also be able to mitigate negative reactions to undesirable outcomes. In this case, although they cannot offer any "official" reassurance, peers and subordinates may be able to demonstrate high levels of interactional justice by sharing their own "unofficial" perspectives on the bad situation that provide comfort through social support via their own explanations and dignified treatment (Greenberg, 2006). In such situations, the unofficial treatment from peers and subordinates may supplement already positive official treatment (when interactional justice from superiors is high), exacerbating its positive effects, or it may counteract negative official treatment (when interactional justice from superiors is low), attenuating its negative effects. Investigations of this issue would be worthwhile in that they promise to shed new light on the dynamics of interactional justice and status. As such, we encourage researchers to make this a priority in future studies.

Promising directions

The research bearing on organizational justice and status has stimulated several particularly fruitful lines of research. Among the most promising are investigations focusing on executive compensation, fair punishment, and cross-national differences.

Executive compensation

In 2008 there was a considerable outcry, from both the US public and President Obama, about bank executives who were paid exorbitant salaries and bonuses despite the fact that they led their institutions so close to collapse that they required government bailouts to stay afloat (Gomstein, 2008). Using equity theory terminology, these high-status people took outcomes that were higher than warranted by their inputs (i.e., they were grossly overpaid). In terms of role schema theory, although their high status entitled top executives to greater outcomes than lower status employees, the magnitude of the differential appeared to violate expectations, especially among those whose low status left them in serious financial straits. From both perspectives the executives in question are considered overpaid.

It appears that the cost of this situation may extend beyond executive overpayment because overpayment at the top tends to cascade down to lower organizational levels. This is illustrated in an ambitious longitudinal survey study by Wade, O'Reilly, and Pollock (2006), who reported that CEOs use their own power not only to raise their own salaries (as also is done regularly by members of the US Congress: Montopoli, 2009), but also to raise their subordinates' salaries. Additionally, these researchers found that CEOs functioned as referents against whom lower level employees compared themselves when assessing the fairness of their own outcomes. Specifically, they observed that when employees believed they were overpaid less than their CEOs were overpaid, they responded in one of the most extreme forms described by equity theory – they resigned from their organizations. The Wade, O'Reilly, and Pollock (2006) study is important from a practical perspective because it underscores the importance of refraining from overpaying high-status individuals in an organization. From a theoretical perspective the study is also important because it raises questions about the well-accepted dictum from social comparison theory (Festinger, 1954) that people generally compare themselves to similar individuals (for a review, see Greenberg, Ashton-James, and Ashkanasy, 2007). Lower level employees surely cannot perceive themselves as similar to their companies' CEOs, but they appear to be influenced by them nonetheless. Specifically, it is possible that what executives may have been doing unknowingly by overpaying themselves was promoting an organizational culture in which overpayment is condoned. Organizations in which this occurs may be draining their bottom lines more than those in which overpayment is not commonplace. Research on this topic would appear to be a fruitful investment for future researchers.

Status and fair punishment

Another interesting issue regarding the connection between justice and status relates to the administration of fair punishment. For example, how does status influence people's willingness to forgive transgressors? Are high-status individuals more forgiving than low-status individuals? At least one study suggests that the answer is yes. Specifically, among people playing a series of bargaining games in a laboratory, Fiddick and Cummins (2001) found that high-status participants were more tolerant of cheating than their low-status counterparts (as suggested by their willingness to remain in relationships with them). Referring to the normative obligation for high-status people (nobility) to conduct themselves in a manner befitting their rank, the researchers refer to this as the *noblesse oblige effect*. It is noteworthy that the effect was obtained in these studies because status was manipulated by asking participants to assume a high-status role (a boss) or a low-status role (a worker) in a role-playing exercise. Although the status was not "real" in the sense that it had no meaningful implications outside the artificial laboratory task, participants behaved as if it were real by demonstrating *noblesse oblige*. Given that role-playing studies are effective at highlighting salient societal norms (Greenberg and Eskew, 1993), these findings serve as an indication that the norm for high-status people to be forgiving of low-status people is quite potent.

Extending the notion that status affects the willingness to forgive, additional research has revealed that status also affects the willingness to be forgiven. To explore this issue, the present authors conducted an experiment in which employees of a financial services company were asked to recommend fair levels of punishment for people in their company who committed various infractions (Greenberg and Ganegoda, 2009). These were arranged on a nine-point scale with anchors ranging from one (do nothing) to nine (terminate), as suggested by Trahan and Steiner (1994). Participants were led to believe that their recommendations would be taken into account in the case before them and subsequently in forming organizational policies. The infractions were either major (fraud) or minor (petty theft) and the individuals who committed them were either high in status (a vice president) or low in status (an account manager). The findings were consistent with the classic *status liability effect* reported by Wiggins, Dill, and Schwartz (1965). Specifically, in the case of major infractions, high-status people were given more severe punishments than low-status people, whereas in the case of minor infractions, high-status people were given less severe punishments. These findings suggest that status is a double-edged sword. As suggested by the notion of *idiosyncrasy credit* (Hollander, 1958), high-status people are "given a break" when they make a mistake, presumably in deference to their otherwise laudable contributions. This occurred only when the wrongdoing was minor. For serious wrongdoings, however, high-status people are "expected to know better" and because they are considered to be the public face of their organizations, they are held to a higher standard and required to "take the fall" for their misdeeds, thereby sending the message that such acts cannot be tolerated, even at the top.

In a second experiment, Greenberg and Ganegoda (2009) followed up on these findings by having a second group of research participants judge the fairness of the levels of punishment recommended in Experiment 1. In other words, they were third-party observers of the judgments made by the actors in Experiment 1. Interestingly, only sometimes did observers believe that the actors (who were trying to be fair) really were fair. Whereas observers believed that the actors punished the low-status wrongdoers fairly, they also indicated that they were too lenient on high-status wrongdoers. Thus, observers were unwilling to give high-status people credit for their high status by being lenient toward them for minor infractions (i.e., they failed to grant idiosyncrasy credit). Observers were *not* attuned to the status liability effect, but focused on the seriousness of the infraction itself regardless of the status of the person who committed it.

Although our data did not shed light on why these findings occurred, we propose that the explanation lies in the different perspectives of actors and observers. Specifically, because actors knew that their decisions mattered, they may have felt pressure to "teach a lesson" to executives guilty of fraud but to "cut them some slack" when their misdeeds were petty. However, observers felt no pressure to differentiate as a function of status. Making their justice judgments more abstractly, observers indicated that fairness demanded higher punishment for more serious infractions regardless of the status of the perpetrator. For them, status was not a salient consideration. This would appear to explain why members of the general public (uninvolved observers) sometimes question the appropriateness of judicial decisions (by actors) regarding high-ranking executives found guilty of serious legal infractions (e.g., Schlesinger, 2009).

It is important to note that because ours was a role-playing study, the findings do not indicate what people actually do, but what people believe to be normative in the situations depicted (Greenberg and Eskew, 1993). For this reason, the findings need to be replicated in settings in which people actually are administering punishment before we can be certain that the status liability effect occurs as suggested. In other words, our findings must be considered preliminary and in need of extension in hedonically relevant and realistic settings.

Cross-national differences

Based on the fact that one of Hofstede's (2001) cultural dimensions, *power distance*, appears to be related to status, we believe it would be potentially fruitful to study cross-national differences with respect to the role of status in organizational justice. Specifically, power distance refers to the extent to which less powerful individuals (and often those with lower levels of status and prestige) accept the fact that power is distributed unequally and believe this to be legitimate. In nations in which such beliefs predominate (e.g., Malaysia, Guatemala, Panama, and the Philippines) we would expect that people will accept reward distributions that differentiate between status levels to be fair and that they will be more inclined to make such differentiations when attempting to be fair than people in nations in which power distance is low (e.g., Austria, Israel, Denmark, and New Zealand). Likewise, in high-power distance countries, we would expect fair procedures to acknowledge status differences and for people to be especially likely to show deference and respect to high-status individuals.

To our knowledge, only one study (Leung and Lind, 1986) has examined status and justice in a cross-national context (comparing participants from the US and Hong Kong), but its findings are complex and not particularly relevant to our analyses. Several other studies relating to justice and status have included participants from outside the US, but these have not been comparative in nature. Specifically, these investigations have included participants from the Netherlands (De Cremer, 2003; Van Prooijen, Van den Bos, and Wilke, 2002, 2005), China (Begley, Lee, and Hui, 2006), Finland (Lipponen, Koivisto, and Olkkonen, 2005) and Turkey (Erdogan, Kraimer, and Liden, 2001). Although these nations vary with respect to power distance (e.g., China is relatively high, the Netherlands and Finland are relatively low, and Turkey is intermediate), methodological limitations (e.g., the small number of studies) preclude making post hoc comparisons (e.g., through meta-analyses). However, we cannot help but wonder about the extent to which the generalizability of the findings of these studies is restricted by their cultural contexts. To address these limitations, we believe that future researchers should conduct cross-cultural studies that are theoretically guided (on this, see Greenberg, 2010a). Investigations of this nature would appear to provide important contextual insight into our understanding of status and organizational justice, leading us to recommend making them a priority among future researchers.

Conclusion

As suggested by our analyses, the connections between organizational justice and status are richly nuanced but underdeveloped. To date, bridges have been drawn but only in pencil. Research in this area has been informed by various complementary theories germane to distributive justice and procedural justice, framing similar issues in different ways. In the case of interactional justice, only a small number of studies have been conducted at all. Despite these limitations, several potentially interesting research questions have already been addressed, but inroads into these issues remain preliminary. However, we believe that developing the rapprochement between organizational justice and status will prove fruitful to promoting our understanding of both concepts. By making the link between organizational justice and status salient in this chapter, we hope to have inspired our colleagues to pursue this direction when developing their own research and theories.

Notes

1 In keeping with the literature, we use the terms *justice* and *fairness* interchangeably in this chapter.
2 This applies to *achieved status* (i.e., status earned by virtue of accomplishments) rather than *ascribed status* (i.e., status resulting from one's inherited position in stratified society) (Foladare, 1969; Linton, 1936). In organizations, ascription is less likely to be the basis of status than achievement. As such, our discussion (and the research on which it is based) focuses on achieved status.
3 We acknowledge that status and organizational rank may not be identical in all contexts because, as Pearce, Ramirez, and Branyiczki (2001) caution, "those occupying higher hierarchical positions may not be the most honored and respected members of the organization" (p. 157). Despite this, because high status is generally associated with attaining high levels in an organizational hierarchy, in this chapter we follow the practice of taking organizational rank as a proxy for status (Driskell and Salas, 1993).

References

Adams, J. S. 1965. "Inequity in social exchange," in L. Berkowitz (ed.), *Advances in Experimental Social Psychology*, Vol. II. New York: Academic Press, pp. 267–299.
Adams, J. S. and Freedman, S. 1976. "Equity theory revisited: Comments and annotated bibliography," in L. Berkowitz and E. Walster (eds.), *Advances in Experimental Social Psychology*, Vol. XIII. New York: Academic Press, pp. 43–90.

Aquino, K., Galperin, B. L., and Bennett, R. J. 2004. "Social status and aggressiveness as moderators of the relationship between interactional justice and workplace deviance." *Journal of Applied Social Psychology* 34: 1001–1029.

Aryee, S., Budhwar, P., and Chen, Z. X. 2002. "Trust as a mediator of the relationship between organizational justice and work outcomes: Test of a social exchange model." *Journal of Organizational Behavior* 23: 267–285.

Begley, T. M., Lee, C., and Hui, C. 2006. "Organizational level as a moderator of the relationship between justice perceptions and work-related reactions." *Journal of Organizational Behavior* 27: 705–721.

Benne, K. and Sheats, P. 1948. "Functional roles of group members." *Journal of Social Issues* 4: 41–49.

Bennett, R. J. and Robinson, S. L. 2000. "The development of a measure of workplace deviance." *Journal of Applied Psychology* 85: 349–360.

Bies, R. J. 2001. "Interactional (in)justice: The sacred and the profane," in J. Greenberg and R. Cropanzano (eds.), *Advances in Organizational Justice*. Palo Alto, CA: Stanford University Press, pp. 89–118.

Bies, R. J. and Moag, J. F. 1986. "Interactional justice: Communication criteria of fairness," in R.J. Lewicki, B. H. Sheppard, and M. H. Bazerman (eds.), *Research on Negotiations in Organizations*, Vol. I. Greenwich, CT: JAI Press, pp. 43–55.

Chen, Y., Brockner, J., and Greenberg, J. 2003. "When is it 'A pleasure to do business with you'? The effects of status, outcome favorability, and procedural fairness." *Organizational Behavior and Human Decision Processes* 92: 1–21.

Colquitt, J. A. 2001. "On the dimensionality of organizational justice: A construct validation of a measure." *Journal of Applied Psychology* 86: 386–400.

Colquitt, J. A., Conlon, D. E., Wesson, M. J., Porter, O. L. H., and Ng, K. Y. 2001. "Justice at the millennium: A meta-analytic review of 25 years of organizational justice research." *Journal of Applied Psychology* 86: 425–445.

De Cremer, D. 2002. "Respect and cooperation in social dilemmas: The importance of feeling included." *Personality and Social Psychology Bulletin* 28: 1335–1341.

2003. "How self-conception may lead to inequality: Effect of hierarchical roles on the equality rule in organizational resource-sharing tasks." *Group & Organization Management* 28: 282–302.

Deutsch, M. 1975. "Equity, equality, and need: What determines which value will be used as basis of distributive justice." *Journal of Social Issues* 31: 137–149.

Diekmann, K. A., Sondak, H., and Bearsness, Z. I. 2007. "Does fairness matter more to some than to others? The moderating role of workplace status on the relationship between procedural fairness perceptions and job satisfaction." *Social Justice Research* 20: 161–180.

Driskell, J. E. and Salas, E. 1993. "Group decision making under stress." *Journal of Applied Psychology* 76: 473–478.

Edelman, M. 1978. *Space and Social Order.* Madison, WI: University of Wisconsin, Institute for Research on Poverty.

Erdogan, B., Kraimer, M. L., and Liden, R. C. 2001. "Procedural justice as a two-dimensional construct: An examination in the performance appraisal context." *Journal of Applied Behavioral Science* 37: 205–222.

Feather, N. 1994. "Attitudes toward high achievers and reactions to their fall: Theory and research concerning tall poppies," in M. P. Zanna (ed.), *Advances in Experimental Social Psychology*, Vol. XXVI. San Diego, CA: Academic Press, pp. 1–73.

Festinger, L. 1954. "A theory of social comparison processes." *Human Relations* 7: 117–140.

Fiddick, L. and Cummins, D. D. 2001. "Reciprocity in ranked relationships: Does social structure influence social reasoning?" *Journal of Bioeconomics* 3: 149–170.

Fiske, S. T. 1993. "Social cognition and social perceptions," in M. R. Rosenzweig and L. W. Porter (eds.), *Annual Review of Psychology*, Vol. XLIV. Palo Alto, CA: Annual Reviews, pp. 155–194.

Foladare, I. S. 1969. "A clarification of 'ascribed status' and 'achieved status.'" *Sociological Quarterly* 10: 53–61.

Gomstein, A. 2008. Bailout outcry: Stop big pay packages for bank execs. *ABC News*, September 24. Accessed online at http://abcnews.go.com/Business/Economy/ story?id=5870983&page=1.

Goodsell, C. T. 1977. "Bureaucratic manipulation of physical symbols. An empirical study." *American Journal of Political Science* 21: 79–91.

Gouldner, A. W. 1960. "The norm of reciprocity: A preliminary statement." *American Sociological Review* 25: 161–178.

Greenberg, J. 1982. "Approaching equity and avoiding inequity in groups and organizations," in J. Greenberg and R. L. Cohen (eds.), *Equity and Justice in Social Behavior.* New York: Academic Press, pp. 389–435.

1987. "A taxonomy of organizational justice theories." *Academy of Management Review* 12: 9–22.

1988. "Equity and workplace status: A field experiment." *Journal of Applied Psychology* 73: 606–613.

1990. "Employee theft as a reaction to underpayment inequity: The hidden cost of pay cuts." *Journal of Applied Psychology* 75: 561–568.

1993a. "The social side of fairness: Interpersonal and informational classes of organizational justice," in R. Cropanzano (ed.), *Justice in the Workplace: Approaching Fairness in Human Resource Management*. Hillsdale, NJ: Erlbaum, pp. 79–103.

1993b. "Stealing in the name of justice: Informational and interpersonal moderators of theft reactions to underpayment inequity." *Organizational Behavior and Human Decision Processes* 54: 81–103.

2006. "Losing sleep over organizational injustice: Attenuating insomniac reactions to underpayment inequity with supervisory training in interactional justice." *Journal of Applied Psychology* 91: 58–69.

2010a. "Organizational justice: The dynamics of fairness in the workplace," in S. Zedeck (ed.), *Handbook of Industrial/Organizational Psychology*, Vol. III. Washington, D.C.: American Psychological Association.

2010b. *Insidious Workplace Behavior*. New York: Psychology Press.

Greenberg, J. and Alge, B. 1998. "Aggressive reactions to workplace injustice," in R. W. Griffin, A. O'Leary-Kelly, and J. Collins (eds.), *Dysfunctional Behavior in Organizations, Volume 1: Violent Behaviors in Organizations*. Greenwich, CT: JAI Press, pp. 119–145.

Greenberg, J., Ashton-James, C., and Ashkanasy, N. 2007. "Social comparison processes in organizations." *Organizational Behavior and Human Decision Processes* 102: 22–41.

Greenberg, J. and Eskew, D. E. 1993. "The role of role playing in organizational research." *Journal of Management* 19: 221–241.

Greenberg, J. and Folger, R. 1988. *Controversial Issues in Social Research Methods*. New York: Springer-Verlag.

Greenberg, J. and Ganegoda, D. B. 2009. "Actor-observer differences in perceived fairness of status liability effects," in J. L. Pearce (Chair), *Status: The Neglected Motive in Industrial/Organizational Psychology*. Symposium presented at the annual meeting of the Society for Industrial and Organizational Psychology, New Orleans, LA.

Greenberg, J. and Ornstein, S. 1983. "High status job title as compensation for underpayment: A test of equity theory." *Journal of Applied Psychology* 68: 285–297.

Greenberg, J. and Tomlinson, E. C. 2004. "Situated experiments in organizations: Transplanting the lab to the field." *Journal of Management* 30: 703–724.

Hofstede, G. 2001. *Culture's Consequences*, 2nd edn. Thousand Oaks, CA: Sage.

Hogg, M. A. and Van Knippenberg, D. J. 2003. "Social identity and leadership processes in groups," in L. Berkowitz (ed.), *Advances in Experimental Social Psychology*, Vol. XXXV. San Diego, CA: Academic Press, pp. 1–52.

Hollander, E. P. 1958. "Conformity, status, and idiosyncrasy credit." *Psychological Review* 65: 117–127.

Homans, G. C. 1961. *Social Behavior: Its Elementary Forms.* New York: Harcourt.

Jost, J. T. 1997. "An experimental replication of the depressed-entitlement effect among women." *Psychology of Women Quarterly* 21: 40–45.

Konar, E. and Sundstrom, E. 1985. "Status demarcation in the office," in J. Wineman (ed.), *Behavioral Issues in Office Design.* New York: Van Nostrand, pp. 48–66.

Lavelle, J. J., Rupp, D. E., and Brockner, J. 2007. "Taking a multifoci approach to the study of justice, social exchange, and citizenship behavior: The target similarity model." *Journal of Management* 33: 841–866.

Lerner, M. J. and Miller, D. T. 1978. "Just world research and the attribution process: Looking back and ahead." *Psychological Bulletin* 85: 1030–1051.

Leung, K. and Lind, E. A. 1986. "Procedural justice and culture: Effects of culture, gender, and investigator status on procedural preferences." *Journal of Personality and Social Psychology* 50: 1134–1140.

Leventhal, G. S. 1976. "The distribution of rewards and resources in groups and organizations," in L. Berkowitz (ed.), *Advances in Experimental Social Psychology*, Vol IX. New York: Academic Press, pp. 91–131.

1980. "What should be done with equity theory? New approaches to the study of fairness in social relationships," in K. Gergen, M. Greenberg, and R. Willis (eds.), *Social Exchange: Advances in Theory and Research.* New York: Plenum, pp. 27–55.

Lind, E. A. and Tyler, T. R. 1988. *The Social Psychology of Procedural Justice.* New York: Plenum.

Linton, R. 1936. *The Study of Man: An Introduction.* New York: Appleton-Century.

Lipponen, J., Koivisto, T. S., and Olkkonen, M.-E. 2005. "Procedural justice and status judgements: The moderating role of leader ingroup prototypicality." *Leadership Quarterly* 16: 517–528.

Lord, R. G. 1977. "Functional leadership behavior: Measurement and relations to social power and leadership perceptions." *Administrative Science Quarterly* 22: 114–133.

Lord, R. G., Foti, R. J., and De Vader, C. L. 1984. "A test of leadership categorization theory: Internal structure, information processing, and leadership perceptions." *Organizational Behavior and Human Performance* 34: 343–378.

Major, B. 1994. "From social inequality to personal entitlement: The role of social comparisons, legitimacy appraisals, and group membership," in L. Berkowitz (ed.), *Advances in Experimental Social Psychology*, Vol. XXVI. New York: Academic Press, pp. 293–355.

Major, B., McFarlin, D. B., and Gagnon, D. 1989. "Overworked and underpaid: On the nature of gender differences in personal entitlement." *Journal of Personality and Social Psychology* 47: 1399–1412.

Masterson, S. S., Lewis, K., Goldman, B. M., and Taylor, M. S. 2000. "Integrating justice and social exchange: The differing effects of fair procedures and treatment on work relationships." *Academy of Management Journal* 43: 738–748.

McClendon, M. J. 1976. "The occupational status attainment processes of males and females." *American Sociological Review* 41: 52–64.

Montopoli, B. 2009. Congress keeps automatic pay raises. *CBS News*, March 13. Accessed at http://www.cbsnews.com/blogs/2009/03/13/politics/ politicalhotsheet/entry4863877.shtml.

Moorman, R. H. 1991. "The relationship between organizational justice and organizational citizenship behavior: Do fairness perceptions influence employee citizenship?" *Journal of Applied Psychology* 76: 845–855.

Orrison, A., Schotter, A., and Weigelt, K. 2004. "Multiperson tournaments: An experimental examination." *Management Science* 50: 268–279.

Pearce, J. L., Ramirez, P. R., and Branyiczki, I. 2001. "Leadership and the pursuit of status: Effects of globalization and economic transformation," in W. H. Mobley and M. W. McCall (eds.), *Advances in Global Leadership*, Vol. II. Greenwich, CT: JAI Press, pp. 153–178.

Pelham, B. W. and Hetts, J. 2001. "Underworked and overpaid: Elevated entitlement in men's self pay." *Journal of Experimental Social Psychology* 37: 93–103.

Schlesinger, J. 2009. Madoff: 150 years doesn't seem like enough. *The Huffington Post*, June 29. Accessed at http://www.huffingtonpost.com/jill-schlesinger/madoff-150-years-doesnt-s_b_222353.html.

Schminke, M., Ambrose, A. L., and Cropanzano, R. S. 2000. "The effect of organizational structure on perceptions of procedural fairness." *Journal of Applied Psychology* 85: 294–304.

Schminke, M., Cropanzano, R., and Rupp, D. E. 2002. "Organization structure and fairness perceptions: The moderating effects of organizational level." *Organizational Behavior and Human Decision Processes* 89: 881–905.

Steele, F. 1973. *Physical Settings and Organizational Development*. Reading, MA: Addison-Wesley.

Stryker, S. and Macke, A. S. 1978. "Status inconsistency and role conflict." in R. H. Turner, J. Coleman, and R. C. Fox (eds.), *Annual Review of Sociology*, Vol. IV. Palo Alto, CA: Annual Reviews, pp. 57–90.

Tajfel, H. and Turner, J. 1979. "An integrative theory of intergroup conflict," in W. G. Austin and S. Worchel (eds.), *The Social Psychology of Intergroup Relations*. Monterey, CA: Brooks-Cole, pp. 94–109.

Thibaut, J. W. and Kelley, H. H. 1959. *The Social Psychology of Groups*. New York: Wiley.

Thibaut, J. and Walker, L. 1975. *Procedural Justice: A Psychological Analysis*. Hillsdale, NJ: Erlbaum.

Trahan, W. A. and Steiner, D. D. 1994. "Factors affecting supervisors' use of disciplinary actions following poor performance." *Journal of Organizational Behavior* 15: 129–139.

Tyler, T. R. 1984. "The role of perceived injustice in defendants' evaluations of their courtroom experience." *Law & Society Review* 18: 51–74.

1989. "The psychology of procedural justice: A test of the group-value model." *Journal of Personality and Social Psychology* 57: 830–838.

1997. "The psychology of legitimacy: A relational perspective on voluntary deference to authorities." *Personality and Social Psychology Review* 1: 323–345.

1999. "Why people cooperate with organizations: An identity-based perspective," in B. M. Staw and R. Sutton (eds.), *Research in Organizational Behavior*, Vol. XXI. Greenwich, CT: JAI Press, pp. 201–246.

Tyler, T. R. and Lind, E. A. 1992. "A relational model of authority in groups," in M. P. Zanna (ed.), *Advances in Experimental Social Psychology*, Vol. XXV. San Diego, CA: Academic Press, pp. 115–191.

Van Dijke, M. and De Cremer, D. 2008. "How leader prototypicality affects followers' status: The role of procedural fairness." *European Journal of Work and Organizational Psychology* 17: 226–250.

Van Prooijen, J., Van den Bos, K., and Wilke, H. A. M. 2002. "Procedural justice and status: Status salience as antecedent of procedural fairness effects." *Journal of Personality and Social Psychology* 83: 1353–1361.

2005. "Procedural justice and intragroup status: Knowing where we stand in a group enhances reactions to procedures." *Journal of Experimental Social Psychology* 41: 664–676.

Wade, J. B., O'Reilly, C. A., and Pollock, T. G. 2006. "Overpaid CEOs and underpaid managers: Fairness and executive compensation." *Organization Science* 17: 527–544.

Webster, M., Jr. and Hysom, S. J. 1998. "Creating status characteristics." *American Sociological Review* 63: 351–378.

Wiesenfeld, B. M., Brockner, J., and Thibaut, V. 2000. "Procedural justice, managers' self-esteem, and managerial behaviors following a layoff." *Organizational Behavior and Human Decision Processes* 83: 1–32.

Wiggins, J. A., Dill, F., and Schwartz, R. 1965. "On 'status liability.'" *Sociometry* 28: 197–209.

Yukl, G. 2009. *Leadership in Organizations*, 7th edn. Upper Saddle River, NJ: Prentice Hall.

11 | Resolving conflicts between status and distinctiveness in individual identity: A framework of multiple identity displays

KIMBERLY D. ELSBACH

In this chapter I discuss how a person might respond to conflicts between status and distinctiveness in individual identity. In particular, I look at how one might affirm an individual identity that is status-enhancing but distinctiveness-threatening on one level (e.g., being categorized as an "attorney" is high status, but not distinctive) and is distinctiveness-enhancing but status-threatening on another level (e.g., being categorized as a public defender for the poor in rural South Dakota is distinctiveness-enhancing, but low in status). I begin by examining the concept of individual identity and extant research that suggests how such identity may be threatened.

Individual identity and identity threats

Researchers of individual identity in organizations have suggested that a person's self-concept may be defined by the categories chosen to define himself or herself. As Hogg and Abrams (1988, pp. 24–25) define it:

The self-concept comprises the totality of self-descriptions and self-evaluations subjectively available to the individual. It is not just a catalogue of evaluative self-descriptions, it is textured and structured into circumscribed and relatively distinct constellations called *self-identifications* ... [where] self identifications are essentially self-categorizations.

Self-categorizations are defined as claims that individuals use to denote similarities to and differences from specific classes of stimuli (Hogg and Abrams, 1988; Turner, 1987). Thus, self-categorizations indicate that a person is defined by various classes of groups, characteristics, traits, or roles. As Thoits and Virshup (1997, p. 107) note, self-categorizations may:

refer to *socio-demographic characteristics* (e.g., male, African-American), *group/organizational membership* (Little League member, church member), *social roles* (stepfather, attorney), *social types of person* (intellectual, leader) and, in some cases, *personality or character traits* (optimist, caring) [emphasis added].

Psychological research also suggests that such self-categorizations confer both *status* based on the legitimacy and rank associated with a category, and *distinctiveness* based on inclusion or exclusion from specific categories (Brewer, 1991).[1] In other words, self-categorizations may say something about how one is distinct and how one ranks compared to others (Brickson, 2000). It is important to note that status and distinctiveness self-categorizations are not separate constructs from identity, but are dimensions of it. As Brewer *et al.* (1993) have noted, both dimensions can influence the value of identities.

Not surprisingly, because self-categorizations are used to affirm and sustain individual identities, substantial research has also shown that events that call into question established self-categorizations may threaten those identities. Thus, identity threats may arise from information, behavior, physical markers, or thoughts that contradict an established self-categorization that signifies status or distinctiveness (Pratt *et al.*, 2006; Beyer and Hannah, 2002; Kreiner *et al.*, 2006; Elsbach, 2001). For example, a professor who self-categorizes herself as a "top-notch scholar" may perceive a threat to that identity after she receives the fifth rejection of one of her research articles from an academic journal. The same professor may also perceive an identity threat if she finds herself devoting more of her time to teaching than to research, or if her colleagues introduce her to others as "our best teacher," but never mention research when talking about her.

In response to these threats, the professor may make identity claims through deliberate behaviors that highlight desired self-categorizations (i.e., introducing herself as a researcher, or changing her website to highlight her research interests rather than her teaching). Deliberate self-categorization is one of the most common means of responding to identity threats (Tesser *et al.*, 2000; Mussweiler *et al.*, 2000), and has been shown as an effective response in a number of laboratory (e.g., Dietz-Uhler and Murrell, 1998; Ellemers *et al.*, 1993) and field studies (Mummendey *et al.*, 1999; Elsbach and Kramer, 1996) of identity threat.

Self-categorizations in response to individual identity threats

In examining the use of self-categorizations in response to identity threats, it appears that the most widely used tactic is to change the level of inclusiveness of self-categorizations to highlight positive and desired dimensions of individual identity (Blanz *et al.*, 1998). This identity management strategy has two possible forms: (1) claiming more exclusive self-categorizations, or (2) claiming more inclusive self-categorizations.

Claiming more exclusive self-categorizations. In general, more exclusive or lower order self-categorizations are thought to be more subjectively important to individuals (e.g., individuals identify more strongly with their intimate work group than their entire organization) (Ashforth and Johnson, 2001). Psychologists suggest that one important reason for this finding is that exclusive groups are more likely to provide individuals with distinctiveness (Brewer, 1991).

In line with this reasoning, researchers have shown that individuals may claim exclusive self-categorizations to accentuate their valued and distinctive traits, especially if those distinctive traits are threatened (Swann and Hill, 1982). For example, in a study of "part-time" workers, Smithson (2005) found that some participants objected to the categorization of "part-timer" because it obscured the fact that they actually had two jobs in the organization. As a result, although they were technically a "part-timer" in each job, they considered themselves as full-timers with multiple job responsibilities. One worker in this group then claimed the more exclusive self-categorization of "full-timer in a part-time job" as a means of preserving his distinctive identity (Smithson, 2005, p. 285). Similarly, in a study of California State legislative staff, Elsbach (2001) found that staffers who worked on policy formulation as opposed to political campaigns preferred the more exclusive self-categorization of "policy-wonk" to the more inclusive categorization of "staffer." This exclusive categorization separated them from the "political hacks" who were viewed as mainly involved in campaign fundraising and more concerned with achieving their own political aspirations than producing policy that would benefit the greater public.

At the same time, researchers have shown that claiming or making salient more exclusive self-categorizations may protect individuals from threats to status. This outcome may arise in part because dividing a superordinate category into smaller subordinate categories may be an effective way to redefine the relevant comparison groups. For example, in a study of higher education in the UK, Bourhis and Hill (1982) found that polytechnic lecturers (who worked at vocational schools) were widely perceived as lower in research excellence and prestige than their counterparts at research universities (i.e., university lecturers) and were made aware of this lower status during an institutional change process. In response, polytechnic lecturers emphasized their relative superiority in teaching skills by categorizing their group in more exclusive ways that made teaching quality more salient. In another case, Elsbach and Kramer (1996) found that members of low-ranked business schools often responded to these threats to their status and self-esteem by highlighting their superiority in a more exclusive category that was not measured by the rankings. For example, some members of public institutions claimed that their ranking among this subset (i.e., business schools at public universities) would be very high and that their status should not be judged compared to the larger category, which contained both public and private business schools, because the latter did not have the same mission to serve the needs of the state as did the former.

Claiming more inclusive self-categorizations. By contrast, claiming membership in a more superordinate category has been found to primarily protect individuals against threats to status. For example, in a study of identity management strategies, Mummendey *et al.* (1999) found that individuals living in the former East Germany (who were widely perceived to be a low-status group compared to those living in the former West Germany) were likely to categorize themselves in the superordinate category of "Germans" to escape this threat to low status, as long as they did not strongly identify as East Germans. In a similar study, Hornsey and Hogg (2000) found that college students who were in majors categorized as lower status (e.g., humanities) were more likely than those in majors categorized as higher status (e.g., math-science) to self-categorize at a more status-enhancing superordinate level (e.g., university X student). The authors interpreted this finding as evidence that self-categorization at a superordinate level was an effective tactic for escaping the poor self-concept associated with the lower status category.

Conflicts between motives in identity affirmation

However, problems may occur if individuals find themselves in situations in which they have to choose between receiving status-enhancing but distinctiveness-threatening vs. distinctiveness-enhancing but status-threatening information related to a single yet important dimension of one's identity (e.g., one's career) (see Hornsey and Hogg, 2000, 2002). For instance, a woman living in Los Angeles may find it status-affirming to claim the higher order self-categorization of attorney, but such a self-categorization may be distinctiveness-threatening because there are so many attorneys in that city. Yet, if, as a means of affirming distinctiveness, the same woman claims the lower order self-categorization of being a public defender in South Central Los Angeles, she may perceive threats to the status of her identity.

These same conflicts are likely to occur in organizational contexts (Van Knippenberg and Van Leeuwen, 2001). For example, following an organizational merger between lower status and higher status firms, an individual who previously belonged to the lower status firm may find it status-enhancing but distinctiveness-threatening to claim to be an employee of the new merged organization. In contrast, these same individuals may find it distinctiveness-enhancing but status-threatening to continue to claim they were employees of their previous organization, which is now essentially defunct.

As these cases illustrate, the use of typical identity management strategies described by psychologists (i.e., changing the level of one's self-categorizations to be more or less inclusive – see Blanz *et al.*, 1998) may not be effective in resolving these types of identity conflicts, because if one affirms a lower order self-categorization that focuses on enhancing distinctiveness, it will threaten status, while affirming a higher order self-categorization that enhances status may threaten distinctiveness.

In support of this notion, extant research has shown that if both status and distinctiveness are threatened, individuals are reluctant to trade off one for the other. For example, as mentioned above, Hornsey and Hogg (2002) found that college students in subject majors categorized as lower status (e.g., humanities) were more likely than those in majors categorized as higher status (e.g., math-science) to self-categorize at a more status-enhancing superordinate level (e.g., university X student), but *only* if their distinctive subject majors were also recognized. If these distinctive categorizations were not affirmed, low-status students were not more likely than high-status students to self-categorize at the superordinate level. As Hornsey and Hogg (2002, p. 210) note:

> It appears, then, that low-status participants may require some assurance that the distinctiveness of their subgroup identity will be protected before using superordinate categorization as an identity-enhancement strategy.

At the same time, Hornsey and Hogg (2002) also found that higher status students who were categorized only at the superordinate level were more likely to show bias toward the lower status students (e.g., downgrade the lower status students) than those higher status students who were also categorized at the level of their distinctiveness-enhancing major. These findings show that even high-status group members may be threatened by a loss of distinctiveness and may seek ways to regain that distinctiveness.

In these cases, Hornsey and Hogg (2002) suggest that individuals be categorized at multiple levels at the same time as a strategy to reduce both status and distinctiveness threat. Yet, they also concede that maintaining both subgroup and superordinate group identities at the same time violates some of the basic tenets of social categorization theory (SCT: see Turner, 1987). As Hornsey and Hogg (2002, p. 216) note, SCT explicitly precludes the notion that subgroup and superordinate identities can be salient at the same time. The notion of functional antagonism (Turner, 1987) dictates that as the salience of one level of self-categorization increases, the salience of the other levels decreases; thus, identification at a superordinate level reconfigures subgroup differences into intragroup similarities.

Alternatively, I argue that a display approach to identity management (i.e., displaying multiple physical markers and salient actions to signal multiple identity categorizations) may be more effective than relying on purely cognitive tactics to affirm identity in these cases. I assert that an individual may simultaneously display cues that signal both status and distinctiveness categorizations (e.g., wearing a uniform signals status while discussing a personal issue that signals distinctiveness). As a result, the display of multiple physical markers and salient behaviors may allow individuals to more readily affirm both status and distinctiveness through distinct identity categorizations. This perspective is grounded in more recent studies of strategic self-verification (Swann *et al.*, 2002), identity management among professional workers (Elsbach, 2003, 2004), and work on the roles of the physical environment and objects in organizations (Rafaeli and Pratt, 2006).

In the following sections I describe how individuals may use identity displays as a means of resolving conflicts between affirming status and distinctiveness in their individual identities. I begin by describing the two most common display tactics apparent in organizational research on identity management. I illustrate these tactics by describing their use in a number of qualitative case studies of identity work following identity threats. Based on these tactics, I then outline a framework that reveals how individuals in organizations may use multiple displays to simultaneously affirm both status and distinctiveness in situations in which these two identity dimensions appear to be in conflict.

Display tactics for affirming identity

Psychological research on "self-identifications" (Schlenker *et al.*, 1996) and strategic self-verifications (Swann *et al.*, 2002) suggests that individuals may customize their behaviors across social interactions to elicit situation-specific affirmations of their identities. In some cases, such as romantic relationships, individuals may engage in behaviors designed to elicit highly positive, but less accurate affirmations of "attractiveness" identity dimensions (Swann *et al.*, 2002). Yet, these same individuals may engage in other behaviors designed to elicit more accurate, but less positive affirmations of other identity dimensions, such as musical ability and common sense (Swann *et al.*, 2002). These findings suggest that individuals are willing to display "situated identities" (Alexander and Lauderdale, 1977; Ibarra, 1999) that reveal only those sides of themselves that allow them to meet their current objectives (e.g., appearing attractive to a romantic partner). Further, they suggest that individuals may be quite savvy at presenting themselves in ways that affirm specific identity dimensions.

In support of these suggestions, organizational researchers have found extensive evidence that individuals engage in strategic identity management behaviors in real-life settings. This research reveals two common tactics that individuals in organizations use to affirm their identities: (1) behavioral displays, and (2) physical marker displays.

Qualitative case study evidence of these two tactics is summarized in Table 11.1. I describe this research below.

Behavioral displays

Psychologists and organizational identity researchers have found that engaging in salient behaviors may be effective means of signaling identity in social contexts (Swann Jr. *et al.*, 2003). For example, a growing number of social psychologists have recognized the role of non-verbal behavior as a means of self-presentation in small groups (see Leary, 1995 for a review). These researchers suggest that visible behavior, such as seating preferences (Reiss and Rosenfeld, 1980), doing favors (Baumeister, 1982), aggressive body language (Bandura, 1973), engaging in sports (Leary, 1992), public eating habits (Pliner and Chaiken, 1990), and risky activities (Brockner *et al.*, 1981) are often used to convey images of power, compassion, control, and youth to other group members.

Similarly, a number of organizational researchers have recently examined how individuals use and interpret role-normative behavior as a means of developing new workplace identities as their work roles change (Ely, 1995; Coveleski *et al.*, 1998; Ibarra, 1999). This work has shown how employees adapt their in-role behavior to fit (or resist) normative role expectations. Over time, such modeling becomes aligned with the employee's workplace identity and alters that person's perceptions of the central and distinctive traits that define him or her at work (Ibarra, 1999).

Finally, sociologists in the field of symbolic interactions (Goffman, 1967) have long discussed the role of interaction rituals as a means of creating and maintaining "selves." For example, Goffman (1967, p. 34) discussed the role of face work, "actions taken by a person to make whatever he [or she] is doing consistent with his [or her] social image." More specifically, he described how aggressive face work, such as encouraging compliments, elitist snubs, and jokes, can be useful in demonstrating one's superiority and status relative to others. He also suggested (p. 25) that it is not only the verbal content but also the behavior in these interactions that helps to maintain an individual's image: "In aggressive interchanges, the winner not only succeeds in introducing information favorable to himself … but also demonstrates that as an interactant, he can handle himself better than his adversaries."

Table 11.1. *Qualitative case studies of identity displays following identity threats*

Reference	Setting	Identity conflict/threat	Distinctiveness affirming displays	Status affirming displays
Kreiner, Hollensbe, and Sheep (2006)	Study of Episcopalian priests' identity work	Conflicts between signaling one's unique individual identity and the expected role-identity of a priest	– Engaging in secular activities such as refereeing youth softball – Interacting with people outside the church or parish – Infusing personality dimensions into tasks of their roles, such as having parishioners call them by their first names, or bringing personal experiences into their weekly sermons	– Putting on priests' collar and robes to signal the status of their role-identity
Pratt, Rockmann, and Kaufmann (2006)	Study of medical residents' identity work	Conflicts between signaling identities related to distinctive medical specialties (e.g., surgery, radiology) and the actual work of residents (e.g., "scut work")	– Surgical residents referring to themselves as the "most complete doctors in the hospital" and talking about how they value putting the patients first	– Surgical residents wearing the white surgeon's coat and pants, even though other residency programs had abandoned them, to signal tradition and status – Surgical residents talking about how tough their program is and citing how high the divorce rate among residents is as evidence

Elsbach (2003)	Study of employee responses to a move from traditional to non-territorial workspace	Identity threats due to an inability to display physical markers that signaled status and distinctiveness at work	– Display of portable artifacts such as photos – Display of prohibited permanent artifacts, such as equipment and clothing in offices – Display of allowed permanent artifacts in common areas – Display of prohibited behaviors such as "squatting" in offices or occupying same office every day	– Display of allowed permanent artifacts in public areas – Creation of group boundaries through furniture arrangement in common areas
Beyer and Hannah (2002)	Study of socialization of engineers and technical professionals in semiconductor consortium	Potential threats to personal identities that were developed from past work experience in new work setting. Threats may come from inability to express established personal identities	– Fitting behavior to new company culture, rather than holding on to old company culture – Finding ways to do the same things at the new company that were done at the old company – Resisting learning new things that conflict with existing identity – Rejecting pressures to do new things that conflict with existing identity	

Table 11.1. (*cont.*)

Reference	Setting	Identity conflict/threat	Distinctiveness affirming displays	Status affirming displays
Elsbach (2001)	Study of long-time California legislative staffers working for organization with low approval ratings	Threat to social identities of policy wonks from working in an organization also populated by negatively perceived political hacks	– Displaying counter-stereotype behavior that distances them from undesired group (political hacks) – Selecting identity markers, such as business cards, that indicate policy identification and not political affiliation	
Ibarra (1999)	Study of newly hired professionals in consulting firms and investment banks	Threats to professional identities from lack of skills in profession, although being portrayed as having those skills	– Selectively imitating others while maintaining some behaviors that are true to oneself	– Gaining legitimacy in role by developing prototypes of good role models and matching behavior to those prototypes

Pratt and Rafaeli (1997)	Study of nurses in rehabilitation unit of a large hospital	Threats to professional identity due to possibility of being incorrectly categorized as "acute care" or "rehabilitation" nurses	– Using appropriate dress (e.g., street clothes vs. scrubs) to signal identity as either acute care or rehabilitation nurses
Ely (1995)	Study of women associates in law firms	Conflict between feminine gender identity and gender expectations of women in law firms with low proportion of senior women	– To get ahead, women perceive the need to enact behaviors that counter stereotypes of women and appear more like stereotypes of men (appearing more professional, less feminine, more confident, less insecure)

In the following sections, I describe research that specifically illustrates how behavioral displays may be used to affirm either distinctiveness or status dimensions of identity in organizational settings.

Use of behavioral displays to affirm distinctiveness. Several
researchers have found that individuals will use behavioral displays
to affirm a pre-existing, distinctive identity when they are faced with
pressures to abandon that identity or act in ways that run counter
to that identity. In this vein, Beyer and Hannah (2002) found that
engineers and technical professionals who had joined a new semiconductor consortium used behavioral displays to affirm pre-existing
professional identities that were developed at their previous employers. For instance, some engineers resisted learning new routines and
processes that conflicted with their existing identities, while others
rejected pressures to engage in new behaviors that were at odds with
their pre-existing professional identities. Similarly, in their study of
identity work by Episcopalian priests, Kreiner *et al.* (2006) found that
to affirm their unique individual identities, priests commonly engage
in secular activities, such as refereeing youth softball and socializ-
ing with people outside of their church or parish. These priests also
infused distinctive identity dimensions into their professional tasks,
such as bringing personal experiences into their weekly sermons.

In other cases, researchers have shown that individuals will signal
their distinctive identities by engaging in behaviors prototypical of
a desired distinctive category and/or unprototypical of an undesired
category. For example, Pratt *et al.* (2006) described how groups of
medical residents (e.g., radiologists and surgeons) customized their
professional identities through the use of behavior and language (e.g.,
relating stories about the "brutality" of a surgery residency) that fitted
the prototype of their chosen specialty. By contrast, Elsbach (2001)
found that California legislative staffers who considered themselves
"policy wonks" engaged in behaviors unprototypical of the alternative distinctive identity of "political hacks" (i.e., they never attached
themselves to legislation associated with tobacco, alcohol, or gambling
interests) to distance themselves from this undesired categorization.

Use of behavioral displays to affirm status. Research on new or
"freshly minted" professionals has shown that behavioral displays
may be used to affirm professional identities that are threatened by
an inability to competently enact the skills and traits of a profession.
In other words, behavioral displays are used to signal that one has the
status of a legitimate professional. For example, Ibarra's (1999) study

of management consultants and investment bankers illustrated how, as a means of growing into appropriate professional identities, "rookies" in these fields "tried on" and symbolically portrayed the professional identities they were expected to hold – even before they actually perceived themselves as holding such identities. Ibarra described how management consultants used the language and informal behaviors of seasoned practitioners as a means of responding to these identity threats. As one young consultant in her study noted:

> I can't talk about some sport I'm not interested in. But you have to be able to talk to clients in an informal setting. That is something I'm still working on ... You learn different styles from your colleagues. (Ibarra, 1999, p. 777)

In other studies, researchers have found that individuals may use behavioral displays to signal an identity that is prototypical of a successful individual within a firm. In this manner, Ely (1995) discussed how female lawyers often used behavior to socially construct higher status identities within their law firms. Some women in her study used traditionally masculine behavior to mark themselves as "accommodators" (e.g., women willing to display aggressive behavior to meet the firms' norms for success), even when the profile went against their own behavioral preferences. In these cases, the women clearly used behavior to send a signal about their workplace identities. Ely (1995, p. 619) quoted one woman as noting that she had stopped showing her insecurities in an attempt to signal a more high-status, "masculine" identity: "Men don't do that. So I've stopped doing that. But that was a pretty easy rule to follow: Do not wear your heart on your sleeve." In response, many of these lawyers received clear feedback about the correctness of their adopted gender identities for success within their firms.

Physical marker displays

Belk (1988, p. 139) drew on findings from psychology, consumer research, psychoanalytic theory, material and popular culture studies, feminist studies, history, medicine, anthropology, and sociology to support the conclusion that "we are what we have." Belk further noted (1988, p. 150) that the functions such possessions play in the extended self involve "the creation, enhancement, and preservation of a sense of identity," including personal and social identities. In this vein, researchers have shown that perceptions of personal distinctiveness and status can be managed through the acquisition and display of personal possessions such as expensive household appliances or furniture (Ames, 1984), and business attire such as expensive watches, business shoes, and attaché cases (Solomon and Anand, 1985). More recently, scholars have described the use of artifacts and objects as a primary means of constructing and signaling distinctive identities, as well as legitimate and high-status identities (see Rafaeli and Pratt, 2006 for examples).

The benefit of physical markers over behavioral markers for identity affirmation is that displaying them does not require constant cognitive attention or vigilance. A person can display a physical identity marker on his or her desk or wall that denotes status (e.g., an award or diploma) and forget about it. Likewise, a person can dress in the morning with the intention of displaying a distinctive identity dimension (e.g., an artistic identity denoted by an unusual shirt or tie) and not pay attention to it during the rest of the workday. As Elsbach (2004, p. 104) notes about physical identity markers in corporate office settings:

[M]any physical markers exist *independent* of the displayer (i.e., décor may be displayed in a workers' office even if he or she is not present). Consequently, physical identity markers are likely to be viewed and assessed even in situations where the displayer is not present or able to explain them. Such markers may even be the first information an observer receives about a person (i.e., one may view a co-worker's workspace before meeting its inhabitant) ... [Also] many physical identity markers in corporate settings are *relatively permanent* (i.e., they remain in place in an office over long periods of time). As a result, choice and display of physical markers may be interpreted as a deliberate act (versus a quirky one-time act, or temporary lapse of judgment) and may be repeatedly viewed, and reinforced over time as a strong indicator of a stable personality or identity (Fiske and Taylor, 1991). In addition, this opportunity for repeat observations may mitigate the effects of cognitive processing capacity on assessments of physical (vs. behavioral) identity markers.

Using physical marker displays to affirm distinctiveness. Researchers have identified the use of a diverse array of physical markers, including photos, business cards, mementoes, artwork, and furnishings as means of signaling distinctive identities (Rafaeli and Pratt, 2006). Yet, the most common physical marker studied in the workplace appears to be individual dress (Rafaeli and Pratt, 1993; Harquail, 2006).

Recent research on the symbolic effects of dress by medical professionals (Pratt and Rafaeli, 1997) and administrative assistants (Rafaeli *et al.*, 1997) suggests that choices in clothing and accessories provide employees with a salient means of affirming and expressing social distinctiveness and social status categorizations. Dress markers such as lab coats and surgical scrubs indicate the status and distinctiveness of medical professionals through their different colors (e.g., surgeons wear green or blue, while nurses wear pink) and styles (physicians wear lab coats, while nurses almost never do), and may help employees adapt to changes in their workplace identities, such as a move from formal to more informal relationships between medical professionals and patients (Pratt and Rafaeli, 1997).

A common finding of these studies is that employees often use portable markers to reflect new workplace identities that they adopt as a result of job changes, geographic moves, and role evolutions. For example, in the area of professional dress, Pratt and Rafaeli (1997) found that nurses, when confronted with a choice of workplace identities because of the evolving nature of healthcare, used dress to signal the identity they chose to maintain. Nurses who maintained a more traditional identity of "acute care professional" wore traditional white uniforms, surgical scrubs, and lab coats. As one nurse reported, "We take care of sick patients ... So we should look like medical professionals, we should be dressed in scrubs" (Pratt and Rafaeli, 1997, p. 862). By contrast, nurses who maintained the more modern identity of "rehabilitation professional" wore street clothes like those of their patients. Another nurse described this approach: "If they [patients] and their caretakers wear street clothes, patients will think of themselves as moving out of the sick role and into rehabilitation. They will be ready for life outside the hospital. This is the rehab philosophy, and this is what makes this unit unique" (Pratt and Rafaeli, 1997, p. 862). Dress markers, then, provided salient cues about the workplace identities different nurses intended to affirm in a more diverse environment. Appropriate organizational dress helped these employees feel like their identities fit their work roles and provided them with added confidence and psychological comfort in carrying out those roles.

In addition, a few studies have examined how individuals in organizations cope with threats to their professional identities in contexts where they believe those identities may be mistaken. For example, Pratt and Rafaeli (1997) described how nurses in a hospital rehabilitation unit used dress (i.e., scrubs vs. street clothes) as a means of affirming desired professional identities when more than one professional identity existed (e.g., rehabilitator vs. caregiver), and nurses perceived that they may be categorized as the wrong type. Similarly, Elsbach (2001) showed how state legislative staffers used language, business cards, office personalization, and selection of work projects to affirm their professional identities as either "policy wonks" or "political hacks" when they believed those two identities might have been mistaken.

In a similar manner, researchers have identified the use of photos, business cards, mementoes, artwork, and furnishings as means of signaling distinctive identities (Baruch, 2006; Cappetta and Gioia, 2006). Much like the studies of dress, these studies illustrate how the symbolic meaning of common physical artifacts may be used to affirm distinctive self-concepts at work.

Using physical marker displays to affirm status. In a study of identity threat among employees moved from a traditional to a non-territorial office space (i.e., an office space in which employees do not have permanent offices, but reserve cubicles or offices on a daily basis and must completely vacate those workspaces at the end of each workday), Elsbach (2003) found that employees used the display of personal or group artifacts in common areas after such display in personal offices was no longer convenient. For example, one highly educated employee, who no longer displayed his diplomas in his office (because he no longer had a permanent office), displayed his books in the mailroom to affirm his status. As he noted: "Everyone's got a little shelf near their mailbox. I put my business books up there. And they're a symbol of my education" (Elsbach, 2003, p. 637). In another case, an employee changed the look of her business cards to be more status-oriented when she could no longer display her sales awards in her office. Because these business cards were prominently displayed in the reception area of the office, this was an easy way for the employee to signal her status through physical markers. As she noted:

When you've made [a high performance sales club] for five years, you can get a little emblem embossed on your business card. So I changed my business card to have that emblem on it. So now, mine is the only one in this entire office that has that emblem on it. And all the cards are sitting out in the reception area anyway. And some people have noticed. They think it's pretty awesome. They go, "you know you're the only one that has the five-year sticker on your business card?" So that's how I am emoting my success without having a lot of plaques up on the wall. (Elsbach, 2003, p. 645)

Responding to identity conflicts with multiple display tactics

While Table 11.1 illustrates numerous studies of effective identity work or identity management in response to identity threats, none of these studies (perhaps with the exception of Kreiner *et al.* [2006]) address the particular identity conflicts described in the introduction, i.e., when affirming a status dimension disaffirms a distinctiveness dimension, or when affirming a distinctiveness dimension disaffirms a status dimension. Nevertheless, these studies provide some clues about how such identity conflicts might be resolved through multiple identity displays. In particular, they suggest that individuals might simultaneously display behaviors and physical markers to affirm complex identities in which status and distinctiveness appear to conflict.

I propose three primary strategies by which identity displays might be combined to this end: (1) displaying physical markers of distinctiveness, while enacting behaviors of status, (2) displaying physical markers of status, while enacting behaviors of distinctiveness, and (3) displaying physical markers of both status and distinctiveness. These tactics are illustrated in Figure 11.1 and summarized below.

Tactic 1: Displaying physical markers of distinctiveness, while enacting behaviors of status. As shown in Figure 11.1, this tactic may be effective when a person desires to affirm an identity dimension that is high on distinctiveness, but low on status. For example, a professor may want to affirm her distinctive identity as an innovator in the use of multiple research methods by highlighting her published papers using these methods. Yet, if these papers were published in low-status journals, drawing attention to them may also hurt her status as a top-notch researcher.

A hypothetical example of this tactic might be related to Ibarra's (1999) study of rookie investment bankers and consultants. As noted earlier, many of these rookies copied the behaviors of seasoned veterans when discussing a project, as a means of signaling and affirming their status as legitimate professionals, worthy of their high fees. At the same time, some of these same rookies lost the ability to affirm their own distinctive management styles and personalities. If these rookies were to continue to copy the prototypes of high-status

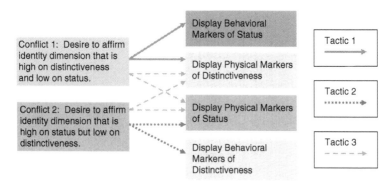

Figure 11.1 Display tactics for resolving identity conflicts

professionals in their behaviors, but also display physical markers that affirmed a distinctive personality dimension, they could avoid this trade-off. For example, a newly minted consultant could follow the script for discussing a project with a new client, but could display distinctive physical markers in her office that affirmed her experience working for the Peace Corps in South America (e.g., photos of work projects in Argentina). These physical markers might allow the consultant to portray herself as unique and distinctive at the same time as her behavior allowed her to come across as high status (e.g., she becomes the high-profile consultant with a social conscience).

Tactic 2: Displaying physical markers of status, while enacting behaviors of distinctiveness. In other cases, as shown in Figure 11.1, individuals may desire to affirm an identity dimension that is high on status, but low on distinctiveness. For example, in trying to obtain a client for a consulting project, a manager may wish to affirm his or her expertise as a certified human resource manager (a high-status identity dimension) but not appear to be just the same as many other consultants who have this same certification. In this case, drawing attention to the high-status identity dimension may also draw attention to its undistinctiveness.

When faced with such a dilemma, the manager may wish to use behavioral markers (i.e., talking about a specific expertise or experience in human resource management) to affirm the distinctiveness dimension, because such behavioral displays are dynamic and thus likely to be salient and draw attention of the observer (Fiske and Taylor, 1991). Yet, at the same time, this manager may display physical markers that affirm status, such as noting his human resource certification on his business cards, since status is less threatened in this case. Physical markers may not be as salient as the behavioral markers – because they are not dynamic – but may be visually prominent enough to be noticed. If the identity dimension is already high in status, such physical markers should be sufficient for affirming distinctiveness.

An example of this strategy may be seen in the study of Episcopalian priests studied by Kreiner *et al.* (2006). Priests in this study confronted identity threats due to conflicts between desires to affirm their individual personalities, with all their distinctiveness, and desires to enact the formal role of the priest, with all its status and trappings. In responding to these conflicts or threats, the priests engaged in a number of different "identity work" tactics, including differentiating or separating these two identity dimensions, and attempting to integrate these two dimensions. Yet, in some of the examples, priests' comments suggest that they were able to use physical markers, such as their formal priestly garments, to signal their status as a priest, while infusing their sermons with individual personality, such as discussing personal hobbies or interests, as a means of affirming their distinctiveness. As one priest in their study commented:

How I live out the vocation emerges out of who I am ... For the most part I feel I bring myself to the task. So how I am as a priest emerges out of who I am. (Kreiner *et al.*, 2006, p. 1047)

As this example illustrates, when the important issue is to affirm an identity that is typically high on status but low on distinctiveness (i.e., the identity of a priest), the use of behavior to focus attention on distinctive identity dimensions is often a natural response. The trappings of status are already established in this case and require less effort and attention to affirm.

Tactic 3: Displaying physical markers of status and physical markers of distinctiveness. Because physical markers require low attention once they are displayed, it may also be effective to affirm both status and distinctiveness through the display of different physical markers. In this manner, Elsbach (2004) describes how office workers displayed a number of different physical markers – some used to signal status and others used to signal distinctiveness – to affirm their identities at work. While this study did not examine or illustrate the use of these tactics in response to identity conflicts *per se*, these tactics may be used as a response to such conflicts.

For example, if a clothing designer wants to communicate status to a new client as a means of gaining legitimacy, but also wants to communicate creative distinctiveness as a means of differentiating herself from competitors, the display of multiple physical markers may be useful. Diplomas and awards may be prominently displayed to affirm her status and legitimacy in the field of design, while unusual and distinctive dress (e.g., quirky glasses, interesting jewelry, casual clothes, and funky shoes) may be used to affirm her unique perspective and attention to style (Harquail, 2006). Similarly, an advertising manager who is interviewing job candidates may decorate his office with dark-colored woods and formal furnishings to affirm his status in the company, while also displaying unusual and interesting drawings or prototypes of past projects to affirm his distinctive perspective and talents in commercial campaigns.

The use of multiple physical markers to affirm both status and distinctiveness appears relatively common and effective for individuals with multi-faceted identities (Fiol and O'Connor, 2006; Elsbach, 2004; Elsbach, 2003). Further, researchers have shown that the display of physical markers in workspaces or in dress is commonly perceived as a deliberate signal of identity (Elsbach, 2006) even if that is not the intention of the displayer.

Conclusion

The desire to affirm complex individual identities may be a common goal of many organizational members, but also may engender conflicts between needs for status and needs for distinctiveness. Further, many times, these conflicts cannot be easily resolved by changing the level of self-categorization, as is typically suggested in social psychological research. Instead, individuals who wish to affirm identities that are high in status but low in distinctiveness, or high in distinctiveness but low in status may need to affirm two different levels of self-categorization at the same time. In these cases, I have argued that the display of multiple identity markers – including some physical markers and some behavioral markers – may be an effective way to affirm both status and distinctiveness in individual identity. These arguments have implications for theory and practice.

In terms of theoretical implications, my arguments demonstrate that identity displays may be a means to developing new category "subgroups" that provide positive but distinct identities for their displayers (Richards and Hewstone, 2001). In other words, by using multiple identity displays, individuals may deliberately create new subgroups (e.g., approachable priests, socially responsible consultants) that are contained within existing, superordinate groups (e.g., priests, consultants).

Most extant research on category subgroups (see Richards and Hewstone, 2001 for a review) suggests that subgrouping creates a more differentiated view of a superordinate group and is therefore a positive act. For example, researchers have argued that the more subgroups a person can generate for a superordinate group, the less likely that person is to stereotype members of the superordinate group (Park *et al.*, 1992). In this way, subgrouping is distinct from subtyping (which is commonly used to preserve a group stereotype by portraying exceptions to the stereotype as "special cases" that exist outside the stereotyped group [Hewstone, 1994]). The current arguments suggest that these positive effects of subgrouping may be helped along by individuals who purposefully develop and affirm new subgroups through multiple identity displays.

Extant research also suggests that the development of subgroups is dependent on the ability of perceivers to form coherent and meaningful subgroups based on some key traits or distinctive attributes (Richards and Hewstone, 2001). For example, Park *et al.* (1992) found that engineering students created subgroups of themselves by differentiating the primary motivation for hard work (e.g., money, parental expectations, environmental goals). The present theorizing provides a means (i.e., identity displays) by which individuals may help observers (and themselves) to see new but meaningful subgroups within an existing superordinate group.

In terms of practical implications, my arguments suggest that individuals may use a repertoire of identity markers to affirm complex individual identities, and suggest that it may be important for organizations to allow members opportunities to display a variety of these markers (Elsbach, 2003). Physical markers can be viewed repeatedly and independent of the displayer, but behavioral markers can be more easily adapted to a specific situation. For example, a manager can make claims about his or her technical skills when talking to engineers and about his or her people skills when talking to sales staff. At the same time, this manager can keep diplomas and awards visible in the office to affirm status to both sets of co-workers. Individuals who maintain and use a variety of identity markers may adapt more easily to threats to their identity self-perceptions and to situations that call for an alteration in their displayed identity (Elsbach, 2003).

Notes

1 I should note that, although being ranked as #1 in a category is, by definition, a "distinctive" categorization (i.e., because there is no one else at that ranking), in this chapter I refer to distinctiveness as a qualitative difference between categories (i.e., apples vs. oranges), rather than a simple numerical uniqueness.

References

Alexander, C. N. and Lauderdale, P. 1977. "Situated identities and social influence." *Social Psychology Quarterly* 40: 225–233.

Ames, K. L. 1984. "Material culture as nonverbal communication: A historical case study," in E. Mayo (ed.), *American Material Culture: The Shape of Things Around Us*. Bowling Green, OH: Bowling Green University Popular Press, pp. 25–47.

Ashforth, B. E. and Johnson, S.A. 2001. "Which hat to wear? The relative salience of multiple identities in organizational contexts," in M. A. Hogg and D. J. Terry (eds.), *Social Identity Processes in Organizational Contexts*. Philadelphia, PA: Psychology Press, pp. 31–48.

Bandura, A. 1973. *Aggression: A Social Learning Analysis*. Oxford: Prentice Hall.

Baruch, Y. 2006. "On logos and business cards: The case of UK universities," in A. Rafaeli and M. G. Pratt (eds.), *Artifacts and Organizations: Beyond Mere Symbolism*. Mahwah, NJ: Lawrence Erlbaum, pp. 181–198.

Baumeister, R. F. 1982. "A self-presentational view of social phenomena." *Psychological Bulletin* 91: 3–26.

Belk, R. W. 1988. "Possessions and the extended self." *Journal of Consumer Research* 15: 139–168.

Beyer, J. M. and Hannah, D. R. 2002. "Building on the past: Enacting established personal identities in a new work setting." *Organization Science* 13: 636–652.

Blanz, M., Mummendey, R. M., and Klink, R. M. 1998. "Responding to negative social identity: A taxonomy of identity management strategies." *European Journal of Social Psychology* 28: 697–729.

Bourhis, R. Y. and Hill, P. 1982. "Intergroup perceptions in British higher education: A field study," in H. Tajfel (ed.), *Social Identity and Intergroup Relations*. Cambridge University Press, pp. 24–40.

Brewer, M. B. 1991. "The social self: On being the same and different at the same time." *Personality and Social Psychology Bulletin* 17: 475–482.

Brewer, M. B., Manzi, J. M., and Shaw, J. S. 1993. "In-group identification as a function of depersonalization, distinctiveness, and status." *Psychological Science* 4: 88–92.

Brickson, S. L. 2000. "The impact of identity orientation on individual and organizational outcomes in demographically diverse settings." *Academy of Management Review* 25: 82–101.

2005. "Organizational identity orientation: Forging a link between organizational identity and organizations' relations with stakeholders." *Administrative Science Quarterly* 50: 576–609.

Brockner, J., Rubin, J. Z., and Lang, E. 1981. "Face-saving and entrapment." *Journal of Experimental Social Psychology* 17: 68–79.

Cappetta, R., and Gioia, D. 2006. "Fine fashion: Using symbolic artifacts, sensemaking, and sensegiving to construct identity and image," in A. Rafaeli and M. G. Pratt (eds.), *Artifacts and Organizations: Beyond Mere Symbolism*. Mahwah, NJ: Lawrence Erlbaum, pp. 199–219.

Coveleski, M. A., Dirsmith, M. W., Heian, J. B., and Sajay, S. 1998. "The calculated and the avowed: Techniques of discipline and struggles over identity in big six public accounting firms." *Administrative Science Quarterly* 43: 293–327.

Dietz-Uhler, B. and Murrell, A. 1998. "Effects of social identity and threat on self-esteem and group attributions." *Group Dynamics: Theory, Research, and Practice* 2: 24–35.

Ellemers, N., Wilke, H., and Van Knippenberg, A. 1993. "Effects of the legitimacy of low group or individual status on individual and collective status-enhancement strategies." *Journal of Personality and Social Psychology* 64: 766–778.

Elsbach, K. D. 2001. "Coping with hybrid organizational identities: Evidence from California leglislative staff." *Advances in Qualitative Organizational Research* 3: 59–90.

2003. "Relating physical environment to self-categorizations: A study of identity threat and affirmation in a non-territorial office space." *Administrative Science Quarterly* 48: 622–654.

2004. "Interpreting workplace identities: The role of office decor." *Journal of Organizational Behavior* 25: 99–128.

2006. "Perceptual biases and mis-interpretation of artifacts," in A. Rafaeli and M. G. Pratt (eds.), *Artifacts and Organizations: Beyond Mere Symbolism*. Mahwah, NJ: Lawrence Erlbaum, pp. 61–81.

Elsbach, K. D. and Kramer, R. M. 1996. "Members' responses to organizational identity threats: Encountering and countering the Business Week rankings." *Administrative Science Quarterly* 41: 442–476.

Ely, R. J. 1995. "The power in demography: Women's social constructions of gender identity at work." *Academy of Management Journal* 38: 589–634.

Fiol, M. and O'Connor, E. 2006. "Stuff matters: Artifacts, social identity, and legitimacy in the U.S. medical profession," in A. Rafaeli and M. G. Pratt (eds.), *Artifacts and Organizations: Beyond Mere Symbolism.* Mahwah, NJ: Lawrence Erlbaum, pp. 241–258.

Fiske, S. and Taylor, S. 1991. *Social Cognition.* New York: McGraw-Hill.

Goffman, E. 1967. *Interaction Ritual.* New York: Pantheon Books.

Harquail, C. V. 2006. "Symbolizing identity: When brand icons become organizational icons." *Academy of Management Proceedings*, H1–H6.

Hewstone, M. 1994. "Revision and change in stereotypic beliefs: In search of the elusive subtyping model," in W. Strobe and M. Hewstone (eds.), *European Review of Social Psychology*, Vol. V. Chichester: Wiley, pp. 69–109.

Hogg, M. A. and Abrams, D. 1988. *Social Identifications: A Social Psychology of Intergroup Relations and Group Processes.* London: Routledge.

Hornsey, M. and Hogg, M. A. 2000. "Intergroup similarity and subgroup relations: Some implications for assimilation." *Personality and Social Psychology Bulletin* 26: 948–958.

  2002. "The effects of status on subgroup relations." *British Journal of Social Psychology* 41: 203–218.

Ibarra, H. 1999. "Provisional selves: Experimenting with image and identity in professional adaptation." *Administrative Science Quarterly* 44: 764–791.

Kreiner, G. E., Hollensbe, E. C., and Sheep, M. L. 2006. "Where is the 'me' among the 'we'? Identity work and the search for optimal balance." *Academy of Management Journal* 49: 1031–1057.

Leary, M. R. 1992. "Self-presentational processes in exercise and sport." *Journal of Sport and Exercise Psychology* 14: 339–351.

  1995. *Self-Presentation: Impression Management and Interpersonal Behavior.* Madison, WI: Brown & Benchmark.

Mummendey, A., Klink, A., Mielke, R., Wenzel, M., and Blanz, M. 1999. "Socio-structural characteristics of intergroup relations and identity management strategies: Results from a field study in East Germany." *European Journal of Social Psychology* 29: 259–285.

Mussweiler, T., Gabriel, S., and Bodenhausen, G. V. 2000. "Shifting social identities as a strategy for deflecting threatening social comparisons." *Journal of Personality and Social Psychology* 79: 398–409.

Park, B., Ryan, C. S., and Judd, C. M. 1992. "The role of meaningful sub-groups in explaining differences in perceived variability for in-groups and out-groups." *Journal of Personality and Social Psychology* 63: 553–567.

Pliner, P. and Chaiken, S. 1990. "Eating, social motives, and self-presentation in women and men." *Journal of Experimental Social Psychology* 26: 240–254.

Pratt, M. G. and Rafaeli, A. 1997. "Organizational dress as a symbol of multilayered social identities." *Academy of Management Journal* 40: 862–898.

Pratt, M. G., Rockmann, K. W., and Kaufman, J. B. 2006. "Constructing professional identity: The role of work and identity learning cycles in the customization of identity among medical residents." *Academy of Management Journal* 49: 235–262.

Rafaeli, A., Dutton, J., Harquail, C. V., and Mackie-Lewis, S. 1997. "Navigating by attire: The use of dress by female administrative employees." *Academy of Management Journal* 40: 9–45.

Rafaeli, A. and Pratt, M. G. 1993. "Tailored meanings: On the meaning and impact of organizational dress." *Academy of Management Review* 18: 32–55.

2006. *Artifacts and Organizations: Beyond Mere Symbolism.* Mahwah, NJ: Lawrence Erlbaum.

Reiss, M. and Rosenfeld, P. 1980. "Seating preferences as nonverbal communication: A self-presentational analysis." *Journal of Applied Communication Research* 8: 22–30.

Richards, Z. and Hewstone, M. 2001. "Subtyping and subgrouping: Processes for the prevention and promotion of stereotype change." *Personality and Social Psychology Review* 5: 52–73.

Schlenker, B. R., Britt, T. W., and Pennington, J. 1996. "Impression regulation and management: Highlights of a theory of self-identification," in R. M. Sorrentino and E. T. Higgins (eds.), *Handbook of Motivation and Cognition, Volume 3: The Interpersonal Context.* New York: Guilford Press, pp. 118–147.

Smithson, J. 2005. "'Full-timer in a part-time job': Identity negotiation in organizational talk." *Feminism & Psychology* 15: 275–293.

Solomon, M. and Anand., P. 1985. "Ritual costumes and status transition: The female business suit as totemic emblem," in E. C. Hirschman and M. B. Holbrook (eds.), *Advances in Consumer Research*, Vol. XII. Provo, UT: Association for Consumer Research, pp. 315–318.

Swann, W. B., Jr., Bosson, J. K., and Pelham, B. W. 2002. "Different partners, different selves: Strategic verification of circumscribed identities." *Personality and Social Psychology Bulletin* 28: 1215–1228.

Swann, W. B. and Hill, C. A. 1982. "When our identities are mistaken: Reaffirming self-concepts through social interaction." *Journal of Personality and Social Psychology* 43: 59–66.

Swann, W. B., Jr., Rentfrow, P. J., and Guinn, J. S. 2003. "Self-verification: The search for coherence," in M. R. Leary and J. P. Tangney (eds.), *Handbook of Self and Identity*. New York: Guilford Press, pp. 367–383.

Tesser, A., Crepaz, N., Beach, S. R. H., Cornell, D., and Collins, J. C. 2000. "Confluence of self-esteem regulation mechanisms: On integrating the self-zoo." *Personality and Social Psychology Bulletin* 26: 1476–1489.

Thoits, P. A. and Virshup, L. K. 1997. "Me's and we's. Forms and functions of social identities," in R. D. Ashmore and L. Jussim (eds.), *Self and Identity. Fundamental Issues*. Oxford University Press, pp. 106–133.

Turner, J. C. 1987. *Rediscovering the Social Group: A Self-categorization Theory*. Oxford: Basil Blackwell.

Van Knippenberg, D. and Van Leeuwen, E. 2001. "Organizational identity after a merger: Sense of continuity as the key to postmerger identification," in M. A. Hogg and D. J. Terry (eds.), *Social Identity Processes in Organizational Contexts*. Philadelphia, PA: Psychology Press, pp. 249–264.

PART VI

Developing status and management knowledge

12 | The value of status in management and organization research: A theoretical integration

JONE L. PEARCE

Status does matter. All the authors in this volume have demonstrated its value in advancing our understanding of current problems in management and organizational scholarship, and in furthering our understanding of how status affects workplace, organizational, and marketplace actions. In this concluding chapter I highlight a few of the contributions their work on status makes to their fields, address their contributions to our understanding of status more generally, and highlight a few practical implications of their work.

How status enriches organization and management theories

Strategy scholarship

All of the authors help to illuminate the developing consensus that the absence of attention to status can lead to impoverished theories. For example, these authors note that an overemphasis on individual firms as isolated utility maximizers in markets has led to incomplete understandings and possibly misleading theory. This point certainly has been made before. However, most of those making it have sought to emphasize pro-social, cooperative motives in interaction. Scholars of status enrich strategy theory by emphasizing that the social environments of firms are as much arenas of competition as they are for cooperation.

In Chapter 5 Michael Nippa identified this flaw in tournament theories of incentives. He persuasively argued that people do not just attend to the rewards they personally receive, but also want to know how what they have received compares to what others get. This means that winner-take-all tournaments, with their large reward disparities among participants that may have only miniscule differences in their performance, often foster anger and resentment that can destroy cooperation. This feature of tournaments accounts for the absence of tournament incentive systems in actual organizations which cannot rely on one-time-only interactions among people who would not need to cooperate or assist one another. As Nippa so cogently observed, no one actually uses such dysfunctional organizational incentive systems in organizations. He concludes that the only real purpose of tournament theories of organizational compensation is ideological: scientistic rationalizations for executives' misuse of their status and power to expropriate exorbitant compensation for themselves.

In Chapter 4 Michael Jensen, Bo Kyung Kim, and Heeyon Kim made two powerful contributions to strategy theory. First, they made a strong case that a firm's status in the marketplace cannot be reduced solely to the firm's product or service quality as Podolny (1993) proposed, and as so many other scholars have assumed. They used this insight as the basis for building a theory of firm identity signaling and then used those ideas to make several provocative propositions about firm diversification strategies. Second, they noted that relative status within an industry or strategic niche can be a powerful explanation of firms' strategic diversification. Previously, theories of diversification have focused on the individual firm and markets it is evaluating. Yet, they highlighted the very powerful strategic advantages that status provides and proposed that executives wishing to enhance and maintain their firm's status will select strategic niches and diversification based on the potential to gain higher status, or will use their high status to exploit niches without high-status participants. They provided a powerful, testable set of propositions that can and will change the way we understand strategy. The authors of both chapters emphasized that firms are not socially isolated, but attend to their status among other firms.

Status provides so many advantages to firms, and firms, like people, expend great energy to attain and defend it. These chapters help to illustrate that status is simply too important for strategists to ignore, and point to fruitful areas for future research.

Innovation scholarship

The future success of innovations is inherently uncertain and status scholarship supports the idea that we rely on social status cues in the absence of confident performance information. Yet, previously, status has played a surprisingly small role in innovation theorizing. Tyler Wry, Michael Lounsbury, and Royston Greenwood, and Kim Saxton and Todd Saxton have pioneered valuable new directions in understanding how innovations are developed and exploited.

In Chapter 6 the authors discovered that earlier research finding that attention and influence to (high-status) star scientists drives much innovation may only be the case in settled fields where culture and relative status have become aligned and mutually supportive. By contrast, in the emerging nanotechnology industry, they found that star scientists' patents only received the expected attention and use if the star scientists were working in a highly central field (one attended to by those working in numerous different areas). Interestingly, they found that work conducted in the high-status firms did not benefit from their status in the same ways that individual scientists do. The innovations from high-status firms were underused, they proposed, because these large firms operated in numerous different industries and so did not sustain their attention to applications of their scientists' earlier work to a level necessary to lead innovation. Much more effective were individual scientists whose careers were invested in a particular range of nanotechnology applications. These scientists expended more effort pursuing development and promoting their innovations. In other words, for large firms operating in multiple markets and using a variety of technologies, their scientific developments did not receive the strategic attention that they could in more focused firms, with powerful implications for why large firms so often fail to capitalize on their scientific technical innovations.

In Chapter 7 Kim Saxton and Todd Saxton drew on status scholarship to theorize why some emerging ventures are better able to capture the attention and support of critical actors such as venture capitalists, angel groups, and advisors. Technology-based emerging ventures are not yet viable enterprises and so do not have customers, and often no developed products. This means that any assessment of their future performance is highly uncertain. They build on status research that has established that status considerations are the most powerful in the absence of confident performance information, making status a particularly powerful predictor of who receives vital support at the ambiguous emerging stage of their ventures. More attention to status and how it drives which ventures receive the support they need to develop their ideas into viable firms is particularly important to the many nations and regions that are seeking to develop technology-based entrepreneurship. It also matters to venture capital decision makers. They need to be concerned that non-performance-based social status is dominating their decision making, so they can be sure that any status considerations are based on performance-relevant assessments.

Influence scholarship

As we saw in Chapter 1, those with higher status are more influential, not only in their areas of established expertise, but also in areas where their status is not performance-relevant. Much organizational work, whether in governing boards, project teams, or management meetings, involves individuals seeking to influence one another. We are only now beginning to understand the ways in which status might undermine reliance on useful expertise or task-relevant knowledge by giving undue influence to those with performance-irrelevant status.

Chapter 8, by Stuart Bunderson and Michelle Barton, illuminated the ways that ascriptive (performance-irrelevant) characteristics of social status interfere with and undermine accurate assessments of co-workers' and colleagues' expertise. With so much work done increasingly by people in ad hoc teams, or virtually across organizational and national borders, learning who has what knowledge and skills, and whether or not you should defer to their judgment can become highly uncertain. Such uncertainty breeds deference to ascriptive and other non-performance-based status cues, cues that can be devastating to performance. The authors proposed that because expertise is not visible, co-workers will turn to cues of varying reliability and validity, too often basing their judgments on what can best be assessed (reliability) rather than what may more accurately reflect the individual's expertise. They developed persuasive theory that individuals will rely more on diffuse cues and on personal attributes rather than behaviors, when the work is novel or face-to-face interaction is limited.

In Chapter 2 Bilian Ni Sullivan and Daniel Stewart found that the long-held assumption that interaction among individuals leads to a convergence of opinions and evaluations does not apply if that interaction is electronically mediated. In their online open-source software, community raters' increasing tenure in the community led to more diverse evaluations of others' contributions. It could well be that the pressure toward consensus among those who interact face-to-face is driven by something fundamental about that type of interaction. With so much organizational (and other social) interaction today via electronic means, their discovery has important implications for how we understand the formation of group-level expectations, evaluations, attitudes, and beliefs. However, while Gibson and Gibbs (2006) found that participants in virtual teams built trust in one another the longer they worked together, in the open-source community increased trust was not associated with increased consensus in their evaluations of their fellow developers' performance. Convergence has been explained in the literature as an exchange of information, but it may be that this is not true. Information was exchanged in these online communities but convergence did not take place. Is there something about face-to-face interaction that compels acquiescence? Is the information exchange epiphenomenal to the real processes driving consensus in face-to-face interaction? Their work suggests that further research is necessary to better understand influence processes in electronically mediated environments, as well as how and why electronically mediated social processes might differ from scholarly knowledge, now wholly situated in face-to-face interaction.

Justice scholarship

In Chapter 10 Jerald Greenberg and Deshani Ganegoda advanced justice theory by marshaling a powerful collection of studies to make the case that procedural justice operates differently for those with high workplace status than it does for those with low status. They proposed that, while those holding divergent statuses all value being treated in procedurally fair ways, those with high status expect fair treatment as their due, while those with low status see it as a source of security. This means that those with high status react more emotionally to unfair treatment, but that those with low status are more likely to respond with deviant acts such as theft and violence. Treating people in procedurally and interactionally just ways is a strong signal of a respected status and such status threats or supports become powerful motives for action.

Theories of workplace discrimination

A major research stream in organizational behavior over the past decades has been the study of racial, gender, ethnic, or other prejudice based on ascriptive characteristics in workplaces. Much has been written about such biases, and many practical interventions have been developed to address these dysfunctions, with only limited success. One reason for such limited success may have been the neglect of the relative status of ascriptive characteristics. Several authors in this volume have illuminated the insights into differences and the theories used to explain them by drawing on status scholarship.

The primary theory used to study workplace differences has been identity theory, and in Chapter 11 Kimberly Elsbach suggested that one of the central premises in its applications to workplaces may be flawed. She has contributed to an understanding of complex self-categorizations in identity theory by drawing on her fieldwork to develop theory about how individuals can manage the desires for both distinctiveness and status when these identities are in conflict. She has made a persuasive case that, contrary to previous scholars' contentions, individuals in practice are not forced to choose among self-categorizations when faced with identity threats. Rather, they can balance workplace displays and actions to simultaneously convey complex multi-faceted identities. She provides rich illustrations of how people at work blend tactics to claim status and distinctiveness via expressing central values, countering stereotypes, and the use of dress and office decorations. Because self-categorization theory has become dominant in many areas of organizational behavior, to the extent that scholars assume zero-sum conflicts among possible identities to drive their theorizing, Elsbach has provided persuasive evidence that individuals do not have to choose, but easily sustain multiplex, and even conflicting, identities at work.

Chapters 3 and 9 drew on status scholarship to provide the basis for powerful theoretical explanations for the continued and persistent presence of racial, ethnic, and gender discrimination in organizations. James O'Brien and Joerg Dietz introduced Social Dominance Theory to the management literature, noting its usefulness in explaining persistent workplace discrimination. Melissa Thomas-Hunt and Katherine Phillips developed new theory of how professionals who are members of low-status ascriptive groups may or may not signal status in a way that damages others' judgments of their competence. Despite decades of sensitivity and diversity training, such discrimination persists (see Brief, 2008 for a recent review). They emphasized that people occupying different demographic and cultural groupings are not merely different, but their differences are often arrayed in status hierarchies. Seeking and maintaining high status is such a powerful motivational force that it can overwhelm attempts to reduce discrimination through programs focused on merely understanding others' experiences and ways of perceiving without recognizing the status implications.

These chapters parallel other current work finding that status can serve as a more powerful explanation of demographic differences than widely assumed explanations. For example, research in relational demography has established an impressive body of empirical relationships (Tsui and Gutek, 1999; William and O'Reilly, 1998). For example, the more members differ in race and gender from one another in task, the lower the innovation and employee task and contextual performance, the lower the member commitment, and the greater the absenteeism and turnover intentions (Baugh and Graen, 1997; Chatman *et al.*, 1998; Chattopadhyay, 1999; Riordan and Shore, 1997; Tsui, Egan, and O'Reilly, 1992). The dominant theoretical explanation for this effect has been the similarity-attraction explanation (Byrne, 1971) – that people tend to be more attracted to, and prefer to be with, those who are more similar to themselves. However, recent work has found that status, not a preference for associating with those with higher status, can overwhelm similarity-attraction (Pearce and Xu, 2010; Ridgeway *et al.*, 1998; Umphress *et al.*, 2007). In other words, the value of gaining higher status through association with higher status others can be more powerful than the attraction of associating with those who are like you. This suggests that previous research, which had lumped those with status-enhancing differences in with those with status-threatening differences, seems to have jumped to the wrong theoretical explanation for this well-documented problem. Taken with the status-based theories of discrimination presented here by the authors of these two chapters, this work, which places status at the center of understanding the persistent attachment to non-performance relevant characteristics at work, points the way to more sophisticated and effective research on workplace discrimination.

Understanding status

By delving deeply into intellectual problems of organizations and management, these authors have also helped to advance our understanding of the concept and functioning of social status more generally. Because the work of these authors originates in such diverse social science fields, their points of commonality build on and reinforce one another's arguments.

One of the important roles of status in organizations and markets is its use as a signal of individual expertise (Chapter 8) and of firm quality (Chapter 4). In the absence of unambiguous performance information, actors will rely on status as a signal of quality. However, these chapters have emphasized that status is not the same as information-based reputation, but is imbued with many received, unarticulated assumptions about others. The well-documented status signals of race and gender, so well described by the Social Dominance Theorists introduced by O'Brien and Dietz, makes painfully clear that ascriptive status is a very poor signal of quality. Status is a signal that observers use; it can represent many different qualities and skills, but it is not a perfect surrogate for any one of them. As noted in Chapter 1, too many in management and organization research have simply equated status with constructs that differ in important ways: power, hierarchical position, speaking style, among many others. The careful work presented here has demonstrated that such confounding is misleading, and it is hoped that it will lead to future research that distinguishes among these diverse concepts.

The authors of Chapters 2, 6, 7, 8, and 9 have all advanced our understanding of how status influences action when the performance of other organizations or individuals is uncertain. Tyler Wry and his colleagues emphasized how important engagement is to high-status individuals' influence, while indifference to their status undercuts its effects. Melissa Thomas-Hunt and Katherine Phillips noted the importance of enacting the core behaviors of the high-status group, while Stuart Bunderson and Michelle Barton highlighted that diffuse ascriptive characteristics can trump actions when the work is novel. Although status research developed in the study of stable social settings, these authors have demonstrated that it may be most powerful under fluid, ambiguous circumstances. Status should be increasingly important in the study of organizations increasingly dependent on innovation, virtual teams, and fluid net-works and communities.

The authors of Chapters 8, 9, and 11 developed masterful theor-izing about what happens when status cues are in conflict with one another. One of the advantages of studying status in organizations and markets is that individuals and firms in these settings can rarely be easily categorized by one status marker alone. After all, a defin-ing feature of modern societies is the multitude and changeability of groups and roles. When status has been used to understand manage-ment and organizational problems, a fundamental question is how different status markers are combined or mixed. Blau (1977, 1994) proposed that ascriptive statuses will trump ascribed statuses because they are more immutable. However, this was speculative; Kimberly Elsbach, Melissa Thomas-Hunt and Katherine Phillips, and Stuart Bunderson and Michelle Barton marshaled data and insight based on years of scholarship to propose that people can and do hold sophis-ticated complex assessments of others' status. Bunderson and Barton proposed that when status cues conflict, people are more likely to rely more on what they can reliably see than they are on what the per-son does. Their work suggests valuable avenues for research on how observers and actors interpret and understand conflicting statuses.

The authors of Chapter 4 set their model of horizontal and vertical status in the contexts of organizations operating in markets; how-ever, it may be fruitfully applied to individuals. Like organizations, individuals may make strategic choices about occupations, employers, and careers based on a combination of vertical and horizontal status considerations. Like firms, individuals must make trade-offs and do not have infinite time and resources. Their work suggests that it is not enough to say that individuals make these kinds of choice based on the pursuit and defense of status; they must make trade-offs and work from the social space in which they find themselves at any point in time. Their work suggests as many fruitful possible research projects exploring the choices that individuals make at work as it does the strategic choices that firms make.

Finally, the authors of Chapters 3, 4, and 7 all have helped further refine and distinguish status and related concepts such as product or service quality, legitimacy, reputation, and ascriptive and achieved status, all critical distinctions in organization and management research. Scholars can now avoid conflating status with authority hierarchy, discrimination and achievement, which will help further the use of status in understanding organization and management phenomena.

Taking action: practical implications of status

Scholars in management and organization address practical problems and so it seems fitting to end this volume with some practical implications of the scholarship presented here. Michael Jensen, Bo Kyung Kim, and Heeyon Kim provided powerful insights into the risks of ignoring relative status in strategic expansions. They have made a strong case that organizations attend to their status in their various markets and are unlikely to undertake an acquisition or merger that might undercut their status. Stuart Bunderson and Michelle Barton, and Kimberly Elsbach highlighted the importance of being articulate about the various status categories we all occupy. Because status provides so many benefits, the ability to articulate one's own identity in status-enhancing ways becomes useful. For example, in the US, Ivy League universities have higher status than state universities, and being affiliated with the former accrues more status than affiliation with the latter. However, those categories need not be accepted but can be reframed. For example, faculty members at state universities can state how much they enjoy being involved in an institution that serves upward mobility and economic development rather than serving as gatekeepers and supports for elites.

The authors of Chapters 3 and 9 suggest how workplace discrimination can be more effectively addressed by both employers, who need to better attend to the status implications of diversity, and by individuals who seek ways to succeed in the face of discrimination. Bilian Ni Sullivan and Daniel Stewart propose that new industries and communities, particularly when the participants do not interact face-to-face, develop social structures in fundamentally different ways from those with more stable face-to-face interaction. The Internet has made these communities increasingly common, and their work suggests we need to direct more attention to understanding how performance and influence is understood by the participants in these settings. Kim and Todd Saxton provided specific advice on where to focus at each developmental stage for emerging ventures seeking funding and advice. And Michael Nippa directly addressed an issue that at the time of writing is at the top of the agenda for policy makers in Europe and North America – has the extraordinarily rapid recent growth in the salaries of corporate executives really been a result of a functional tournament approach to compensation, or an exploitation of status and power?

Conclusion

Taken as a whole, what is clear from this new work is that too much historical research has focused on status in comparatively stable social settings. This new research focuses on emergent, innovative, virtual, and changing workplaces and markets, finding that the ambiguity of such settings makes social status an important anchor of perceptions and evaluations. Because there are few indicators of performance, the attainment and defense of status is both more important and more complex in these ambiguous and shifting environments.

In other words, status matters, and it matters more the more the situation is uncertain, ambiguous, or shifting. As the new financiers quoted at the beginning of Chapter 1 have learned, status cannot be reduced to money, nor is it the power to coerce others. Status matters to management and organization theorizing because it matters so much to the people acting in and for organizations. It brings them numerous advantages and it is pursued with much guile and effort. Something so important to people was ignored for too long in management and organizations research, and the work presented here suggests that the future payoff from making status more central to our research holds great promise.

References

Baugh, S. G. and Graen, G. B. 1997. "Effects of team gender and racial composition on perceptions of team performance in cross-functional teams." *Group and Organization Management* 22: 366–383.

Blau, P. M. 1977. *Inequality and Heterogeneity*. New York: The Free Press.

1994. *Structural contexts of opportunities*. University of Chicago Press.

Brief, A. P. (ed.). 2008. *Diversity at Work*. Cambridge University Press.

Byrne, D. 1971. *The Attraction Paradigm*. New York: Academic Press.

Chatman, J. A., Polzer, J. T., Barsade, S. G., and Neale, M. A. 1998. "Being different yet feeling similar: The influence of demographic composition and organizational culture on work processes and outcomes." *Administrative Science Quarterly* 43: 749–780.

Chattopadhyay, P. 1999. "Beyond direct and symmetrical effects: The influence of demographic dissimilarity on organizational citizenship behavior." *Academy of Management Journal* 42: 273–287.

Gibson, C. B. and Gibbs, J. L. 2006. "Unpacking the concept of virtuality." *Administrative Science Quarterly* 51: 451–495.

Pearce, J. L. and Xu, Q. J. 2010. "Rating performance or contesting status: A test of a Social Dominance Theory of supervisor demographic skew in performance ratings." Merage School Working Paper, University of California, Irvine.

Podolny, J. M. 1993. "A status-based model of market competition." *American Journal of Sociology* 98: 829–872.

Ridgeway, C. L., Boyle, E. H., Kuipers, K. J., and Robinson, D. T. 1998. "How do status beliefs develop? The role of resources and interactional experience." *American Sociological Review* 63: 331–350.

Riordan, C. and Shore, L. 1997. "Demographic diversity and employee attitudes: Examination of relational demography within work units." *Journal of Applied Psychology* 82: 342–358.

Tsui, A. S., Egan, T. D, and O'Reilly, C. A., III. 1992. "Being different: Relational demography and organizational attachment." *Administrative Science Quarterly* 37: 549–579.

Tsui, A. S. and Gutek, B. A. 1999. *Demographic Differences in Organizations: Current Research and Future Directions.* Lanham, MD: Lexington Books.

Umphress, E. E., Smith-Crowe, K., Brief, A. P., Dietz, J., and Watkins, M. B. 2007. "When birds of a feather flock together and when they do not: Status composition, social dominance orientation, and organizational attractiveness." *Journal of Applied Psychology* 92: 396–409.

Williams, K. Y. and O'Reilly, C. A., III. 1998. "Demography and diversity in organizations," in B. M. Staw and R. I. Sutton (eds.), *Research in Organizational Behavior.* Greenwich, CT: JAI Press, pp. 77–140.

Index

Printed in Great Britain
by Amazon